The Straube Pioneers
The Descendants of Johan Augustus Stroube and Francis Feagen

by Samuel E. Hargadine, V.

The Straube Pioneers
The Descendants of Johan Augustus Stroube and Francis Feagen

Samuel Emmett Hargadine, V.
Fifth Great Grandson of Johann Augustus Stroube

Compass Flower Press
Compass Flower Press
Columbia, Missouri

Cover Photo left to right:
Ada Straube Pollard, Hershel Pollard, Everet James Straube, Lewis (Last name unknown)
Circa1908, From family archives

Library of Congress Control Number: 2024914770
ISBN: 978-1-951960-63-6

This book is dedicated to my brother.

John Everett Hargadine was named after John W. Willis (1791-1897) and Everett James Straube (1885-1968). Most of the family calls him John, however at work most call him Everett. There are usually a couple of Johns in every office, however there are few Everetts.

John has had my back my entire life. A friend recently told me that he was envious of my relationship with my brother. This friend has several sisters and the last few years have been strained since their parents passed. That has not happened between John and me and I have never told John how much I appreciate him and love him. Until now!

Foreword

General Erich Straube (1887-1971) was a German general in the Wehrmacht during World War II. Karl Straube (1873-1950) was a notable organist and conductor. Alive today is a famous soccer player, an actress, author, painter, and several CEOs all bearing the name Straube. The Straube name originated in Germany and there are many that live there today.

This book starts with Johann Augustus Stroube who was born in Bavaria, Germany and died in Augusta, Bracken County, Kentucky. Johann had five children that we know of each with long lines of descendants. I have listed Johann A. Stroube along with his immediate family, but my research focuses on Christian Straube (1791-1867), his descendants, and the hundreds who have married in to the Christian Straube family. The Straubes were my maternal side along with the Morris, Willis, Mudd and Myers lines. There are hundreds of surnames that married into these families. The two spellings are interconnected. My family line stayed with the Straube spelling with Christian. Two families in the Christian Straube line changed their name to Strauby and Straubie for unknown reasons, but they were born Straube.

My interest in family genealogy started in the early days of the internet. Websites like ancestry.com and findagrave.com were in their infancy and not particularly good. Prior to these sites becoming what they are today, researchers used Family Group Sheets that were xeroxed over and over, so the quality of the print was faint, and you were lucky if you received one that was typed. My original mentors were family members that researched our history decades before I was interested in it, and they called people on the phone, wrote to people the old-fashioned way, which is now referred to as "snail mail." This was before cell phones were even thought of, and long distance was relatively expensive.

This work is published as a means of furthering the work of any person engaged in genealogical research on the family lines listed. It does not represent complete research into all available sources. It has been said that genealogy work is never done. As you are reading this there is no doubt that there are recent discoveries, and you may even have facts of which I am not aware. I certainly hope so, and you are welcome to communicate discrepancies or additions to the author.

While my research spans a couple of decades, it was not continuous, non-stop work. It is a hobby that lends itself to winter when you are stuck inside, and in between the demands of family and career. As I type this, I am semi-retired, the family is grown and gone, and I have picked up where I left off. The information on the internet is much more complete and easier to find. It still requires due diligence because there are hundreds of people with the same name.

The Christian Straube line and related families are located throughout the United States, however the largest concentration is in the Missouri counties of Audrain, Montgomery, Marion, and Pike. The largest concentration of burials is in the Siloam Primitive Baptist Church Cemetery, Pike County, Missouri. There are at least 100 buried in Siloam.

The information in this genealogical effort came from many sources in addition to those shown in footnotes. Since contributions came from many individuals, some of the original source materials were not noted, but are believed to be true, thus are included with documented material. These may include:

- Oral interviews of family members.
- Federal, state, county, city, and township census records.
- Public court records, military records.
- Church records, funeral and crematory service records, cemetery records.
- Family records including family Bibles, birth certificates, marriage certificates, death certificates, and estate documents.

Many thanks to the following people who have contributed, collaborated, and traded family history over the years. Without these cousins, some more distant than others, this effort would never have ended up being what it is at this moment.

Lillie **(Aunt Lil)** Mae Dieckmann Straube *

Garland Frederick (**Fred**) Smith Jr.

Donna **Gail** Hartman

* Genealogy researchers long before the internet was invented.

Contents

Introduction

The following pages list data for all known family members as of April 26, 2024.

Each immediate family is presented in their own section that contains a graphical family tree as well as a description with information about each referenced person and their children. The child section provides information about the children of the preceding couple. When a child has offspring of their own this is presented in a separate family section for that child. In this case a '+' is used to denote that an individual will appear later in the book as a parent with his/her own children. For children with partners but no offspring, the partner data is given with the reference family. Roman numerals followed by a period are used to indicate the birth order.

In the chapter titled "Family of the Starting Person" the ancestors of Johann Stroube and Francis Feagen are presented in an enhanced Pedigree Chart which displays the graphic representation of their direct-line ancestors and the children of the couple. This chapter contains information about the couple whose offspring are listed in the later chapters.

The chapter titled "Families of his Descendants" provides details (as of the publication date) for the offspring of Johann Stroube and Francis Feagen. There is a chapter for each generation. Relatives are listed in the order of the nearness of their relationship.

If a burial date or cause of death is included then I've actually seen or have a copy of the death certificate. If there is no burial place listed then it can be assumed there is no online reference to where an individual is buried. There are instances where the death certificate will say someone is buried in a specific cemetery but the decedent ends up buried somewhere else. There are also individuals that have two findagrave.com numbers or locations. This is usually because one is a cenotaph and the other is the actual burial location. A common example is a war memorial where someone is listed but not buried there. In the index of places, GPS coordinates are provided if they are known. Some family plots on old farms are not listed.

Sources for the information provided are given in the footnotes.

This document reports the details of 542 individuals, of whom 284 are male and 257 are female. The sex of one individual is unknown. Of the 286 individuals with recorded birth and death dates, the average lifespan was 65.5 years. Of these, 152 males averaged 65.5 years, and 134 females averaged 65.5 years. The longest living male was Walter VanDevener Branstetter (1868–1964), who died aged 95. The longest living female was Lena Heins (1867–1967), who died aged 99.

Editorials and obituaries are denoted with a vertical left margin line.

Momentous events during our ancestors' lives:

Revolutionary War	1775 – 1783
California Gold Rush	1848 - 1855
Civil War	1861 – 1865
Lincoln Assassination	April 15,1865
First flight Kitty Hawk, North Carolina	December 17, 1903
WWI	1914 – 1918
Prohibition Era	1919 – 1933
19th Amendment Ratified Women's Right to Vote	August 18, 1920
Great Depression	1929 - 1939
WWII	1939 – 1945
Attack on Pearl Harbor	December 7, 1941
Korean Conflict	1950 – 1953
Kennedy Assassination	1963
Vietnam War	1954 – 1975
First Man on the Moon	1969
Watergate Scandal	1970
Elvis Presley Dies	1977
World Trade Center Attacked	September 11, 2001
Covid-19 Pandemic	March 11, 2020

Family of the Starting Person

Family of Johann Stroube and Francis Feagen

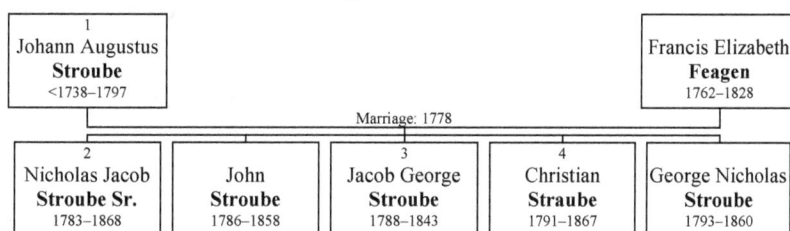

1. **Johann Augustus Stroube** was born before 1738 in Bayern, Imperial, Germany.[1] He died in Augusta, Bracken County, Kentucky, in 1797.[1] His burial details are unknown.

> Took the Oath to the Government in 1754 and had to be at least 16 years old to take the oath. Calculated DOB is before 1738.

Johann Augustus married **Francis Elizabeth Feagen** on Friday, January 02, 1778, in Augusta, Bracken County, Kentucky. They had five sons.

Francis Elizabeth was born in Fauquier County, British Colonial Province of Virginia, in 1762.[1] She was also known as **Fanny**.

Francis Elizabeth reached 66 years of age and died in Augusta, Bracken County, Kentucky, on December 15, 1828.[1] She was buried in Highland Cemetery, Augusta, Bracken County, Kentucky (Find a Grave ID 60236921).[1]

Sons of Johann Augustus Stroube and Francis Elizabeth Feagen:

+ 2   m   I. **Nicholas Jacob Stroube Sr.** was born in Quemahonig, Somerset County, British Colonial Province of Pennsylvania, on January 10, 1783. He died in Augusta, Bracken County, Kentucky, on August 27, 1868, at the age of 85. Nicholas Jacob was buried in Highland Cemetery, Augusta, Bracken County, Kentucky (Find a Grave ID 60235764).

       m   II. **John Stroube** was born in Quemahoning, Somerset County, Pennsylvania, on January 22, 1786. He died in Campbell County, Kentucky, on August 30, 1858, at the age of 72.

+ 3   m   III. **Jacob George Stroube** was born on July 16, 1788. He died in Bracken County, Kentucky, on February 23, 1843, at the age of 54. Jacob George was buried in Pepper Cemetery, Woolcott, Bracken County, Kentucky (Find a Grave ID 63575879).

> No GPS coordinates for this cemetery. It is located on private property. Take AA Highway to Rt #1159 and go north. Take Rt #1159 to Rt #1951 and go .5 miles to a lane on the right-hand side of the road. The cemetery is next to a field.

---

1   Ancestry.com, Public Member Trees (Provo, UT, USA, Ancestry.com Operations, Inc., 2006), Ancestry.com, Record for Christian Straube - Stroube. https://search.ancestry.co.uk/cgi-bin/sse.dll?db=1030&h=42086980514&indiv=try.

+   4   m   IV.   **Christian Straube** was born in Quemahoning, Somerset County, Pennsylvania, on December 24, 1791.[1–3] He died in Vandalia, Audrain County, Missouri, in 1867 at the age of 75.[1–3] Christian was buried in Fike Cemetery, Audrain County, Missouri (Find a Grave ID 68861781).[1–3]

He was a farmer and lived in the following places:
Pennsylvania (c1789-c1812)
Bracken County, Kentucky (c1812-1813)
Franklin County, Indiana (1813-1839)
Audrain County, Missouri (1839-1863)

Christian Straube's biography appeared in *Pioneer Families of Missouri*, by Wm. S. Bryan and Robert Rose, Montgomery County, p. 289 (originally published in St. Louis, 1876):
"STROBE [sic] — Christian Strobe, of Pennsylvania, removed first to Indiana, and from thence to Audrain County, Mo. His wife was Marry Miller [sic], of Kentucky, and they had — William H., Eliza, James, Isabella, George, Rebecca, Mary, and Christian, Jr., most of whom have families, and live in Audrain and Montgomery counties."

"The Will of Christian Straube." *The First 100 Wills in Audrain County, Missouri*, compiled by the D.A.R., Journal A, p. 322. (Abstract copied and provided by Donna Dawkins Squires.)
Abstract: Christian Straube, Audrain County MO, July 14, 1863. To my wife, Mary, all my estate, real and personal, during her natural life, and at her death to be divided among my heirs as follows:
To my son William H. Straube, $58.89. To my son James E. Straube, $1.00. To my daughter Eliza Straube, wife of Thomas Norris, $134.60. To Isabelle Straube, wife of William Sox, $153.60. To my son George Straube, $150.60. To my daughter Rebecca Straube, wife of Jackson Sox, $132.60. To my daughter Mary Straube, Wife of Almerane Davis, $163.30. The remainder of my estate to be equally divided among my named children. I appoint Cornelius H. Cawfield Administrator of this last will.

[Journal A, p. 322]

NOTE: Moneys total $794.59.

---

2   FamilySearch.org, FamilySearch Family Tree, FamilySearch, "Family Tree," database, <i>FamilySearch</i> (http://familysearch.org : modified 14 April 2022, 19:32), entry for Christian Straube (PID https://familysearch.org/ark:/61903/4:1:KJMH-N7D); contributed by various users. PersonID KJMH-N7D.

3   FamilySearch.org, FamilySearch Family Tree, FamilySearch.

m   V. **George Nicholas Stroube** was born in Quemahoning, Somerset County, Pennsylvania, on April 26, 1793. He died in Augusta, Bracken County, Kentucky, on June 11, 1860, at the age of 67. His burial details are unknown.

Families of his Descendants

1st Generation

Nicholas Stroube

2.   **Nicholas Jacob Stroube Sr.** was born on Friday, January 10, 1783, in Quemahonig, Somerset County, British Colonial Province of Pennsylvania. He was the son of Johann Augustus Stroube (1) and Francis Elizabeth Feagen.

Nicholas Jacob died in Augusta, Bracken County, Kentucky, on August 27, 1868, at the age of 85. He was buried in Highland Cemetery, Augusta, Bracken County, Kentucky (Find a Grave ID 60235764).

Marriages with Mary Seal and (unknown given name) Catherine (Page 22) are known.

Family of Nicholas Stroube and Mary Seal

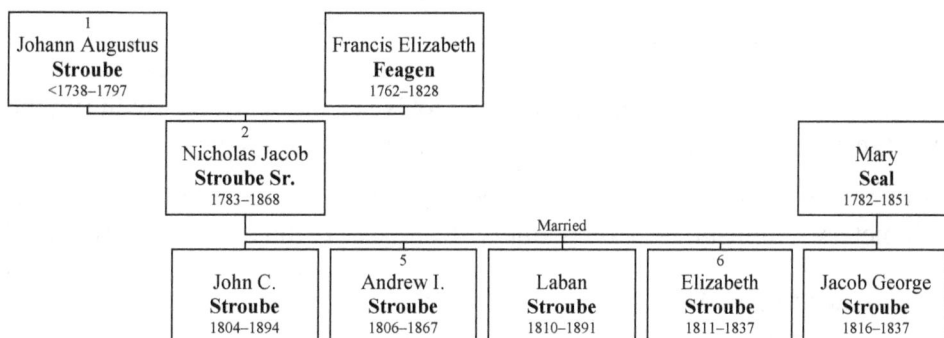

```
┌────────────────────┐          ┌────────────────────┐
│          1         │          │                    │
│  Johann Augustus   │          │  Francis Elizabeth │
│     Stroube        │          │      Feagen        │
│    <1738–1797      │          │     1762–1828      │
└────────────────────┘          └────────────────────┘
        ┌────────────────────┐                          ┌────────────────────┐
        │          2         │                          │                    │
        │  Nicholas Jacob    │                          │       Mary         │
        │   Stroube Sr.      │                          │       Seal         │
        │    1783–1868       │                          │     1782–1851      │
        └────────────────────┘                          └────────────────────┘
                                       Married
  ┌──────────┐  ┌──────────┐  ┌──────────┐  ┌──────────┐  ┌──────────┐
  │          │  │    5     │  │          │  │    6     │  │          │
  │ John C.  │  │ Andrew I.│  │  Laban   │  │Elizabeth │  │Jacob George│
  │ Stroube  │  │ Stroube  │  │ Stroube  │  │ Stroube  │  │ Stroube  │
  │1804–1894 │  │1806–1867 │  │1810–1891 │  │1811–1837 │  │1816–1837 │
  └──────────┘  └──────────┘  └──────────┘  └──────────┘  └──────────┘
```

Here are the details about **Nicholas Jacob Stroube Sr.'s** first marriage, with Mary Seal. You can read more about Nicholas Jacob on page 21.

Nicholas Jacob Stroube Sr. married **Mary Seal**. They had five children.

Mary was born in Augusta, Bracken County, Kentucky, on Thursday, October 24, 1782. She reached 69 years of age and died on November 04, 1851. Mary was buried in Highland Cemetery, Augusta, Bracken County, Kentucky (Find a Grave ID 60235796).

Children of Nicholas Jacob Stroube Sr. and Mary Seal:

	m	I. **John C. Stroube** was born in Augusta, Bracken County, Kentucky, on July 07, 1804. He died on January 24, 1894, at the age of 89. John C. was buried in Highland Cemetery, Augusta, Bracken County, Kentucky (Find a Grave ID 60237349).
+ 5	m	II. **Andrew I. Stroube** was born on December 06, 1806. He died on June 22, 1867, at the age of 60. Andrew I. was buried in Greenlawn Cemetery, Portsmouth, Scioto County, Ohio (Find a Grave ID 103424510).
	m	III. **Laban Stroube** was born on April 27, 1810. He died on April 30, 1891, at the age of 81. Laban was buried in Augusta Hillside Cemetery, Augusta, Bracken County, Kentucky (Find a Grave ID 147945293).

+ 6   f   IV. **Elizabeth Stroube** was born on March 06, 1811. She died on November 08, 1837, at the age of 26. Elizabeth was buried in Pepper Cemetery, Woolcott, Bracken County, Kentucky (Find a Grave ID 63575739).

     m   V. **Jacob George Stroube** was born on February 28, 1816. He died on December 07, 1837, at the age of 21. Jacob George was buried in Highland Cemetery, Augusta, Bracken County, Kentucky (Find a Grave ID 60236340).

Family of Nicholas Stroube and Catherine

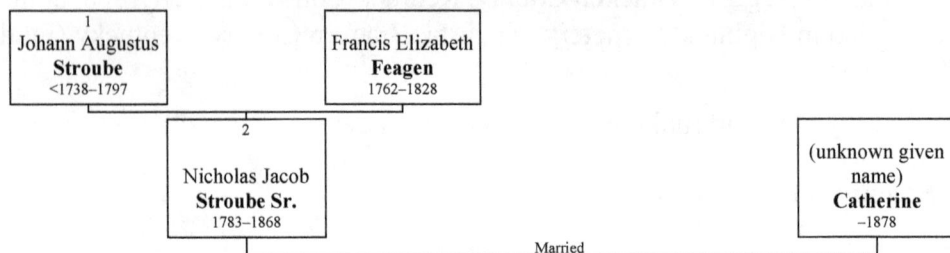

Here are the details about **Nicholas Jacob Stroube Sr.'s** second marriage, with (unknown given name) Catherine. You can read more about Nicholas Jacob on page 21.

Nicholas Jacob Stroube Sr. married **Catherine**. She died on May 28, 1878. She was buried in Highland Cemetery, Augusta, Bracken County, Kentucky (Find a Grave ID 60235870).

Family of Jacob Stroube and Mary Wiley

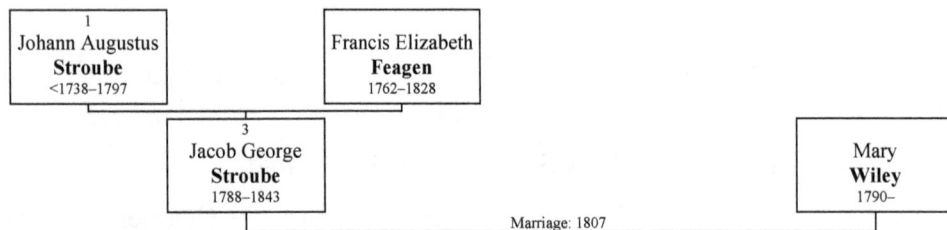

3.   **Jacob George Stroube** was born on Wednesday, July 16, 1788. He was the son of Johann Augustus Stroube (1) and Francis Elizabeth Feagen.

Jacob George died in Bracken County, Kentucky, on February 23, 1843, at the age of 54. He was buried in Pepper Cemetery, Woolcott, Bracken County, Kentucky (Find a Grave ID 63575879).

> No GPS coordinates for this cemetery. It is located on private property. Take AA Highway to Rt #1159 and go north. Take Rt #1159 to Rt #1951 and go .5 miles to a lane on the right-hand side of the road. The cemetery is next to a field.

Jacob George married **Mary Wiley** on Tuesday, December 15, 1807. Mary was born in Franklin Farms, Washington County, Pennsylvania, in 1790. She was also known as **Polly**.

Mary died in Bracken County, Kentucky. She was buried in Pepper Cemetery, Woolcott, Bracken County, Kentucky (Find a Grave ID 90668553).

Family of Christian Straube and Mary Miller

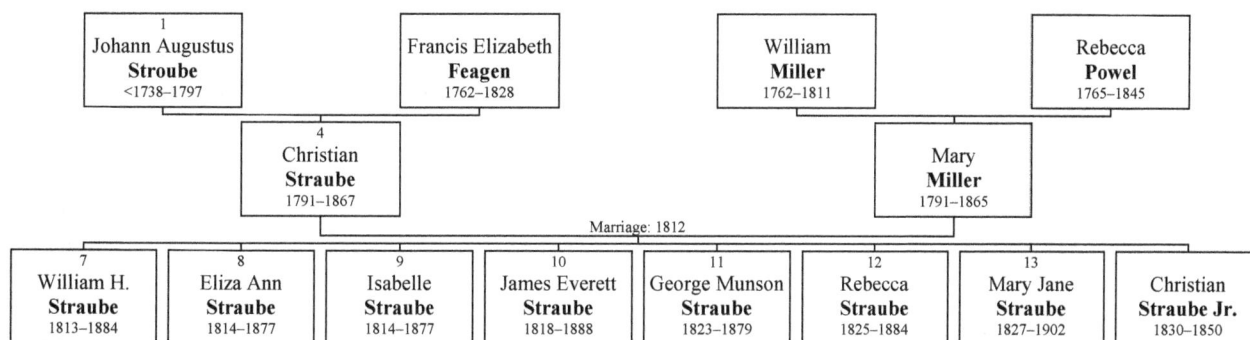

1 Johann Augustus **Stroube** <1738–1797	Francis Elizabeth **Feagen** 1762–1828	William **Miller** 1762–1811	Rebecca **Powel** 1765–1845

4
Christian
Straube
1791–1867

Mary
Miller
1791–1865

Marriage: 1812

7 William H. **Straube** 1813–1884	8 Eliza Ann **Straube** 1814–1877	9 Isabelle **Straube** 1814–1877	10 James Everett **Straube** 1818–1888	11 George Munson **Straube** 1823–1879	12 Rebecca **Straube** 1825–1884	13 Mary Jane **Straube** 1827–1902	Christian **Straube Jr.** 1830–1850

4. **Christian Straube** was born on Saturday, December 24, 1791, in Quemahoning, Somerset County, Pennsylvania.[4–6] He was the son of Johann Augustus Stroube (1) and Francis Elizabeth Feagen.

Christian died in Vandalia, Audrain County, Missouri, in 1867 at the age of 75.[4–6] He was buried in Fike Cemetery, Audrain County, Missouri (Find a Grave ID 68861781).[4–6]

He was a farmer and lived in the following places:
Pennsylvania (c1789-c1812)
Bracken County, Kentucky (c1812-1813)
Franklin County, Indiana (1813-1839)
Audrain County, Missouri (1839-1863)

Christian Straube's biography appeared in *Pioneer Families of Missouri*, by Wm. S. Bryan and Robert Rose, Montgomery County, p. 289 (originally published in St. Louis, 1876):
"STROBE [sic] -- Christian Strobe, of Pennsylvania, removed first to Indiana, and from thence to Audrain County, Mo. His wife was Marry Miller [sic], of Kentucky, and they had -- William H., Eliza, James, Isabella, George, Rebecca, Mary, and Christian, Jr., most of whom have families, and live in Audrain and Montgomery counties."

The Will of Christian Straube. The First 100 Wills in Audrain County, Missouri, compiled by the D.A.R., Journal A, p. 322. (Abstract copied and provided by Donna Dawkins Squires.)

Abstract: Christian Straube, Audrain County MO, July 14, 1863. To my wife, Mary, all my estate, real and personal, during her natural life, and at her death to be divided among my heirs as follows:

4   FamilySearch.org, FamilySearch Family Tree, FamilySearch, "Family Tree," database, <i>FamilySearch</i> (http://familysearch.org : modified 14 April 2022, 19:32), entry for Christian Straube (PID https://familysearch.org/ark:/61903/4:1:KJMH-N7D); contributed by various users. PersonID KJMH-N7D.

5   FamilySearch.org, FamilySearch Family Tree, FamilySearch.

6   Ancestry.com, Public Member Trees (Provo, UT, USA, Ancestry.com Operations, Inc., 2006), Ancestry.com, Record for Christian Straube - Stroube. https://search.ancestry.co.uk/cgi-bin/sse.dll?db=1030&h=42086980514&indiv=try.

To my son William H. Straube, $58.89. To my son James E. Straube, $1.00. To my daughter Eliza Straube, wife of Thomas Norris, $134.60. To Isabelle Straube, wife of William Sox, $153.60. To my son George Straube, $150.60. To my daughter Rebecca Straube, wife of Jackson Sox, $132.60. To my daughter Mary Straube, Wife of Almerane Davis, $163.30. The remainder of my estate to be equally divided among my named children. I appoint Cornelius H. Cawfield Administrator of this last will.

[Journal A, p. 322]

NOTE: Moneys total $794.59.

More facts and events for Christian Straube:

Individual Note: March 17, 1818 Received a U.S. patent for property with John Straube, SW1/4,Sec18, Tsp9, R1.

Individual Note: May 15, 1852 Received a U.S. patent for property (Certificate No. 26070) SE1/4 SE1/4 T51N, R5W, Sec.31, Audrain County, MO, 40 acres, in Audrain County, MO.

At the age of 20, Christian married **Mary Miller** on Thursday, July 02, 1812, in Bracken County, Kentucky, when she was 21 years old. They had eight children.

Mary was born in Bracken County, Kentucky, on Tuesday, March 01, 1791. She was the daughter of William Miller and Rebecca Powel. She was also known as **Polly**.

Mary reached 74 years of age and died in Audrain County, Missouri, on April 18, 1865. She was buried in Fike Cemetery, Audrain County, Missouri (Find a Grave ID 68862024).

Children of Christian Straube and Mary Miller:

+ 7   m   I. **William H. Straube** was born in Bracken County, Kentucky, on April 14, 1813. He died in Elsberry, Lincoln County, Missouri, on January 02, 1884, at the age of 70. His cause of death was uremia with the complication of cystitis with enlarged prostate. He was buried in Palmer Cemetery, Elsberry, Lincoln County, Missouri, on January 03, 1884 (Find a Grave ID 83937996).

Listed in Lincoln County, MO Death Register as 70 yrs, 8 mos, 18 days.

+ 8   f   II. **Eliza Ann Straube** was born in Springfield, Franklin County, Indiana, on December 12, 1814. She died in Audrain County, Missouri, on February 08, 1877, at the age of 62. Eliza Ann was buried in Fike Cemetery, Audrain County, Missouri (Find a Grave ID 70608410).

Eliza Ann Straube was born 12 Dec 1814 in Springfield, Franklin County, Indiana, and died 08 Feb 1877 in Audrain County, Missouri. She married (1) Isaac Smalley 05 Sep 1833 in Springfield, Franklin County, Indiana. He died before Mar 1839 in Franklin County, Indiana. She married (2) Thomas Norris 28 Sep 1838 in Franklin County, Indiana. He was born about 1814 in Ohio, and died about 04 Nov 1879 in Louisville, Denton County, Texas.

+ 9   f   III. **Isabelle Straube** was born in Springfield Township, Franklin County, Indiana, on December 12, 1814.[7, 8] She was also known as **Isabela**.

Isabelle died in Audrain County, Missouri, on February 08, 1877, at the age of 62.[7, 8] She was buried in Kansas City, Wyandotte County, Kansas.[8]

+ 10   m   IV. **James Everett Straube** was born in Indiana, USA, on January 08, 1818. He died in On Indian Creek, Middletown, Montgomery County, Missouri, on January 23, 1888, at the age of 70. James Everett was buried in Siloam Primitive Baptist Church Cemetery, Ashley, Pike County, Missouri (Find a Grave ID 68990713).

Head of household in 1840 Census- Audrain County
Head of household in 1850 Census- Audrain County
Head of household in 1860 Census- Middletown, Montgomery County, Missouri
Head of household in 1870 Census- New Harmony, Pike County, Missouri

(Death Notices from   *The Montgomery Standard* Newspaper, Montgomery City, 1880-89, abstracted by Alma Jane Eulbe Wheeler);

Jan 23, 1888 James Straube Sr. at his home on Indian Creek, near Middletown (10 Feb 1888). Copy provided by Donna Dawkins Squires, Camdenton, MO, 1994.

James Everett Straube was born on January 8, 1818 in Indiana and is the son of Christian Straube and Mary "Polly" Miller Straube.

James Everett Straube married Rebecca Ann Gregg on June 30, 1836 in Franklin County, Indiana. Rebecca Ann Gregg was born in Cincinnati, Hamilton County, Ohio, and was a cousin to William McKinley, the 25th President of the United States. McKinley was a Republican, and James Everett was never proud of that fact. As a result, there were mixed political feelings among the family.

+ 11   m   V. **George Munson Straube** was born in Franklin County, Indiana, on October 15, 1823. He died in Montgomery County, Missouri, on August 06, 1879, at the age of 55. George Munson was buried in Wellsville Cemetery, Wellsville, Montgomery County, Missouri (Find a Grave ID 83904546).

+ 12   f   VI. **Rebecca Straube** was born in Springfield Township, Franklin County, Indiana, in 1825. She died in Audrain County, Missouri, in 1884 at the age of 59. Her burial details are unknown (Find a Grave ID 250850235).

---

7   Ancestry.com, Public Member Trees (Provo, UT, USA, Ancestry.com Operations, Inc., 2006), Ancestry.com, Record for Isabel Flood. https://search.ancestry.co.uk/cgi-bin/sse.dll?db=1030&h=202148572135&indiv=try.

8   Ancestry.com, Public Member Trees (Provo, UT, USA, Ancestry.com Operations, Inc., 2006), Ancestry.com, Record for Joseph Flood. https://search.ancestry.co.uk/cgi-bin/sse.dll?db=1030&h=34222407661&indiv=try.

+ 13   f   VII. **Mary Jane Straube** was born in Springfield Township, Franklin County, Indiana, on February 12, 1827. She died in Miami, Roberts County, Texas, on February 10, 1902, at the age of 74. Mary Jane was buried in Miami Cemetery, Miami, Roberts County, Texas (Find a Grave ID 18004777).

   m   VIII. **Christian Straube Jr.** was born in Franklin County, Indiana, in April 1830. He died in Audrain County, Missouri, in February 1850 at the age of 19. Christian was buried in Fike Cemetery, Audrain County, Missouri (Find a Grave ID 70608020).

2nd Generation

Family of Andrew Stroube and Eleanor Linn

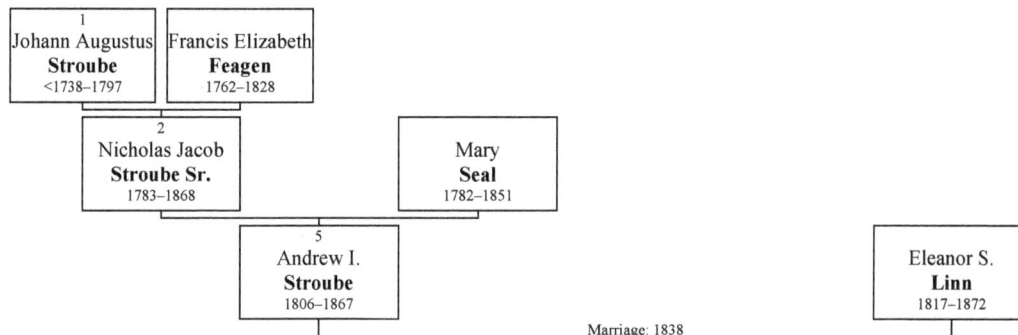

5. **Andrew I. Stroube** was born on Saturday, December 06, 1806. He was the son of Nicholas Jacob Stroube Sr. (2) and Mary Seal.

Andrew I. died on June 22, 1867, at the age of 60. He was buried in Greenlawn Cemetery, Portsmouth, Scioto County, Ohio (Find a Grave ID 103424510).

At the age of 31, Andrew I. married **Eleanor S. Linn** on Tuesday, February 13, 1838, in Brown County, Ohio, when she was 20 years old. Eleanor S. was born on Monday, April 07, 1817.

She reached 55 years of age and died in Scioto County, Ohio, on November 01, 1872. Eleanor S. was buried in Greenlawn Cemetery, Portsmouth, Scioto County, Ohio (Find a Grave ID 102822486).

Family of Elizabeth Stroube and Jacob Hickman

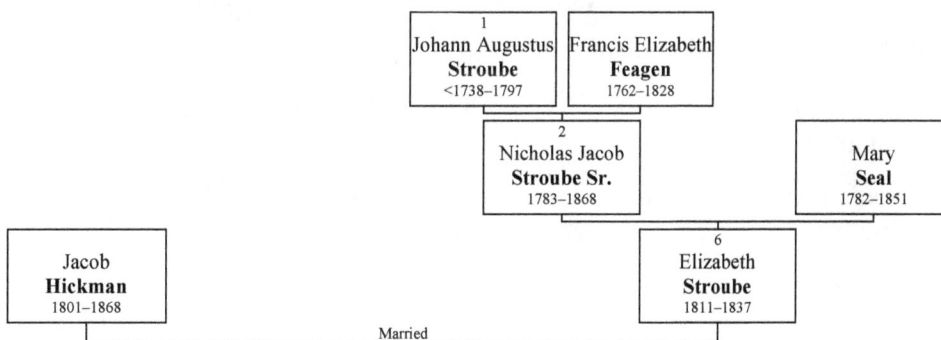

6. **Elizabeth Stroube** was born on Wednesday, March 06, 1811. She was the daughter of Nicholas Jacob Stroube Sr. (2) and Mary Seal.

Elizabeth died on November 08, 1837, at the age of 26. She was buried in Pepper Cemetery, Woolcott, Bracken County, Kentucky (Find a Grave ID 63575739).

She married **Jacob Hickman**. Jacob was born on Sunday, November 01, 1801.

He reached 66 years of age and died in August 1868. Jacob was buried in Bethel Baptist Church Cemetery, Palmyra, Marion County, Missouri (Find a Grave ID 9032502).

Family of William Straube and Phoebe Norris

1 Johann Augustus **Stroube** <1738–1797	Francis Elizabeth **Feagen** 1762–1828	William **Miller** 1762–1811	Rebecca **Powel** 1765–1845

4 Christian **Straube** 1791–1867	Mary **Miller** 1791–1865	John **Norris** 1786–1858	Jane **Hannah** 1790–1869

7 William H. **Straube** 1813–1884	Phoebe **Norris** 1813–1880

Marriage: 1836

14 Samuel Norris **Straube** 1837–1923	Nancy E. **Straube** 1839–	**15** Emeline **Straube** 1840–1886	**16** Elizabeth J. **Straube** 1844–1894	**17** Caleb Sylvester **Straube** 1844–1879	**18** William Martillus **Straube** 1846–1888	**19** Phoebe Leticia **Straube** 1851–	**20** Martha Isabell **Straube** 1853–1928

7.   **William H. Straube** was born on Wednesday, April 14, 1813, in Bracken County, Kentucky. He was the son of Christian Straube (4) and Mary Miller.

William H. served in the military on April 30, 1863 and was relieved of duty. He served in the military on August 12, 1864 and enlisted for one year at Wellsville MO (CW Union) - Co.B, 49th Reg. Inf. Vols. William H. served in the military at Civil War, Union, 49th Regiment, Missouri Infantry in Missouri, USA, on September 15, 1864.

He died in Elsberry, Lincoln County, Missouri, on January 02, 1884, at the age of 70. His cause of death was uremia with the complication of cystitis with enlarged prostate. He was buried in Palmer Cemetery, Elsberry, Lincoln County, Missouri, on January 03, 1884 (Find a Grave ID 83937996).

Listed in Lincoln County, MO Death Register as 70 yrs, 8 mos, 18 days.

William H. married **Phoebe Norris** in 1836. They had eight children.

Phoebe was born in Ohio, USA, in 1813.[9] She was the daughter of John Norris and Jane Hannah.

Phoebe reached 67 years of age and died in Missouri, USA, in 1880.[9] Her burial details are unknown (Find a Grave ID 230195992).

Children of William H. Straube and Phoebe Norris:

+   14   m   I. **Samuel Norris Straube** was born in Brookfield, Shelby County, Indiana, on September 22, 1837. He died in Moberly, Randolph County, Missouri, on October 31, 1923, at the age of 86. His cause of death was brain hemorrhage. He was buried in Wellsville Cemetery, Wellsville, Montgomery County, Missouri, on November 01, 1923 (Find a Grave ID 42562959).

---

9   Ancestry.com, Public Member Trees (Provo, UT, USA, Ancestry.com Operations, Inc., 2006), Ancestry.com, Record for Phebe Norris. https://search.ancestry.co.uk/cgi-bin/sse.dll?db=1030&h=280087509291&indiv=try.

The following is a newspaper article from the *Montgomery Standard* of Montgomery City, MO:

November 9, 1923 p. 6/1

WELLSVILLE STARS.

N. Straube, a former resident of Wellsville, died at the home of his daughter, Mrs. L. Wullschlager, in Moberly Wednesday. Besides Mrs. Wullschlager he leaves one daughter, Mrs Addie Morris of Pueblo, Colo., and one son, Melvin Straube of Madison, MO. The remains were brought to this city Thursday and interment was made in the Wellsville cemetery.

The following is a newspaper article from the *Moberly Monitor Index* in Moberly, MO:

October 31, 1923 p. 7/4

SAMUEL N. STRAUBE 86, DIES

Funeral will be held in Morning Burial at Wellsville

Samuel N. Straube, 86 years old, died at 1 o'clock this afternoon at the home of his daughter. Mrs. L. C. Wullschleger, 608 West Coates Street, where he had made his home for the last four and a half years. He formerly made his home in Wellsville.

The following is a newspaper article from the *Wellsville Optic-News* in Wellsville, MO:

November 2, 1923 p. 1/1

FORMER RESIDENT OF WELLSVILLE DIED IN MOBERLY WEDNESDAY

S. N. STRAUBE, 86, WAS BURIED IN THE WELLSVILLE CEMETERY THURSDAY AFTERNOON.

Samuel Norris Strabue, one of Wellsville's old and well known citizens departed this life October 31, 1923. His age was 86 years, 1 month, and 9 days.

Mr. Straube was born in the state of Indiana September 22, 1837, and his parents afterward came to Missouri where they reared a family of eight children. He spent most of his early life in Middletown until he moved to Wellsville in 1879. After residing in Wellsville almost 40 years he retired to Moberly and spent the last few years with his oldest daughter Mrs. Jessie Wullschleger.

In 1861 Mr. Straube was married to Susan H. Fox, who died in 1866. In 1871 he was married to Iva A. Allen who died in 1873. On Dec 5, 1875 he was married to [Sarah Ada] Ada Hammett who died December 12, 1915. He was the father of seven children four of whom preceded him to the grave.. The three that survive him are Melvin M. Straube of Madison Mo, Mrs. Jessie Wullschleger of Moberly and Mrs. Addie Morris of Pueblo, County.

At the age of 18 he united with the Christian church to which he remained a faithful member until his death. For many years he was an elder and leader in the church at Wellsville until his declining health confined him more closely to privacy. While he took considerable interest in reading and discussing the political affairs of the day his main interest seemed to be taken up in discussing the spiritual condition of the world in regard to death and immortality. In the last few years of his life he claimed that sectarianism had become corrupt and that great troubles would soon come up-on the earth which would force the world to righteousness and usher in the millennium.

He was the father of Edward Straube who died in this city a few years ago with influenza.

There are few men who lived purer and nobler lives than Mr. Straube, and the devoted Christian died as he had lived.

His three children were at the cemetery at the time of his burial including several ladies who were friends of Mrs. Wullschleger, of Moberly, and several relatives and old acquaintances of this city.

The body arrived in Wellsville Thursday and interment was made in the Wellsville City cemetery that afternoon.

Many citizens of this place extend their sympathy to the bereaved ones who mourn the loss of the noble man.

Besides Mrs. Wullschleger, he is survived by one other daughter , Mrs. Addie Harrison of Pueblo, Colo.; one son H. M. Straube of Madison, MO; two grandchildren, and two sisters, Mrs. Bell Angell of Middletown, MO., and Mrs. Bettie Miller of Clinton, MO.

This afternoon short services will be conducted at 9:15 o'clock tomorrow morning after which the body will be shipped on Wabash train No. 10 to Wellsville for burial.

		f	II. **Nancy E. Straube** was born in Angola, Steuben County, Indiana, in 1839.
+	15	f	III. **Emeline Straube** was born in Missouri, USA, in 1840. She was also known as **Pulina**.

Emeline died in Lincoln County, Missouri, on March 25, 1886, at the age of 46. She was buried in Winfield Cemetery, Winfield, Lincoln County, Missouri (Find a Grave ID 83970824).

+	16	f	IV. **Elizabeth J. Straube** was born in Missouri, USA, in 1844.[10–13] She was also known as **Eliza Strawby**.

Elizabeth J. died in Clinton, Henry County, Missouri, on November 30, 1894, at the age of 50.[14] Her burial details are unknown.

+	17	m	V. **Caleb Sylvester Straube** was born in 1844. He died in 1879 at the age of 35. His burial details are unknown.
+	18	m	VI. **William Martillus Straube** was born in Missouri, USA, on November 27, 1846.[11, 12, 15, 16] He died in Wellsville, Montgomery County, Missouri, on December 31, 1888, at the age of 42.[15] William Martillus was buried in Fairmount Cemetery, Middletown, Montgomery County, Missouri (Find a Grave ID 84020789).[15]
+	19	f	VII. **Phoebe Leticia Straube** was born in Missouri, USA, in 1851.[17] She was also known as **Lettie**.

Her burial details are unknown.

+	20	f	VIII. **Martha Isabell Straube** was born in Missouri, USA, on February 04, 1853. She died in Saint Louis, Saint Louis County, Missouri, on December 30, 1928, at the age of 75. Martha was buried in Fairmount Cemetery, Middletown, Montgomery County, Missouri (Find a Grave ID 157112047).

10 FamilySearch.org, Missouri State and Territorial Census Records, 1732-1933, FamilySearch, "Missouri State and Territorial Census Records, 1732-1933", , <i>FamilySearch</i> (https://www.familysearch.org/ark:/61903/1:1:QPHW-DYLT : Wed Oct 04 14:24:15 UTC 2023), Entry for W J Sanders and A C Sanders, 1876.

11 FamilySearch.org, United States Census, 1860, FamilySearch, "United States Census, 1860", , <i>FamilySearch</i> (https://www.familysearch.org/ark:/61903/1:1:MHZR-B95 : Thu Oct 05 13:34:30 UTC 2023), Entry for William H Straly and Phebe Straly, 1860.

12 FamilySearch.org, United States Census, 1850, FamilySearch, "United States Census, 1850", , <i>FamilySearch</i> (https://www.familysearch.org/ark:/61903/1:1:MDZS-YKV : Fri Oct 06 14:26:49 UTC 2023), Entry for William H Strawby and Phebe Strawby, 1850.

13 FamilySearch.org, United States Census, 1880, FamilySearch, "United States Census, 1880", , <i>FamilySearch</i> (https://www.familysearch.org/ark:/61903/1:1:M6X7-R2C : Thu Oct 05 10:37:01 UTC 2023), Entry for Wm. Sanders and Eliza J. Sanders, 1880.

14 Ancestry.com, Public Member Trees (Provo, UT, USA, Ancestry.com Operations, Inc., 2006), Ancestry.com, Record for Eliza J Strawbe. https://search.ancestry.co.uk/cgi-bin/sse.dll?db=1030&h=18572195325&indiv=try.

15 FamilySearch.org, Find A Grave Index, FamilySearch, "Find A Grave Index," database, <i>FamilySearch</i> (https://www.familysearch.org/ark:/61903/1:1:QVL9-V8M4 : 16 June 2020), William Straube, 1888; Burial, , ; citing record ID , <i>Find a Grave</i>, http://www.findagrave.com.

16 FamilySearch.org, United States Census, 1880, FamilySearch, "United States Census, 1880", , <i>FamilySearch</i> (https://www.familysearch.org/ark:/61903/1:1:M6XY-42P : Tue Oct 03 22:41:12 UTC 2023), Entry for Wm. H. Straube and Martha D. Straube, 1880.

17 Ancestry.com, Public Member Trees (Provo, UT, USA, Ancestry.com Operations, Inc., 2006), Ancestry.com, Record for Phebe Leticia Straube, Strawby, Strawbe (Miller). https://search.ancestry.co.uk/cgi-bin/sse.dll?db=1030&h=32297777406&indiv=try.

Eliza Straube

8.　　**Eliza Ann Straube** was born on Monday, December 12, 1814, in Springfield, Franklin County, Indiana. She was the daughter of Christian Straube (4) and Mary Miller.

Eliza Ann died in Audrain County, Missouri, on February 08, 1877, at the age of 62. She was buried in Fike Cemetery, Audrain County, Missouri (Find a Grave ID 70608410).

Eliza Aan Straube was born 12 Dec 1814 in Springfield, Franklin County, Indiana, and died 08 Feb 1877 in Audrain County, Missouri. She married (1) Isaac Smalley 05 Sep 1833 in Springfield, Franklin County, Indiana. He died before Mar 1839 in Franklin County, Indiana. She married (2) Thomas Norris 28 Sep 1838 in Franklin County, Indiana. He was born about1814 in Ohio, and died about 04 Nov 1879 in Louisville, Denton County, Texas.

Marriages with Isaac Smalley and Thomas Norris (Page 33) are known.

Family of Eliza Straube and Isaac Smalley

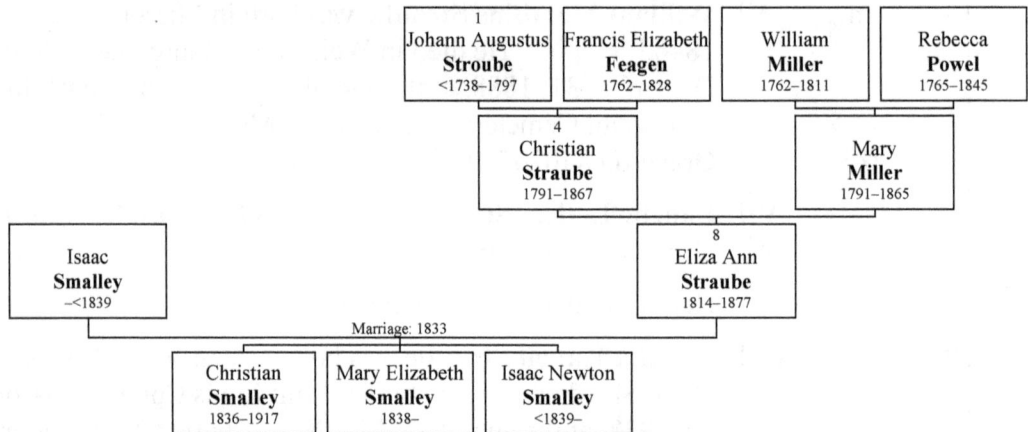

Here are the details about **Eliza Ann Straube's** first marriage, with Isaac Smalley. You can read more about Eliza Ann on page 32.

Eliza Ann Straube married **Isaac Smalley** on Thursday, September 05, 1833, in Springfield, Franklin County, Indiana. They had three children.

Isaac died in Franklin County, Indiana, before March 1839.

Children of Eliza Ann Straube and Isaac Smalley:

m　　　　I. **Christian Smalley** was born in Indiana, USA, in 1836. He died in Los Angeles County, California, on May 17, 1917, at the age of 81. Christian's burial details are unknown (Find a Grave ID 231022845).

f　　　　II. **Mary Elizabeth Smalley** was born in Indiana, USA, in 1838.[18]

m　　　　III. **Isaac Newton Smalley** was born before 1839.

18　　Ancestry.com, Public Member Trees (Provo, UT, USA, Ancestry.com Operations, Inc., 2006), Ancestry.com, Record for Mary Elizabeth Smalley. https://search.ancestry.co.uk/cgi-bin/sse.dll?db=1030&h=27343989416&indiv=try.

Family of Eliza Straube and Thomas Norris

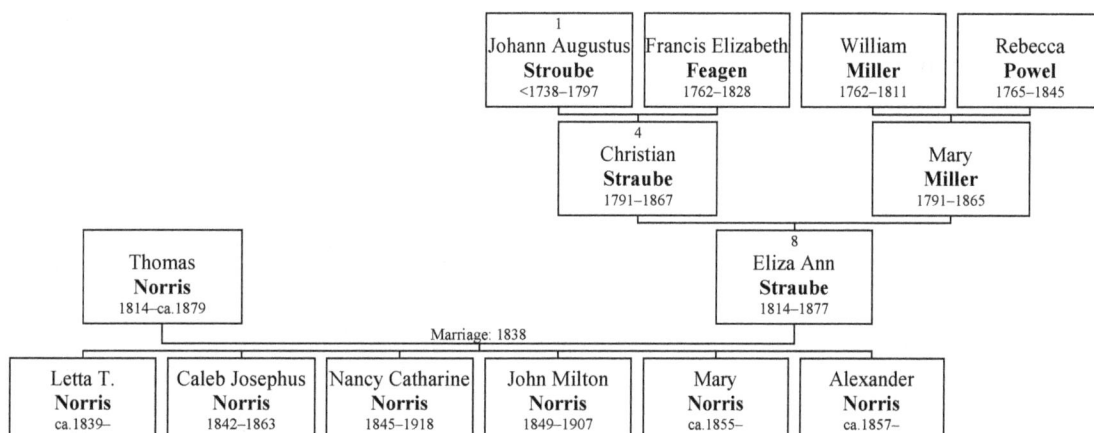

	1 Johann Augustus **Stroube** <1738–1797	Francis Elizabeth **Feagen** 1762–1828	William **Miller** 1762–1811	Rebecca **Powel** 1765–1845

	4 Christian **Straube** 1791–1867	Mary **Miller** 1791–1865

Thomas **Norris** 1814–ca.1879	8 Eliza Ann **Straube** 1814–1877

Marriage: 1838

Letta T. **Norris** ca.1839–	Caleb Josephus **Norris** 1842–1863	Nancy Catharine **Norris** 1845–1918	John Milton **Norris** 1849–1907	Mary **Norris** ca.1855–	Alexander **Norris** ca.1857–

Here are the details about **Eliza Ann Straube's** second marriage, with Thomas Norris. You can read more about Eliza Ann on page 32.

Eliza Ann Straube married **Thomas Norris** on Friday, September 28, 1838, in Franklin County, Indiana. They had six children.

Thomas was born in Ohio, USA, in 1814. He reached 65 years of age and died in Louisville, Denton County, Texas, about November 04, 1879. Thomas' burial details are unknown (Find a Grave ID 231099518).

Children of Eliza Ann Straube and Thomas Norris:

f   I.   **Letta T. Norris** was born about 1839. She was also known as **Letty**.

m   II. **Caleb Josephus Norris** was born on November 22, 1842. He died in Missouri, USA, on September 01, 1863, at the age of 20. Caleb Josephus was buried in Fike Cemetery, Audrain County, Missouri (Find a Grave ID 83891880).

f   III. **Nancy Catharine Norris** was born on February 22, 1845. She died in Adair, Mayes County, Oklahoma, on July 27, 1918, at the age of 73.

m   IV. **John Milton Norris** was born in Audrain County, Missouri, on November 05, 1849. He died on July 01, 1907, at the age of 57.

f   V.   **Mary Norris** was born about 1855.

m   VI. **Alexander Norris** was born about 1857.

Isabelle Straube

9.   **Isabelle Straube** was born on Monday, December 12, 1814, in Springfield Township, Franklin County, Indiana.[19, 20] She was the daughter of Christian Straube (4) and Mary Miller. She was also known as **Isabela**.

---

19   Ancestry.com, Public Member Trees (Provo, UT, USA, Ancestry.com Operations, Inc., 2006), Ancestry.com, Record for Isabel Flood. https://search.ancestry.co.uk/cgi-bin/sse.dll?db=1030&h=202148572135&indiv=try.

20   Ancestry.com, Public Member Trees (Provo, UT, USA, Ancestry.com Operations, Inc., 2006), Ancestry.com, Record for Joseph Flood. https://search.ancestry.co.uk/cgi-bin/sse.dll?db=1030&h=34222407661&indiv=try.

Isabelle died in Audrain County, Missouri, on February 08, 1877, at the age of 62.[19, 20] She was buried in Kansas City, Wyandotte County, Kansas.[20]

Marriages with Joseph Flood, William Sox (Page 34) and William T. Angel (Page 35) are known.

Family of Isabelle Straube and Joseph Flood

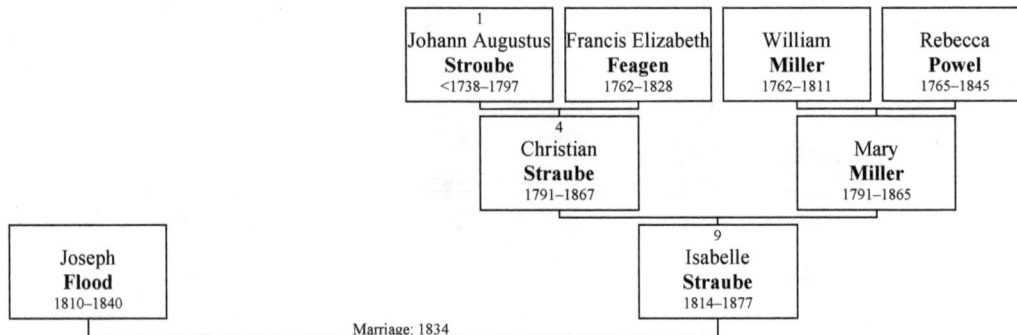

Here are the details about **Isabelle Straube's** first marriage, with Joseph Flood. You can read more about Isabelle on page 33.

Isabelle Straube married **Joseph Flood** on Thursday, July 31, 1834, in Franklin County, Indiana.[20] Joseph was born in 1810.[20]

He reached 30 years of age and died in 1840.[20]

Family of Isabelle Straube and William Sox

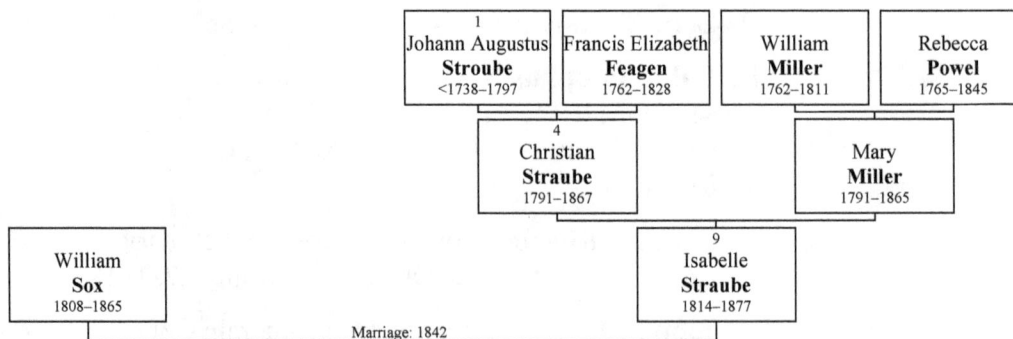

Here are the details about **Isabelle Straube's** second marriage, with William Sox. You can read more about Isabelle on page 33.

At the age of 27, Isabelle Straube married **William Sox** on Sunday, July 31, 1842, in Audrain County, Missouri, when he was 33 years old. William was born in Northampton County, Pennsylvania, on Tuesday, August 16, 1808.[21, 22] He was also known as **William Saxe**.

William reached 56 years of age and died in Audrain County, Missouri, on July 15, 1865.[21, 22]

---

21 Ancestry.com, Public Member Trees (Provo, UT, USA, Ancestry.com Operations, Inc., 2006), Ancestry.com, Record for William Saxe/Sox. https://search.ancestry.co.uk/cgi-bin/sse.dll?db=1030&h=372294096674&indiv=try.

22 Ancestry.com, Public Member Trees (Provo, UT, USA, Ancestry.com Operations, Inc., 2006), Ancestry.com, Record for William Saxe. https://search.ancestry.co.uk/cgi-bin/sse.dll?db=1030&h=182026347058&indiv=try.

Descendants of Johann Stroube and Francis Feagen

Family of Isabelle Straube and William Angel

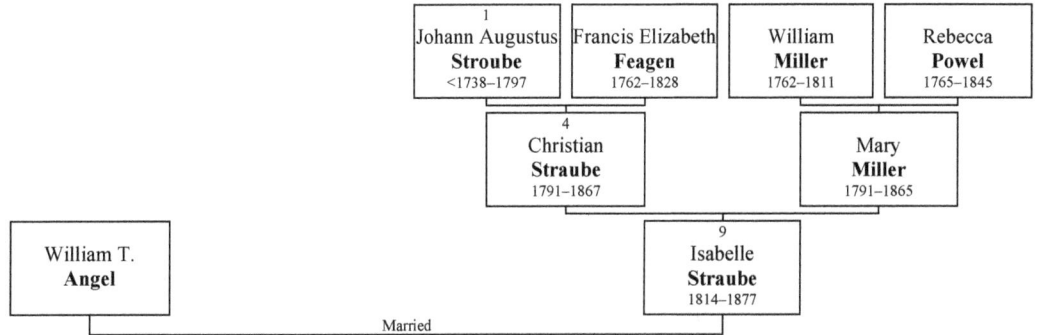

```
┌─────────────┬─────────────┐ ┌─────────────┬─────────────┐
│      1      │Francis      │ │   William   │  Rebecca    │
│Johann       │Elizabeth    │ │   Miller    │   Powel     │
│Augustus     │  Feagen     │ │  1762–1811  │  1765–1845  │
│  Stroube    │  1762–1828  │ │             │             │
│  <1738–1797 │             │ │             │             │
└─────────────┴─────────────┘ └─────────────┴─────────────┘
         ┌─────────────┐           ┌─────────────┐
         │      4      │           │    Mary     │
         │  Christian  │           │   Miller    │
         │   Straube   │           │  1791–1865  │
         │  1791–1867  │           │             │
         └─────────────┘           └─────────────┘
┌─────────────┐              ┌─────────────┐
│ William T.  │              │      9      │
│    Angel    │              │  Isabelle   │
│             │              │   Straube   │
│             │              │  1814–1877  │
└─────────────┘              └─────────────┘
              Married
```

Here are the details about **Isabelle Straube's** third marriage, with William T. Angel. You can read more about Isabelle on page 33.

Isabelle Straube married **William T. Angel**.

Family of James Straube and Rebecca Gregg

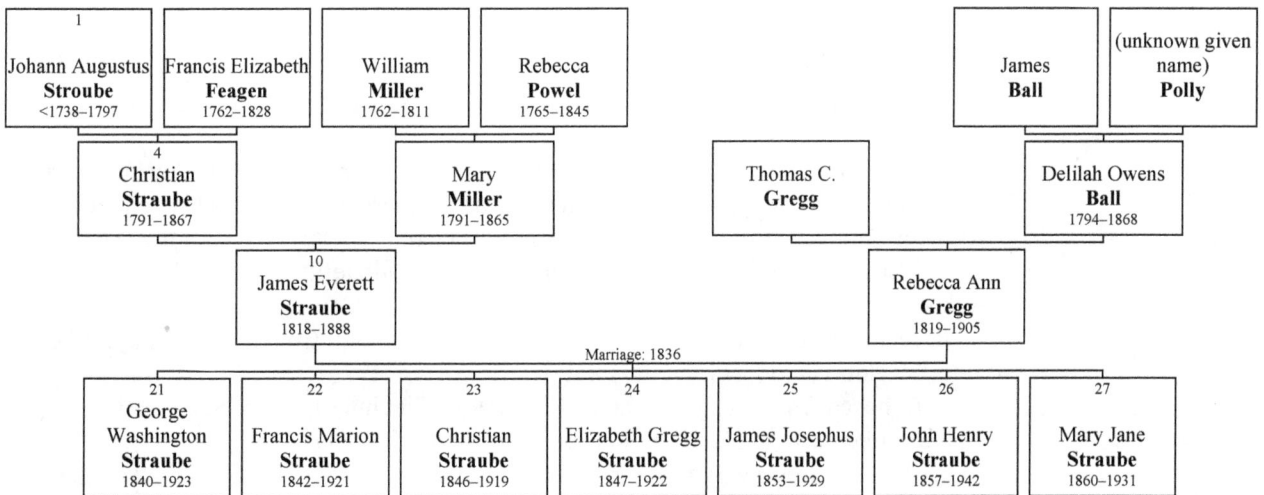

```
┌─────────────┬─────────────┐ ┌─────────────┬─────────────┐        ┌─────────────┬─────────────┐
│      1      │Francis      │ │   William   │  Rebecca    │        │    James    │(unknown     │
│Johann       │Elizabeth    │ │   Miller    │   Powel     │        │    Ball     │given name)  │
│Augustus     │  Feagen     │ │  1762–1811  │  1765–1845  │        │             │   Polly     │
│  Stroube    │  1762–1828  │ │             │             │        │             │             │
│  <1738–1797 │             │ │             │             │        │             │             │
└─────────────┴─────────────┘ └─────────────┴─────────────┘        └─────────────┴─────────────┘
         ┌─────────────┐           ┌─────────────┐      ┌─────────────┐     ┌─────────────┐
         │      4      │           │    Mary     │      │  Thomas C.  │     │Delilah Owens│
         │  Christian  │           │   Miller    │      │    Gregg    │     │    Ball     │
         │   Straube   │           │  1791–1865  │      │             │     │  1794–1868  │
         │  1791–1867  │           │             │      │             │     │             │
         └─────────────┘           └─────────────┘      └─────────────┘     └─────────────┘
              ┌─────────────┐                              ┌─────────────┐
              │     10      │                              │ Rebecca Ann │
              │James Everett│                              │    Gregg    │
              │   Straube   │                              │  1819–1905  │
              │  1818–1888  │                              │             │
              └─────────────┘                              └─────────────┘
                            Marriage: 1836
```

21	22	23	24	25	26	27
George Washington **Straube** 1840–1923	Francis Marion **Straube** 1842–1921	Christian **Straube** 1846–1919	Elizabeth Gregg **Straube** 1847–1922	James Josephus **Straube** 1853–1929	John Henry **Straube** 1857–1942	Mary Jane **Straube** 1860–1931

10. **James Everett Straube** was born on Thursday, January 08, 1818, in Indiana, USA. He was the son of Christian Straube (4) and Mary Miller.

James Everett died in On Indian Creek, Middletown, Montgomery County, Missouri, on January 23, 1888, at the age of 70. He was buried in Siloam Primitive Baptist Church Cemetery, Ashley, Pike County, Missouri (Find a Grave ID 68990713).

> Head of household in 1840 Census- Audrain County
> Head of household in 1850 Census- Audrain County
> Head of household in 1860 Census- Middletown, Montgomery County, Missouri
> Head of household in 1870 Census- New Harmony, Pike County, Missouri

- 35 -

(Death Notices from *The Montgomery Standard* Newspaper, Montgomery City, 1880-89, abstracted by Alma Jane Eulbe Wheeler); Jan 23, 1888 James Straube Sr. at his home on Indian Creek, near Middletown (10 Feb 1888).

Copy provided by Donna Dawkins Squires, Camdenton, MO, 1994.

> James Everett Straube was born on January 8, 1818 in Indiana and is the son of Christian Straube and Mary "Polly" Miller Straube.
>
> James Everett Straube married Rebecca Ann Gregg on June 30, 1836 in Franklin County, Indiana. Rebecca Ann Gregg was born in Cincinnati, Hamilton County, Ohio, and was a cousin to William McKinley, the 25th President of the United States. McKinley was a Republican, and James Everett was never proud of that fact. As a result, there were mixed political feelings among the family.
>
> To this union was born George Washington Straube, b. 10 Mar 1840, (near) Middletown, Montgomery County, Missouri; d. 10 Jul 1923, Audrain County, Missouri. Francis M. Straube, b. 1842. Christian Straube, b. 23 May 1846, Missouri; d. 15 Jan 1919. Elizabeth Straube, b. 12 Oct 1847, Missouri; d. 13 Jul 1922. James Josephus Straube, b. 03 Apr 1853 in Middletown, Montgomery County, Missouri; d. 20 Sep 1929. John Straube, b. 1856. Mary Jane Straube, b. 12 Oct 1860.

February 2, 1888 edition of the *Bowling Green Times* researched by Marie Haught:

> James Straubie, Sr., aged 73, died Tuesday night and was buried Wednesday at Siloam cemetery.
> At the age of 18, James Everett married Rebecca Ann Gregg on Thursday, June 30, 1836, in Franklin County, Indiana, when she was 17 years old. They had seven children.
> Rebecca Ann was born in Cincinnati, Hamilton County, Ohio, on Monday, March 22, 1819.[23] She was the daughter of Thomas C. Gregg and Delilah Owens Ball.
> Rebecca Ann reached 85 years of age and died in Pike County, Missouri, on January 28, 1905. She was buried in Siloam Primitive Baptist Church Cemetery, Ashley, Pike County, Missouri (Find a Grave ID 68990965).
> Born Rebecca Ann Gregg on March 22, 1819 in Cincinnati, Ohio. She married James Everett Straube on June 30, 1836, in Franklin County, Indiana.
> Rebecca Ann Gregg was a cousin to William McKinley, the 25th President of the United States. McKinley was a Republican, and James Everett was never proud of that fact. As a result, there were mixed political feelings among the family, which continues today. Gravesite Details: No grave marker or tombstone.

---

[23]   GREGG-1819.FTW, Date of Import: Jun 25, 2000.

Children of James Everett Straube and Rebecca Ann Gregg:

+ 21 m I. **George Washington Straube** was born in Middletown, Montgomery County, Missouri, on May 16, 1840. He was also known as **Strauby**.

George Washington died in Mexico, Audrain County, Missouri, on July 10, 1923, at the age of 83. He was buried in Siloam Primitive Baptist Church Cemetery, Ashley, Pike County, Missouri (Find a Grave ID 77428850).

Headstone is spelled Strauby, wife Joanah applied for a Civil War pension and it was spelled Straube.

+ 22 m II. **Francis Marion Straube** was born in Cuvire Twp., Audrain County, Missouri, on September 28, 1842.[24] He was also known as **Frank**.

Francis Marion died in Laramie, Albany County, Wyoming, on March 07, 1921, at the age of 78.[24] He was buried in Greenhill Cemetery, Laramie, Albany County, Wyoming (Find a Grave ID 79607962).

Luther through Lura show up in the Boulder, Colorado 1900 US Census with month and year of birth. It's not known if Nebraska is accurate as their listed birthplace.

Francis M. Straube is listed as a gunsmith and bicycle repairman. He also was given a patent for a tool which resembles a modern-day vice grip plier.

+ 23 m III. **Christian Straube** was born in Middletown, Montgomery County, Missouri, on May 23, 1846. He died in Saint James, Phelps County, Missouri, on January 15, 1919, at the age of 72. Christian was buried in Saint James Veterans Home Cemetery, Saint James, Phelps County, Missouri, on January 16, 1919 (Find a Grave ID 10851139).

Listed as a farmer with wife Mary J. in 1850 U.S. Census, Indian Creek, Pike County, Missouri. James T. is also listed as 1 year old.

49th REGIMENT MO INFANTRY.

Organized at Warrenton, Mexico, Macon and St. Louis, Mo., August 31,1864, to February 5, 1865. Attached to District of North Missouri, Dept, of Missouri, to February, 1865. 2nd Brigade, 3rd Division, 16th Army Corps (New), Military District of West Mississippi, to August, 1865. Dept. of Alabama to December, 1865.
SERVICE.-Duty in Northern Missouri line of Northern Missouri Railroad, till January 30, 1865. Moved to St. Louis, Mo., January 30-February 1, thence to New Orleans, LL, February 10-21. Campaign against Mobile, Ala., and its defenses March 17-April 12. Siege of Spanish Fort and Fort Blakely March 26-April 8. Assault and capture

of Fort Blakely April 9. Occupation of Mobile April 12. March to Montgomery April 1325, and duty there till July 14, Companies "A," "B," "C," "D," "E," "F," "G" and "I" ordered to St. Louis, Mo., and mustered out August.2, 1865. Companies' "H" and "K" on duty at Eufaula, Ala., till December, 1865. Mustered out December 20, 1865.

Regiment lost during service 4 enlisted men killed and mortally wounded and 96 enlisted men by disease. Total 100.

Source of Data: *A Compendium of the War of the Rebellion, V.III* by Frederick H. Dyer, c1908, p.1338
Missouri Commandery
Military Order of the Loyal Legion of the US.

+ 24   f   IV. **Elizabeth Gregg Straube** was born in Audrain County, Missouri, on October 12, 1847. She died in Pike County, Missouri, on July 13, 1922, at the age of 74. Elizabeth Gregg was buried in Siloam Primitive Baptist Church Cemetery, Ashley, Pike County, Missouri (Find a Grave ID 84022584).

+ 25   m   V. **James Josephus Straube** was born in Montgomery County, Missouri, on April 03, 1853.[25] He died in Hartford, Pike County, Missouri, on September 20, 1929, at the age of 76. His cause of death was aortic inefficiency. He was buried in Siloam Primitive Baptist Church Cemetery, Ashley, Pike County, Missouri, on September 21, 1929 (Find a Grave ID 68743487).

> James Josephus was born on Sunday, April 3, 1853 in Middletown, Montgomery County, Missouri and died at age 76 on Friday, September 20, 1929 of aortic inefficiency and chronic myocarditis in New Hartford, Pike County, Missouri. On Sunday, February 6, 1876 at the home of Joshua Martin Morris in Pike County, Missouri James and Lucy Frances Morris were married by Reverend Melton Sears. Lucy was born on Saturday, February 25, 1854 in Pike County, Missouri and died at age 84 on Saturday, March 5, 1938 of cardiac failure, arteriosclerosis, chronic interstitial and chronic myocarditis at the home of her son, Luther Joshua Straube, in Bellflower, Montgomery County, Missouri. She is the daughter of Joshua Martin Morris and Louisa Frances Willis.
>
> On November 14, 1914 James Josephus and Lucy Frances Straube purchased 20 acres of land that was part of 80 acres known as East one-half of the Northwest quarter of Section one (1), Township (51) North, Range four (4) West, in Pike County, Missouri from their son, Everett James Straube for $700. On February 15, 1928, Everett and his

---

[25]   Death Certificate.

wife, Mary Anna Willis Straube, purchased the land back from his parents for $525 and was held until his death in 1968.

+   26   m   VI. **John Henry Straube** was born in Missouri, USA, in August 1857.[26] He died in Harvey, Cook County, Illinois, on October 01, 1942, at the age of 85.[26] John Henry was buried in Homewood Memorial Gardens, Homewood, Cook County, Illinois (Find a Grave ID 220097456).

+   27   f   VII. **Mary Jane Straube** was born in Middleton, Pike County, Missouri, on October 12, 1860. She died in Ashley, Pike County, Missouri, on May 12, 1931, at the age of 70. Mary Jane was buried in Concord Cemetery, Pike County, Missouri, on May 13, 1931 (Find a Grave ID 8320150).

Family of George Straube and Mariah Enslen

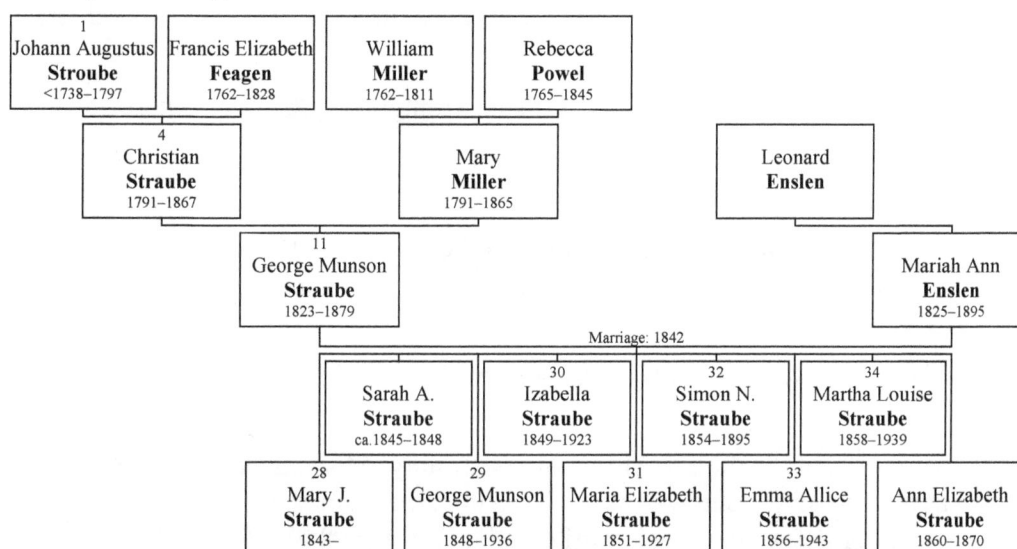

1 Johann Augustus **Stroube** <1738–1797	Francis Elizabeth **Feagen** 1762–1828	William **Miller** 1762–1811	Rebecca **Powel** 1765–1845		Leonard **Enslen**	
4 Christian **Straube** 1791–1867		Mary **Miller** 1791–1865				
11 George Munson **Straube** 1823–1879					Mariah Ann **Enslen** 1825–1895	

Marriage: 1842

	Sarah A. **Straube** ca.1845–1848	30 Izabella **Straube** 1849–1923	32 Simon N. **Straube** 1854–1895	34 Martha Louise **Straube** 1858–1939	
28 Mary J. **Straube** 1843–	29 George Munson **Straube** 1848–1936	31 Maria Elizabeth **Straube** 1851–1927	33 Emma Allice **Straube** 1856–1943	Ann Elizabeth **Straube** 1860–1870	

11.   **George Munson Straube** was born on Wednesday, October 15, 1823, in Franklin County, Indiana. He was the son of Christian Straube (4) and Mary Miller.

George Munson died in Montgomery County, Missouri, on August 06, 1879, at the age of 55. He was buried in Wellsville Cemetery, Wellsville, Montgomery County, Missouri (Find a Grave ID 83904546).

At the age of 19, George Munson married **Mariah Ann Enslen** on Sunday, November 27, 1842, in Audrain County, Missouri, when she was 17 years old. They had nine children.

Mariah Ann was born in Luzerne County, Pennsylvania, on Tuesday, October 11, 1825. She was the daughter of Leonard Enslen.

Mariah Ann reached 69 years of age and died in Wellsville, Montgomery County, Missouri, on August 15, 1895. She was buried in Wellsville Cemetery, Wellsville, Montgomery County, Missouri (Find a Grave ID 83904643).

---

26   Ancestry.com, Public Member Trees (Provo, UT, USA, Ancestry.com Operations, Inc., 2006), Ancestry.com, Record for John Henry Straube. https://search.ancestry.co.uk/cgi-bin/sse.dll?db=1030&h=322059795869&indiv=try.

Children of George Munson Straube and Mariah Ann Enslen:

+   28   f   I. **Mary J. Straube** was born in Audrain County, Missouri, on September 17, 1843.

           f   II. **Sarah A. Straube** was born in Missouri, USA, about February 28, 1845. She died in Missouri, USA, on August 30, 1848, at the age of 3. Sarah A. was buried in Payne-Seeley Cemetery, Audrain County, Missouri (Find a Grave ID 83902864).

+   29   m   III. **George Munson Straube** was born in Audrain County, Missouri, on January 06, 1848. He was also known as **G.M.**.

                     George Munson died in Wellsville, Montgomery County, Missouri, on April 27, 1936, at the age of 88. He was buried in Wellsville Cemetery, Wellsville, Montgomery County, Missouri, on April 29, 1936 (Find a Grave ID 83904859).

                     Children info from 1910 U.S. Census, Montgomery County, Missouri

+   30   f   IV. **Izabella Straube** was born in Audrain County, Missouri, on September 06, 1849. She was also known as **Bell**.

                     Izabella died in Washington, USA, on February 02, 1923, at the age of 73. She was buried in Washington Lawn Cemetery, Centralia, Lewis County, Washington (Find a Grave ID 93369474).

+   31   f   V. **Maria Elizabeth Straube** was born on July 10, 1851. She was also known as **Lizzie**.

                     Maria Elizabeth died in Montgomery County, Missouri, on June 18, 1927, at the age of 75. She was buried in Wellsville Cemetery, Wellsville, Montgomery County, Missouri (Find a Grave ID 84026491).

+   32   m   VI. **Simon N. Straube** was born in Missouri, USA, on January 04, 1854. He died in Wellsville, Montgomery County, Missouri, on December 26, 1895, at the age of 41. Simon N. was buried in Wellsville Cemetery, Wellsville, Montgomery County, Missouri (Find a Grave ID 83904986).

+   33   f   VII. **Emma Allice Straube** was born in Audrain County, Missouri, in 1856. She was also known as **Emily**.

                     Emma Allice died in Dustin, Hughes County, Oklahoma, in 1943 at the age of 87. She was buried in Fairview Cemetery, Dustin, Hughes County, Oklahoma (Find a Grave ID 26561634).

+   34   f   VIII. **Martha Louise Straube** was born in Montgomery County, Missouri, on March 10, 1858. She was also known as **Mattie**.

                     Martha Louise died in Wellsville, Montgomery County, Missouri, on April 27, 1939, at the age of 81. She was buried in Wellsville Cemetery, Wellsville, Montgomery County, Missouri (Find a Grave ID 166222795).

           f   IX. **Ann Elizabeth Straube** was born in Missouri, USA, on April 03, 1860. She died in Missouri, USA, on June 16, 1870, at the age of 10. Ann Elizabeth was buried in Payne-Seeley Cemetery, Audrain County, Missouri (Find a Grave ID 83902982).

Family of Rebecca Straube and Jackson Saxe

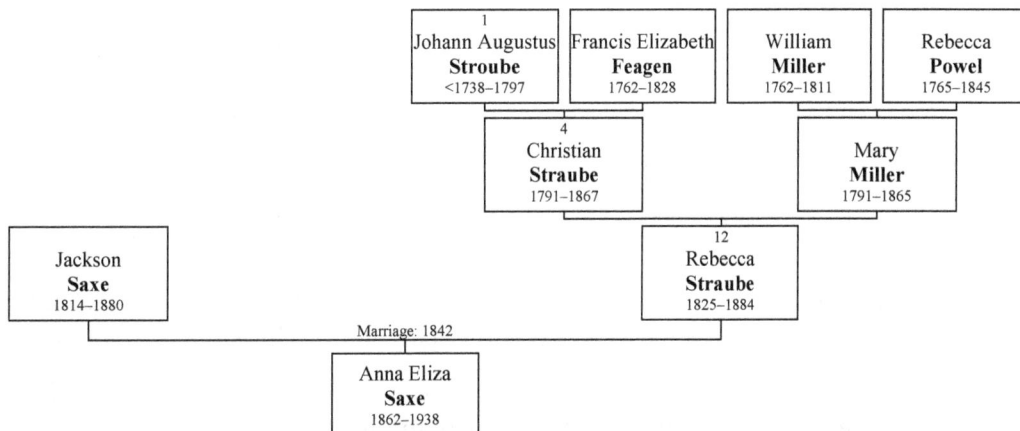

12.   **Rebecca Straube** was born in 1825 in Springfield Township, Franklin County, Indiana. She was the daughter of Christian Straube (4) and Mary Miller.

Rebecca died in Audrain County, Missouri, in 1884 at the age of 59. Her burial details are unknown (Find a Grave ID 250850235).

Rebecca married **Jackson Saxe** on Sunday, July 24, 1842, in Audrain County, Missouri. They had one daughter.

Jackson was born in Pennsylvania, USA, in 1814. He reached 66 years of age and died in Audrain County, Missouri, in 1880. His burial details are unknown (Find a Grave ID 250850362).

Spelled both Saxe and Sox.

Daughter of Rebecca Straube and Jackson Saxe:

f   I. **Anna Eliza Saxe** was born in Audrain County, Missouri, on February 24, 1862. She died in Wellsville, Montgomery County, Missouri, on September 08, 1938, at the age of 76. Anna Eliza was buried in Wellsville Cemetery, Wellsville, Montgomery County, Missouri, on September 11, 1938 (Find a Grave ID 120591791).

Family of Mary Straube and Almarien Davis

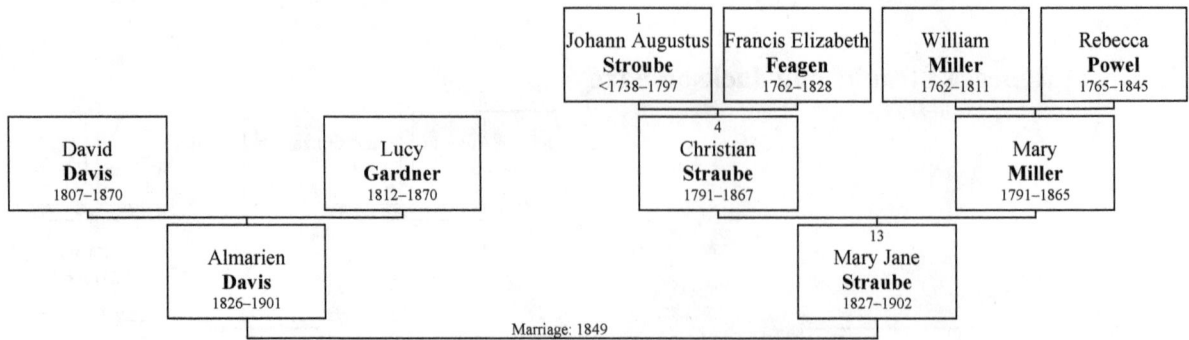

| | | Johann Augustus **Stroube** <1738–1797 | Francis Elizabeth **Feagen** 1762–1828 | William **Miller** 1762–1811 | Rebecca **Powel** 1765–1845 |

David **Davis** 1807–1870

Lucy **Gardner** 1812–1870

1

4
Christian **Straube** 1791–1867

Mary **Miller** 1791–1865

Almarien **Davis** 1826–1901

13
Mary Jane **Straube** 1827–1902

Marriage: 1849

13. **Mary Jane Straube** was born on Monday, February 12, 1827, in Springfield Township, Franklin County, Indiana. She was the daughter of Christian Straube (4) and Mary Miller.

Mary Jane died in Miami, Roberts County, Texas, on February 10, 1902, at the age of 74. She was buried in Miami Cemetery, Miami, Roberts County, Texas (Find a Grave ID 18004777).

At the age of 21, Mary Jane married **Almarien Davis** on Thursday, January 18, 1849, in Cuivre Township, Audrain County, Missouri, when he was 22 years old. Almarien was born in Indiana, USA, on Monday, June 12, 1826. He was the son of David Davis and Lucy Gardner.

Almarien reached 74 years of age and died on May 23, 1901. He was buried in Miami Cemetery, Miami, Roberts County, Texas (Find a Grave ID 18004705).

3rd Generation

Samuel Straube

14.   **Samuel Norris Straube** was born on Friday, September 22, 1837, in Brookfield, Shelby
      County, Indiana. He was the son of William H. Straube (7) and Phoebe Norris.

      Samuel Norris died in Moberly, Randolph County, Missouri, on October 31, 1923, at the
      age of 86. His cause of death was brain hemorrhage. Samuel Norris was buried in Wellsville
      Cemetery, Wellsville, Montgomery County, Missouri, on November 01, 1923 (Find a Grave
      ID 42562959).

      Marriages with Susan A. Fox, Iva A. Allen (Page 44) and Sarah Ada Hammett (Page 45) are
      known.

Family of Samuel Straube and Susan Fox

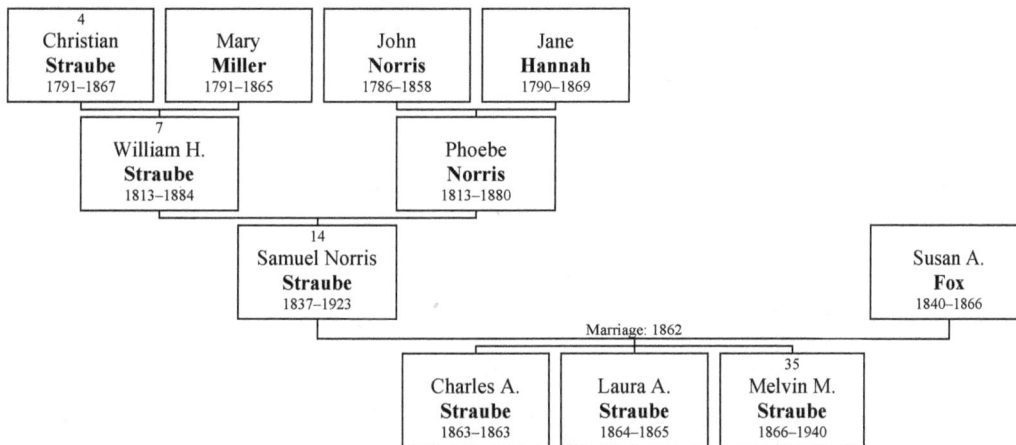

Here are the details about **Samuel Norris Straube's** first marriage, with Susan A. Fox. You
can read more about Samuel Norris on page 43.

Samuel Norris Straube married **Susan A. Fox** on Thursday, May 01, 1862, in Audrain
County, Missouri. They had three children.

Susan A. was born in 1840. She reached 26 years of age and died in Montgomery County,
Missouri, on November 30, 1866. Susan A. was buried in Fairmount Cemetery,
Middletown, Montgomery County, Missouri (Find a Grave ID 84066793).

Children of Samuel Norris Straube and Susan A. Fox:

m   I.   **Charles A. Straube** was born in Missouri, USA, in 1863. He died in
           Missouri, USA, on April 22, 1863. Charles A. was buried in Fairmount
           Cemetery, Middletown, Montgomery County, Missouri (Find a Grave ID
           84066872).

f   II. **Laura A. Straube** was born in Missouri, USA, in September 1864. She
           died in Missouri, USA, on August 23, 1865. Laura A. was buried in
           Fairmount Cemetery, Middletown, Montgomery County, Missouri (Find a
           Grave ID 84066962).

+   35   m   III. **Melvin M. Straube** was born in Montgomery County, Missouri, on August 28, 1866. He died in Paris, Monroe County, Missouri, on August 25, 1940, at the age of 73. Melvin M. was buried in Sunset Hill Cemetery, Madison, Monroe County, Missouri (Find a Grave ID 83946574).

Family of Samuel Straube and Iva Allen

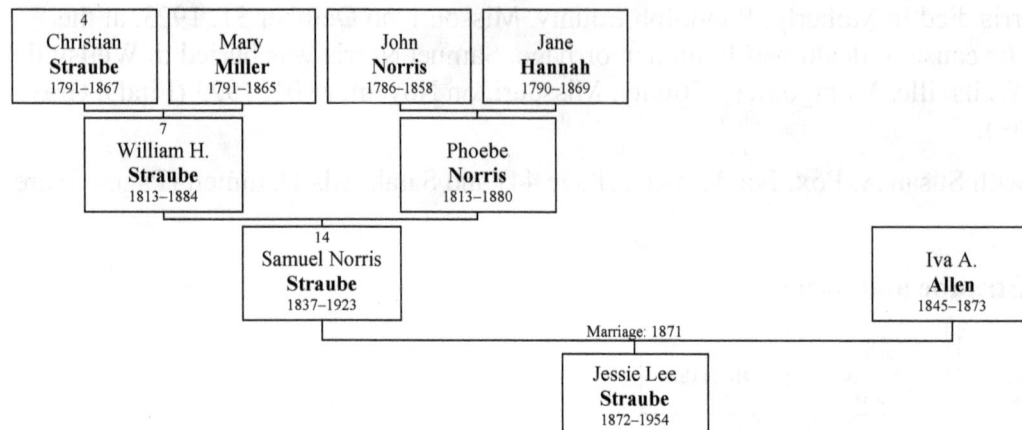

Here are the details about **Samuel Norris Straube's** second marriage, with Iva A. Allen. You can read more about Samuel Norris on page 43.

Samuel Norris Straube married **Iva A. Allen** on Thursday, April 06, 1871, in Montgomery County, Missouri. They had one daughter.

Iva A. was born in 1845.[27] She reached 28 years of age and died in 1873.[27]

Daughter of Samuel Norris Straube and Iva A. Allen:

f   I. **Jessie Lee Straube** was born in Wellsville, Montgomery County, Missouri, on March 14, 1872. She died in Moberly, Randolph County, Missouri, on May 19, 1954, at the age of 82. Jessie Lee was buried in Oakland Cemetery, Moberly, Randolph County, Missouri (Find a Grave ID 29401995).

---

27   Ancestry.com, Public Member Trees (Provo, UT, USA, Ancestry.com Operations, Inc., 2006), Ancestry.com, Record for Iva A. Allen. https://search.ancestry.co.uk/cgi-bin/sse.dll?db=1030&h=172063275779&indiv=try.

Family of Samuel Straube and Sarah Hammett

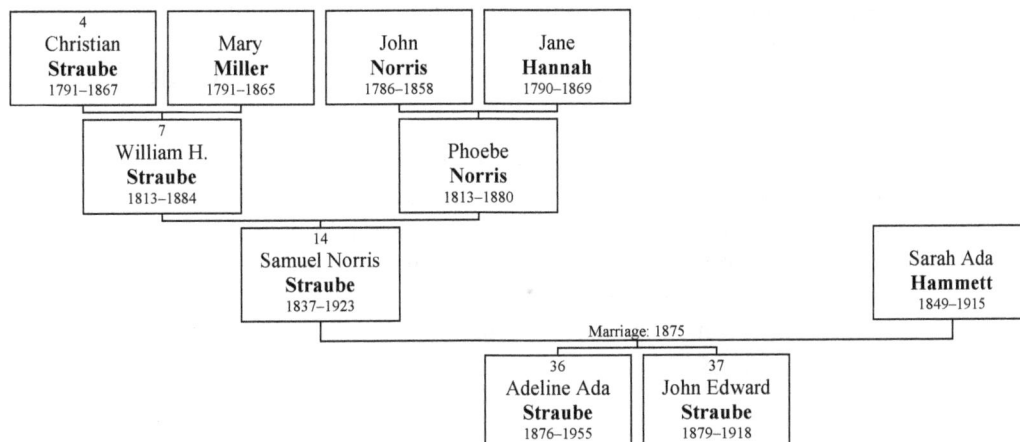

Here are the details about **Samuel Norris Straube's** third marriage, with Sarah Ada Hammett. You can read more about Samuel Norris on page 43.

At the age of 38, Samuel Norris Straube married **Sarah Ada Hammett** on Sunday, December 05, 1875, in Montgomery County, Missouri, when she was 26 years old. They had two children.

Sarah Ada was born in Millwood, Lincoln County, Missouri, on Wednesday, January 17, 1849. She reached 66 years of age and died in Montgomery County, Missouri, on December 12, 1915. Sarah Ada was buried in Wellsville Cemetery, Wellsville, Montgomery County, Missouri (Find a Grave ID 42563294).

Children of Samuel Norris Straube and Sarah Ada Hammett:

+ 36   f   I. **Adeline Ada Straube** was born in Wellsville, Montgomery County, Missouri, in 1876. She died in Pueblo County, Colorado, on February 01, 1955, at the age of 79. Adeline Ada was buried in Mountain View Cemetery, Pueblo, Pueblo County, Colorado (Find a Grave ID 63512638).

+ 37   m   II. **John Edward Straube** was born in Wellsville, Montgomery County, Missouri, on January 23, 1879. He was also known as **Ed**.

John Edward died in Wellsville, Montgomery County, Missouri, on December 07, 1918, at the age of 39. He was buried in Wellsville Cemetery, Wellsville, Montgomery County, Missouri (Find a Grave ID 42563523).

> December 13, 1918 p. 1/4
>
> DEATH OF J. E. STRAUBE
> HIGHLY RESPECTED RESIDENT PASSED AWAY AT HOME SATURDAY AFTER A SHORT ILLNESS
>
> J. E. Straube died at his home in this city Saturday December 7th after an illness of pneumonia. Ed, as he was popularly known, was born January 23rd 1879. He was married to Miss Lee Irvin on

Dec. 8, 1901. In his departure the city loses one of its highly respected, energetic and popular characters. At the time of his death, he was employed at the C. W. Reed & Bros. Mercantile. Co., and bore the esteem of both his employers and many friends.

He is survived by his widow, his father, one brother and one sister , Mrs. Addie Wuelschlaeger, a number of relatives and a host of friends. He united with the Christian church early in life and was an active worker until the time of his death. He was also a prominent member of the Knights of Pythias Lodge. The funeral service was conducted at the home by Rev. B. G. Reavis of Mexico, after which the body was buried in the Wellsville City Cemetery. The Knights of Pythias burial rites were performed at the grave.

Family of Emeline Straube and James Yates

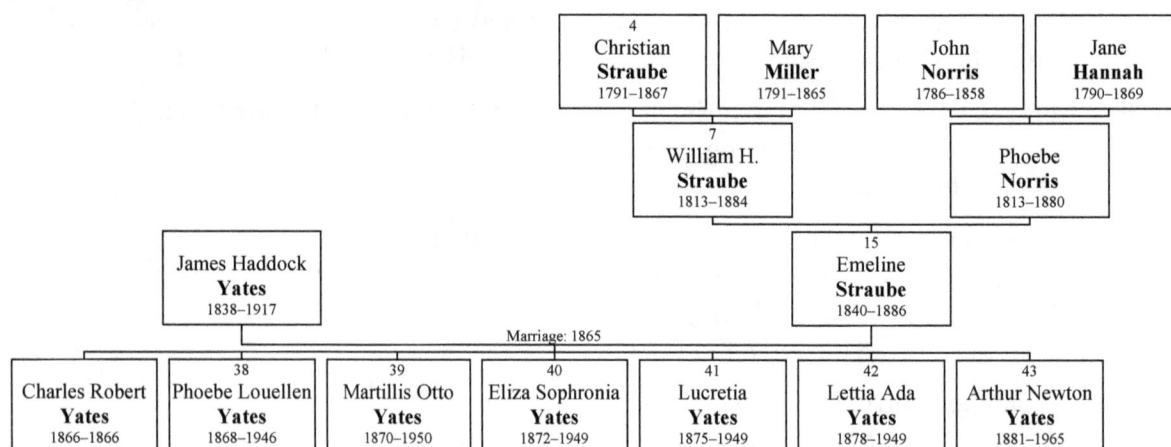

4 Christian **Straube** 1791–1867	Mary **Miller** 1791–1865	John **Norris** 1786–1858	Jane **Hannah** 1790–1869

7 William H. **Straube** 1813–1884	Phoebe **Norris** 1813–1880

James Haddock **Yates** 1838–1917	15 Emeline **Straube** 1840–1886

Marriage: 1865

37 Charles Robert **Yates** 1866–1866	38 Phoebe Louellen **Yates** 1868–1946	39 Martillis Otto **Yates** 1870–1950	40 Eliza Sophronia **Yates** 1872–1949	41 Lucretia **Yates** 1875–1949	42 Lettia Ada **Yates** 1878–1949	43 Arthur Newton **Yates** 1881–1965

15. **Emeline Straube** was born in 1840 in Missouri, USA. She was the daughter of William H. Straube (7) and Phoebe Norris. She was also known as **Pulina**.

Emeline died in Lincoln County, Missouri, on March 25, 1886, at the age of 46. She was buried in Winfield Cemetery, Winfield, Lincoln County, Missouri (Find a Grave ID 83970824).

At the age of 25, Emeline married **James Haddock Yates** on Thursday, November 16, 1865, in Montgomery County, Missouri, when he was 27 years old. They had seven children.

James Haddock was born in Shelbyville, Shelby County, Kentucky, on Saturday, October 20, 1838. He served in the military. Confederacy, Co. B, 1st Missouri Infantry.

James Haddock reached 79 years of age and died in Louisiana, Pike County, Missouri, on November 04, 1917. He was buried on November 05, 1917, in Winfield Cemetery, Winfield, Lincoln County, Missouri (Find a Grave ID 10152918).

James Haddock Yates: Military

He was twenty-three years of age when trained with Union troops began arriving in Missouri in July 1861, and on July 20, 1861, Missouri ruled under martial law for the next three years without a free election or a vote except from those deemed 'loyal' by a non-elected provisional government. Ten days after martial law was declared, the Missouri State Guard officially organized 30 Jul 1861.

James joined Bruce's Regiment in the Missouri State Guard, serving in County G, and he was probably with that regiment when he fought his first battle of record for the Confederate cause at Lexington MO in 12-20 September 1861. The Confederates won an overwhelmingly victorious battle against the Union troops.

On November 25, 1861, General Price told his men that the Confederate government would receive into service as many troops from Missouri as would volunteer to serve twelve months. So, on the Sac River in St. Clair County, 9 Dec 1861, James enlisted in the Confederate Army under General Sterling Price as a private and agreed to serve twelve months.

Before the war was over, that twelve months had extended into more than three years. He is recorded as serving from September 1861 to December 1864. His name then later appears on the Historic Roll of County B., 2 Reg't Missouri Infantry, dated 28 Feb 1865.

James was born 20 October 1838 in Shelby County, Kentucky, and moved to Missouri in 1851, living in Audrain, Callaway, Montgomery, Pike and Lincoln counties.

He married twice, first to Mary Ann FREEMAN on 20 December 1857, and second to Emeline STRAUBE on 16 November 1865.

He died 4 November 1917 in Pike County, Missouri and is buried beside his second wife.
His military record lists his service with the Confederacy in County B, 1st Missouri Infantry, latterly known as County B, 2nd Missouri Infantry.

Children of Emeline Straube and James Haddock Yates:

m   I. **Charles Robert Yates** was born in Pilot Knob, Iron County, Missouri, on July 14, 1866.[28] He died in Ironton, Iron County, Missouri, on August 03, 1866.[28]

+ 38   f   II. **Phoebe Louellen Yates** was born in Middletown, Montgomery County, Missouri, on November 29, 1868. She was also known as **Lou**.

---

28   Ancestry.com, Public Member Trees (Provo, UT, USA, Ancestry.com Operations, Inc., 2006), Ancestry.com, Record for Charles Robert Yates. https://search.ancestry.co.uk/cgi-bin/sse.dll?db=1030&h=172003664651&indiv=try.

Phoebe Louellen died in Saint Louis, Saint Louis County, Missouri, on July 12, 1946, at the age of 77. She was buried in Winfield Cemetery, Winfield, Lincoln County, Missouri, on July 15, 1946 (Find a Grave ID 83972471).

+ 39   m   III. **Martillis Otto Yates** was born in Missouri, USA, on November 16, 1870. He died in Tacoma, Pierce County, Washington, on December 05, 1950, at the age of 80. Martillis Otto was buried in Woodbine Cemetery, Puyallup, Pierce County, Washington, on December 07, 1950 (Find a Grave ID 83977270).

+ 40   f   IV. **Eliza Sophronia Yates** was born in Middletown, Montgomery County, Missouri, on August 30, 1872. She died in Dodge City, Ford County, Kansas, on August 23, 1949, at the age of 76. Eliza Sophronia was buried in Bucklin Cemetery, Ford County, Kansas, on August 26, 1949 (Find a Grave ID 83977626).

+ 41   f   V. **Lucretia Yates** was born in Middletown, Montgomery County, Missouri, on August 17, 1875. She was also known as **Cretia**.

Lucretia died in Hannibal, Marion County, Missouri, on January 20, 1949, at the age of 73. She was buried in Mount Olivet Cemetery, Hannibal, Marion County, Missouri, on January 22, 1949 (Find a Grave ID 83989993).

+ 42   f   VI. **Lettia Ada Yates** was born in Middletown, Montgomery County, Missouri, on September 14, 1878. She was also known as **Lettie**.

Lettia Ada died in Alton, Madison County, Illinois, on December 25, 1949, at the age of 71. She was buried in Oakwood Cemetery, Alton, Madison County, Illinois, on December 28, 1949 (Find a Grave ID 83990159).

+ 43   m   VII. **Arthur Newton Yates** was born in Clarksville, Pike County, Missouri, on February 23, 1881. He died in Winfield, Lincoln County, Missouri, on March 27, 1965, at the age of 84. Arthur Newton was buried in Winfield Cemetery, Winfield, Lincoln County, Missouri, on March 29, 1965 (Find a Grave ID 84020357).

Family of Elizabeth Straube and William Sanders

```
  ┌──────────────┐ ┌──────────────┐   ┌──────────────┐ ┌──────────────┐
  │      4       │ │              │   │              │ │              │
  │  Christian   │ │    Mary      │   │    John      │ │    Jane      │
  │  Straube     │ │   Miller     │   │   Norris     │ │   Hannah     │
  │  1791–1867   │ │  1791–1865   │   │  1786–1858   │ │  1790–1869   │
  └──────────────┘ └──────────────┘   └──────────────┘ └──────────────┘
           ┌──────────────┐              ┌──────────────┐
           │      7       │              │              │
           │  William H.  │              │   Phoebe     │
           │   Straube    │              │   Norris     │
           │  1813–1884   │              │  1813–1880   │
           └──────────────┘              └──────────────┘
  ┌──────────────┐              ┌──────────────┐
  │              │              │     16       │
  │William Jasper│              │ Elizabeth J. │
  │   Sanders    │              │   Straube    │
  │  1836–1909   │              │  1844–1894   │
  └──────────────┘              └──────────────┘
                      Married
```

16.   **Elizabeth J. Straube** was born in 1844 in Missouri, USA.[29–32] She was the daughter of William H. Straube (7) and Phoebe Norris. She was also known as **Eliza Strawby**.

Elizabeth J. died in Clinton, Henry County, Missouri, on November 30, 1894, at the age of 50.[33] Her burial details are unknown.

She married **William Jasper Sanders**. William Jasper was born in Montgomery City, Montgomery County, Missouri, in October 1836.[33]

He reached 72 years of age and died in Henry County, Missouri, in 1909.[33] William Jasper's burial details are unknown.

Family of Caleb Straube and Mary Muse

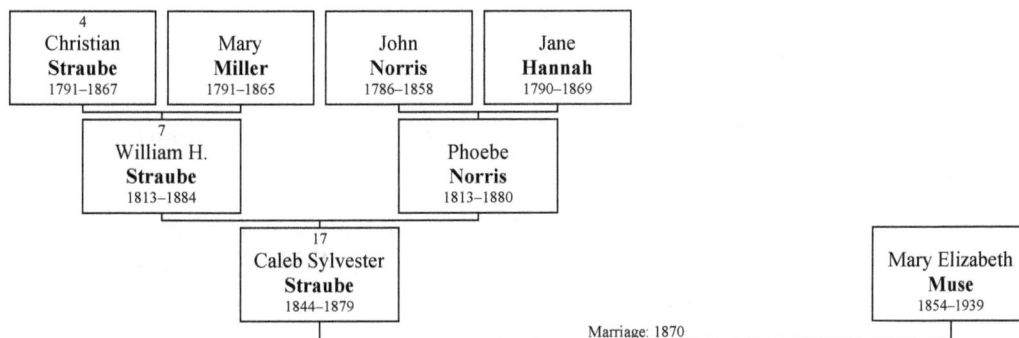

17.   **Caleb Sylvester Straube** was born in 1844. He was the son of William H. Straube (7) and Phoebe Norris.

Caleb Sylvester died in 1879 at the age of 35. Possibly in Civil War.

Caleb Sylvester married **Mary Elizabeth Muse** in 1870. Mary Elizabeth was born in Bowling Green, Pike County, Missouri, on Thursday, June 01, 1854.

She reached 84 years of age and died in Schuyler, Colfax County, Nebraska, in 1939. Mary Elizabeth was buried in Schuyler Cemetery, Schuyler, Colfax County, Nebraska (Find a Grave ID 66417784).

29   FamilySearch.org, Missouri State and Territorial Census Records, 1732-1933, FamilySearch, "Missouri State and Territorial Census Records, 1732-1933", , <i>FamilySearch</i> (https://www.familysearch.org/ark:/61903/1:1:QPHW-DYLT : Wed Oct 04 14:24:15 UTC 2023), Entry for W J Sanders and A C Sanders, 1876.

30   FamilySearch.org, United States Census, 1860, FamilySearch, "United States Census, 1860", , <i>FamilySearch</i> (https://www.familysearch.org/ark:/61903/1:1:MHZR-B95 : Thu Oct 05 13:34:30 UTC 2023), Entry for William H Straly and Phebe Straly, 1860.

31   FamilySearch.org, United States Census, 1850, FamilySearch, "United States Census, 1850", , <i>FamilySearch</i> (https://www.familysearch.org/ark:/61903/1:1:MDZS-YKV : Fri Oct 06 14:26:49 UTC 2023), Entry for William H Strawby and Phebe Strawby, 1850.

32   FamilySearch.org, United States Census, 1880, FamilySearch, "United States Census, 1880", , <i>FamilySearch</i> (https://www.familysearch.org/ark:/61903/1:1:M6X7-R2C : Thu Oct 05 10:37:01 UTC 2023), Entry for Wm. Sanders and Eliza J. Sanders, 1880.

33   Ancestry.com, Public Member Trees (Provo, UT, USA, Ancestry.com Operations, Inc., 2006), Ancestry.com, Record for Eliza J Strawbe. https://search.ancestry.co.uk/cgi-bin/sse.dll?db=1030&h=18572195325&indiv=try.

Family of William Straube and Martha Gibson

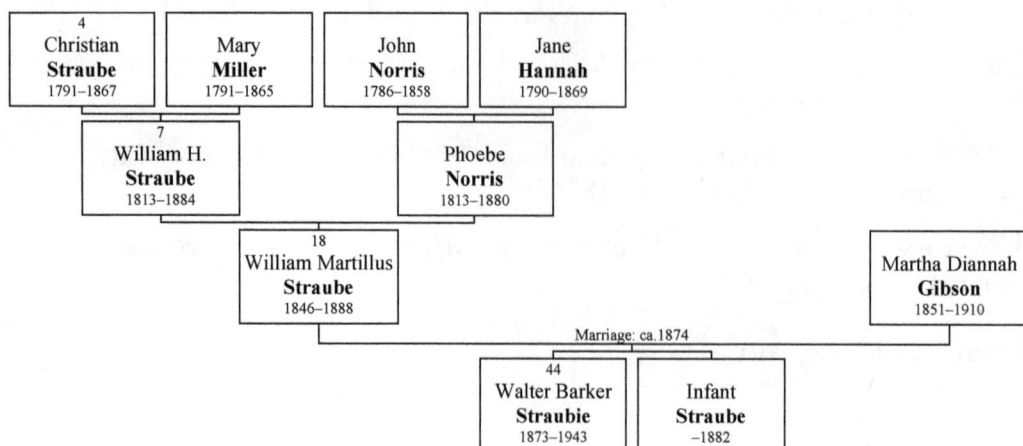

18. **William Martillus Straube** was born on Friday, November 27, 1846, in Missouri, USA.[34–37] He was the son of William H. Straube (7) and Phoebe Norris.

William Martillus died in Wellsville, Montgomery County, Missouri, on December 31, 1888, at the age of 42.[36] He was buried in Fairmount Cemetery, Middletown, Montgomery County, Missouri (Find a Grave ID 84020789).[36]

William Martillus married **Martha Diannah Gibson** about 1874. They had two sons.

Martha Diannah was born in Montgomery County, Missouri, on Monday, August 04, 1851. She was also known as **Mattie**.

Martha Diannah reached 59 years of age and died in Jackson County, Arkansas, on December 31, 1910. She was buried in Dowells Chapel Cemetery, Tuckerman, Jackson County, Arkansas (Find a Grave ID 68246337).

Sons of William Martillus Straube and Martha Diannah Gibson:

+ 44 m I. **Walter Barker Straubie** was born in Middletown, Montgomery County, Missouri, on October 15, 1873. William Martillus Straube was his stepfather.

He died in Little Rock, Pulaski County, Arkansas, on June 10, 1943, at the age of 69. Walter Barker was buried in Roselawn Memorial Park, Little

---

34 FamilySearch.org, United States Census, 1860, FamilySearch, "United States Census, 1860", , <i>FamilySearch</i> (https://www.familysearch.org/ark:/61903/1:1:MHZR-B95 : Thu Oct 05 13:34:30 UTC 2023), Entry for William H Straly and Phebe Straly, 1860.

35 FamilySearch.org, United States Census, 1850, FamilySearch, "United States Census, 1850", , <i>FamilySearch</i> (https://www.familysearch.org/ark:/61903/1:1:MDZS-YKV : Fri Oct 06 14:26:49 UTC 2023), Entry for William H Strawby and Phebe Strawby, 1850.

36 FamilySearch.org, Find A Grave Index, FamilySearch, "Find A Grave Index," database, <i>FamilySearch</i> (https://www.familysearch.org/ark:/61903/1:1:QVL9-V8M4 : 16 June 2020), William Straube, 1888; Burial, , ; citing record ID , <i>Find a Grave</i>, http://www.findagrave.com.

37 FamilySearch.org, United States Census, 1880, FamilySearch, "United States Census, 1880", , <i>FamilySearch</i> (https://www.familysearch.org/ark:/61903/1:1:M6XY-42P : Tue Oct 03 22:41:12 UTC 2023), Entry for Wm. H. Straube and Martha D. Straube, 1880.

Rock, Pulaski County, Arkansas, on June 11, 1943 (Find a Grave ID 176587695).

Both death certificate and gravestone have a spelling of Straubie.

m   II. **Infant Straube**. Infant died in Missouri, USA, on November 19, 1882. He was buried in Fairmount Cemetery, Middletown, Montgomery County, Missouri (Find a Grave ID 98278092).

Family of Phoebe Straube and George Miller

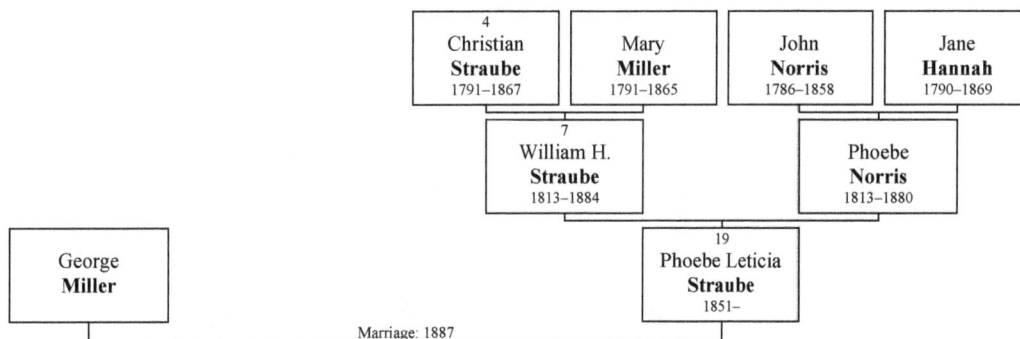

19.   **Phoebe Leticia Straube** was born in 1851 in Missouri, USA.[38] She was the daughter of William H. Straube (7) and Phoebe Norris. She was also known as **Lettie**.

Phoebe Leticia's burial details are unknown.

Phoebe Leticia married **George Miller** on Sunday, February 20, 1887, in Clinton, Henry County, Missouri. George's burial details are unknown.

Family of Martha Straube and William Angel

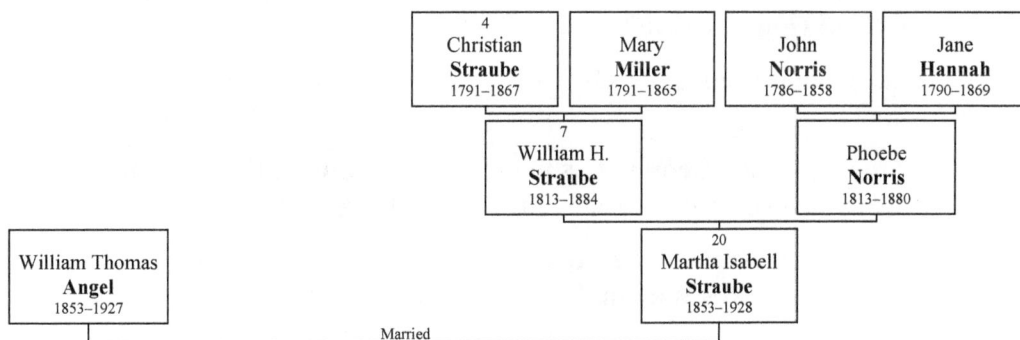

20.   **Martha Isabell Straube** was born on Friday, February 04, 1853, in Missouri, USA. She was the daughter of William H. Straube (7) and Phoebe Norris.

Martha Isabell died in Saint Louis, Saint Louis County, Missouri, on December 30, 1928, at the age of 75. She was buried in Fairmount Cemetery, Middletown, Montgomery County, Missouri (Find a Grave ID 157112047).

38   Ancestry.com, Public Member Trees (Provo, UT, USA, Ancestry.com Operations, Inc., 2006), Ancestry.com, Record for Phebe Leticia Straube, Strawby, Strawbe (Miller). https://search.ancestry.co.uk/cgi-bin/sse.dll?db=1030&h=32297777406&indiv=try.

She married **William Thomas Angel**. William Thomas was born in Missouri, USA, on Wednesday, November 23, 1853.

He reached 73 years of age and died in Middletown, Montgomery County, Missouri, on June 02, 1927. William Thomas was buried in Fairmount Cemetery, Middletown, Montgomery County, Missouri (Find a Grave ID 137225097).

Family of George Straube and Joannah Willis

4 Christian **Straube** 1791–1867	Mary **Miller** 1791–1865	Thomas C. **Gregg**	Delilah Owens **Ball** 1794–1868	John William **Willis** 1791–1849	Rhoda A. **Farmer** 1792–1878	Daniel **Wilhoit** 1781–1835	Eva Crisler **Matilda** 1790–1835

10 James Everett **Straube** 1818–1888 — Rebecca Ann **Gregg** 1819–1905 ; James William **Willis** 1820–1850 — Mary Matilda **Wilhoit** 1817–1904

21 George Washington **Straube** 1840–1923 — Joannah **Willis** 1845–1934 (Marriage: 1863)

45 Mary Belle **Straube** 1864–1941	46 Matilda Ann **Straube** 1865–1944	47 Porter Coe **Straube** 1867–1958	48 Amanda Catherine **Straube** 1869–1943	49 Ora Lee **Straube** 1871–1963

21. George Washington Straube was born on Saturday, May 16, 1840, in Middletown, Montgomery County, Missouri. He was the son of James Everett Straube (10) and Rebecca Ann Gregg. He was also known as **Strauby**.

George Washington died in Mexico, Audrain County, Missouri, on July 10, 1923, at the age of 83. He was buried in Siloam Primitive Baptist Church Cemetery, Ashley, Pike County, Missouri (Find a Grave ID 77428850).

Headstone is spelled Strauby, wife Joanah applied for a Civil War pension and it was spelled Straube.

At the age of 22, George Washington married **Joannah Willis** on Wednesday, February 25, 1863, when she was 17 years old. They had five children.

Joannah was born in Pike County, Missouri, on Sunday, June 22, 1845. She was the daughter of James William Willis and Mary Matilda Wilhoit.

Joannah reached 89 years of age and died in Wellsville, Montgomery County, Missouri, on August 10, 1934. She was buried on August 12, 1934, in Siloam Primitive Baptist Church Cemetery, Ashley, Pike County, Missouri (Find a Grave ID 77428544).

Children of George Washington Straube and Joannah Willis:

+ 45 f I. **Mary Belle Straube** was born in Pike County, Missouri, on March 13, 1864. She died in Pike County, Missouri, on July 26, 1941, at the age of 77. Mary Belle was buried in Siloam Primitive Baptist Church Cemetery, Ashley, Pike County, Missouri (Find a Grave ID 83685374).

+ 46 f II. **Matilda Ann Straube** was born in Pike County, Missouri, on November 23, 1865. She died in Hannibal, Marion County, Missouri, on November 10, 1944, at the age of 78. Matilda Ann was buried in Grand View Burial Park, Hannibal, Ralls County, Missouri (Find a Grave ID 87226120).

+ 47 m III. **Porter Coe Straube** was born in Pike County, Missouri, on October 23, 1867. He died in Bowling Green, Pike County, Missouri, on May 31, 1958, at the age of 90. Porter Coe was buried in Siloam Primitive Baptist Church Cemetery, Ashley, Pike County, Missouri, on June 04, 1958 (Find a Grave ID 83753603).

Spelled Strauby on headstone like his father George.

+ 48 f IV. **Amanda Catherine Straube** was born in Pike County, Missouri, on September 01, 1869. She died in Saskatchewan, Canada, on January 23, 1943, at the age of 73. Amanda Catherine was buried in Shamrock Cemetery, Shamrock, Moose Jaw Census Division, Saskatchewan, Canada (Find a Grave ID 227021571).

+ 49 f V. **Ora Lee Straube** was born in Pike County, Missouri, on April 21, 1871. She died in Mexico, Audrain County, Missouri, on March 12, 1963, at the age of 91. Ora Lee was buried in Wellsville Cemetery, Wellsville, Montgomery County, Missouri (Find a Grave ID 135220399).

Francis Straube

22. **Francis Marion Straube** was born on Wednesday, September 28, 1842, in Cuvire Twp., Audrain County, Missouri.[39] He was the son of James Everett Straube (10) and Rebecca Ann Gregg. He was also known as **Frank**.

Francis Marion died in Laramie, Albany County, Wyoming, on March 07, 1921, at the age of 78.[39] He was buried in Greenhill Cemetery, Laramie, Albany County, Wyoming (Find a Grave ID 79607962).

Luther through Lura show up in the Boulder, Colorado 1900 US Census with month and year of birth. It's not known if Nebraska is accurate as their listed birthplace.

Francis M. Straube is listed as a gunsmith and bicycle repairman. He also was given a patent for a tool which resembles a modern-day vice-grip plier.

Marriages with Mary Elizabeth Mulherin and Alice A. Martin (Page 55) are known.

---

[39] Ancestry.com, Public Member Trees (Provo, UT, USA, Ancestry.com Operations, Inc., 2006), Ancestry.com, Record for Francis M. Straube. https://search.ancestry.co.uk/cgi-bin/sse.dll?db=1030&h=172022640561&indiv=try.

Family of Francis Straube and Mary Mulherin

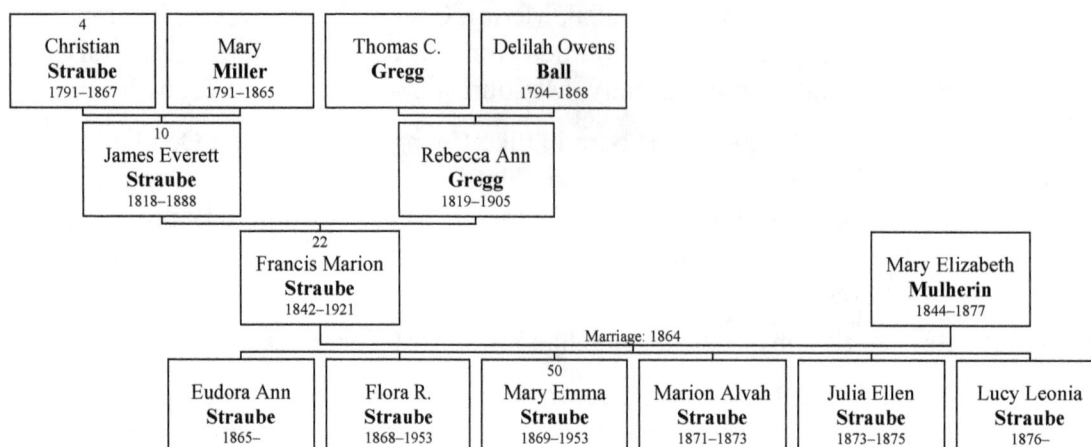

4 Christian **Straube** 1791–1867	Mary **Miller** 1791–1865	Thomas C. **Gregg**	Delilah Owens **Ball** 1794–1868

10 James Everett **Straube** 1818–1888	Rebecca Ann **Gregg** 1819–1905

22 Francis Marion **Straube** 1842–1921	Mary Elizabeth **Mulherin** 1844–1877

Marriage: 1864

Eudora Ann **Straube** 1865–	Flora R. **Straube** 1868–1953	50 Mary Emma **Straube** 1869–1953	Marion Alvah **Straube** 1871–1873	Julia Ellen **Straube** 1873–1875	Lucy Leonia **Straube** 1876–

Here are the details about **Francis Marion Straube's** first marriage, with Mary Elizabeth Mulherin. You can read more about Francis Marion on page 53.

At the age of 21, Francis Marion Straube married **Mary Elizabeth Mulherin** on Saturday, August 06, 1864, when she was 19 years old. They had six children.

Mary Elizabeth was born in Pike County, Missouri, on Sunday, December 08, 1844. She reached 32 years of age and died in Montgomery County, Missouri, on November 21, 1877. Mary Elizabeth's burial details are unknown (Find a Grave ID 255545505).

Daughter of John M. Mulherin & Ann D. Watts

Children of Francis Marion Straube and Mary Elizabeth Mulherin:

f   I. **Eudora Ann Straube** was born in Missouri, USA, on April 26, 1865. She was also known as **Udora**.

f   II. **Flora R. Straube** was born in Independence, Jackson County, Missouri, on October 02, 1868. She died in 1953 at the age of 84. Flora R. was buried in Vernon Cemetery, Vernon, Marion County, Illinois (Find a Grave ID 102188774).

> Marriage to John G. Graham on Nov. 6th, 1894. John died in Atlas Twp, Pike, Illinois on 27 Mar 1905.
> Marriage to John Steele (1863-) by the 1920 census
> Children: Earl G. Graham

+ 50   f   III. **Mary Emma Straube** was born in Pike County, Missouri, on January 20, 1869. She died in Greeley, Weld County, Colorado, on November 04, 1953, at the age of 84. Mary Emma was buried in Linn Grove Cemetery, Greeley, Weld County, Colorado (Find a Grave ID 65216731).

m   IV. **Marion Alvah Straube** was born in Missouri, USA, on June 13, 1871. He died on October 06, 1873, at the age of 2.

f   V. **Julia Ellen Straube** was born in Missouri, USA, on August 24, 1873. She died on October 23, 1875, at the age of 2.

f   VI. **Lucy Leonia Straube** was born in Missouri, USA, on January 05, 1876.

May have died before 1880 as she is not listed on the census with her parents that year.

Family of Francis Straube and Alice Martin

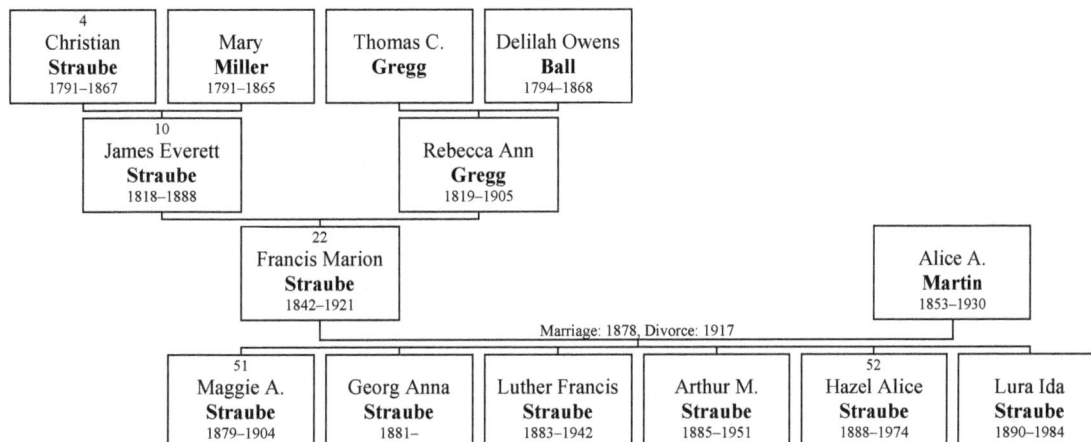

```
┌──────────┐ ┌──────────┐ ┌──────────┐ ┌──────────────┐
│    4     │ │          │ │          │ │ Delilah Owens│
│ Christian│ │  Mary    │ │ Thomas C.│ │    Ball      │
│ Straube  │ │  Miller  │ │  Gregg   │ │              │
│1791-1867 │ │1791-1865 │ │          │ │  1794-1868   │
└──────────┘ └──────────┘ └──────────┘ └──────────────┘
    ┌───────────────┐        ┌───────────────┐
    │      10       │        │  Rebecca Ann  │
    │ James Everett │        │    Gregg      │
    │   Straube     │        │               │
    │  1818-1888    │        │   1819-1905   │
    └───────────────┘        └───────────────┘
           ┌───────────────┐              ┌──────────────┐
           │      22       │              │   Alice A.   │
           │ Francis Marion│              │   Martin     │
           │   Straube     │              │              │
           │  1842-1921    │              │  1853-1930   │
           └───────────────┘              └──────────────┘
                    Marriage: 1878, Divorce: 1917
```

| 51 Maggie A. Straube 1879-1904 | Georg Anna Straube 1881- | Luther Francis Straube 1883-1942 | Arthur M. Straube 1885-1951 | 52 Hazel Alice Straube 1888-1974 | Lura Ida Straube 1890-1984 |

Here are the details about **Francis Marion Straube's** second marriage, with Alice A. Martin. You can read more about Francis Marion on page 53.

Francis Marion Straube married **Alice A. Martin** on Thursday, August 22, 1878, in Montgomery County, Missouri. They were divorced in York County, Nebraska, on March 21, 1917. They had six children.

Alice A. was born in Carroll County, Maryland, in 1853. She reached 77 years of age and died in Hall County, Nebraska, on July 14, 1930. Alice A. was buried in Soldiers And Sailors Cemetery, Grand Island, Hall County, Nebraska (Find a Grave ID 39843986).

When she married Francis, she already had a son Mosley McElfresh who is named as Francis' stepson in the 1880 census.

Children of Francis Marion Straube and Alice A. Martin:

+ 51   f   I. **Maggie A. Straube** was born in Missouri, USA, on July 10, 1879. She died in Boulder, Boulder County, Colorado, on February 28, 1904, at the age of 24. Her cause of death was edematous laryngitis. She was buried in Columbia Cemetery, Boulder, Boulder County, Colorado (Find a Grave ID 67848393).

When Maggie L. Straube was born on 16 July 1879, in Greeley, Weld, Colorado, United States, her father, Francis M Straube, was 35 and her mother, Alice M. Martin, was 26.

She married William Robert McGill on 8 November 1899, in Greeley, Weld, Colorado. She lived in Prairie Township, Montgomery, Missouri, United States in 1880. She died on 28 February 1904, in Boulder, Colorado, at the age of 24, and was buried in Columbia Cemetery, Boulder, Boulder County, Colorado.

f   II. **Georg Anna Straube** was born in Missouri, USA, on March 27, 1881.

m   III. **Luther Francis Straube** was born in Schuyler, Colfax County, Nebraska, on May 16, 1883. He died in Manhattan, New York County, New York, on May 15, 1942, at the age of 58. Luther Francis' burial details are unknown (Find a Grave ID 232399085).

m   IV. **Arthur M. Straube** was born in Nebraska, USA, on September 05, 1885. He died in Los Angeles County, California, on March 18, 1951, at the age of 65. Arthur's burial details are unknown (Find a Grave ID 232399598).

+ 52 f   V. **Hazel Alice Straube** was born in Nebraska, USA, on October 10, 1888. She died on December 22, 1974, at the age of 86. Hazel Alice was buried in Forest Lawn Memorial Park, Glendale, Los Angeles County, California (Find a Grave ID 85527613).

f   VI. **Lura Ida Straube** was born in Nebraska, USA, on August 28, 1890. She died in Grand Island, Hall County, Nebraska, on April 20, 1984, at the age of 93. Lura Ida was buried in Grand Island, Hall County, Nebraska (Find a Grave ID 100736426).

Christian Straube

23. **Christian Straube** was born on Saturday, May 23, 1846, in Middletown, Montgomery County, Missouri. He was the son of James Everett Straube (10) and Rebecca Ann Gregg.

Christian served in the military. 49th Missouri Infantry, Co. B. He died in Saint James, Phelps County, Missouri, on January 15, 1919, at the age of 72. Christian was buried in Saint James Veterans Home Cemetery, Saint James, Phelps County, Missouri, on January 16, 1919 (Find a Grave ID 10851139).

> Listed as a farmer with wife Mary J. in 1850 U.S. Census, Indian Creek, Pike County, Missouri. James T. is also listed as 1 year old.

> Military: 49th REGIMENT MO INFANTRY.

> Organized at Warrenton, Mexico, Macon and St. Louis, Mo., August 31,1864, to February 5, 1865. Attached to District of North Missouri, Dept, of Missouri, to February, 1865. 2nd Brigade, 3rd Division, 16th Army Corps (New), Military District of West Mississippi, to August, 1865. Dept. of Alabama to December, 1865.

> SERVICE.-Duty in Northern Missouri line of Northern Missouri Railroad, till January 30, 1865. Moved to St. Louis, Mo., January 30-February 1, thence to New Orleans, LL, February 10-21. Campaign against Mobile, Ala., and its defenses March 17-April 12. Siege of Spanish Fort and Fort Blakely March 26-April 8. Assault and capture of Fort Blakely April 9. Occupation of Mobile April 12. March to Montgomery April 1325, and duty there till July 14 Companies "A," "B," "C", "D," "E," "F", "G," and "I" ordered to St. Louis, Mo., and mustered out August 2, 1865. Companies "H" and "K" on duty at Eufaula, Ala., till December, 1865. Mustered out December 20, 1865.

Regiment lost during service 4 Enlisted men killed and mortally wounded and 96 Enlisted men by disease. Total 100.

Source of Data: *A Compendium of the War of the Rebellion, V.III* by Frederick H. Dyer, c1908, p.1338

Missouri Commandery
Military Order of the Loyal Legion of the US.

Marriages with Mary J. Woodson and Mary Ellen Blane (Page 58) are known.

Family of Christian Straube and Mary Woodson

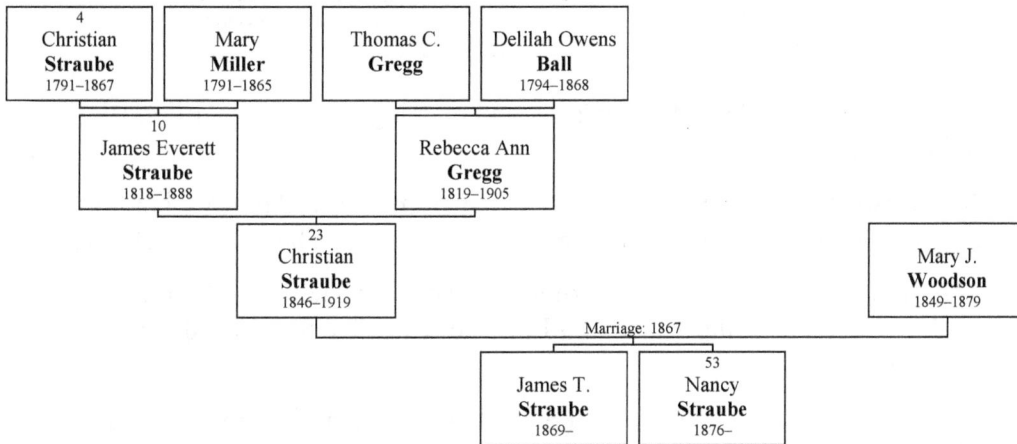

Here are the details about **Christian Straube's** first marriage, with Mary J. Woodson. You can read more about Christian on page 56.

Christian Straube married **Mary J. Woodson** in 1867. They had two children.

Mary J. was born in Missouri, USA, in 1849. She reached 30 years of age and died in Missouri, USA, on July 23, 1879. Mary J. was buried in Kilby Cemetery, Curryville, Pike County, Missouri (Find a Grave ID 199443564).

Children of Christian Straube and Mary J. Woodson:

        m   I. **James T. Straube** was born in Missouri, USA, in 1869.

+   53   f   II. **Nancy Straube** was born in Missouri, USA, in 1876.

Family of Christian Straube and Mary Blane

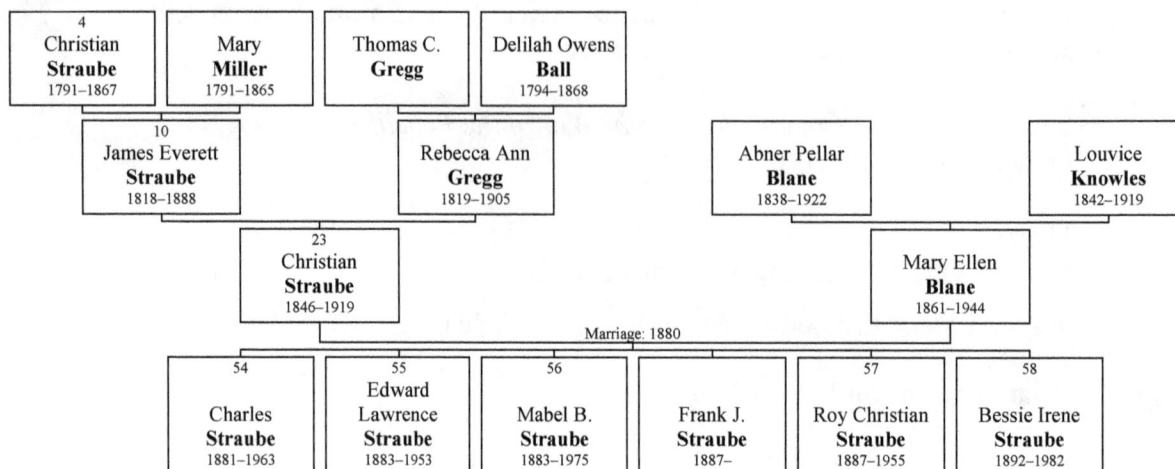

4 Christian **Straube** 1791–1867	Mary **Miller** 1791–1865	Thomas C. **Gregg**	Delilah Owens **Ball** 1794–1868

10 James Everett **Straube** 1818–1888	Rebecca Ann **Gregg** 1819–1905	Abner Pellar **Blane** 1838–1922	Louvice **Knowles** 1842–1919

23 Christian **Straube** 1846–1919	Mary Ellen **Blane** 1861–1944

Marriage: 1880

54 Charles **Straube** 1881–1963	55 Edward Lawrence **Straube** 1883–1953	56 Mabel B. **Straube** 1883–1975	Frank J. **Straube** 1887–	57 Roy Christian **Straube** 1887–1955	58 Bessie Irene **Straube** 1892–1982

Here are the details about **Christian Straube's** second marriage, with Mary Ellen Blane. You can read more about Christian on page 56.

At the age of 34, Christian Straube married **Mary Ellen Blane** on Friday, October 08, 1880, in Menard, Randolph County, Illinois, when she was 19 years old. They had six children.

Mary Ellen was born in Greenview, Menard County, Illinois, on Tuesday, October 08, 1861. She was the daughter of Abner Pellar Blane and Louvice Knowles. She was also known as **Molly**.

Mary Ellen reached 82 years of age and died in Saint James, Phelps County, Missouri, on January 01, 1944. She was buried in Mount Hope Cemetery, Belleville, St. Clair County, Illinois (Find a Grave ID 120993787).

Children of Christian Straube and Mary Ellen Blane:

+ 54 m I. **Charles Straube** was born in Havana, Mason County, Illinois, on July 02, 1881. He died in San Mateo County, California, on February 15, 1963, at the age of 81. Charles was buried in Golden Gate National Cemetery, San Bruno, San Mateo County, California (Find a Grave ID 3638225).

+ 55 m II. **Edward Lawrence Straube** was born in Greenview, Menard County, Illinois, on February 12, 1883.[40] He died in Belleville, St. Clair County, Illinois, on April 30, 1953, at the age of 70. Edward Lawrence was buried in Valhalla Gardens of Memory and Mausoleum, Belleville, St. Clair County, Illinois (Find a Grave ID 131224039).

+ 56 f III. **Mabel B. Straube** was born in Illinois, USA, on July 08, 1883. She died in Highland, Madison County, Illinois, on November 29, 1975, at the age of 92. Mabel B. was buried in Glen Carbon Cemetery, Glen Carbon, Madison County, Illinois (Find a Grave ID 143748265).

---

40   Ancestry.com, U.S., Social Security Applications and Claims Index, 1936-2007 (Provo, UT, USA, Ancestry.com Operations, Inc., 2015), Ancestry.com, Record for Edward L Straube. https://search.ancestry.co.uk/cgi-bin/sse.dll?db=60901&h=4476572&indiv=try.

Married Joseph Garrish Moore on February 10, 1904 St. Clair
County, Illinois
They were the parents of:
Herold Moore
Ruby Juanita Moore Sweeney 1908-1994
Harriet Clara Moore Deltour 1910-2006
Arthur Woodrow Moore 1912-1985

From the *Edwardsville Intelligencer*, Edwardsville, Madison
County, Illinois, Wednesday, December 3, 1975, page 15:

> Mrs. Mabel Moore, 91, of the Madison County Shelter Home, died
> Saturday at St. Joseph's Hospital, Highland. Graveside services
> were held at 2 p.m. Monday at the Glen Carbon City Cemetery.

m   IV. **Frank J. Straube** was born in Illinois, USA, in October 1887.

+ 57   m   V. **Roy Christian Straube** was born in Macon City, Missouri, on October 16, 1887. He died in Saint Louis, Saint Louis County, Missouri, on October 20, 1955, at the age of 68. Roy Christian was buried in Jefferson Barracks National Cemetery, Lemay, St. Louis County, Missouri, on October 24, 1955 (Find a Grave ID 25769841).

+ 58   f   VI. **Bessie Irene Straube** was born in Illinois, USA, in October 1892.[41] She died in Belleville, St. Clair County, Illinois, on February 01, 1982, at the age of 89.[41] Bessie Irene was buried in Mount Hope Cemetery, Belleville, St. Clair County, Illinois (Find a Grave ID 255614555).[41]

Family of Elizabeth Straube and Robert Wilhoit

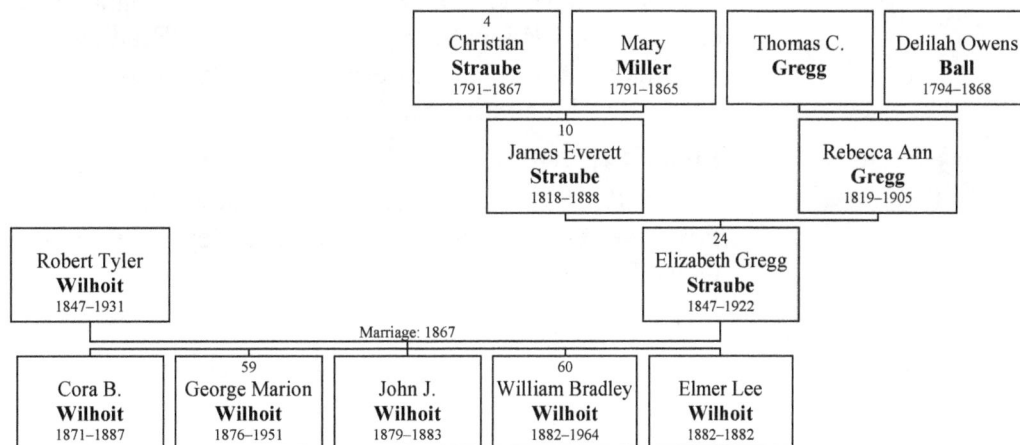

	4 Christian **Straube** 1791–1867	Mary **Miller** 1791–1865	Thomas C. **Gregg**	Delilah Owens **Ball** 1794–1868
	10 James Everett **Straube** 1818–1888		Rebecca Ann **Gregg** 1819–1905	

Robert Tyler **Wilhoit** 1847–1931

24 Elizabeth Gregg **Straube** 1847–1922

Marriage: 1867

59		60	
Cora B. **Wilhoit** 1871–1887	George Marion **Wilhoit** 1876–1951	John J. **Wilhoit** 1879–1883	William Bradley **Wilhoit** 1882–1964	Elmer Lee **Wilhoit** 1882–1882

24.   **Elizabeth Gregg Straube** was born on Tuesday, October 12, 1847, in Audrain County, Missouri. She was the daughter of James Everett Straube (10) and Rebecca Ann Gregg.

---

41   Ancestry.com, U.S., Find a Grave® Index, 1600s-Current (Lehi, UT, USA, Ancestry.com Operations, Inc., 2012), Ancestry.com, Record for Bessie Irene Prather. https://search.ancestry.co.uk/cgi-bin/sse.dll?db=60525&h=226633466&indiv=try.

Elizabeth Gregg died in Pike County, Missouri, on July 13, 1922, at the age of 74. She was buried in Siloam Primitive Baptist Church Cemetery, Ashley, Pike County, Missouri (Find a Grave ID 84022584).

At the age of 20, Elizabeth Gregg married **Robert Tyler Wilhoit** on Monday, November 18, 1867, when he was 20 years old. They had five children.

Robert Tyler was born in Pike County, Missouri, on Monday, September 20, 1847. He reached 83 years of age and died in Montgomery County, Missouri, on March 22, 1931. Robert Tyler was buried in Siloam Primitive Baptist Church Cemetery, Ashley, Pike County, Missouri (Find a Grave ID 84022440).

Children of Elizabeth Gregg Straube and Robert Tyler Wilhoit:

	f	I.	**Cora B. Wilhoit** was born on April 30, 1871. She died on August 24, 1887, at the age of 16. Cora B. was buried in Siloam Primitive Baptist Church Cemetery, Ashley, Pike County, Missouri (Find a Grave ID 84022714).
+ 59	m	II.	**George Marion Wilhoit** was born in New Hartford, Pike County, Missouri, on February 06, 1876. He died in Montgomery County, Missouri, on March 21, 1951, at the age of 75. George Marion was buried in Fairmount Cemetery, Middletown, Montgomery County, Missouri (Find a Grave ID 145395055).
	m	III.	**John J. Wilhoit** was born on December 14, 1879. He died on November 23, 1883, at the age of 3. John J. was buried in Siloam Primitive Baptist Church Cemetery, Ashley, Pike County, Missouri (Find a Grave ID 84022903).
+ 60	m	IV.	**William Bradley Wilhoit** was born in New Hartford, Pike County, Missouri, on March 06, 1882. He died in Louisiana, Pike County, Missouri, on April 29, 1964, at the age of 82. William Bradley was buried in Siloam Primitive Baptist Church Cemetery, Ashley, Pike County, Missouri (Find a Grave ID 84025086).
	m	V.	**Elmer Lee Wilhoit** was born in New Hartford, Pike County, Missouri, on March 06, 1882. He died on June 24, 1882. Elmer Lee was buried in Siloam Primitive Baptist Church Cemetery, Ashley, Pike County, Missouri (Find a Grave ID 84022819).

Family of James Straube and Lucy Morris

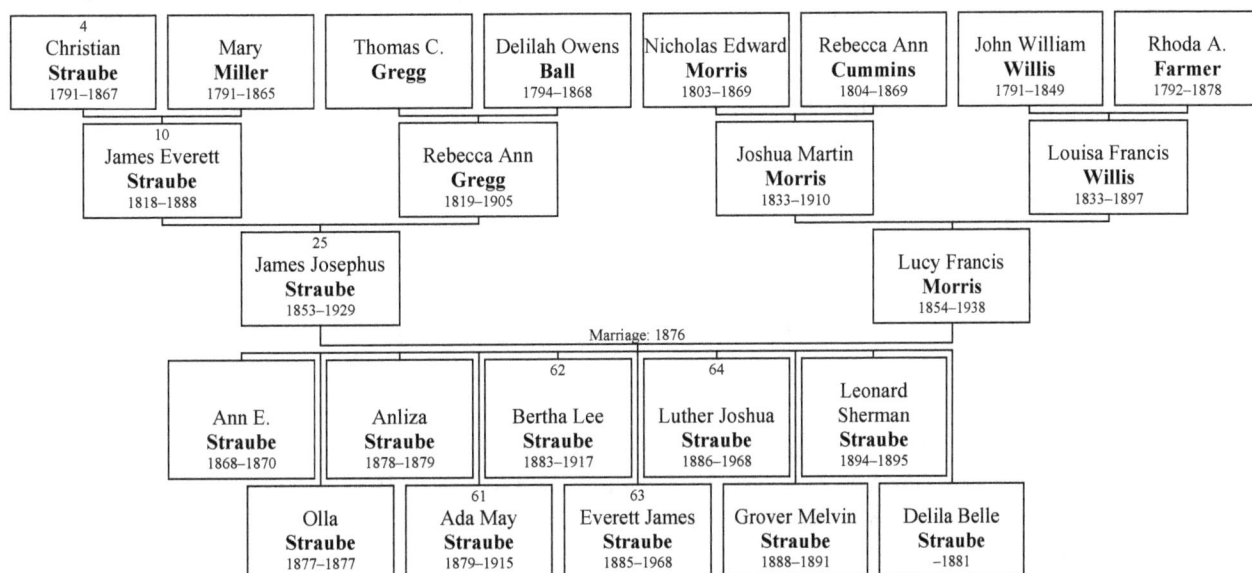

```
┌─────────────┬─────────────┬─────────────┬─────────────┬─────────────┬─────────────┬─────────────┬─────────────┐
│      4      │             │             │             │             │             │             │             │
│  Christian  │    Mary     │  Thomas C.  │Delilah Owens│Nicholas Edward│ Rebecca Ann │John William │  Rhoda A.   │
│  Straube    │   Miller    │   Gregg     │    Ball     │   Morris    │  Cummins    │   Willis    │   Farmer    │
│  1791–1867  │  1791–1865  │             │  1794–1868  │  1803–1869  │  1804–1869  │  1791–1849  │  1792–1878  │
└─────────────┴─────────────┴─────────────┴─────────────┴─────────────┴─────────────┴─────────────┴─────────────┘
```

- 4 Christian **Straube** 1791–1867
- Mary **Miller** 1791–1865
- Thomas C. **Gregg**
- Delilah Owens **Ball** 1794–1868
- Nicholas Edward **Morris** 1803–1869
- Rebecca Ann **Cummins** 1804–1869
- John William **Willis** 1791–1849
- Rhoda A. **Farmer** 1792–1878

- 10 James Everett **Straube** 1818–1888
- Rebecca Ann **Gregg** 1819–1905
- Joshua Martin **Morris** 1833–1910
- Louisa Francis **Willis** 1833–1897

- 25 James Josephus **Straube** 1853–1929
- Lucy Francis **Morris** 1854–1938

Marriage: 1876

- Ann E. **Straube** 1868–1870
- Anliza **Straube** 1878–1879
- 62 Bertha Lee **Straube** 1883–1917
- 64 Luther Joshua **Straube** 1886–1968
- Leonard Sherman **Straube** 1894–1895

- Olla **Straube** 1877–1877
- 61 Ada May **Straube** 1879–1915
- 63 Everett James **Straube** 1885–1968
- Grover Melvin **Straube** 1888–1891
- Delila Belle **Straube** –1881

25.   **James Josephus Straube** was born on Sunday, April 03, 1853, in Montgomery County, Missouri.[42] He was the son of James Everett Straube (10) and Rebecca Ann Gregg.

James Josephus died in Hartford, Pike County, Missouri, on September 20, 1929, at the age of 76. His cause of death was aortic inefficiency. James Josephus was buried in Siloam Primitive Baptist Church Cemetery, Ashley, Pike County, Missouri, on September 21, 1929 (Find a Grave ID 68743487).

> James Josephus was born on Sunday, April 3, 1853 in Middletown, Montgomery County, Missouri and died at age 76 on Friday, September 20, 1929 of aortic inefficiency and chronic myocarditis in New Hartford, Pike County, Missouri. On Sunday, February 6, 1876 at the home of Joshua Martin Morris in Pike County, Missouri James and Lucy Frances Morris were married by Reverend Melton Sears. Lucy was born on Saturday, February 25, 1854 in Pike County, Missouri and died at age 84 on Saturday, March 5, 1938 of cardiac failure, arteriosclerosis, chronic interstitial and chronic myocarditis at the home of her son, Luther Joshua Straube, in Bellflower, Montgomery County, Missouri. She is the daughter of Joshua Martin Morris and Louisa Frances Willis.
>
> On November 14, 1914 James Josephus and Lucy Frances Straube purchased 20 acres of land that was part of 80 acres known as East one-half of the Northwest quarter of Section one (1), Township (51) North, Range four (4) West, in Pike County, Missouri from their son, Everett James Straube for $700. On February 15, 1928, Everett and his wife, Mary Anna Willis Straube, purchased the land back from his parents for $525 and was held until his death in 1968.

---

42   Death Certificate.

At the age of 22, James Josephus married **Lucy Francis Morris** on Tuesday, February 01, 1876, in Pike County, Missouri, when she was 21 years old.[43] They had ten children.

Lucy Francis was born in Pike County, Missouri, on Saturday, February 25, 1854.[44] She was the daughter of Joshua Martin Morris and Louisa Francis Willis.

Lucy Francis reached 84 years of age and died in Bellflower, Montgomery County, Missouri, on March 05, 1938. Her cause of death was cardiac failure. Lucy Francis was buried in Siloam Primitive Baptist Church Cemetery, Ashley, Pike County, Missouri (Find a Grave ID 68743411).

Obituary of Lucy Straube as copied from *The Bowling Green Times*, issue 03-10-1938:

> Lucy Frances Morris, daughter of Joshua and Luiza Morris, was born near New Hartford February 25, 1854 and died March 5, 1938 being at the time of her death 84 years and 10 days.
>
> She was married to James J. Straube in February 1876. To this union eight children were born, six of which preceded her in death, four in early childhood, and Ada May, wife of H. W. Pollard, September 1915, and Bertha Lee, also the wife of H. W. Pollard, September 1917. Those who remain to mourn her passing are Everett James and Luther Joshua Straube with their families; sixteen grandchildren; twelve great grandchildren; two sisters, Mrs. Joel Moore and Mrs. Vineyard James of Gazette; two brothers, Joshua Morris of Sacramento, Calif. and Thomas Morris of Pawhuska, Oklahoma; and a host of other relatives and friends.
>
> She united with the regular Baptist Church at Siloam in October 1910, of which she remained a consistent member until death. She was a true wife, a loving mother and grandmother and a kind obliging neighbor. Funeral services were conducted Sunday Morning at eleven o'clock at Siloam Church by Rev. Dobbs with interment in the Siloam Cemetery. We extend sympathy.

> Lived 84 years and 10 days

> Lucy Frances was born on Saturday, February 25, 1854 in Pike County, Missouri and died at age 84 on Saturday, March 5, 1938 of cardiac failure, arteriosclerosis, chronic interstitial and chronic myocarditis at the home of her son, Luther Joshua Straube, in Bellflower, Montgomery County, Missouri. On Sunday, February 6, 1876 at the home of Joshua Martin Morris in Pike County, Missouri Lucy married James Josephus Straube. Reverend Melton Sears officiated. James Josephus was born on Sunday, April 3, 1853 in Middletown, Montgomery County, Missouri and is the son of James Everett Straube and Rebecca Ann Gregg. James died at age 76 on Friday, September 20, 1929 of aortic inefficiency and chronic myocarditis in New Hartford, Pike County, Missouri. Lucy and James are buried at Siloam Cemetery, Pike County, Missouri. Plot: Row 11 Ward 11 Graves 3 & 4.

---

43   The Church of Jesus Christ of Latter-day Saints, International Genealogical Index (R), Copyright (c) 1980, 1997, data as of February 1997.

44   Death Certificate, Certificate #11548. Informant was Everett Straube.

Lucy is the daughter of Joshua Martin Morris. He was born on Saturday, January 5, 1833 in Robertson County, Tennessee and died at age 77 on Tuesday, June 21, 1910 in Vandalia, Audrain County, Missouri. [1] On Thursday, December 18, 1851, at Siloam, Pike County, Missouri married Louisa Frances Willis. She was born on Sunday, April 7, 1833 in New Hartford, Pike County, Missouri and died at age 64 on Tuesday, May 25, 1897 in Pike County, Missouri and is the daughter of William Willis and Rhoda A. Farmer. Louisa was baptized Saturday, October 26, 1861 at Siloam Church.

The Morris family came to Lincoln County, Missouri from Robertson County, Tennessee when Joshua Martin Morris was about 4 years old. Joshua was raised and educated in Lincoln County, but soon after completing his education, Joshua engaged in farming with his father. In the spring of 1850, at the age of 17, Joshua came to New Hartford in Pike County. He owned 160 acres of land he self-improved and on which he farmed and raised stock. He also had a fine orchard of choice fruit, which completely surrounded the home. In 1860 he crossed the plains to Pike's Peak where he remained after mining for some months. Later he returned home to Pike County.

He united with the Baptist Church in 1858. He was considered of fine reputation and a good businessman. [2] On Wednesday, September 28, 1898 in Olney, Lincoln County, Missouri Joshua married Isabelle B. Parsons who was born on Tuesday, February 5, 1850 in Missouri and died at age 81 on Thursday, March 5, 1931 of hypertension nephritis in Cooper County, Missouri. Isabelle is the daughter of William Shelton Parsons, FAG# 37324899 and Mary Margaret Johnston, FAG# 34984376. Joshua, FAG# 44946020 and Louisa, FAG# 44946067 are buried at Siloam Cemetery, Pike County, Missouri. Plot: Row 8 Ward 21 Graves 2 & 1. Isabelle, FAG# 22529511 is buried at Union Cemetery, Pettis County, Missouri.

Children of James Josephus Straube and Lucy Francis Morris:

f   I. **Ann E. Straube** was born on August 30, 1868. She died on August 01, 1870, at the age of 1. Ann E. was buried in Siloam Primitive Baptist Church Cemetery, Ashley, Pike County, Missouri (Find a Grave ID 100290136).

f   II. **Olla Straube** was born in New Hartford, Pike County, Missouri, on February 05, 1877. She was also known as **Olie**.

Olla died in New Hartford, Pike County, Missouri, on November 25, 1877. She was buried in Siloam Primitive Baptist Church Cemetery, Ashley, Pike County, Missouri (Find a Grave ID 70940272).

Aged 9 months, 20 days

f   III. **Anliza Straube** was born in New Hartford, Pike County, Missouri, on April 19, 1878. She was also known as **Anne E. Straube**.

Anliza died in New Hartford, Pike County, Missouri, on August 01, 1879, at the age of 1. She was buried in Siloam Primitive Baptist Church Cemetery, Ashley, Pike County, Missouri (Find a Grave ID 70941478).

Anliza is the name as written in the Bible of her mother, Lucy Frances Morris Straube, but the name Ann E. is inscribed on tombstone.

+ 61   f   IV. **Ada May Straube** was born on November 17, 1879.[45] She died in Saint Louis, Saint Louis County, Missouri, on September 21, 1915, at the age of 35. Her cause of death was hepatic abscess. She was buried in Siloam Primitive Baptist Church Cemetery, Ashley, Pike County, Missouri, on September 22, 1915 (Find a Grave ID 69238769).

> Ada May Straube was born near New Hartford, Missouri, on November 17, 1879. She is the daughter and 3rd child of James Josephus Straube and Lucy Francis Morris.
>
> Ada's siblings are as follows and are on this site: Olie # 70940272, Anliza # 70941478, Bertha Lee # 69240088, Everett James # 68075841, Luther Joshua # 69533077, Grover Melvin # 70964070 and Lenard Sherman # 70964138.
>
> Ada was converted and joined the Baptist Church at Siloam September 22, 1909 where she was devoted member until death.
>
> Ada May married Hershel Weaver Pollard on Jamary 1, 1899. To this union were born four children, two dying in infancy. Two survive her, Cleo, age 12 and Ralph age 9 months.
>
> She passed away on September 21, 1915, age: 35 years, 10 months, 4 days; as a result of a hepatic abscess (liver infection) and appendicitis at Missouri Baptist Sanatorium in Saint Louis, Missouri.
>
> Ada's funeral was conducted by her pastor, Reverend Huff, of Moberly, Mo., on September 22 at 2 p.m. at Siloam Church, after which the remains were laid to rest in the Siloam cemetery to await the resurrection morn.
>
> Note: The spelling of Hershel here is correct and is found on several documents including the 1940 Census however spelled "Hearschel" on Ada's tombstone at Siloam and spelled "Herchel" on his Death Certificate. After Ada died, Hershel married Ada's sister, Bertha Lee Straube. Following Bertha's death Hershel married Louvenia Pearl Jackson and following Louvenia's death he married Lutetia Pearl Jackson; both are buried in Bowling Green Cemetery alongside Hershel.

+ 62   f   V. **Bertha Lee Straube** was born on January 02, 1883.[46] She died in Hartford Township, Pike County, Missouri, on August 30, 1917, at the age of 34. Her cause of death was rupture of gall bladder. She was buried in Siloam

---

[45]   Death Certificate, Certificate # 29236, Reg. # 7942.

[46]   Death Certificate, Certificate # 29516.

Primitive Baptist Church Cemetery, Ashley, Pike County, Missouri, on August 31, 1917 (Find a Grave ID 69240088).

> Bertha Lee Straube was born near New Hartford, Missouri, on January 2, 1883. She is the daughter and 4th child of James Josephus Straube and Lucy Francis Morris.
>
> Bertha's siblings are as follows and are on this site: Olie # 70940272, Anliza # 70941478, Ada May # 69238769, Everett James # 68075841, Luther Joshua # 69533077, Grover Melvin # 70964070 and Lenard Sherman # 70964138.
>
> Bertha Lee united with the Baptist Church at New Hartford in October 1914, later changing her membership to Siloam Baptist Church.
>
> Bertha Lee married Hershel Weaver Pollard (see note) on September 28, 1916. Bertha Lee passed away on August 30, 1917, age: 34 years, 7 months, 28 days, only being married 11 months as a result of a ruptured gall bladder.
>
> Bertha Lee leaves behind her husband, Hershel; two step-children, Cleo and Ralph; a father, James J., and mother, Lucy F. Straube; and two brothers, Everett James and Luther Joshua Straube.
>
> Funeral services were conducted by her pastor, Rev. Carter of Moberly, Mo., after which she was laid to rest beside her beloved sister, Ada May, who preceded her to the grave two years before.

+ 63   m   VI. **Everett James Straube** was born in New Hartford, Pike County, Missouri, on January 17, 1885. He died in Bowling Green, Pike County, Missouri, on December 29, 1968, at the age of 83. His cause of death was coronary occlusion, arteriosclerosis. He was buried in Memorial Gardens Cemetery, Bowling Green, Pike County, Missouri, on December 31, 1968 (Find a Grave ID 68075841).

> From *People Places & Pikers* page 639:
>
> > Everett James Straube, was born January 17, 1885, near New Hartford. He lived his boyhood on the farm and was a talented fiddler and singer. Everett and Anna established their home near Siloam Church in the New Hartford-Farmer community. Around 1943 Everett and Anna moved to Bowling Green. They purchased the B.B. Springs Hotel in 1945. They lived at the B. B. Springs and operated it as a nursing home until their retirement in 1962. Everett and Anna remained in Bowling Green until their deaths. Both are buried in Bowling Green Memorial Gardens. They were members of the Second Baptist Church in Bowling Green.

One of the first Straube families to settle in Pike County was that of James E. Straube. James E., of German ancestry, was married to Rebecca Ann Greg, cousin of William McKinley, 25th President of the United States.

Everett James Straube was born near New Hartford, Missouri, on Saturday, January 17, 1885. He is the son of James Josephus Straube and Lucy Francis Morris.

Everett was the 5th born of 8 children. His siblings are as follows and are listed on this site: Olie # 70940272, Anliza # 70941478, Ada May # 69238769, Bertha Lee # 69240088, Luther Joshua # 69533077, Grover Melvin # 70964070 and Lenard Sherman # 70964138.

In 1909, Everett united with the Primitive Baptist Church at Siloam, near New Hartford, and later transferred his membership to the Second Baptist Church in Bowling Green. Everett was a farmer and accomplished at playing the fiddle by ear and he and his sister, Ada, and her husband, Herschel Pollard, often provided the music for the dances in the area.

On August 12, 1910, the Reverend Wiley J. Patrick married Everett James Straube and Mary Anna Willis, the daughter of John William Willis and Mary Elizabeth "Lizzie" Mudd. Everett, 25, dressed in a navy suit with a white shirt and tie, was a well-built handsome farmer with dark hair and eyes. Anna, 22, with pure white skin, beautiful reddish hair and blue eyes, wore a delicate high neck white laced wedding dress.

To this union was born Tressa Jean, July 1, 1911; Bennett Clark, fondly known as "Ike", December 7, 1912; Lucy Gladys, September 17, 1914; Walter Scott, September 26, 1916; Hazel Elizabeth, October 13, 1918 and Everett James Jr. called by his initials "E.J.", April 13, 1920.

They made their home on a farm in the New Hartford area near Farmer. Mrs. Straube taught school in Pike County for over 30 years. In 1944 they moved to Bowling Green and in 1945 purchased the BB Springs Rest Home and in 1946 purchased the Cottage Hotel in Bowling Green and operated both until they retired in 1962. Mrs. Straube passed away on Saturday, April 8, 1967.

Everett James Straube passed away at the Straube Rest Home on Sunday, December 29, 1968, at the age of 83 years, 11 months and 12 days as a result of coronary occlusion and arteriosclerosis. Funeral services were held on Tuesday, December 31, at the Second Baptist Church of Bowling Green with the Reverends Joe Barbour and G.E. Rittenhouse officiating. "The Old Rugged Cross" and "In The Sweet Bye and Bye" were sung by Reverend Barbour with Mrs. Chester C. Coddington accompanist.

Surviving Everett James Straube are his six children: Tressa (Floyd) Chamberlain, Ike (Shirley) Straube, Gladys Straube Myers, Scott (Ann) Straube, Sr., Hazel (Garland) Smith and E.J. (Lil) Straube, Jr.; twenty-five grandchildren: Shirley Jean Chamberlain (Ted) Mummert, Georganna Myers (Sam) Hargadine, Tanya Straube (Tom) Cunningham, Scott Straube, Jr., Duane (Mary Kay) Straube, Fred Smith, Christine Smith

(Jacques) McCormack, Robert Straube, Elaine Straube (Clem) Deters, Rosetta Straube (William) Pagnella, Stephen Smith, David Straube, Annice Straube (R. J.) Allensworth, Michael Straube, Pam Chamberlain, Jerry Straube, Chris (Vickie) Straube, Karen Straube, Willis Straube, Bruce Smith, Joyce Straube, Lucy Straube, Cheryl Straube, Elizabeth Smith and Dewey Straube; thirteen great grandchildren: Paula Henderson, Marsha Henderson, Susan Henderson, Sam Hargadine, John Hargadine, Troy Straube, Calvin Mummert, Floyd Mummert, Bob Cunningham, Sharlene Mummert, Crystal Straube, Terri Cunningham and Brian Pagnella.

Mr. Straube was laid to rest by his Grandsons Duane, Chris, Willis and David Straube and Fred and Bruce Smith. Burial was at Memorial Gardens in Bowling Green, Missouri. The Family was served by the Mudd Funeral Home.

+ 64 m VII. **Luther Joshua Straube** was born in New Hartford, Pike County, Missouri, on June 20, 1886. He died in Bowling Green, Pike County, Missouri, on December 14, 1968, at the age of 82. Luther Joshua was buried in Siloam Primitive Baptist Church Cemetery, Ashley, Pike County, Missouri, on December 17, 1968 (Find a Grave ID 69533077).

Luther Joshua Straube was born near New Hartford, Missouri, on June 20, 1886. He is the son and 6th child of James Josephus Straube and Lucy Francis Morris.

Luther's siblings are as follows and are on this site: Olie # 70940272, Anliza # 70941478, Ada May # 69238769, Bertha Lee # 69240088, Everett James # 68075841, Luther Joshua # 69533077, Grover Melvin # 70964070 and Lenard Sherman # 70964138.

Luther married Rosa Shelton Lewis on December 1, 1907. To this union were born Melvin Joshua, Leonard Shelton, Irene Frances, Ogle Edward "Tutor", Carroll Wilson, Claude A., Glen Whitt and Bobby Edwin.

Children of LUTHER STRAUBE and ROSA LEWIS are:

• MELVIN JOSHUA STRAUBE, b. 16 Aug 1908, Gazette, Pike County, Missouri; d. 11 May 1996, Vandalia, Audrain County, Missouri.
• LEONARD STRAUBE, b. 11 Feb 1910; d. May 1971.
• IRENE STRAUBE, b. about 1913; d. before 11 Apr 1996.
• OGLE E. STRAUBE.
• CARROL STRAUBE, b. about 1917; d. before 11 Apr 1996.
• CLAUDE A. STRAUBE, b. 08 Dec 1921; d. 09 Mar 1979 Burial:

Fairmount Cemetery, Middletown, Montgomery County, Missouri; m. BEATRICE P..

- GLEN STRAUBE.
- ROBERT STRAUBE.

m   **VIII.** **Grover Melvin Straube** was born in New Hartford, Pike County, Missouri, on October 31, 1888. He was also known as **Mevion**.

Grover Melvin died in New Hartford, Pike County, Missouri, on March 05, 1891, at the age of 2. He was buried in Siloam Primitive Baptist Church Cemetery, Ashley, Pike County, Missouri (Find a Grave ID 70964070).

Shares a headstone with brother Lenord (Leonard) Sherman.

Grover Melvin was born October 31, 1888 and is the son and 7th child of James Josephus and Lucy Francis Straube.

According to the *Louisiana Press Journal* dated 3-27-1891: Grover accidently turned over a kettle of soft soap (lye) on himself on Tuesday 3-24-1891 and was so badly burned he died the next day, Wednesday 3-25-1891. He was age 2 years, 4 months, 25 days.

m   **IX.** **Leonard Sherman Straube** was born in New Hartford, Pike County, Missouri, on August 25, 1894. He was also known as **Lenord**.

Leonard Sherman died in New Hartford, Pike County, Missouri, on February 01, 1895. He was buried in Siloam Primitive Baptist Church Cemetery, Ashley, Pike County, Missouri (Find a Grave ID 70964138).

Shares a head stone with brother Grover.

f   **X.** **Delila Belle Straube**. Delila Belle died on March 21, 1881. She was buried in Siloam Primitive Baptist Church Cemetery, Ashley, Pike County, Missouri.

Not listed in Find a Grave. (3/20/2023)

Family of John Straube and Alice Mummey

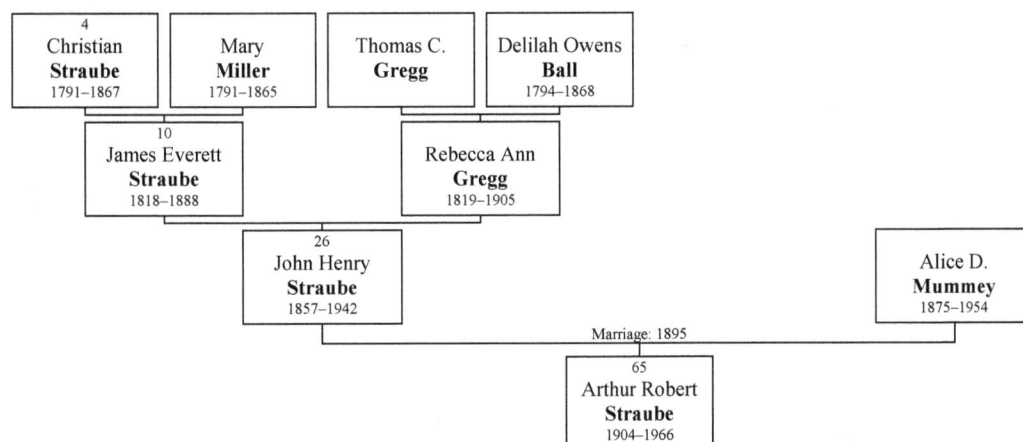

26. **John Henry Straube** was born in August 1857 in Missouri, USA.[47] He was the son of James Everett Straube (10) and Rebecca Ann Gregg.

John Henry died in Harvey, Cook County, Illinois, on October 01, 1942, at the age of 85.[47] He was buried in Homewood Memorial Gardens, Homewood, Cook County, Illinois (Find a Grave ID 220097456).

John Henry married **Alice D. Mummey** in 1895.[47] They had one son.

Alice D. was born in Illinois, USA, in 1875.[47] She reached 79 years of age and died in 1954. Alice D. was buried in Homewood Memorial Gardens, Homewood, Cook County, Illinois (Find a Grave ID 220097421).

Son of John Henry Straube and Alice D. Mummey:

+ 65 m I. **Arthur Robert Straube** was born in Barry, Pike County, Illinois, on July 20, 1904. He died in Harvey, Cook County, Illinois, on October 03, 1966, at the age of 62. Arthur Robert was buried in Homewood Memorial Gardens, Homewood, Cook County, Illinois (Find a Grave ID 197513801).

Family of Mary Straube and Jacob Renner

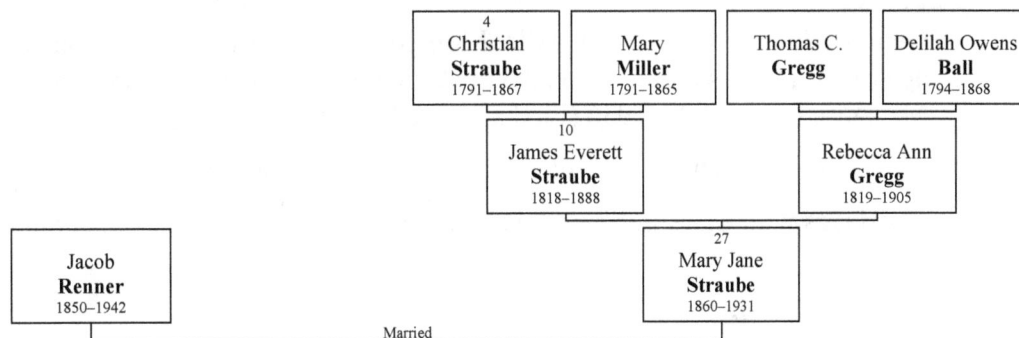

---

47 Ancestry.com, Public Member Trees (Provo, UT, USA, Ancestry.com Operations, Inc., 2006), Ancestry.com, Record for John Henry Straube. https://search.ancestry.co.uk/cgi-bin/sse.dll?db=1030&h=322059795869&indiv=try.

27. **Mary Jane Straube** was born on Friday, October 12, 1860, in Middleton, Pike County, Missouri. She was the daughter of James Everett Straube (10) and Rebecca Ann Gregg.

Mary Jane died in Ashley, Pike County, Missouri, on May 12, 1931, at the age of 70. She was buried in Concord Cemetery, Pike County, Missouri, on May 13, 1931 (Find a Grave ID 8320150).

She married **Jacob Renner**. Jacob was born in Ashley, Pike County, Missouri, on Saturday, December 28, 1850.

He reached 91 years of age and died in Hannibal, Marion County, Missouri, on January 28, 1942. Jacob was buried in Concord Cemetery, Pike County, Missouri (Find a Grave ID 8320141).

Family of Mary Straube and George Davis

```
                    ┌──────────────┐  ┌──────────┐  ┌──────────┐
                    │      4       │  │   Mary   │  │ Leonard  │
                    │  Christian   │  │  Miller  │  │  Enslen  │
                    │   Straube    │  │1791–1865 │  │          │
                    │  1791–1867   │  └──────────┘  └──────────┘
                    └──────────────┘
                        ┌──────────────────┐        ┌──────────────┐
                        │        11        │        │  Mariah Ann  │
                        │  George Munson   │        │    Enslen    │
                        │     Straube      │        │  1825–1895   │
                        │    1823–1879     │        └──────────────┘
                        └──────────────────┘
                              ┌──────────────┐
  ┌──────────────┐           │      28      │
  │    George    │           │   Mary J.    │
  │    Davis     │           │   Straube    │
  │              │           │    1843–     │
  └──────────────┘           └──────────────┘
              Marriage: <1870
```

28. **Mary J. Straube** was born on Sunday, September 17, 1843, in Audrain County, Missouri. She was the daughter of George Munson Straube (11) and Mariah Ann Enslen.

Mary J. married **George Davis** before 1870.

George Straube

29. **George Munson Straube** was born on Thursday, January 06, 1848, in Audrain County, Missouri. He was the son of George Munson Straube (11) and Mariah Ann Enslen. He was also known as **G.M.**.

George Munson died in Wellsville, Montgomery County, Missouri, on April 27, 1936, at the age of 88. He was buried in Wellsville Cemetery, Wellsville, Montgomery County, Missouri, on April 29, 1936 (Find a Grave ID 83904859).

Children referenced from 1910 U.S. Census, Montgomery County, Missouri.

Marriages with Clara E. Shipperd and Alice Jane Rezner (Page 72) are known.

Family of George Straube and Clara Shipperd

Here are the details about **George Munson Straube's** first marriage, with Clara E. Shipperd. You can read more about George Munson on page 70.

George Munson Straube married **Clara E. Shipperd** in 1875. They had two children.

Clara E. was born in Freeport, Stephenson County, Illinois, on Tuesday, August 26, 1856. She reached 23 years of age and died on November 16, 1879. Clara E. was buried in Wellsville Cemetery, Wellsville, Montgomery County, Missouri (Find a Grave ID 130017998).

Children of George Munson Straube and Clara E. Shipperd:

f   I.   **Maude S. Straube** was born in Wellsville, Montgomery County, Missouri, on December 25, 1876. She died in Wellsville, Montgomery County, Missouri, on March 23, 1942, at the age of 65. Maude S. was buried in Wellsville Cemetery, Wellsville, Montgomery County, Missouri (Find a Grave ID 166344766).

m   II.   **Clarel Shipperd Straube** was born in Wellsville, Montgomery County, Missouri, on November 07, 1879. He died in Wellsville, Montgomery County, Missouri, on November 20, 1951, at the age of 72. Clarel Shipperd was buried in Wellsville Cemetery, Wellsville, Montgomery County, Missouri (Find a Grave ID 84074092).

Family of George Straube and Alice Rezner

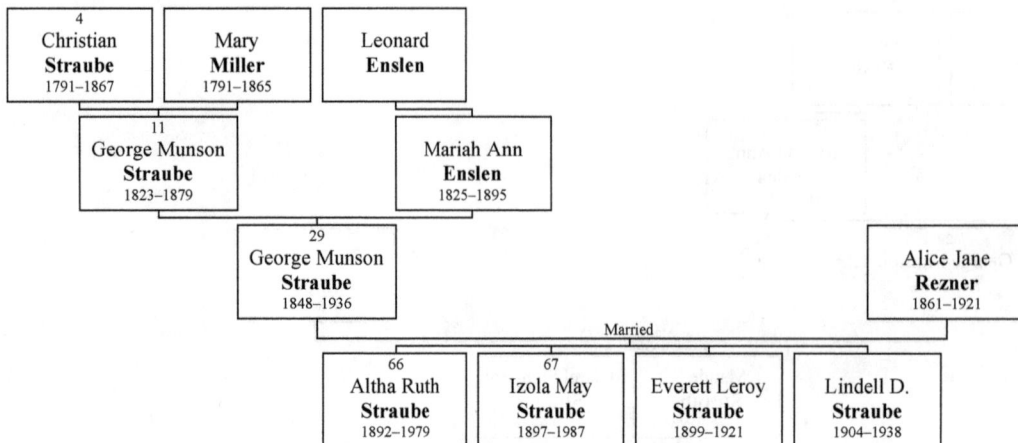

Here are the details about **George Munson Straube's** second marriage, with Alice Jane Rezner. You can read more about George Munson on page 70.

George Munson Straube married **Alice Jane Rezner**. They had four children.

Alice Jane was born in Freeport, Stephenson County, Illinois, on Tuesday, February 19, 1861. She reached 59 years of age and died in Mexico, Audrain County, Missouri, on January 10, 1921. Alice Jane was buried in Wellsville Cemetery, Wellsville, Montgomery County, Missouri (Find a Grave ID 93984968).

Children of George Munson Straube and Alice Jane Rezner:

+ 66 f I. **Altha Ruth Straube** was born in Wellsville, Montgomery County, Missouri, on November 02, 1892.[48] She died in Grand Haven, Ottawa County, Michigan, on August 15, 1979, at the age of 86.[48] Altha Ruth was buried in Saint Joseph Valley Memorial Park, Mishawaka, St. Joseph County, Indiana (Find a Grave ID 54901512).[48]

48 Ancestry.com, Public Member Trees (Provo, UT, USA, Ancestry.com Operations, Inc., 2006), Ancestry.com, Record for Altha Ruth Straube. https://search.ancestry.co.uk/cgi-bin/sse.dll?db=1030&h=40424591245&indiv=try.

+	67	f	II. **Izola May Straube** was born in Missouri, USA, on May 12, 1897.[49–54] She died on June 25, 1987, at the age of 90.[51] Her burial details are unknown.
		m	III. **Everett Leroy Straube** was born in Wellsville, Montgomery County, Missouri, on March 10, 1899. He died in Wellsville, Montgomery County, Missouri, on March 01, 1921, at the age of 21. His cause of death was accidental gun discharge killing him instantly. He was buried in Wellsville Cemetery, Wellsville, Montgomery County, Missouri (Find a Grave ID 84035901).
		m	IV. **Lindell D. Straube** was born in Montgomery City, Montgomery County, Missouri, in 1904. He died in Boulder, Boulder County, Colorado, on August 28, 1938, at the age of 34.

More facts and events for Lindell D. Straube:

Individual Note: Dentist

Family of Izabella Straube and John Card

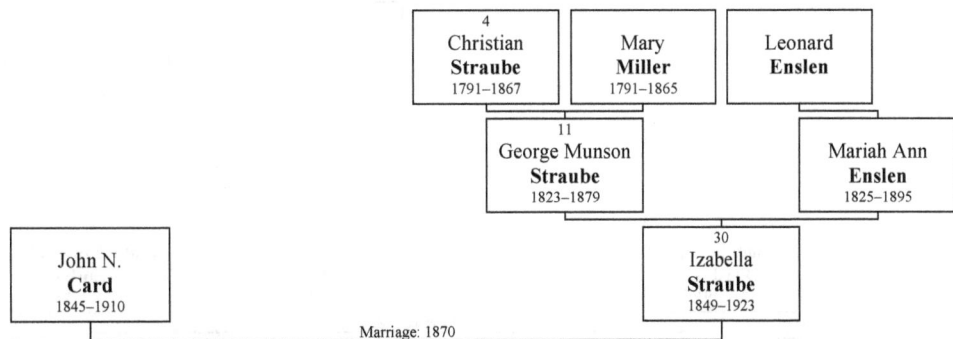

30.   **Izabella Straube** was born on Thursday, September 06, 1849, in Audrain County, Missouri. She was the daughter of George Munson Straube (11) and Mariah Ann Enslen. She was also known as **Bell**.

49   FamilySearch.org, United States Census, 1940, FamilySearch, "United States Census, 1940", , <i>FamilySearch</i> (https://www.familysearch.org/ark:/61903/1:1:K7HN-43L : Tue Oct 03 09:55:28 UTC 2023), Entry for Emma L Brinkmann and I Zala Alvey, 1940.

50   FamilySearch.org, United States Census, 1930, FamilySearch, "United States Census, 1930", , <i>FamilySearch</i> (https://www.familysearch.org/ark:/61903/1:1:XHV6-2MM : Thu Oct 05 09:11:41 UTC 2023), Entry for Raymond Alvey and Izola Alvey, 1930.

51   FamilySearch.org, United States Social Security Death Index, FamilySearch, "United States Social Security Death Index," database, <i>FamilySearch</i> (https://familysearch.org/ark:/61903/1:1:JLPS-XY4 : 10 January 2021), Izola Alvey, Jun 1987; citing U.S. Social Security Administration, <i>Death Master File</i>, database (Alexandria, Virginia: National Technical Information Service, ongoing).

52   FamilySearch.org, United States Census, 1920, FamilySearch, "United States Census, 1920", , <i>FamilySearch</i> (https://www.familysearch.org/ark:/61903/1:1:M8CZ-8WH : Wed Oct 04 20:42:20 UTC 2023), Entry for T M Stroube and Alice Stroube, 1920.

53   FamilySearch.org, United States Census, 1910, FamilySearch, "United States Census, 1910", , <i>FamilySearch</i> (https://www.familysearch.org/ark:/61903/1:1:M2B8-RGC : Thu Oct 05 19:55:14 UTC 2023), Entry for George M Straube and Alice J Straube, 1910.

54   FamilySearch.org, United States Census, 1900, FamilySearch, "United States Census, 1900", , <i>FamilySearch</i> (https://www.familysearch.org/ark:/61903/1:1:M3ZT-B7Q : Thu Oct 05 06:04:36 UTC 2023), Entry for Geo M Straube and Alice J Straube, 1900.

Izabella died in Washington, USA, on February 02, 1923, at the age of 73. She was buried in Washington Lawn Cemetery, Centralia, Lewis County, Washington (Find a Grave ID 93369474).

Izabella married **John N. Card** on Thursday, February 24, 1870, in Audrain County, Missouri. John N. was born in Rhode Island, USA, in 1845.

He reached 65 years of age and died in Centralia, Lewis County, Washington, on September 18, 1910. John N. was buried in Washington Lawn Cemetery, Centralia, Lewis County, Washington (Find a Grave ID 86512758).

> Civil War Veteran
> 3rd Regiment Company D Heavy Artillery
> Rhode Island
> Father J. P. Card
> Mother Mary Nichols

Family of Maria Straube and William Frisbie

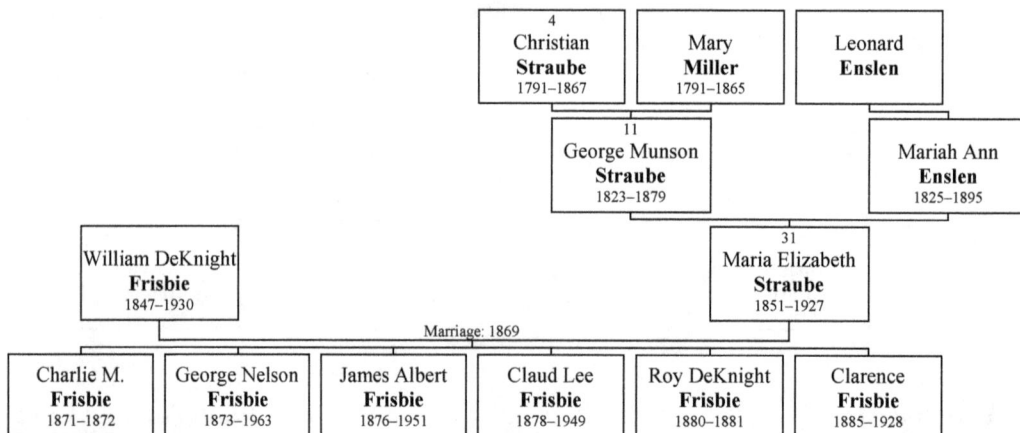

31. **Maria Elizabeth Straube** was born on Thursday, July 10, 1851. She was the daughter of George Munson Straube (11) and Mariah Ann Enslen. She was also known as **Lizzie**.

Maria Elizabeth died in Montgomery County, Missouri, on June 18, 1927, at the age of 75. She was buried in Wellsville Cemetery, Wellsville, Montgomery County, Missouri (Find a Grave ID 84026491).

At the age of 18, Maria Elizabeth married **William DeKnight Frisbie** on Thursday, December 23, 1869, in Audrain County, Missouri, when he was 22 years old. They had six sons.

William DeKnight was born in Burlington, Hartford County, Connecticut, on Friday, December 03, 1847. He was also known as **FRISBY**.

William DeKnight reached 82 years of age and died in Hannibal, Marion County, Missouri, on July 15, 1930. He was buried in Wellsville Cemetery, Wellsville, Montgomery County, Missouri (Find a Grave ID 84026702).

Sons of Maria Elizabeth Straube and William DeKnight Frisbie:

m   I. **Charlie M. Frisbie** was born on August 12, 1871. He died on August 05, 1872. Charlie M. was buried in Payne-Seeley Cemetery, Audrain County, Missouri (Find a Grave ID 84026953).

m   II. **George Nelson Frisbie** was born in Audrain County, Missouri, on February 09, 1873. He died in Columbia, Boone County, Missouri, on December 16, 1963, at the age of 90. George Nelson was buried in Wellsville Cemetery, Wellsville, Montgomery County, Missouri (Find a Grave ID 139927533).

m   III. **James Albert Frisbie** was born in Montgomery County, Missouri, on December 15, 1876. He died in Saint Louis, Saint Louis County, Missouri, on September 29, 1951, at the age of 74. James Albert was buried in Wellsville Cemetery, Wellsville, Montgomery County, Missouri (Find a Grave ID 166169650).

m   IV. **Claud Lee Frisbie** was born in Wellsville, Montgomery County, Missouri, on April 28, 1878. He died in Mexico, Audrain County, Missouri, on August 24, 1949, at the age of 71. Claud Lee was buried in Elmwood Cemetery, Mexico, Audrain County, Missouri (Find a Grave ID 100542690).

m   V. **Roy DeKnight Frisbie** was born in Missouri, USA, on January 16, 1880. He died in Missouri, USA, on October 01, 1881, at the age of 1. Roy DeKnight was buried in Wellsville Cemetery, Wellsville, Montgomery County, Missouri (Find a Grave ID 84026807).

m   VI. **Clarence Frisbie** was born in Missouri, USA, on March 14, 1885. He died on April 29, 1928, at the age of 43. Clarence was buried in Wellsville Cemetery, Wellsville, Montgomery County, Missouri (Find a Grave ID 94047306).

Family of Simon Straube and Lou Nelson

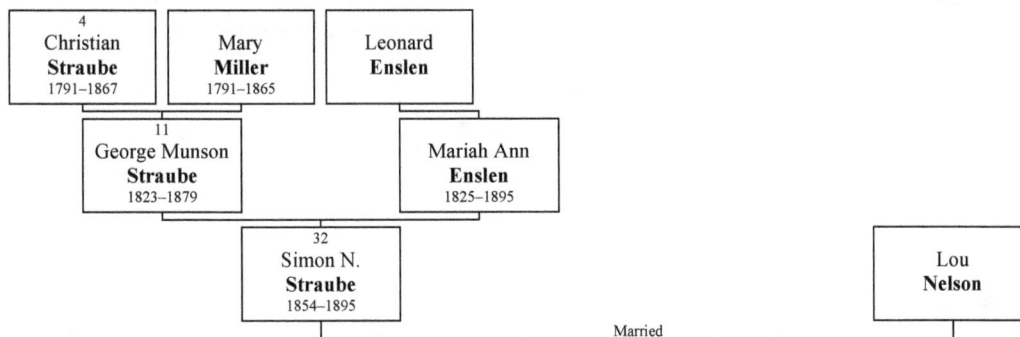

32.   **Simon N. Straube** was born on Wednesday, January 04, 1854, in Missouri, USA. He was the son of George Munson Straube (11) and Mariah Ann Enslen.

Simon N. died in Wellsville, Montgomery County, Missouri, on December 26, 1895, at the age of 41. He was buried in Wellsville Cemetery, Wellsville, Montgomery County, Missouri (Find a Grave ID 83904986).

He married **Lou Nelson**.

Family of Emma Straube and Leroy Myers

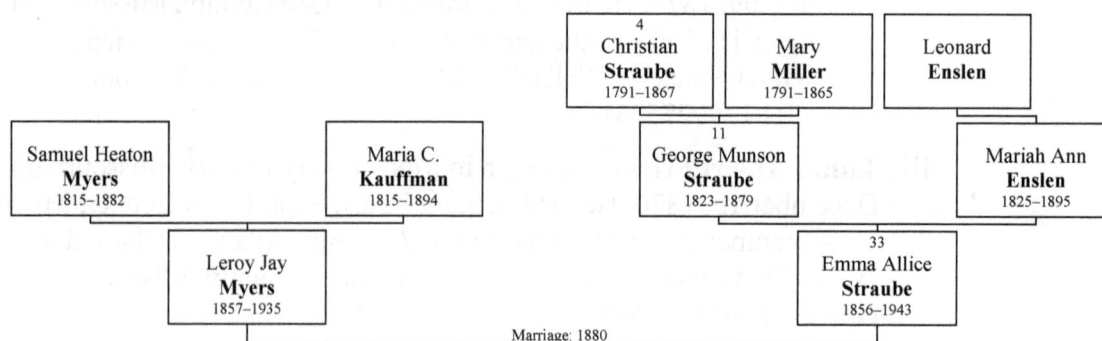

33. **Emma Allice Straube** was born in 1856 in Audrain County, Missouri. She was the daughter of George Munson Straube (11) and Mariah Ann Enslen. She was also known as **Emily**.

Emma Allice died in Dustin, Hughes County, Oklahoma, in 1943 at the age of 87. She was buried in Fairview Cemetery, Dustin, Hughes County, Oklahoma (Find a Grave ID 26561634).

At the age of 24, Emma Allice married **Leroy Jay Myers** on Thursday, May 20, 1880, in Montgomery County, Missouri, when he was 23 years old. Leroy Jay was born in Shelby, Ohio, USA, on Wednesday, March 11, 1857. He was the son of Samuel Heaton Myers and Maria C. Kauffman. He was also known as **Lee**.

Leroy Jay reached 77 years of age and died in Dustin, Hughes County, Oklahoma, on January 27, 1935. He was buried in Fairview Cemetery, Dustin, Hughes County, Oklahoma (Find a Grave ID 26561633).

Family of Martha Straube and Frederick Blattner

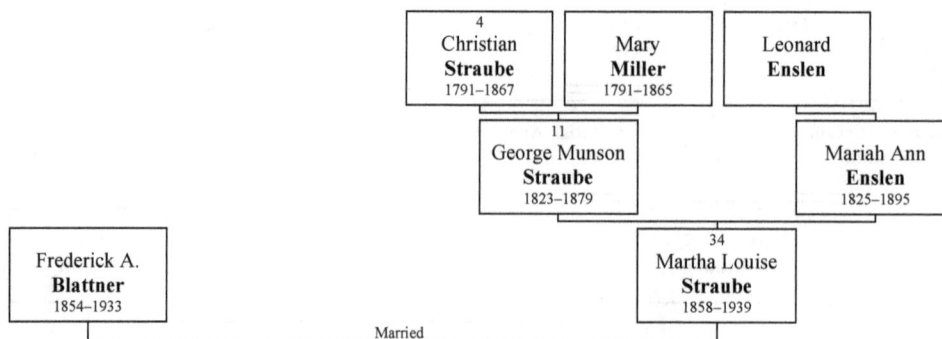

34. **Martha Louise Straube** was born on Wednesday, March 10, 1858, in Montgomery County, Missouri. She was the daughter of George Munson Straube (11) and Mariah Ann Enslen. She was also known as **Mattie**.

Martha Louise died in Wellsville, Montgomery County, Missouri, on April 27, 1939, at the age of 81. She was buried in Wellsville Cemetery, Wellsville, Montgomery County, Missouri (Find a Grave ID 166222795).

She married **Frederick A. Blattner**. Frederick A. was born in Warren County, Missouri, on Friday, February 24, 1854.

He reached 79 years of age and died in Wellsville, Montgomery County, Missouri, on August 31, 1933. Frederick A. was buried in Wellsville Cemetery, Wellsville, Montgomery County, Missouri (Find a Grave ID 166222771).

4th Generation

Family of Melvin Straube and Betty Brown

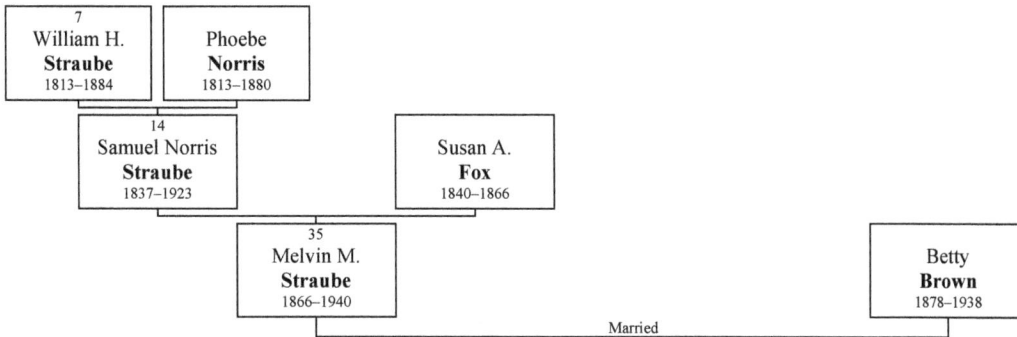

```
┌──────────────┐ ┌──────────────┐
│      7       │ │   Phoebe     │
│ William H.   │ │   Norris     │
│  Straube     │ │  1813–1880   │
│  1813–1884   │ │              │
└──────────────┘ └──────────────┘
   ┌──────────────┐    ┌──────────────┐
   │     14       │    │  Susan A.    │
   │ Samuel Norris│    │    Fox       │
   │  Straube     │    │  1840–1866   │
   │  1837–1923   │    │              │
   └──────────────┘    └──────────────┘
        ┌──────────────┐         ┌──────────────┐
        │     35       │         │   Betty      │
        │  Melvin M.   │         │   Brown      │
        │  Straube     │         │  1878–1938   │
        │  1866–1940   │         │              │
        └──────────────┘         └──────────────┘
                        Married
```

35. **Melvin M. Straube** was born on Tuesday, August 28, 1866, in Montgomery County, Missouri. He was the son of Samuel Norris Straube (14) and Susan A. Fox.

Melvin M. died in Paris, Monroe County, Missouri, on August 25, 1940, at the age of 73. He was buried in Sunset Hill Cemetery, Madison, Monroe County, Missouri (Find a Grave ID 83946574).

He married **Betty Brown**. Betty was born in Monroe County, Missouri, in 1878.

She reached 60 years of age and died in Madison, Monroe County, Missouri, on September 05, 1938. Betty was buried in Sunset Hill Cemetery, Madison, Monroe County, Missouri (Find a Grave ID 84070418).

Adeline Straube

36. **Adeline Ada Straube** was born in 1876 in Wellsville, Montgomery County, Missouri. She was the daughter of Samuel Norris Straube (14) and Sarah Ada Hammett.

Adeline Ada died in Pueblo County, Colorado, on February 01, 1955, at the age of 79. She was buried in Mountain View Cemetery, Pueblo, Pueblo County, Colorado (Find a Grave ID 63512638).

Marriages with Robert J. Wullschleger and Sam Kalyniak (Page 80) are known.

Family of Adeline Straube and Robert Wullschleger

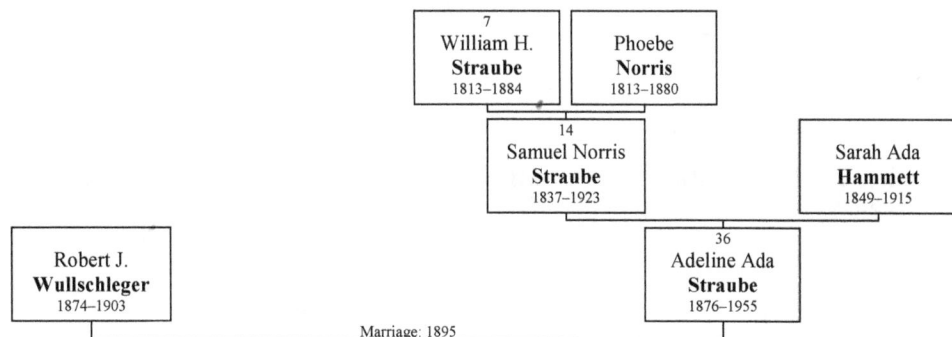

```
                    ┌──────────────┐ ┌──────────────┐
                    │      7       │ │   Phoebe     │
                    │ William H.   │ │   Norris     │
                    │  Straube     │ │  1813–1880   │
                    │  1813–1884   │ │              │
                    └──────────────┘ └──────────────┘
                       ┌──────────────┐    ┌──────────────┐
                       │     14       │    │  Sarah Ada   │
                       │ Samuel Norris│    │  Hammett     │
                       │  Straube     │    │  1849–1915   │
                       │  1837–1923   │    │              │
                       └──────────────┘    └──────────────┘
   ┌──────────────┐         ┌──────────────┐
   │  Robert J.   │         │     36       │
   │ Wullschleger │         │ Adeline Ada  │
   │  1874–1903   │         │  Straube     │
   │              │         │  1876–1955   │
   └──────────────┘         └──────────────┘
              Marriage: 1895
```

Here are the details about **Adeline Ada Straube's** first marriage, with Robert J. Wullschleger. You can read more about Adeline Ada on page 79.

At the age of 19, Adeline Ada Straube married **Robert J. Wullschleger** on Wednesday, November 20, 1895, in Montgomery County, Missouri, when he was 21 years old. Robert J. was born in Wentzville, St. Charles County, Missouri, on Sunday, February 08, 1874.

He reached 29 years of age and died in Montgomery County, Missouri, on April 29, 1903. His cause of death was train accident. He was buried in Wellsville Cemetery, Wellsville, Montgomery County, Missouri (Find a Grave ID 144057594).

Ironton County Register, Ironton, Missouri-May 7, 1903:

> Robert J. Wullschleger stepped to his death in the dark.
>
> The engine and tender of a Wabash freight train in charge of Conductor R.J. Wullschler became uncoupled from the balance of the train, at night, at the east approach of the St. Charles bridge. The train arrived at the station in St. Charles before the fact became known.
>
> On returning for the balance of the train the conductor was found lying on the track dead, is head was badly crushed, his right arm severed. Robert, not knowing the that the train was uncoupled and it being very dark stepped off one of the cars to his death.
>
> The deceased was 28 years, 2 months and 27 days old. He leaves a widow and child, in Moberly, to mourn his passing.

Family of Adeline Straube and Sam Kalyniak

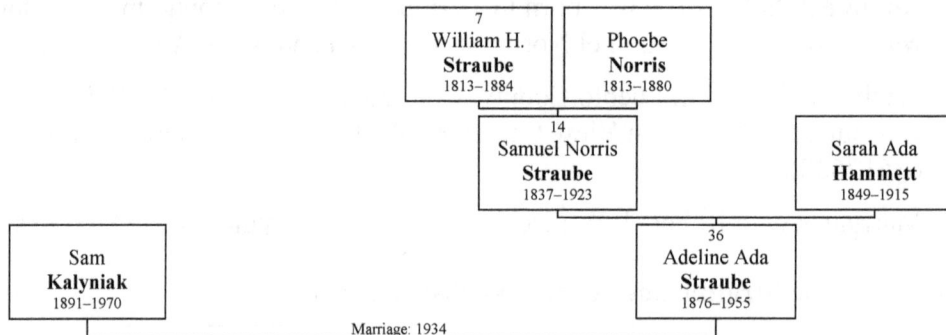

Here are the details about **Adeline Ada Straube's** second marriage, with Sam Kalyniak. You can read more about Adeline Ada on page 79.

Adeline Ada Straube married **Sam Kalyniak** in 1934. Sam was born in Ostrynia, Poland, on Wednesday, July 22, 1891.

He reached 79 years of age and died in Colorado, USA, on October 07, 1970. Sam was buried in Mountain View Cemetery, Pueblo, Pueblo County, Colorado (Find a Grave ID 63512663).

Family of John Straube and Lottie Irwin

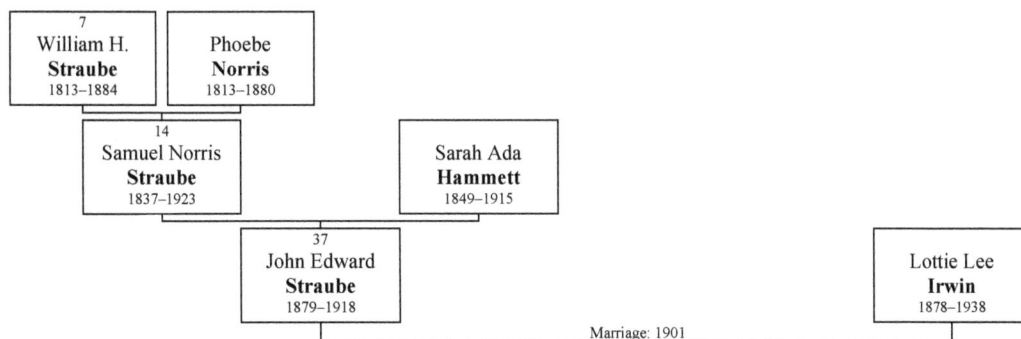

37.   **John Edward Straube** was born on Thursday, January 23, 1879, in Wellsville, Montgomery County, Missouri. He was the son of Samuel Norris Straube (14) and Sarah Ada Hammett. He was also known as **Ed**.

John Edward died in Wellsville, Montgomery County, Missouri, on December 07, 1918, at the age of 39. He was buried in Wellsville Cemetery, Wellsville, Montgomery County, Missouri (Find a Grave ID 42563523).

December 13, 1918 p. 1/4

> DEATH OF J. E. STRAUBE
> HIGHLY RESPECTED RESIDENT PASSED AWAY AT HOME
> SATURDAY AFTER A SHORT ILLNESS
>
> J. E. Straube died at his home in this city Saturday December 7th after an illness of pneumonia. Ed, as he was popularly known, was born January 23rd 1879. He was married to Miss Lee Irvin Dec. 8, 1901. In his departure the city loses one of its highly respected, energetic and popular characters. At the time of his death, he was employed at the C. W. Reed & Bros. Mercantile. Co., and bore the esteem of both his employers and many friends.
>
> He is survived by his widow, his father, one brother and one sister, Mrs. Addie Wuelschlaeger, a number of relative and a host of friends. He united with the Christian church early in life and was an active worker until the time of his death. He was also a prominent member of the Knights of Pythias Lodge. The funeral service was conducted at the home by Rev. B. G. Reavis of Mexico, after which the body was buried in the Wellsville City Cemetery. The Knights of Pythias burial rites were performed at the grave.

At the age of 22, John Edward married **Lottie Lee Irwin** on Sunday, December 08, 1901, in Callaway County, Missouri, when she was 23 years old. Lottie Lee was born in Callaway County, Missouri, on Saturday, June 15, 1878.

She reached 60 years of age and died in Montgomery County, Missouri, on December 29, 1938. Lottie Lee was buried in Wellsville Cemetery, Wellsville, Montgomery County, Missouri (Find a Grave ID 42563799).

Family of Phoebe Yates and William Sitton

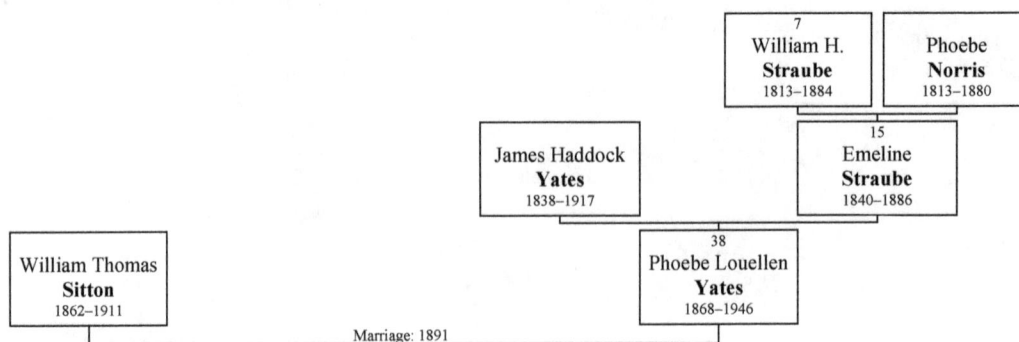

38.   **Phoebe Louellen Yates** was born on Sunday, November 29, 1868, in Middletown, Montgomery County, Missouri. She was the daughter of James Haddock Yates and Emeline Straube (15). She was also known as **Lou**.

Phoebe Louellen died in Saint Louis, Saint Louis County, Missouri, on July 12, 1946, at the age of 77. She was buried in Winfield Cemetery, Winfield, Lincoln County, Missouri, on July 15, 1946 (Find a Grave ID 83972471).

At the age of 23, Phoebe Louellen married **William Thomas Sitton** on Wednesday, December 09, 1891, in Lincoln County, Missouri, when he was 28 years old. William Thomas was born in Kings Lake, Lincoln County, Missouri, on Saturday, December 27, 1862.

He reached 48 years of age and died in Winfield, Lincoln County, Missouri, on April 17, 1911. William Thomas was buried in Winfield Cemetery, Winfield, Lincoln County, Missouri (Find a Grave ID 83975933).

Family of Martillis Yates and Leona Angel

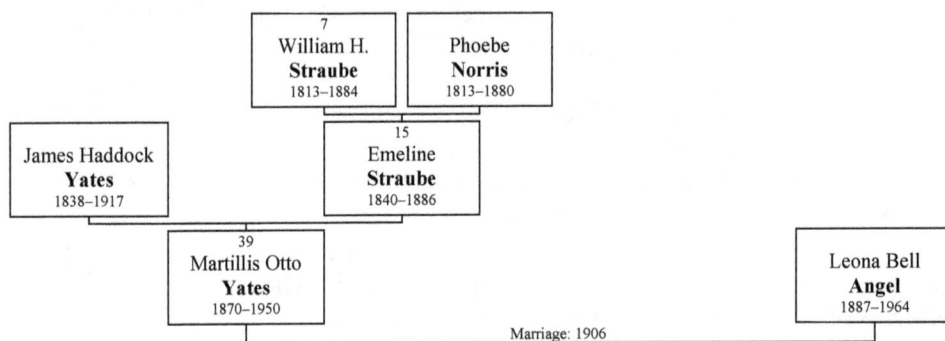

39.   **Martillis Otto Yates** was born on Wednesday, November 16, 1870, in Missouri, USA. He was the son of James Haddock Yates and Emeline Straube (15).

Martillis Otto died in Tacoma, Pierce County, Washington, on December 05, 1950, at the age of 80. He was buried in Woodbine Cemetery, Puyallup, Pierce County, Washington, on December 07, 1950 (Find a Grave ID 83977270).

At the age of 35, Martillis Otto married **Leona Bell Angel** on Sunday, May 27, 1906, in Middleton, Montgomery County, Missouri, when she was 18 years old. Leona Bell was born in Middletown, Montgomery County, Missouri, on Saturday, December 24, 1887. She was also known as **Leonie**.

Leona Bell reached 76 years of age and died in Puyallup, Pierce County, Washington, in 1964. She was buried in Fairmount Cemetery, Middletown, Montgomery County, Missouri (Find a Grave ID 169229130).

Family of Eliza Yates and Wallace Dawkins

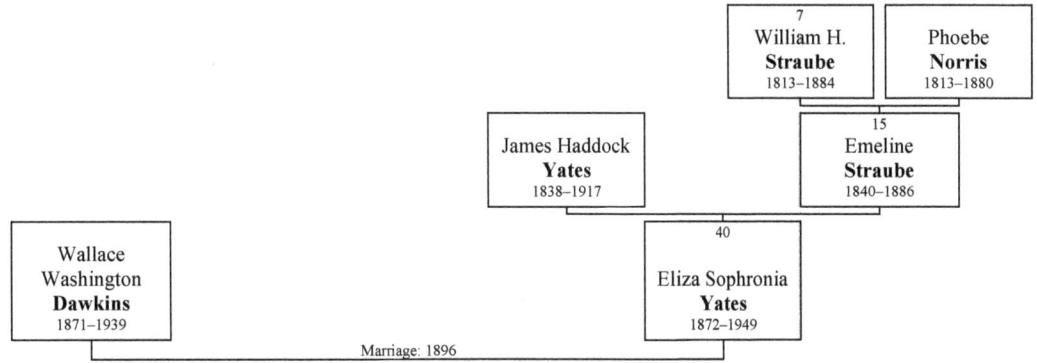

40.   **Eliza Sophronia Yates** was born on Friday, August 30, 1872, in Middletown, Montgomery County, Missouri. She was the daughter of James Haddock Yates and Emeline Straube (15).

Eliza Sophronia died in Dodge City, Ford County, Kansas, on August 23, 1949, at the age of 76. She was buried in Bucklin Cemetery, Ford County, Kansas, on August 26, 1949 (Find a Grave ID 83977626).

At the age of 23, Eliza Sophronia married **Wallace Washington Dawkins** on Sunday, February 02, 1896, in Winfield, Lincoln County, Missouri, when he was 24 years old. Wallace Washington was born in Argentville, Lincoln County, Missouri, on Monday, August 14, 1871.

He reached 68 years of age and died in Bucklin, Ford County, Kansas, on October 18, 1939. Wallace Washington was buried on October 20, 1939, in Bucklin Cemetery, Ford County, Kansas (Find a Grave ID 83977730).

Family of Lucretia Yates and Edward Dryden

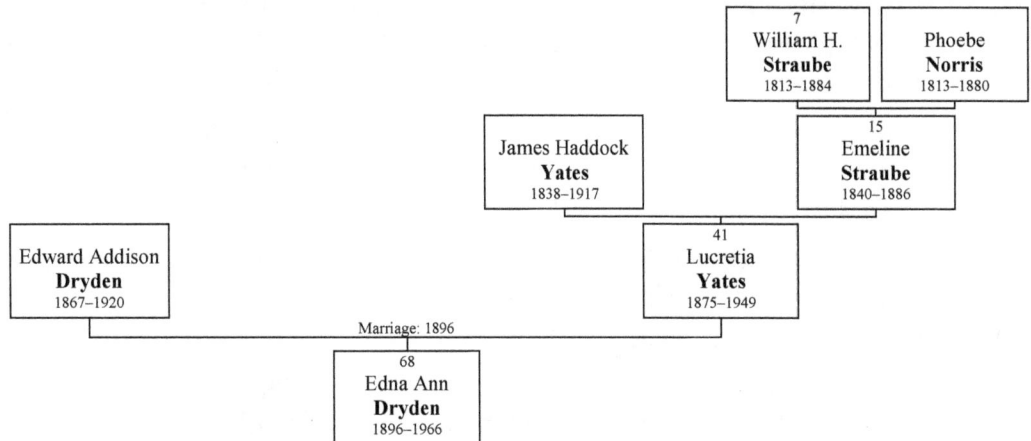

41.   **Lucretia Yates** was born on Tuesday, August 17, 1875, in Middletown, Montgomery County, Missouri. She was the daughter of James Haddock Yates and Emeline Straube (15). She was also known as **Cretia**.

Lucretia died in Hannibal, Marion County, Missouri, on January 20, 1949, at the age of 73. She was buried in Mount Olivet Cemetery, Hannibal, Marion County, Missouri, on January 22, 1949 (Find a Grave ID 83989993).

At the age of 20, Lucretia married **Edward Addison Dryden** on Friday, June 12, 1896, in Lincoln County, Missouri, when he was 29 years old. They had one daughter.

Edward Addison was born in Lincoln County, Missouri, on Monday, January 07, 1867. He reached 53 years of age and died in St. Francois County, Missouri, on January 24, 1920. Edward Addison was buried in Harod Cemetery, Desloge, St. Francois County, Missouri (Find a Grave ID 84027528).

Daughter of Lucretia Yates and Edward Addison Dryden:

+   68   f   I. **Edna Ann Dryden** was born in Winfield, Lincoln County, Missouri, on October 11, 1896. She died in Hannibal, Marion County, Missouri, on January 26, 1966, at the age of 69. Edna Ann was buried in Mount Olivet Cemetery, Hannibal, Marion County, Missouri, on January 27, 1966 (Find a Grave ID 84028044).

Family of Lettia Yates and Samuel Cox

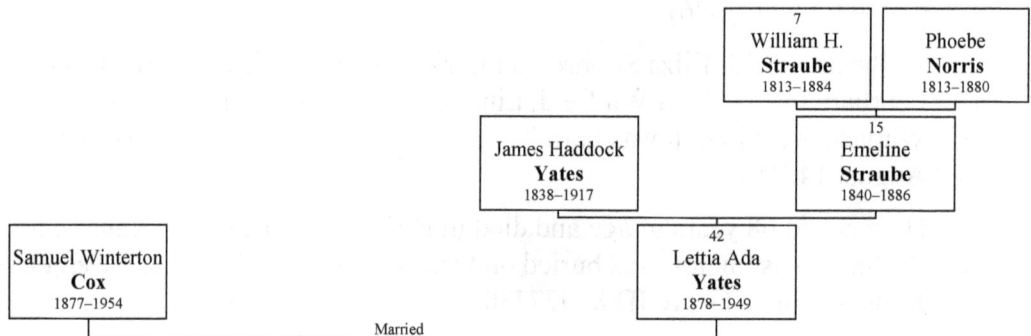

```
                                                  ┌──────────────┬──────────────┐
                                                  │      7       │              │
                                                  │ William H.   │   Phoebe     │
                                                  │  Straube     │   Norris     │
                                                  │  1813–1884   │  1813–1880   │
                                                  └──────────────┴──────────────┘
                                  ┌──────────────┐        ┌──────────────┐
                                  │ James Haddock│        │     15       │
                                  │    Yates     │        │  Emeline     │
                                  │  1838–1917   │        │  Straube     │
                                  └──────────────┘        │  1840–1886   │
                                                          └──────────────┘
        ┌──────────────┐                 ┌──────────────┐
        │Samuel Winterton│               │     42       │
        │     Cox      │                 │ Lettia Ada   │
        │  1877–1954   │                 │   Yates      │
        └──────────────┘                 │  1878–1949   │
                         Married         └──────────────┘
```

42.   **Lettia Ada Yates** was born on Saturday, September 14, 1878, in Middletown, Montgomery County, Missouri. She was the daughter of James Haddock Yates and Emeline Straube (15). She was also known as **Lettie**.

Lettia Ada died in Alton, Madison County, Illinois, on December 25, 1949, at the age of 71. She was buried in Oakwood Cemetery, Alton, Madison County, Illinois, on December 28, 1949 (Find a Grave ID 83990159).

She married **Samuel Winterton Cox**. Samuel Winterton was born in Hamburg, Calhoun County, Illinois, on Thursday, May 03, 1877.

He reached 77 years of age and died in Alton, Madison County, Illinois, on November 01, 1954. Samuel Winterton was buried on November 04, 1954, in Oakwood Cemetery, Alton, Madison County, Illinois (Find a Grave ID 83990310).

Family of Arthur Yates and Lena Heins

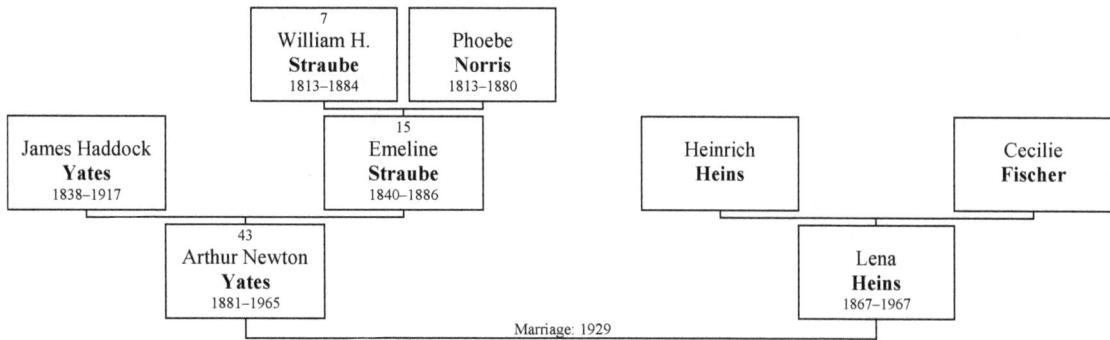

```
                    ┌──────────────┬──────────────┐
                    │      7       │   Phoebe     │
                    │  William H.  │   Norris     │
                    │  Straube     │  1813–1880   │
                    │  1813–1884   │              │
    ┌──────────────┐└──────────────┴──────────────┘              ┌──────────────┐                    ┌──────────────┐
    │ James Haddock│┌─────────────────────────────┐              │  Heinrich    │                    │   Cecilie    │
    │    Yates     ││           15                │              │   Heins      │                    │   Fischer    │
    │  1838–1917   ││        Emeline              │              │              │                    │              │
    │              ││        Straube              │              │              │                    │              │
    └──────────────┘│        1840–1886            │              └──────────────┘                    └──────────────┘
                    └─────────────────────────────┘
               ┌──────────────────────┐                                    ┌──────────────┐
               │          43          │                                    │    Lena      │
               │    Arthur Newton     │                                    │    Heins     │
               │       Yates          │                                    │  1867–1967   │
               │      1881–1965       │                                    │              │
               └──────────────────────┘                                    └──────────────┘
                              Marriage: 1929
```

43. **Arthur Newton Yates** was born on Wednesday, February 23, 1881, in Clarksville, Pike County, Missouri. He was the son of James Haddock Yates and Emeline Straube (15).

Arthur Newton died in Winfield, Lincoln County, Missouri, on March 27, 1965, at the age of 84. He was buried in Winfield Cemetery, Winfield, Lincoln County, Missouri, on March 29, 1965 (Find a Grave ID 84020357).

At the age of 48, Arthur Newton married **Lena Heins** on Saturday, March 23, 1929, in St. Charles, St. Charles County, Missouri, when she was 61 years old. Lena was born in Germany on Tuesday, June 18, 1867. She was the daughter of Heinrich Heins and Cecilie Fischer.

Lena reached 99 years of age and died in Saint Louis, Saint Louis County, Missouri, on May 13, 1967. She was buried on May 16, 1967, in Gatewood Gardens Cemetery, Saint Louis, St. Louis City, Missouri (Find a Grave ID 31942509).

She was married to Arthur Newton Yates and William Patrick O'Donnell. She is buried as Lena O'Donnell.

Family of Walter Straubie and Barbee Craig

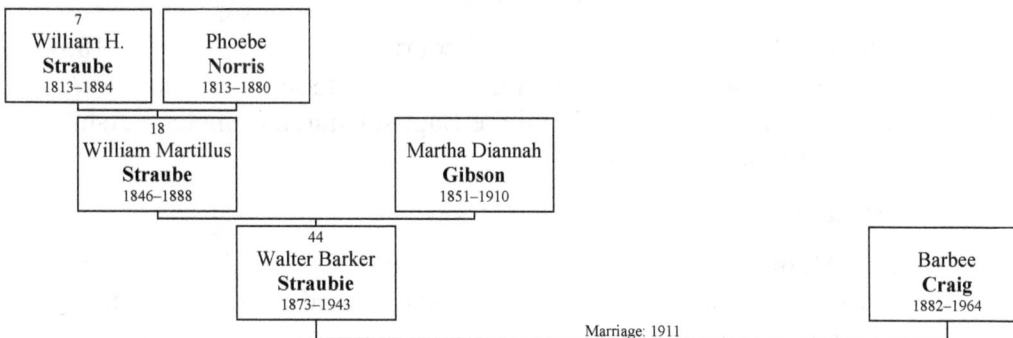

```
┌──────────────┬──────────────┐
│      7       │   Phoebe     │
│  William H.  │   Norris     │
│  Straube     │  1813–1880   │
│  1813–1884   │              │
└──────────────┴──────────────┘
┌─────────────────────────────┐   ┌──────────────┐
│           18                │   │Martha Diannah│
│  William Martillus          │   │   Gibson     │
│     Straube                 │   │  1851–1910   │
│    1846–1888                │   │              │
└─────────────────────────────┘   └──────────────┘
         ┌──────────────────────┐                              ┌──────────────┐
         │          44          │                              │   Barbee     │
         │    Walter Barker     │                              │    Craig     │
         │     Straubie         │                              │  1882–1964   │
         │     1873–1943        │                              │              │
         └──────────────────────┘                              └──────────────┘
                        Marriage: 1911
```

44. **Walter Barker Straubie** was born on Wednesday, October 15, 1873, in Middletown, Montgomery County, Missouri. He was the son of William Martillus Straube (18) and Martha Diannah Gibson. William Martillus Straube was his stepfather.

Walter Barker died in Little Rock, Pulaski County, Arkansas, on June 10, 1943, at the age of 69. He was buried in Roselawn Memorial Park, Little Rock, Pulaski County, Arkansas, on June 11, 1943 (Find a Grave ID 176587695).

Both death certificate and gravestone have a spelling of Straubie.

Walter Barker married **Barbee Craig** in 1911. Barbee was born on Friday, June 16, 1882.

She reached 82 years of age and died on November 11, 1964. Barbee was buried in Roselawn Memorial Park, Little Rock, Pulaski County, Arkansas (Find a Grave ID 208701187).

Family of Mary Straube and John Moore

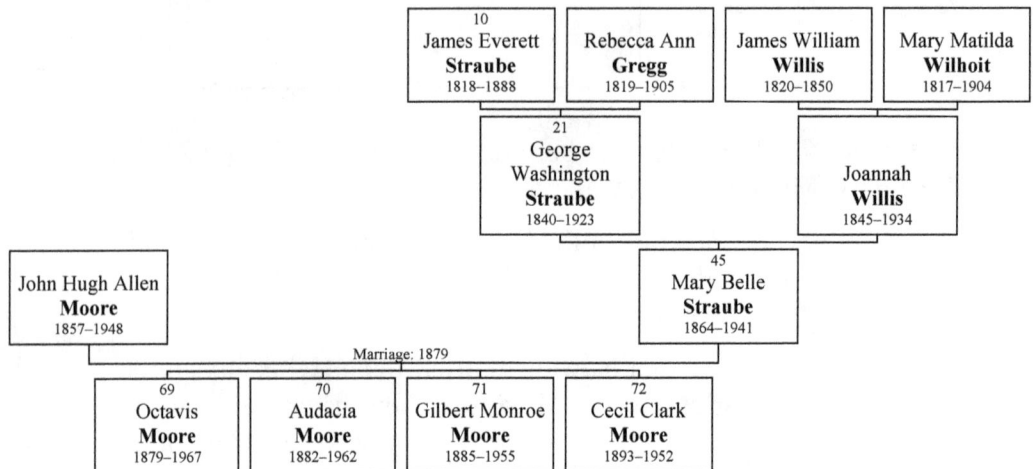

45. **Mary Belle Straube** was born on Sunday, March 13, 1864, in Pike County, Missouri. She was the daughter of George Washington Straube (21) and Joannah Willis.

Mary Belle died in Pike County, Missouri, on July 26, 1941, at the age of 77. She was buried in Siloam Primitive Baptist Church Cemetery, Ashley, Pike County, Missouri (Find a Grave ID 83685374).

At the age of 14, Mary Belle married **John Hugh Allen Moore** on Sunday, February 09, 1879, when he was 21 years old. They had four children.

John Hugh Allen was born in Montgomery County, Missouri, on Tuesday, June 09, 1857. He reached 90 years of age and died in Louisiana, Pike County, Missouri, on March 02, 1948. John Hugh Allen was buried in Siloam Primitive Baptist Church Cemetery, Ashley, Pike County, Missouri (Find a Grave ID 83688641).

Children of Mary Belle Straube and John Hugh Allen Moore:

+ 69 m I. **Octavis Moore** was born in New Hartford, Pike County, Missouri, on July 12, 1879. He died in Chaplin, Saskatchewan, Canada, on November 04, 1967, at the age of 88. Octavis was buried in Droxford Cemetery, Droxford, Moose Jaw Census Division, Saskatchewan, Canada (Find a Grave ID 21372903).

+ 70 f II. **Audacia Moore** was born in New Hartford, Pike County, Missouri, on January 02, 1882. She was also known as **Audie**.

Audacia died in Louisiana, Pike County, Missouri, on May 05, 1962, at the age of 80. She was buried in Siloam Primitive Baptist Church Cemetery, Ashley, Pike County, Missouri (Find a Grave ID 83748464).

+   71   m   III. **Gilbert Monroe Moore** was born in New Hartford, Pike County, Missouri, on June 02, 1885. He died in Hartford Township, Pike County, Missouri, on October 14, 1955, at the age of 70. Gilbert Monroe was buried in Bowling Green City Cemetery, Pike County, Missouri (Find a Grave ID 134950249).

+   72   m   IV. **Cecil Clark Moore** was born in New Hartford, Pike County, Missouri, on August 05, 1893. He died in Saskatchewan, Canada, on April 29, 1952, at the age of 58. Cecil Clark was buried in Droxford Cemetery, Droxford, Moose Jaw Census Division, Saskatchewan, Canada (Find a Grave ID 21400314).

Family of Matilda Straube and Charles Gibbs

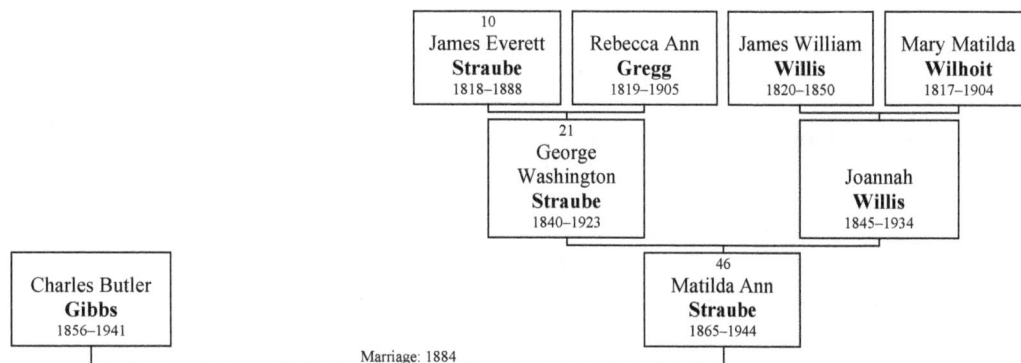

46.   **Matilda Ann Straube** was born on Thursday, November 23, 1865, in Pike County, Missouri. She was the daughter of George Washington Straube (21) and Joannah Willis.

Matilda Ann died in Hannibal, Marion County, Missouri, on November 10, 1944, at the age of 78. She was buried in Grand View Burial Park, Hannibal, Ralls County, Missouri (Find a Grave ID 87226120).

At the age of 19, Matilda Ann married **Charles Butler Gibbs** on Wednesday, December 17, 1884, when he was 28 years old. Charles Butler was born in Pike County, Missouri, on Monday, April 07, 1856. He was also known as **Bates**.

Charles Butler reached 84 years of age and died in Hannibal, Marion County, Missouri, on January 08, 1941. He was buried in Grand View Burial Park, Hannibal, Ralls County, Missouri (Find a Grave ID 87226031).

Family of Porter Straube and Daisie Stuart

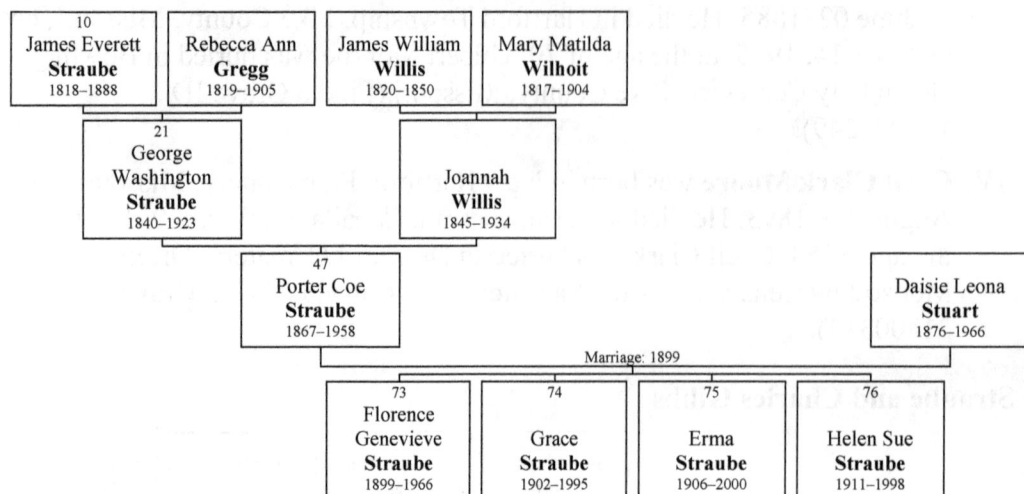

10 James Everett **Straube** 1818–1888	Rebecca Ann **Gregg** 1819–1905	James William **Willis** 1820–1850	Mary Matilda **Wilhoit** 1817–1904

21 George Washington **Straube** 1840–1923

Joannah **Willis** 1845–1934

47 Porter Coe **Straube** 1867–1958

Daisie Leona **Stuart** 1876–1966

Marriage: 1899

| **73** Florence Genevieve **Straube** 1899–1966 | **74** Grace **Straube** 1902–1995 | **75** Erma **Straube** 1906–2000 | **76** Helen Sue **Straube** 1911–1998 |

47. **Porter Coe Straube** was born on Wednesday, October 23, 1867, in Pike County, Missouri. He was the son of George Washington Straube (21) and Joannah Willis.

Porter Coe worked as a judge. He died at B.B. Springs in Bowling Green, Pike County, Missouri, on May 31, 1958, at the age of 90. Porter Coe was buried in Siloam Primitive Baptist Church Cemetery, Ashley, Pike County, Missouri, on June 04, 1958 (Find a Grave ID 83753603).

Spelled Strauby on headstone like his father George.

At the age of 31, Porter Coe married **Daisie Leona Stuart** on Wednesday, February 15, 1899, when she was 22 years old. They had four daughters.

Daisie Leona was born in Menard, Randolph County, Illinois, on Wednesday, November 01, 1876. She reached 89 years of age and died in Bowling Green, Pike County, Missouri, on March 07, 1966. Daisie Leona was buried in Siloam Primitive Baptist Church Cemetery, Ashley, Pike County, Missouri (Find a Grave ID 83753921).

Daughters of Porter Coe Straube and Daisie Leona Stuart:

+ 73   f   I. **Florence Genevieve Straube** was born in Vandalia, Audrain County, Missouri, on November 16, 1899. She died in Missouri, USA, on March 07, 1966, at the age of 66. Florence Genevieve was buried in Siloam Primitive Baptist Church Cemetery, Ashley, Pike County, Missouri (Find a Grave ID 230052577).

+ 74   f   II. **Grace Straube** was born in Farmer, Pike County, Missouri, on April 02, 1902. She died in Norwalk, Los Angeles County, California, on July 08, 1995, at the age of 93. Grace was buried in Park Lawn Memorial Park, Commerce, Los Angeles County, California (Find a Grave ID 184711343).

+ 75   f   III. **Erma Straube** was born in Pike County, Missouri, on April 30, 1906.[55] She died in Bowling Green, Pike County, Missouri, on August 15, 2000, at

---

55   Ancestry.com, Public Member Trees (Provo, UT, USA, Ancestry.com Operations, Inc., 2006), Ancestry.com, Record for Erma L Straube. https://search.ancestry.co.uk/cgi-bin/sse.dll?db=1030&h=30514359916&indiv=try.

the age of 94.[55] Erma was buried in Curryville City Cemetery, Curryville, Pike County, Missouri (Find a Grave ID 100038977).[55]

+ 76   f   IV. **Helen Sue Straube** was born in Farmer, Pike County, Missouri, on February 16, 1911. She died in Louisiana, Pike County, Missouri, on January 05, 1998, at the age of 86. Helen Sue was buried in Curryville City Cemetery, Curryville, Pike County, Missouri (Find a Grave ID 125315606).

Family of Amanda Straube and Merritt Glascock

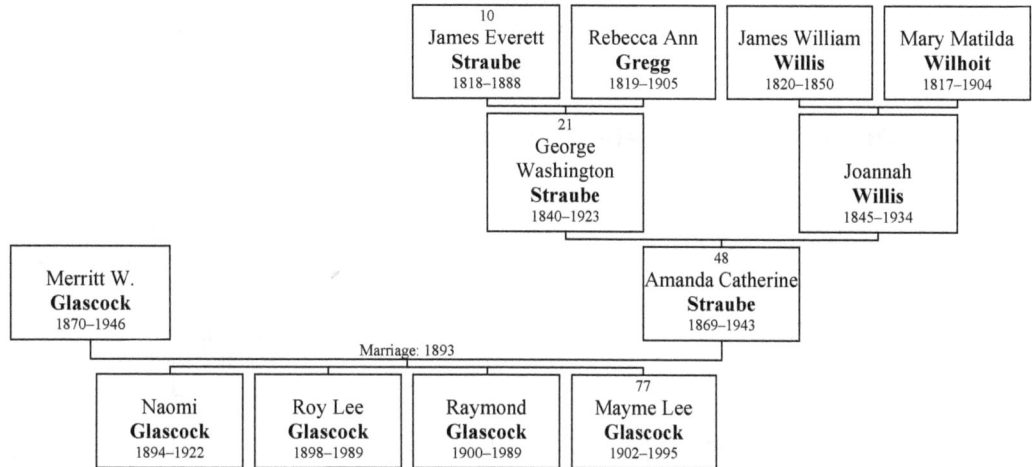

48.   **Amanda Catherine Straube** was born on Wednesday, September 01, 1869, in Pike County, Missouri. She was the daughter of George Washington Straube (21) and Joannah Willis.

Amanda Catherine died in Saskatchewan, Canada, on January 23, 1943, at the age of 73. She was buried in Shamrock Cemetery, Shamrock, Moose Jaw Census Division, Saskatchewan, Canada (Find a Grave ID 227021571).

At the age of 24, Amanda Catherine married **Merritt W. Glascock** on Wednesday, November 08, 1893, when he was 22 years old. They had four children.

Merritt W. was born in Pike County, Missouri, on Wednesday, November 23, 1870. He reached 75 years of age and died in Shamrock, Moose Jaw Census Division, Saskatchewan, Canada, on March 29, 1946. Merritt W. was buried in Shamrock Cemetery, Shamrock, Moose Jaw Census Division, Saskatchewan, Canada (Find a Grave ID 227021586).

Children of Amanda Catherine Straube and Merritt W. Glascock:

f   I. **Naomi Glascock** was born in Gazette, Pike County, Missouri, on August 18, 1894. She died in Chaplin, Moose Jaw Census Division, Saskatchewan, Canada, on March 02, 1922, at the age of 27. Naomi was buried in Bethlehem Hills Cemetery, Shamrock, Moose Jaw Census Division, Saskatchewan, Canada (Find a Grave ID 204234120).

m   II. **Roy Lee Glascock** was born in Vandalia, Audrain County, Missouri, on August 18, 1898. He died in Gravelbourg, Assiniboia Census Division, Saskatchewan, Canada, on February 23, 1989, at the age of 90. Roy Lee was buried in Shamrock Cemetery, Shamrock, Moose Jaw Census Division, Saskatchewan, Canada (Find a Grave ID 227021602).

m   III. **Raymond Glascock** was born in Gazette, Pike County, Missouri, on June 07, 1900. He was also known as **Pete**.

Raymond died in Canada on November 16, 1989, at the age of 89. He was buried in Maple Creek Cemetery, Maple Creek, Maple Creek Census Division, Saskatchewan, Canada (Find a Grave ID 131198867).

+   77   f   IV. **Mayme Lee Glascock** was born in Vandalia, Audrain County, Missouri, on May 03, 1902. She died in Scarborough, Toronto Municipality, Ontario, Canada, on February 05, 1995, at the age of 92. Mayme Lee was buried in Rosedale Cemetery, Moose Jaw, Moose Jaw Census Division, Saskatchewan, Canada (Find a Grave ID 178425272).

Family of Ora Straube and Walter Branstetter

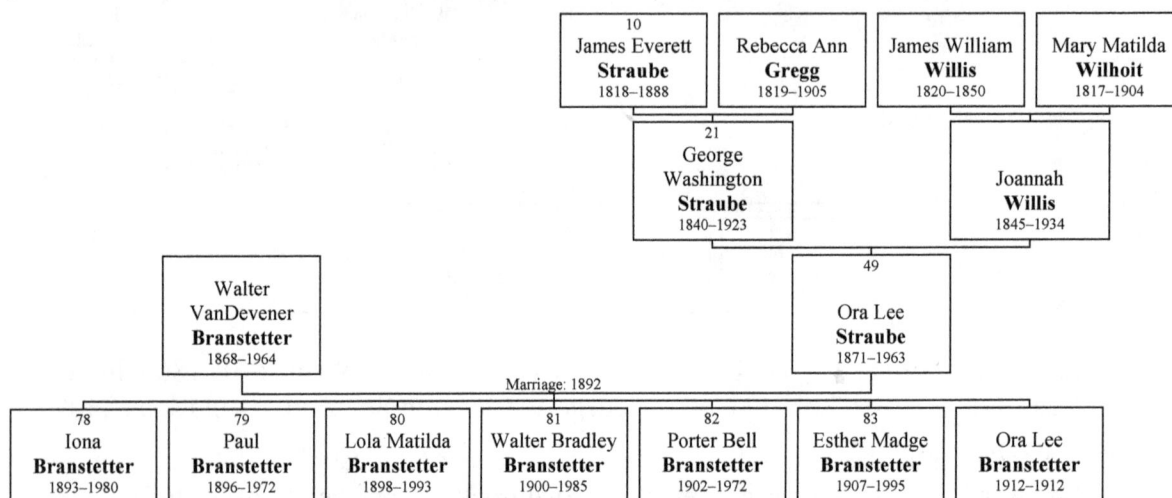

49.   **Ora Lee Straube** was born on Friday, April 21, 1871, in Pike County, Missouri. She was the daughter of George Washington Straube (21) and Joannah Willis.

Ora Lee died in Mexico, Audrain County, Missouri, on March 12, 1963, at the age of 91. She was buried in Wellsville Cemetery, Wellsville, Montgomery County, Missouri (Find a Grave ID 135220399).

At the age of 21, Ora Lee married **Walter VanDevener Branstetter** on Tuesday, October 04, 1892, when he was 24 years old. They had seven children.

Walter VanDevener was born in Audrain County, Missouri, on Wednesday, March 04, 1868. He was also known as **Watt**.

Walter VanDevener reached 95 years of age and died in Mexico, Audrain County, Missouri, on January 12, 1964. He was buried in Wellsville Cemetery, Wellsville, Montgomery County, Missouri (Find a Grave ID 135220639).

Children of Ora Lee Straube and Walter VanDevener Branstetter:

+   78   f   I. **Iona Branstetter** was born in Audrain County, Missouri, on September 11, 1893. She died in Saint Louis, Saint Louis County, Missouri, on August 20,

1980, at the age of 86. Iona was buried in Vandalia Cemetery, Vandalia, Ralls County, Missouri (Find a Grave ID 178435135).

+ 79 m   II. **Paul Branstetter** was born in Middletown, Montgomery County, Missouri, on May 14, 1896. He died in Columbia, Boone County, Missouri, on September 28, 1972, at the age of 76. Paul was buried in Wellsville Cemetery, Wellsville, Montgomery County, Missouri (Find a Grave ID 163850826).

+ 80 f   III. **Lola Matilda Branstetter** was born in Audrain County, Missouri, on December 17, 1898. She died in Golden, Jefferson County, Colorado, on November 22, 1993, at the age of 94. Lola burial details are unknown (Find a Grave ID 197788290).

+ 81 m   IV. **Walter Bradley Branstetter** was born in Middletown, Montgomery County, Missouri, on September 08, 1900. He died in Mexico, Audrain County, Missouri, on October 05, 1985, at the age of 85. Walter Bradley was buried in Callaway Memorial Gardens and Mausoleum, Fulton, Callaway County, Missouri (Find a Grave ID 94163544).

+ 82 m   V. **Porter Bell Branstetter** was born in Audrain County, Missouri, on June 28, 1902. He died in San Bernardino, San Bernardino County, California, on September 21, 1972, at the age of 70. Porter's burial details are unknown (Find a Grave ID 232330628).

+ 83 f   VI. **Esther Madge Branstetter** was born in Wellsville, Montgomery County, Missouri, on July 22, 1907. She died in Jackson, Hinds County, Mississippi, on December 25, 1995, at the age of 88. Esther Madge was cremated (Find a Grave ID 232332133).

   f   VII. **Ora Lee Branstetter** was born in Missouri, USA, on October 31, 1912. She died in Wellsville, Montgomery County, Missouri, on December 04, 1912. Ora Lee was buried in Wellsville Cemetery, Wellsville, Montgomery County, Missouri (Find a Grave ID 135220529).

Family of Mary Straube and Edward Brynn

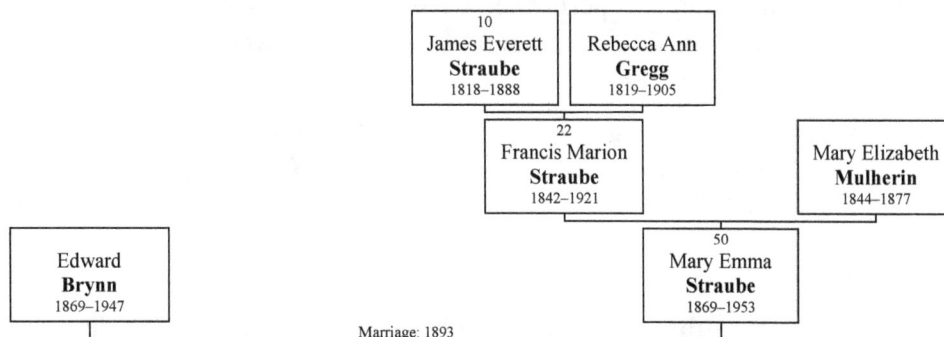

	10 James Everett **Straube** 1818–1888	Rebecca Ann **Gregg** 1819–1905	
	22 Francis Marion **Straube** 1842–1921		Mary Elizabeth **Mulherin** 1844–1877
Edward **Brynn** 1869–1947		50 Mary Emma **Straube** 1869–1953	

Marriage: 1893

50.   **Mary Emma Straube** was born on Wednesday, January 20, 1869, in Pike County, Missouri. She was the daughter of Francis Marion Straube (22) and Mary Elizabeth Mulherin.

Mary Emma died in Greeley, Weld County, Colorado, on November 04, 1953, at the age of 84. She was buried in Linn Grove Cemetery, Greeley, Weld County, Colorado (Find a Grave ID 65216731).

Mary Emma married **Edward Brynn** in 1893. Edward was born in Illinois, USA, in 1869. He reached 78 years of age and died on March 28, 1947. Edward was buried in Linn Grove Cemetery, Greeley, Weld County, Colorado (Find a Grave ID 65216729).

Family of Maggie Straube and William McGill

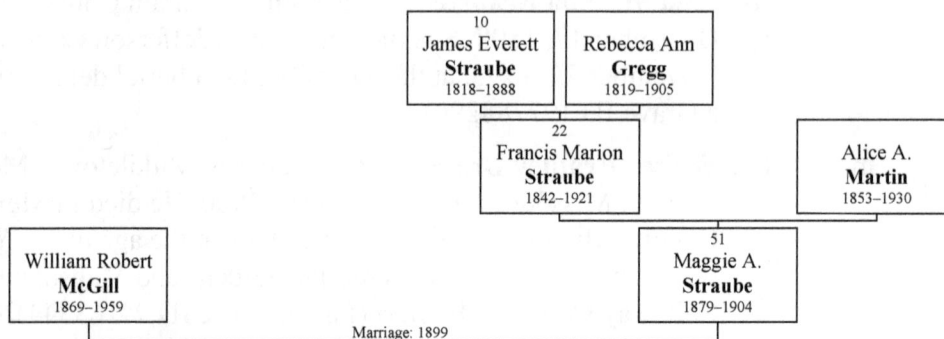

51.   **Maggie A. Straube** was born on Thursday, July 10, 1879, in Missouri, USA. She was the daughter of Francis Marion Straube (22) and Alice A. Martin.

Maggie A. died in Boulder, Boulder County, Colorado, on February 28, 1904, at the age of 24. Her cause of death was edematous laryngitis. Maggie A. was buried in Columbia Cemetery, Boulder, Boulder County, Colorado (Find a Grave ID 67848393).

When Maggie L. Straube was born on 16 July 1879, in Greeley, Weld County, Colorado, her father, Francis M Straube was 35, and her mother, Alice M. Martin was 26.

She married William Robert McGill on 8 November 1899, in Greeley, Weld, Colorado, United States. She lived in Prairie Township, Montgomery, Missouri in 1880. She died on 28 February 1904, in Boulder, Boulder, Colorado, United States, at the age of 24, and was buried in Columbia Cemetery, Boulder, Boulder County, Colorado.

At the age of 20, Maggie A. married **William Robert McGill** on Wednesday, November 08, 1899, at Arthur S. Phelps performed Ceremony in Greeley, Weld County, Colorado, when he was 30 years old. William Robert was born in Beaver County, Pennsylvania, on Monday, September 27, 1869.

He reached 90 years of age and died in Boulder, Boulder County, Colorado, on December 11, 1959. William Robert was buried in Columbia Cemetery, Boulder, Boulder County, Colorado (Find a Grave ID 67848466).

Hazel Straube

52.   **Hazel Alice Straube** was born on Wednesday, October 10, 1888, in Nebraska, USA. She was the daughter of Francis Marion Straube (22) and Alice A. Martin.

Hazel Alice died on December 22, 1974, at the age of 86. She was buried in Forest Lawn Memorial Park, Glendale, Los Angeles County, California (Find a Grave ID 85527613).

Marriages with Frederick August Bieck and Cannon P. Strandlund (Page 93) are known.

Family of Hazel Straube and Frederick Bieck

```
┌──────────────────┬──────────────────┐
│ 10               │ Rebecca Ann      │
│ James Everett    │ Gregg            │
│ Straube          │ 1819–1905        │
│ 1818–1888        │                  │
└──────────────────┴──────────────────┘
         │ 22                      ┌──────────────┐
         │ Francis Marion         │ Alice A.     │
         │ Straube                │ Martin       │
         │ 1842–1921              │ 1853–1930    │
                                  └──────────────┘
┌──────────────────┐        │ 52
│ Frederick August │        │ Hazel Alice
│ Bieck            │        │ Straube
│ 1887–1952        │        │ 1888–1974
└──────────────────┘
              Marriage: 1907
```

Here are the details about **Hazel Alice Straube's** first marriage, with Frederick August Bieck. You can read more about Hazel Alice on page 92.

At the age of 19, Hazel Alice Straube married **Frederick August Bieck** on Wednesday, December 11, 1907, in Denver, Denver County, Colorado, when he was 20 years old. Frederick August was born on Thursday, March 24, 1887. He was also known as **Fred**.

Frederick August reached 65 years of age and died on September 05, 1952. He was buried in Grand Island Cemetery, Grand Island, Hall County, Nebraska (Find a Grave ID 92398709).

Family of Hazel Straube and Cannon Strandlund

```
┌──────────────────┬──────────────────┐
│ 10               │ Rebecca Ann      │
│ James Everett    │ Gregg            │
│ Straube          │ 1819–1905        │
│ 1818–1888        │                  │
└──────────────────┴──────────────────┘
         │ 22                      ┌──────────────┐
         │ Francis Marion         │ Alice A.     │
         │ Straube                │ Martin       │
         │ 1842–1921              │ 1853–1930    │
                                  └──────────────┘
┌──────────────────┐        │ 52
│ Cannon P.        │        │ Hazel Alice
│ Strandlund       │        │ Straube
│ 1891–1975        │        │ 1888–1974
└──────────────────┘
              Married
```

Here are the details about **Hazel Alice Straube's** second marriage, with Cannon P. Strandlund. You can read more about Hazel Alice on page 92.

Hazel Alice Straube married **Cannon P. Strandlund**. Cannon P. was born on Saturday, March 14, 1891.

He reached 83 years of age and died in Los Angeles County, California, on January 04, 1975. Cannon P. was buried in Forest Lawn Memorial Park, Glendale, Los Angeles County, California (Find a Grave ID 115551637).

Family of Nancy Straube and Charles Clark

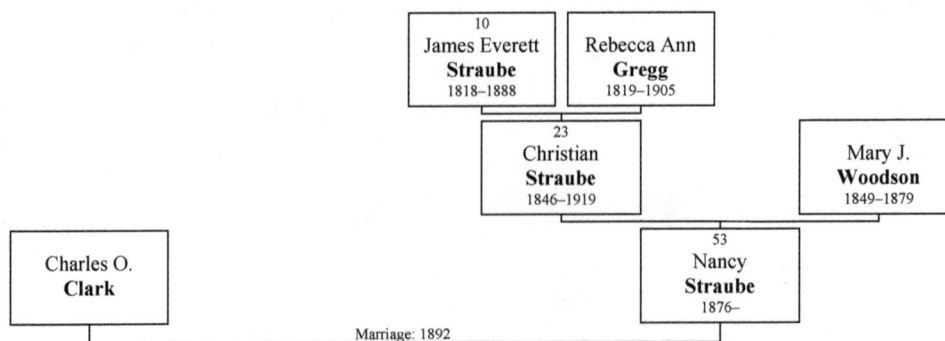

```
                        ┌─────────────────┬─────────────────┐
                        │      10         │                 │
                        │ James Everett   │  Rebecca Ann    │
                        │   Straube       │    Gregg        │
                        │  1818–1888      │  1819–1905      │
                        └─────────────────┴─────────────────┘
                              ┌──────────────────┐
                              │       23         │          ┌─────────────────┐
                              │   Christian      │          │    Mary J.      │
                              │    Straube       │          │   Woodson       │
                              │   1846–1919      │          │  1849–1879      │
                              └──────────────────┘          └─────────────────┘
   ┌─────────────────┐                    ┌──────────────────┐
   │                 │                    │       53         │
   │  Charles O.     │                    │     Nancy        │
   │    Clark        │                    │    Straube       │
   │                 │                    │     1876–        │
   └─────────────────┘                    └──────────────────┘
                        Marriage: 1892
```

53.　　**Nancy Straube** was born in 1876 in Missouri, USA. She was the daughter of Christian Straube (23) and Mary J. Woodson.

Nancy married **Charles O. Clark** on Sunday, May 22, 1892, in Pike County, Missouri.

Family of Charles Straube and Anna Quinlan

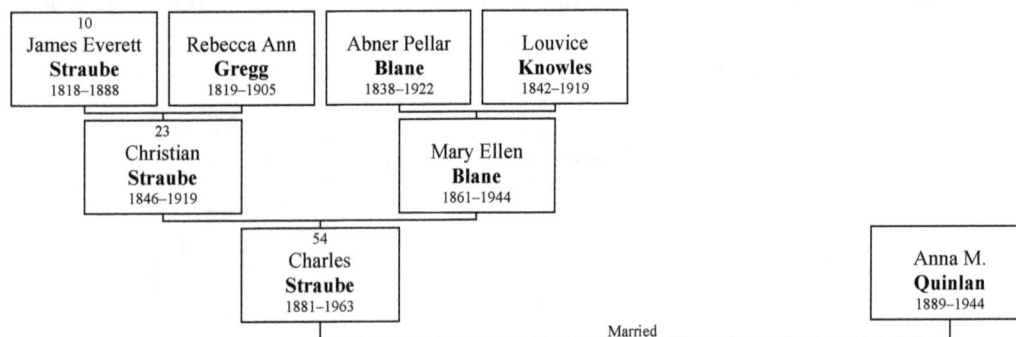

```
┌──────────────┬──────────────┬──────────────┬──────────────┐
│     10       │              │              │              │
│James Everett │ Rebecca Ann  │ Abner Pellar │   Louvice    │
│  Straube     │   Gregg      │    Blane     │   Knowles    │
│ 1818–1888    │ 1819–1905    │  1838–1922   │  1842–1919   │
└──────────────┴──────────────┴──────────────┴──────────────┘
   ┌──────────────┐                ┌──────────────┐
   │     23       │                │  Mary Ellen  │
   │  Christian   │                │    Blane     │
   │   Straube    │                │  1861–1944   │
   │  1846–1919   │                └──────────────┘
   └──────────────┘
          ┌──────────────┐                           ┌──────────────┐
          │     54       │                           │   Anna M.    │
          │   Charles    │                           │   Quinlan    │
          │   Straube    │                           │  1889–1944   │
          │  1881–1963   │                           └──────────────┘
          └──────────────┘
                              Married
```

54.　　**Charles Straube** was born on Saturday, July 02, 1881, in Havana, Mason County, Illinois. He was the son of Christian Straube (23) and Mary Ellen Blane.

Charles served in the U.S. Navy, Spanish American War as a blacksmith. He died in San Mateo County, California, on February 15, 1963, at the age of 81. Charles was buried in Golden Gate National Cemetery, San Bruno, San Mateo County, California (Find a Grave ID 3638225).

He married **Anna M. Quinlan**. Anna M. was born in New Hampshire, USA, on Sunday, September 15, 1889.

She reached 55 years of age and died in San Francisco, San Francisco County, California, on December 21, 1944. Anna M. was buried in Holy Cross Catholic Cemetery, Colma, San Mateo County, California (Find a Grave ID 105113596).

Family of Edward Straube and Elsie Sattig

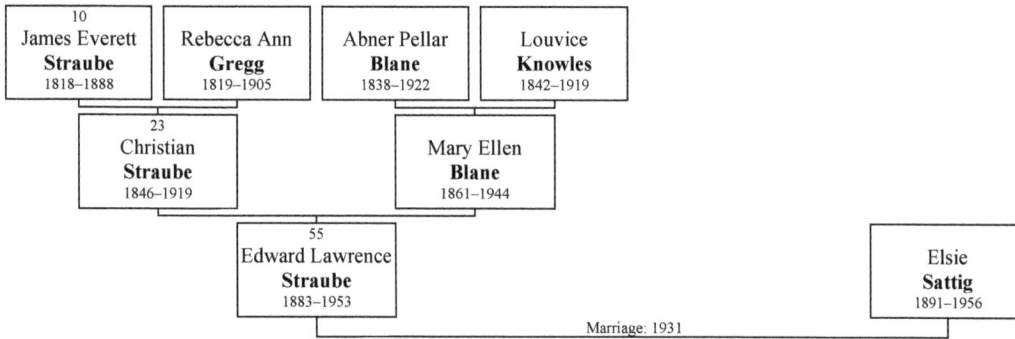

55. **Edward Lawrence Straube** was born on Monday, February 12, 1883, in Greenview, Menard County, Illinois.[56] He was the son of Christian Straube (23) and Mary Ellen Blane.

Edward Lawrence died in Belleville, St. Clair County, Illinois, on April 30, 1953, at the age of 70. He was buried in Valhalla Gardens of Memory and Mausoleum, Belleville, St. Clair County, Illinois (Find a Grave ID 131224039).

Edward Lawrence married **Elsie Sattig** in 1931. Elsie was born in Belleville, St. Clair County, Illinois, on Monday, August 24, 1891.

She reached 64 years of age and died in Belleville, St. Clair County, Illinois, on May 06, 1956. Elsie was buried in Valhalla Gardens of Memory and Mausoleum, Belleville, St. Clair County, Illinois (Find a Grave ID 131224040).

Family of Mabel Straube and Joseph Moore

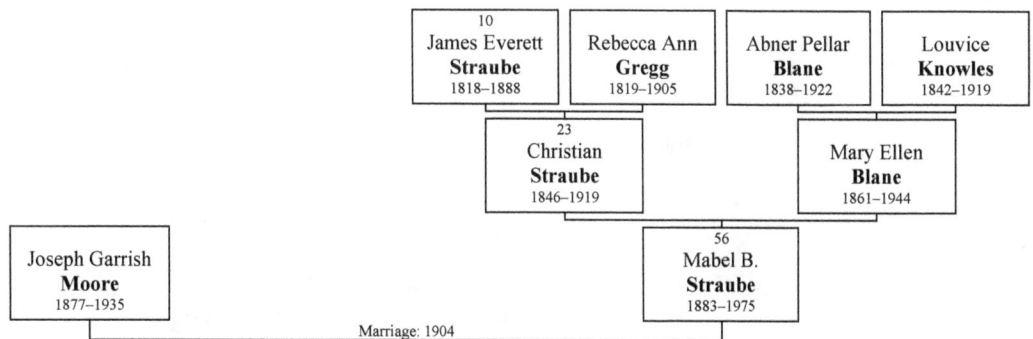

56. **Mabel B. Straube** was born on Sunday, July 08, 1883, in Illinois, USA. She was the daughter of Christian Straube (23) and Mary Ellen Blane.

Mabel B. died in Highland, Madison County, Illinois, on November 29, 1975, at the age of 92. She was buried in Glen Carbon Cemetery, Glen Carbon, Madison County, Illinois (Find a Grave ID 143748265).

Married Joseph Garrish Moore on February 10, 1904 St. Clair County, IL

---

56   Ancestry.com, U.S., Social Security Applications and Claims Index, 1936-2007 (Provo, UT, USA, Ancestry.com Operations, Inc., 2015), Ancestry.com, Record for Edward L Straube. https://search.ancestry.co.uk/cgi-bin/sse.dll?db=60901&h=4476572&indiv=try.

They were the parents of:

- Herold Moore
- Ruby Juanita Moore Sweeney 1908-1994
- Harriet Clara Moore Deltour 1910-2006
- Arthur Woodrow Moore 1912-1985

From the *Edwardsville Intelligencer*, Edwardsville, Madison County, Illinois, Wednesday, December 3, 1975, page 15:

> Mrs. Mabel Moore, 91, of the Madison County Shelter Home, died Saturday at St. Joseph's Hospital, Highland. Graveside services were held at 2 p.m. Monday at the Glen Carbon City Cemetery.

At the age of 20, Mabel B. married **Joseph Garrish Moore** on Wednesday, February 10, 1904, in St. Clair County, Illinois, when he was 26 years old. Joseph Garrish was born in Mount Sterling, Brown County, Illinois, on Sunday, December 09, 1877.

He reached 57 years of age and died in East Saint Louis, St. Clair County, Illinois, on February 17, 1935. Joseph Garrish was buried in Mount Hope Cemetery, Belleville, St. Clair County, Illinois (Find a Grave ID 149604070).

Family of Roy Straube and Martha McNew

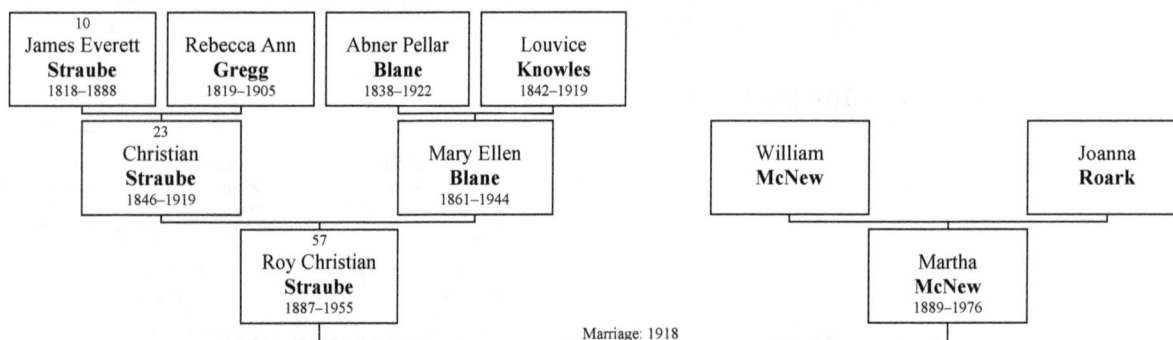

57. **Roy Christian Straube** was born on Sunday, October 16, 1887, in Macon City, Missouri. He was the son of Christian Straube (23) and Mary Ellen Blane.

Roy Christian served in the military between 1908 and 1911. Illinois Regimental Calvary. He died in Saint Louis, Saint Louis County, Missouri, on October 20, 1955, at the age of 68. Roy Christian was buried in Jefferson Barracks National Cemetery, Lemay, St. Louis County, Missouri, on October 24, 1955 (Find a Grave ID 25769841).

At the age of 30, Roy Christian married **Martha McNew** on Monday, February 25, 1918, when she was 28 years old. Martha was born on Wednesday, May 22, 1889. She was the daughter of William McNew and Joanna Roark. She was also known as **Mattie**.

Martha reached 87 years of age and died on June 30, 1976. She was buried in Jefferson Barracks National Cemetery, Lemay, St. Louis County, Missouri (Find a Grave ID 25769884).

Family of Bessie Straube and Ernest Prather

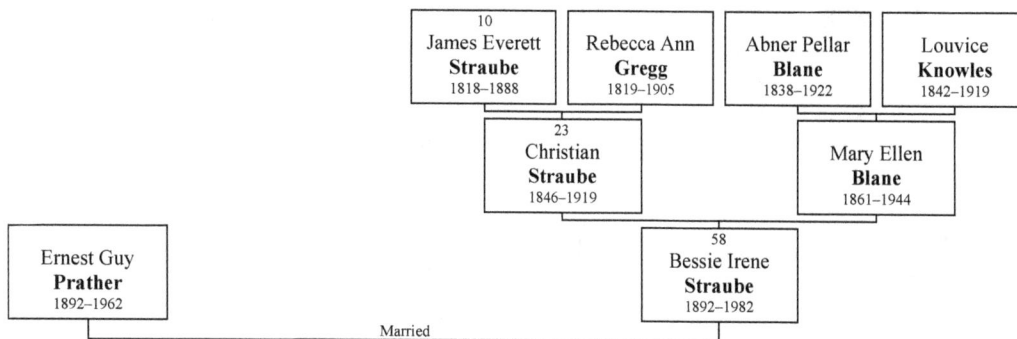

58. **Bessie Irene Straube** was born in October 1892 in Illinois, USA.[57] She was the daughter of Christian Straube (23) and Mary Ellen Blane.

Bessie Irene died in Belleville, St. Clair County, Illinois, on February 01, 1982, at the age of 89.[57] She was buried in Mount Hope Cemetery, Belleville, St. Clair County, Illinois (Find a Grave ID 255614555).[57]

She married **Ernest Guy Prather**. Ernest Guy was born in Sailor Springs, Clay County, Illinois, on Tuesday, July 12, 1892.[57]

He reached 69 years of age and died in Saint Louis, Saint Louis County, Missouri, on January 27, 1962.[57] Ernest Guy was buried in Mount Hope Cemetery, Belleville, St. Clair County, Illinois (Find a Grave ID 255614716).[57]

Family of George Wilhoit and Maggie Fisher

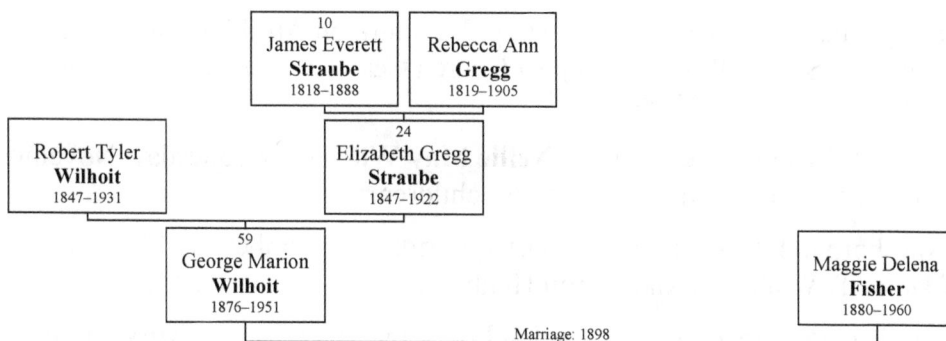

59. **George Marion Wilhoit** was born on Sunday, February 06, 1876, in New Hartford, Pike County, Missouri. He was the son of Robert Tyler Wilhoit and Elizabeth Gregg Straube (24).

George Marion died in Montgomery County, Missouri, on March 21, 1951, at the age of 75. He was buried in Fairmount Cemetery, Middletown, Montgomery County, Missouri (Find a Grave ID 145395055).

57   Ancestry.com, U.S., Find a Grave® Index, 1600s-Current (Lehi, UT, USA, Ancestry.com Operations, Inc., 2012), Ancestry.com, Record for Bessie Irene Prather. https://search.ancestry.co.uk/cgi-bin/sse.dll?db=60525&h=226633466&indiv=try.

At the age of 21, George Marion married **Maggie Delena Fisher** on Wednesday, January 26, 1898, in Pike County, Missouri, when she was 17 years old. Maggie Delena was born in Pike County, Missouri, on Wednesday, February 25, 1880.

She reached 79 years of age and died in Wellsville, Montgomery County, Missouri, on January 04, 1960. Maggie Delena was buried in Fairmount Cemetery, Middletown, Montgomery County, Missouri (Find a Grave ID 145396760).

Family of William Wilhoit and Nellie Willis

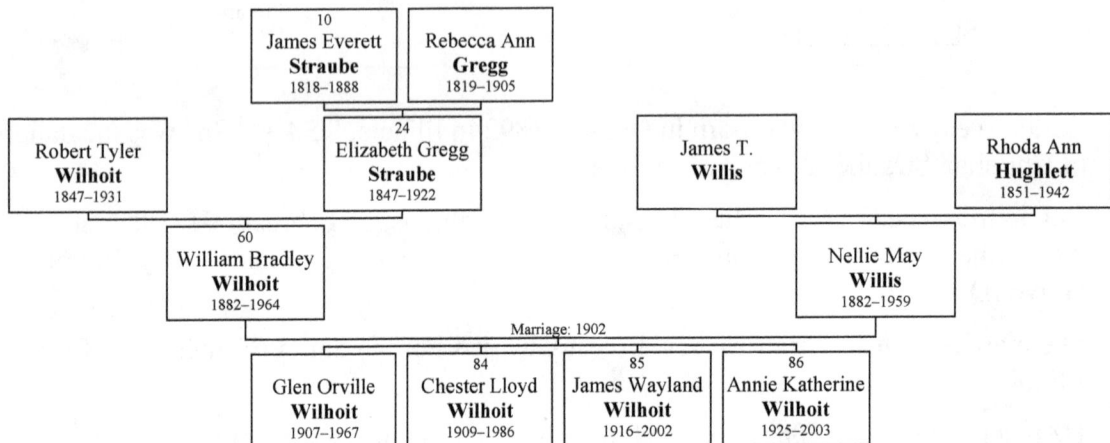

60.   **William Bradley Wilhoit** was born on Monday, March 06, 1882, in New Hartford, Pike County, Missouri. He was the son of Robert Tyler Wilhoit and Elizabeth Gregg Straube (24).

William Bradley died in Louisiana, Pike County, Missouri, on April 29, 1964, at the age of 82. He was buried in Siloam Primitive Baptist Church Cemetery, Ashley, Pike County, Missouri (Find a Grave ID 84025086).

At the age of 20, William Bradley married **Nellie May Willis** on Wednesday, November 19, 1902, when she was 20 years old. They had four children.

Nellie May was born in Pike County, Missouri, on Friday, November 17, 1882. She was the daughter of James T. Willis and Rhoda Ann Hughlett.

Nellie May reached 76 years of age and died in Louisiana, Pike County, Missouri, on February 25, 1959. She was buried in Siloam Primitive Baptist Church Cemetery, Ashley, Pike County, Missouri (Find a Grave ID 84025194).

Children of William Bradley Wilhoit and Nellie May Willis:

m   I. **Glen Orville Wilhoit** was born in Pike County, Missouri, on March 01, 1907. He died in Louisiana, Pike County, Missouri, on November 02, 1967, at the age of 60. Glen Orville was buried in Siloam Primitive Baptist Church Cemetery, Ashley, Pike County, Missouri (Find a Grave ID 99692734).

+ 84   m   II. **Chester Lloyd Wilhoit** was born in Pike County, Missouri, on February 01, 1909. He died on February 13, 1986, at the age of 77. Chester Lloyd was buried in Siloam Primitive Baptist Church Cemetery, Ashley, Pike County, Missouri (Find a Grave ID 84025318).

+ 85 m III. **James Wayland Wilhoit** was born in New Hartford, Pike County, Missouri, on July 16, 1916.[58] He died in Mexico, Audrain County, Missouri, on March 06, 2002, at the age of 85.[58] James Wayland was buried in Siloam Primitive Baptist Church Cemetery, Ashley, Pike County, Missouri (Find a Grave ID 86162887).[58]

+ 86 f IV. **Annie Katherine Wilhoit** was born in Pike County, Missouri, on December 12, 1925. She died in Missouri, USA, on September 09, 2003, at the age of 77. Annie Katherine was buried in Siloam Primitive Baptist Church Cemetery, Ashley, Pike County, Missouri (Find a Grave ID 86166192).

Family of Ada Straube and Hershel Pollard

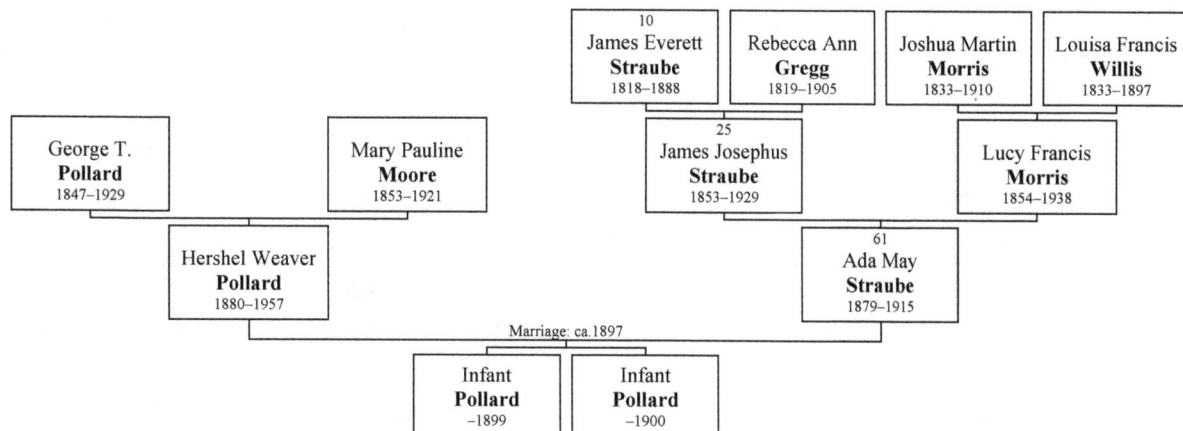

61. **Ada May Straube** was born on Monday, November 17, 1879.[59] She was the daughter of James Josephus Straube (25) and Lucy Francis Morris.

Ada May died at Missouri Baptist Sanitorium in Saint Louis, Saint Louis County, Missouri, on September 21, 1915, at the age of 35. Her cause of death was hepatic abscess. Ada May was buried in Siloam Primitive Baptist Church Cemetery, Ashley, Pike County, Missouri, on September 22, 1915 (Find a Grave ID 69238769).

Ada May Straube was born near New Hartford, Missouri, on November 17, 1879. She is the daughter and 3rd child of James Josephus Straube and Lucy Francis Morris.

Ada's siblings are as follows and are on this site: Olie # 70940272, Anliza # 70941478, Bertha Lee # 69240088, Everett James # 68075841, Luther Joshua # 69553077, Grover Melvin # 70964070 and Lenard Sherman # 70964138.

Ada was converted and joined the Baptist Church at Siloam September 22, 1909 where she was devoted member until death.

---

58 Ancestry.com, U.S., Find a Grave® Index, 1600s-Current (Lehi, UT, USA, Ancestry.com Operations, Inc., 2012), Ancestry.com, Record for James Wayland Wilhoit. https://search.ancestry.co.uk/cgi-bin/sse.dll?db=60525&h=53317179&indiv=try.

59 Death Certificate, Certificate # 29236, Reg. # 7942.

Ada May married Hershel Weaver Pollard on Jamary 1, 1899. To this union were born four children, two dying in infancy. Two survive her, Cleo, age 12 and Ralph age 9 months.

She passed away on September 21, 1915, age: 35 years, 10 months, 4 days; as a result of a hepatic abscess (liver infection) and appendicitis at Missouri Baptist Sanatorium in Saint Louis, Missouri.

Ada's funeral was conducted by her pastor, Reverend Huff, of Moberly, Mo., on September 22 at 2 p.m. at Siloam Church, after which the remains were laid to rest in the Siloam cemetery to await the resurrection morn.

Note: The spelling of Hershel here is correct and is found on several documents including the 1940 Census however spelled "Hearschel" on Ada's tombstone at Siloam and spelled "Herchel" on his Death Certificate. After Ada died, Hershel married Ada's sister, Bertha Lee Straube. Following Bertha's death Hershel married Louvenia Pearl Jackson and following Louvenia's death he married Lutetia Pearl Jackson; both are buried in Bowling Green Cemetery alongside Hershel.

Ada May married **Hershel Weaver Pollard** about 1897. They had two daughters.

Hershel Weaver was born on Saturday, July 17, 1880. He was the son of George T. Pollard and Mary Pauline Moore.

Hershel Weaver reached 77 years of age and died in Bowling Green, Pike County, Missouri, on December 18, 1957. He was buried in Siloam Primitive Baptist Church Cemetery, Ashley, Pike County, Missouri (Find a Grave ID 69241210).

Married and buried with Straube sisters. Hershel's gravestone does not indicate his DOD.

Hershel's first wife was Ada May Straube who died on September 21, 1915 and is buried at Siloam Cemetery. After Ada died, Hershel married Ada's sister, Bertha Lee Straube who died on August 30, 1917 and is also buried at Siloam. Following Bertha's death Hershel married Louvenia Pearl Jackson b. 4-25-1880 d. 4-18-1951; following Louvenia's death he married Lutetia Pearl Jackson b. 1887 d.1967; both are buried in Bowling Green Cemetery alongside Hershel.

NOTE: "Hershel" is the correct spelling of his name that is found in the 1940 Census and on several other documents but spelled "Hearschel" on Ada's tombstone and spelled "Herchel" on his Death Certificate and spelled "Herschel" on Louvenia Pearl Pollards' Death Certificate.

Daughters of Ada May Straube and Hershel Weaver Pollard:

      f   I. **Infant Pollard**. Infant died on August 18, 1899.

      f   II. **Infant Pollard**. Infant died on August 14, 1900.

Family of Bertha Straube and Hershel Pollard

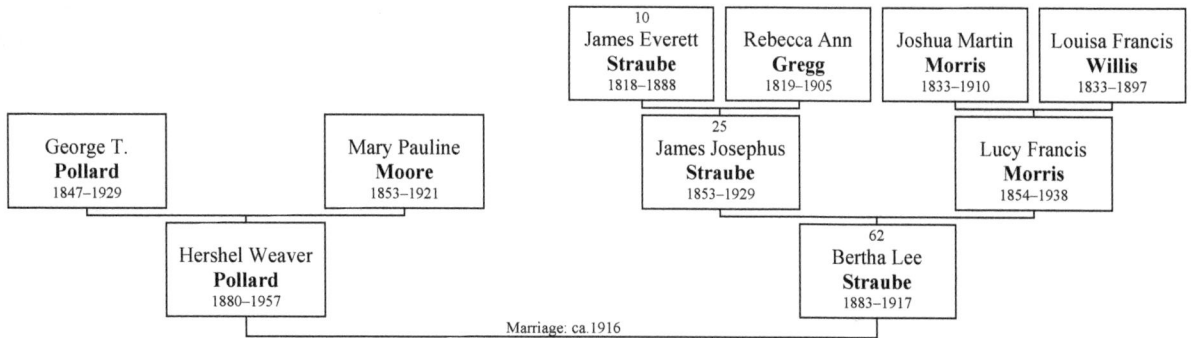

62. **Bertha Lee Straube** was born on Tuesday, January 02, 1883.[60] She was the daughter of James Josephus Straube (25) and Lucy Francis Morris.

Bertha Lee died in Hartford Township, Pike County, Missouri, on August 30, 1917, at the age of 34. Her cause of death was rupture of gall bladder. Bertha Lee was buried in Siloam Primitive Baptist Church Cemetery, Ashley, Pike County, Missouri, on August 31, 1917 (Find a Grave ID 69240088).

> Bertha Lee Straube was born near New Hartford, Missouri, on January 2, 1883. She is the daughter and 4th child of James Josephus Straube and Lucy Francis Morris.
>
> Bertha's siblings are as follows and are on this site: Olie # 70940272, Anliza # 70941478, Ada May # 69238769, Everett James # 68075841, Luther Joshua # 69553077, Grover Melvin # 70964070 and Lenard Sherman # 70964138.
>
> Bertha Lee united with the Baptist Church at New Hartford in October 1914, later changing her membership to Siloam Baptist Church.
>
> Bertha Lee married Hershel Weaver Pollard (see note) on September 28, 1916. Bertha Lee passed away on August 30, 1917, age: 34 years, 7 months, 28 days, only being married 11 months as a result of a ruptured gall bladder.
>
> Bertha Lee leaves behind her husband, Hershel; two step-children, Cleo and Ralph; a father, James J., and mother, Lucy F. Straube; and two brothers, Everett James and Luther Joshua Straube.
>
> Funeral services were conducted by her pastor, Rev. Carter of Moberly, Mo., after which she was laid to rest beside her beloved sister, Ada May, who preceded her to the grave two years before.

Bertha Lee married **Hershel Weaver Pollard** about 1916. Married this sister second. Hershel Weaver was born on Saturday, July 17, 1880.

Hershel Weaver reached 77 years of age and died in Bowling Green, Pike County, Missouri, on December 18, 1957.

Further details about Hershel Weaver may be found on page 101.

---

60   Death Certificate, Certificate # 29516.

Family of Everett Straube and Mary Willis

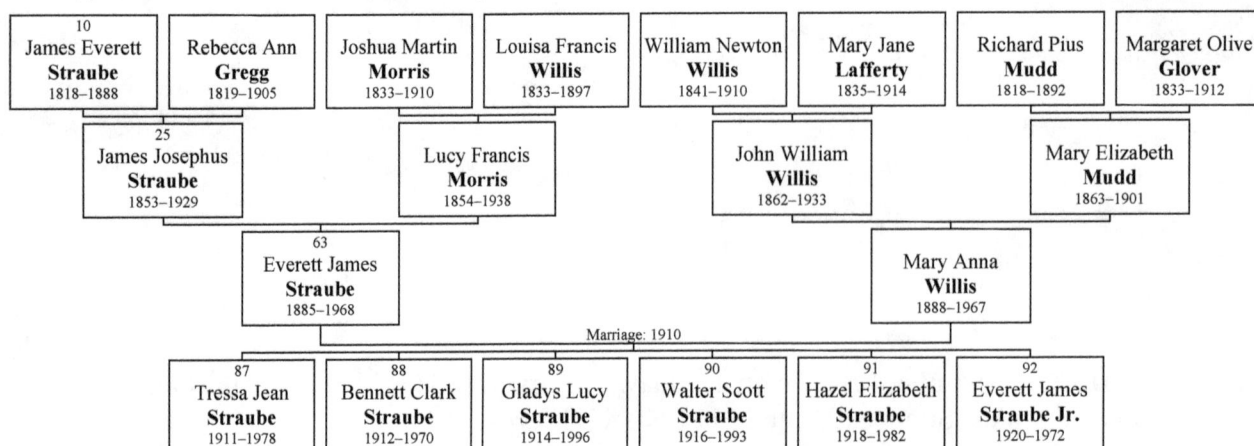

10 James Everett **Straube** 1818–1888	Rebecca Ann **Gregg** 1819–1905	Joshua Martin **Morris** 1833–1910	Louisa Francis **Willis** 1833–1897	William Newton **Willis** 1841–1910	Mary Jane **Lafferty** 1835–1914	Richard Pius **Mudd** 1818–1892	Margaret Olive **Glover** 1833–1912

25 James Josephus **Straube** 1853–1929	Lucy Francis **Morris** 1854–1938	John William **Willis** 1862–1933	Mary Elizabeth **Mudd** 1863–1901

63 Everett James **Straube** 1885–1968	Mary Anna **Willis** 1888–1967

Marriage: 1910

87 Tressa Jean **Straube** 1911–1978	88 Bennett Clark **Straube** 1912–1970	89 Gladys Lucy **Straube** 1914–1996	90 Walter Scott **Straube** 1916–1993	91 Hazel Elizabeth **Straube** 1918–1982	92 Everett James **Straube Jr.** 1920–1972

63. **Everett James Straube** was born on Saturday, January 17, 1885, in New Hartford, Pike County, Missouri. He was the son of James Josephus Straube (25) and Lucy Francis Morris.

Everett James died in Bowling Green, Pike County, Missouri, on December 29, 1968, at the age of 83. His cause of death was coronary occlusion, arteriosclerosis. Everett James was buried in Memorial Gardens Cemetery, Bowling Green, Pike County, Missouri, on December 31, 1968 (Find a Grave ID 68075841).

From *People Places & Pikers* page 639

Everett James Straube, was born January 17, 1885, near New Hartford. He lived his boyhood on the farm and was a talented fiddler and singer. Everett and Anna established their home near Siloam Church in the New Hartford-Farmer community. Around 1943 Everett and Anna moved to Bowling Green. They purchased the B.B. Springs Hotel in 1945. They lived at the B. B. Springs and operated it as a nursing home until their retirement in 1962. Everett and Anna remained in Bowling Green until their deaths. Both are buried in Bowling Green Memorial Gardens. They were members of the Second Baptist Church in Bowling Green. One of the first Straube families to settle in Pike County was that of James E. Straube. James E., of German ancestry, was married to Rebecca Ann Greg, cousin of William McKinley, 25th President of the United States.

Everett James Straube was born near New Hartford, Missouri, on Saturday, January 17, 1885. He is the son of James Josephus Straube and Lucy Francis Morris.

Everett was the 5th born of 8 children. His siblings are as follows and are listed on this site: Olie # 70940272, Anliza # 70941478, Ada May # 69238769, Bertha Lee # 69240088, Luther Joshua # 69553077, Grover Melvin # 70964070 and Lenard Sherman # 70964138.

In 1909, Everett united with the Primitive Baptist Church at Siloam, near New Hartford, and later transferred his membership to the Second Baptist Church in Bowling Green. Everett was a farmer and accomplished at playing the fiddle by ear and he and his sister, Ada, and her husband, Herschel Pollard, often provided the music for the dances in the area.

On August 12, 1910, the Reverend Wiley J. Patrick married Everett James Straube and Mary Anna Willis, the daughter of John William Willis and Mary Elizabeth "Lizzie" Mudd. Everett, 25, dressed in a navy suit with a white shirt and tie, was a well-built handsome farmer with dark hair and eyes. Anna, 22, with pure white skin, beautiful reddish hair and blue eyes, wore a delicate high neck white laced wedding dress.

To this union was born Tressa Jean, July 1, 1911; Bennett Clark, fondly known as "Ike", December 7, 1912; Lucy Gladys, September 17, 1914; Walter Scott, September 26, 1916; Hazel Elizabeth, October 13, 1918 and Everett James Jr. called by his initials "E.J.", April 13, 1920.

They made their home on a farm in the New Hartford area near Farmer. Mrs. Straube taught school in Pike County for over 30 years. In 1944 they moved to Bowling Green and in 1945 purchased the BB Springs Rest Home and in 1946 purchased the Cottage Hotel in Bowling Green and operated both until they retired in 1962. Mrs. Straube passed away on Saturday, April 8, 1967.

Everett James Straube passed away at the Straube Rest Home on Sunday, December 29, 1968, at the age of 83 years, 11 months and 12 days as a result of coronary occlusion and arteriosclerosis. Funeral services were held on Tuesday, December 31, at the Second Baptist Church of Bowling Green with the Reverends Joe Barbour and G.E. Rittenhouse officiating. "The Old Rugged Cross" and "In The Sweet Bye and Bye" were sung by Reverend Barbour with Mrs. Chester C. Coddington accompanist.

Surviving Everett James Straube are his six children: Tressa (Floyd) Chamberlain, Ike (Shirley) Straube, Gladys Straube Myers, Scott (Ann) Straube, Sr., Hazel (Garland) Smith and E.J. (Lil) Straube, Jr.; twenty-five grandchildren: Shirley Jean Chamberlain (Ted) Mummert, Georganna Myers (Sam) Hargadine, Tanya Straube (Tom) Cunningham, Scott Straube, Jr., Duane (Mary Kay) Straube, Fred Smith, Christine Smith (Jacques) McCormack, Robert Straube, Elaine Straube (Clem) Deters, Rosetta Straube (William) Pagnella, Stephen Smith, David Straube, Annice Straube (R. J.) Allensworth, Michael Straube, Pam Chamberlain, Jerry Straube, Chris (Vickie) Straube, Karen Straube, Willis Straube, Bruce Smith, Joyce Straube, Lucy Straube, Cheryl Straube, Elizabeth Smith and Dewey Straube; thirteen great grandchildren: Paula Henderson, Marsha Henderson, Susan Henderson, Sam Hargadine, John Hargadine, Troy Straube, Calvin Mummert, Floyd Mummert, Bob Cunningham, Sharlene Mummert, Crystal Straube, Terri Cunningham and Brian Pagnella.

Mr. Straube was laid to rest by his Grandsons Duane, Chris, Willis and David Straube and Fred and Bruce Smith. Burial was at Memorial Gardens in Bowling Green, Missouri. The Family was served by the Mudd Funeral Home.

At the age of 25, Everett James married **Mary Anna Willis** on Friday, August 12, 1910, in Bowling Green, Pike County, Missouri, when she was 22 years old. They had six children.

Mary Anna was born in New Hartford, Pike County, Missouri, on Friday, January 20, 1888. Mary Anna reached 79 years of age and died in Bowling Green, Pike County, Missouri, on April 08, 1967. Her cause of death was congestive heart failure. Mary Anna was buried on April 11, 1967, in Memorial Gardens Cemetery, Bowling Green, Pike County, Missouri (Find a Grave ID 42093025). Married by Rev. Wiley J. Patrick She was the daughter of John William Willis and Mary Elizabeth Mudd.

Mary Anna Straube was born in the Farmer area of rural Pike County on Friday, January 20, 1888. She is the daughter of John William Willis and Mary Elizabeth "Lizzie" Mudd. Mary Anna was called Anna by her family and siblings, Annie by her husband, mother by her children, "Miss Annie" by her students, Mother Straube by her in-laws and Mrs. Straube by everybody else.

Mary Anna was the 3rd born of 9 children. Her siblings are as follows and are listed on this site: Carrie Louella # 74217135, Ruby # 76200169, William Richard #72668514, Herman # 72668140, Dura Elizabeth #73539241, Buford Newton # 17332884, Viva Leota # 72676555, and Infant Willis # 72667895.

Anna attended a women's college in Virginia where she also played basketball. Upon her return to Missouri, she began her teaching career. Miss Annie, as she was known, taught school in rural Pike County from 1908 until her retirement in 1945. Her teaching record is as follows: Vannoy 1908, 1919, 1929-1936 where she taught fifth, sixth, seventh and eighth grades; Woodlawn 1909; Curryville 1910; Dunn School 1918; Ashburn 1937 taught grades 4 through 8th; Miller 1938-1945.

On August 12, 1910, the Reverend Wiley J. Patrick married Everett James Straube and Mary Anna Willis. Everett, 25, dressed in a navy suit with a white shirt and tie, was a well-built handsome farmer with dark hair and eyes. Anna, 22, with pure white skin, beautiful reddish hair and blue eyes, wore a delicate high neck white laced wedding dress.

To this union was born Tressa Jean, July 1, 1911; Bennett Clark, fondly known as "Ike," on December 7, 1912; Lucy Gladys on September 17, 1914; Walter Scott on September 26, 1916; Hazel Elizabeth on October 13, 1918 and Everett James Jr. called by his initials "E.J.," on April 13, 1920.

They made their home on a farm in the New Hartford area near Farmer. In 1944 they moved to Bowling Green and in 1945 purchased the BB Springs Rest Home and in 1946 they purchased The Cottage Hotel in Bowling Green and operated both until they were sold and retired in 1962.

Mrs. Straube was active in her community, contributing her services to a number of civic organizations including the Business and Professional Women's Club of which she served as president; member of the American Legion Auxiliary, Victory Mothers' Club, Pike County Teachers Association and Farmer-Farmerette Extension Club.

Surviving Mrs. Straube are her six children: Tressa (Floyd) Chamberlain, Ike (Shirley) Straube, Gladys (William "Sie") Myers, Scott (Ann) Straube, Sr., Hazel (Garland) Smith and E.J. (Lil) Straube, Jr.; twenty-five grandchildren: Shirley Jean Chamberlain (Ted) Mummert, Georganna Myers (Sam) Hargadine, Tanya Straube (Tom) Cunningham, Scott Straube, Jr., Duane (Mary Kay) Straube, Fred Smith, Christine Smith (Jacques) McCormack, Robert Straube, Elaine Straube (Clem) Deters, Rosetta Straube, Stephen Smith, David Straube, Annice Straube (R. J.) Allensworth, Michael Straube, Pam Chamberlain, Jerry Straube, Chris Straube, Karen Straube, Willis Straube, Bruce Smith, Joyce Straube, Lucy Straube, Cheryl Straube, Elizabeth Smith and Dewey Straube; ten great grandchildren: Paula Henderson, Marsha Henderson, Susan Henderson, Sam Hargadine, John Hargadine, Troy Straube, Calvin Mummert, Floyd Mummert, Bob Cunningham and Sharlene Mummert: three sisters: Lou (Que) Wylie, Dura (Grover)Tartt and Viva (Ewart) Gunn; one brother: Buford Newton (Vic) Willis.

Mrs. Straube passed away at the Straube Rest Home on Saturday, April 8, 1967, as a result of congestive heart failure and other contributory illnesses. Funeral services were held on Tuesday, April 11, 1967, at the Second Baptist Church in Bowling Green. A large spray of yellow roses (her favorite) was placed on her casket flanked by two large arrangements of yellow roses. She held six yellow rose buds, one for each of her children. The Reverend G. E Rittenhouse officiated with church pastor, Reverend W. Joe Barbour assisting. Songs "How Great Thou Art" and "No Night There" were sung by Reverend Barbour accompanied by Miss Mae Rieman. Mrs. Straube was laid to rest by her Grandsons, Duane, David, Mike and Chris Straube and Fred and Stephen Smith in Memorial Gardens in Bowling Green. The Family was served by the Mudd Funeral Home.

She is gone. That is true. But just as the fragrance of the incense lingers on, so her presence lingers with us, consoles, and encourages us.

Children of Everett James Straube and Mary Anna Willis:

+ 87   f   I. **Tressa Jean Straube** was born in New Hartford, Pike County, Missouri, on July 01, 1911.[61] She died in Bowling Green, Pike County, Missouri, on May 20, 1978, at the age of 66. Tressa Jean was buried in Memorial Gardens Cemetery, Bowling Green, Pike County, Missouri, on May 23, 1978 (Find a Grave ID 68397409).

> Born Tressa Jean Straube on Saturday, July 1, 1911, in rural Pike County near New Harford, Missouri. She is the daughter of Everett James and Mary Anna (Willis) Straube.
>
> Tressa graduated from Bowling Green High School in 1929, attended Hannibal-LaGrange College and was a member of the Second Baptist Church in Bowling Green.

---

61   SSDI.

Tressa married Floyd Willard Chamberlain on December 26, 1929, in Bowling Green. To this union were born at the family home in Curryville, Missouri, Shirley Jean on March 26, 1931, and Pamela Lou on July 16, 1948.

Tressa was a woman of many talents of her time. After W.W. II and the Depression, she was active in Farmer Farmerette Extension Club where the women learned to cold pack foods, sew, cook new recipes and etch aluminum trays, just to name a few skills. She was a 4-H leader and loved to fish and dance. In her later years, she was a teacher's aide for 12 years in the Bowling Green School District, loved to talk politics with her friends and relatives and play bridge till the wee hours of the morning. She learned to drive the car in her 60s after Floyd died.

Tressa passed away on Saturday, May 20, 1978, at the age of 66 years, 10 months and 19 days as a result of respiratory failure, cerebral hemorrhage and infraction of basal ganglia of the brain at the University of Missouri Medical Center in Columbia, Missouri. Funeral services were held on Tuesday, May 23, 1978, at the Second Baptist Church in Bowling Green, with the Reverend G. E. Rittenhouse officiating. Burial was at Memorial Gardens in Bowling Green. Pallbearers were Mike, Willis and Jerry Straube, Fred Smith, R. J. Allensworth and John Hargadine.

Tressa is survived by two daughters, Mrs. Ted (Shirley) Mummert of Ennis, Texas, and Mrs. Wayne (Pam) Korte of Bowling Green, 10 grandchildren; a brother, Scott Straube, of Bowling Green; and two sisters, Gladys Myers of Columbia and Mrs. Garland (Hazel) Smith of Richmond Heights, Missouri.

+   88   m   II. **Bennett Clark Straube** was born in New Hartford, Pike County, Missouri, on December 07, 1912. He was also known as **Ike**.

Bennett Clark died in Hannibal, Marion County, Missouri, on August 14, 1970, at the age of 57. He was buried in Vandalia Cemetery, Vandalia, Audrain County, Missouri, on August 16, 1970 (Find a Grave ID 68885819).

Born Bennett Clark Straube on Saturday, December 7, 1912, in Hartford Township of Pike County, Missouri. Named after James Beauchamp Clark, who is best known as Champ Clark, a prominent lawyer and politician from Bowling Green, Missouri. Clark was a member of the U.S. House of Representatives and was speaker from 1911 to 1919.

Ike grew up on his parent's farm and attended Vannoy School. He enjoyed sports, especially baseball. Ike played on their small community Farmer team. At times, the team was made up of his brothers, Scott and E.J., and many of Ike's cousins. His Uncle Buford Willis was the team coach and manager.

Ike loved to catch catfish by hand. The rare and painful fishing technique called "noodling" was a way of life for many country folks. Often Ike would go to Indian Creek in June and July when catfish are nesting, and he would lie on the bank and stick his arms down dark creek holes surrounded by craggily tree roots and wiggle his fingers around as bait hoping a catfish would latch on. Sometimes Ike hands would get scraped or bloody as a result of those catfish that were resistant to being caught. But that's part of the sport of "noodling."

On March 1, 1941, Ike married Shirley Maxine Livingston. She was born Monday, March 19, 1917, in the home in rural route Curryville in Pike County and was the daughter of Robert and Cora Bennett Livingston. They lived on the Livingston 80 acres, and Ike farmed most of his life. Later he owned his own well drilling company. Ike was a member of the Farmer Methodist Church.

To this union were born Tanya D'Arline on January 16, 1942; Duane Bennett on November 26, 1943; Elaine Rosemary on February 20, 1946; and Michael Dean on March 18, 1948 at the family home in rural route Curryville, Missouri. Cheryl Denise was born on September 8, 1954, and Derwin Leon on October 11, 1956, at Saint Elizabeth's Hospital in Hannibal, Missouri.

Ike passed away at 4:35 PM on Friday, August 14, 1970, at the age of 57 years, 8 months and 7 days as a result of acute congestive heart failure, vague neuritis and a hemorrhaged gastric ulcer at Saint Elizabeth Hospital in Hannibal, Missouri. Funeral services were held on Sunday, August 16, 1970, at the First Baptist Church in Vandalia, Missouri, with the Reverend Walter Hinton officiating. Burial was at Vandalia City Cemetery in Vandalia, Missouri. Pallbearers were Ogle and Melvin Straube, Norbert Grawe, Raymond Dieckmann and J. W. Kohl.

Ike is survived by his wife, Shirley; three sons, Duane Straube of St. Louis, Michael Straube of Columbia and Derwin of the home; three daughters, Mrs. Tom (Tanya) Cunningham of Vandalia, Mrs. Clem (Elaine) Deters of St. Clement and Cheryl Straube of the home. He also leaves two brothers and three sisters, Scott Straube, Sr., E.J. Straube, Jr., Mrs. Floyd (Tressa) Chamberlain, Mrs. Gladys Myers of Bowling Green and Mrs. Garland (Hazel) Smith of St. Louis; and three grandchildren, Crystal Sue Straube of St. Louis and Robert and Terri Ann Cunningham of Vandalia.

+ 89   f   III. **Gladys Lucy Straube** was born in New Hartford, Pike County, Missouri, on September 17, 1914. She was also known as **Tucky**.

Gladys Lucy died in Columbia, Boone County, Missouri, on August 19, 1996, at the age of 81. She was buried in Memorial Gardens Cemetery, Bowling Green, Pike County, Missouri, on August 22, 1996 (Find a Grave ID 68398299).

Graduate of Hannibal-LaGrange College (Associate in Elementary Education) and the University of Missouri-Columbia (B.S. and M.S. in Elementary Education); Alpha Delta Kappa; Delta Pi Epsilon. She was a member of the First Baptist Church, Sneed Class for 25 years. Gladys was a principal at South School in Fulton, and the elementary schools in Frankford and Bowling Green. She taught public School for 37 years, retiring from West Boulevard Elementary School in Columbia. Gladys was a Life Master in American Contract Bridge League and Director of two duplicate contract bridge clubs in Columbia.

Born Lucy Gladys Straube on Thursday, September 17, 1914, in rural Pike County near New Hartford, Missouri. She is the daughter of Everett James and Mary Anna Willis Straube. Gladys was named after her grandmother Lucy Francis Straube. Her nickname was "Tucky."

Gladys married William Barnett Myers on April 28, 1934, in Bowling Green, Missouri. William Barnett was known by his nickname, "Sie," and was born on Sunday, April 5, 1909, in rural Pike County near New Hartford, Missouri. He was a farmer and the son of Ira James Myers and Georgia Thomas Rector. To this union was born Georganna Myers on December 30, 1937, at their home in Farmer, Missouri. Sie also broke horses, and Gladys had a fondness for them. One of her horses was named "Lady," who a beautiful five-gated mare. Gladys also liked to fish and enjoyed going to just about any lake, pond or steam.

Gladys started teaching in 1931 at Prairie View, a one-room rural school in Pike County, Missouri, where she taught all grades with 32 students. In 1941, she taught one year at Allison School, then two years at Vannoy School. Gladys started teaching with 12 hours of college credit and a teacher's examination.

Some of the extra duties teachers had to do were to build a fire in a big old coal stove, sweep and dust the building, cook lunch on many occasions, referee ball games and have the entertainment program for the entire community in the school building.

Like most teachers Gladys went back to college. She got an associate's degree in elementary education from Hannibal-LaGrange College after which she taught three years at Watson School and five years at Bowling Green. In 1955 she moved to Columbia, Missouri, while Georganna was attending the University of Missouri and taught one year at the University Lab School. Gladys earned a Bachelor of Science and a Master of

Science degree in elementary education from the University of Missouri in Columbia and was a member of Alpha Delta Kappa and Delta Pi Epsilon. She was the principal at South School in Fulton, Missouri, for two years. Then moved to Prince George's County in Maryland where she taught one year and also received the "Teacher of the Year" award.

Gladys moved to Bowling Green in 1963. She was the principal at Frankfort Elementary School for two years and Bowling Green Junior High School for seven years and was President of the Pike County Teacher's Association.

She returned to Columbia, Missouri and retired in 1975 from West Boulevard Elementary School. In 1964, Gladys was listed in "Who's Who West of the Mississippi" for education excellence.

When Gladys retired, she taught bridge twice a week- "Once a teacher always a teacher," she said. This was easy for her since she was also Life Master in Contract Bridge League and Director of two duplicate contract bridge clubs in Columbia.

Gladys passed away on Monday, August 19, 1996, at the age of 81 years, 11 months and 2 days at her residence, Candlelight Terrace Apartments, in Columbia, Missouri, from cerebra vascular accident and generalized arteriosclerosis. A funeral service was held at 10:00 AM on Thursday, August 22, 1996, at the First Baptist Church in Columbia, Missouri, with the Reverend Robert Russell officiating. At 2:00 PM a graveside service was held at Memorial Gardens Cemetery in Bowling Green, Missouri, with the Reverend Ed Engle officiating. She was buried alongside Sie. The inscription on the grave marker reads "Together Forever." Pallbearers were Duane, Chris, Jerry and Willis Straube, Wayne Korte and Bill Gates.

Survivors include one daughter, Georganna Beachboard of Jefferson City; two grandsons, Samuel E. Hargadine and John E. Hargadine, both of Columbia; and three great-grandsons.

+ 90   m   IV. **Walter Scott Straube** was born in New Hartford, Pike County, Missouri, on September 26, 1916. He died in Bowling Green, Pike County, Missouri, on December 09, 1993, at the age of 77. Walter Scott was buried in Memorial Gardens Cemetery, Bowling Green, Pike County, Missouri, on December 13, 1993 (Find a Grave ID 68398377).

Born Walter Scott Straube on Tuesday, September 26, 1916, at the home in rural Pike County near New Hartford, Missouri. He is the son of Everett James and Mary Anna Willis Straube.

Scott grew up on his parent's farm where he learned many skills that carried him throughout his life. During spring, summer and fall there were plenty of chores to do, fish to catch and animals to hunt.

Scott attended Vannoy School in rural Pike County through the eighth grade. After graduating from Vannoy, he attended Bowling Green High School and graduated in 1934. During the school week, since the school was miles from his home he boarded with the Smith family. Of the things he did and accomplished in high school, of which is history now, one still remains present. Scott signed the original Future Farmers of America (FFA) Charter that hangs in the Ag building at Bowling Green High School today. After high school, Scott attended the University of Missouri in Columbia, Missouri then later went to work for Bridges Asphalt & Paving Company in Bowling Green.

On July 11, 1942, Scott married Annie Elizabeth Dieckmann. The marriage was performed by Reverend G. O. Baxter at the Second Baptist Church Parsonage at 215 West Locust in Bowling Green. Ann was born on Tuesday, November 7, 1922 near Silex, Missouri and is the fifth child of John Henry Dieckmann (FAG#100414395) and Annie Alvena Neumann (FAG#100414842). To this union seven children were born.

Scott was an excellent baseball player in his own right and played on many ball teams including the Farmer baseball team. At times, players were his brothers, Ike and E.J., and many of Scott's cousins which made up the majority of the team. His Uncle Buford was the team coach and manager.

Scott passed away at their home on Thursday, December 9, 1993, at the age of 77 years, 2 months and 13 days as a result of progressive hypoxia and carcinoma of the lung. Services were held at the Second Baptist Church in Bowling Green on Monday, December 13, 1993, with Reverend Bill Peters officiating. Burial was at Memorial Gardens Cemetery in Bowling Green. Pallbearers were Chris, Willis, Jason and Dewey Straube and Sam and John Hargadine.

Scott is survived by his wife, Ann; four sons, Scott Straube, Jr. of Caruthersville, Robert "Bobby" Straube of Plant City, Florida; David Straube of Henderson, Kentucky and Jerry Straube of Bowling Green; three daughters, Rosetta Pagnella of Bowling Green; Karen Drennan and Joyce Roloff both of Juneau, Alaska; on sister, Gladys Myers of Columbia; 12 grandchildren and two great-grandchildren.

+ 91   f   V. **Hazel Elizabeth Straube** was born in New Hartford, Pike County, Missouri, on October 13, 1918. She died in Saint Louis, Saint Louis

County, Missouri, on April 21, 1982, at the age of 63. Hazel Elizabeth was buried in Oak Hill Cemetery, Kirkwood, St. Louis County, Missouri (Find a Grave ID 68614261).

Born Hazel Elizabeth Straube on Sunday, October 13, 1918, in Hartford Township in rural Pike County, Missouri. She is the daughter of Everett James and Mary Anna Willis Straube.

After graduation from Bowling Green High School in 1935, Hazel taught at Allison School, a one-room schoolhouse, for two years. After two years of teaching, Hazel saved enough money to put herself through Brown Business and Secretarial School in St. Louis to become a stenographer. On April 21, 1939, Hazel graduated and became secretary at Washington University School of Medicine.

Hazel married Garland F. Smith, M. D. on April 17, 1942, at Central Presbyterian Church in Clayton, Missouri. They were married by the Revered Dr. Benjamin Franklin Hall.

To this union were born Garland Frederick (Fred) Jr. on February 4, 1944, at St. Patrick's Hospital, Lake Charles, Louisiana; Hazel Christine on December 4, 1944, at St. Luke's Hospital; Stephen Thomas on November 17, 1946, at DePaul Hospital; Bruce Beaumont on June 30, 1951, at St. Luke's Hospital; and Elizabeth Ellen on September 22, 1954, at St. John's Hospital. All were born in St. Louis except Fred.

Hazel was a member of Central Presbyterian Church in Clayton loved to garden, collect antiques and do volunteer work. She was active in many organizations and clubs including the National Society of the Daughters of the American Revolution (DAR) national number 658345; President of St. Louis Presbytery, 1967-68; Southeast Missouri Presbytery, 1970-71; St. John's Mercy Women's Auxiliary, 1969-71; 9th District of Church Women United, 1973-75 and Central Branch of the American Cancer Society, 1975-76. Hazel also received Honorary Life Membership Awards from Central Presbyterian Women of the Church, 1967; Clayton Garden Club Group I, 1973 and St. John's Mercy Medical Center Auxiliary, 1971. She received Auxilian of the Year Award for St. John's Mercy Auxiliary in 1975 and State Auxiliary Woman of the Year Award for the Missouri Hospital Association in 1975. She also was the recipient of the Mercy Award given by St. John's Mercy Medical Center in 1980.

In October of 1978 Hazel was diagnosed with cancer and had a radical mastectomy followed by chemotherapy treatments. Later the disease spread to the lymphatic area and she passed away on Wednesday, April 21, 1982, at St. John's Mercy Medical Center in Creve Coeur at the age of 63 years, 6 months and 8 days. The cause of death was listed as metastatic cancer of the breast. A funeral service was conducted on Friday, April 23, at the Lupton Chapel, and burial was at Oak Hill Cemetery, Kirkwood, Missouri. The Reverend Dr. Andrew Jumper and Reverend Donald M. Megahan officiated.

Hazel is survived by her husband, Garland F. Smith, M.D.; three sons, Garland F. (Fred) (Karen) Jr. of Florissant, Stephen Thomas (Karen) of Westwood, N.J. and Bruce Beaumont (Ruth) of Annapolis, MD; two daughters, Hazel Christine Smith (Jacques) McCormack of Katonah, NY and Elizabeth Ellen Smith of Chicago; one sister, Gladys Straube Myers of Columbia, MO and one brother, Scott Straube, Sr. of Bowling Green, MO; and two grandchildren, Christiane Elizabeth Smith of Florissant and John Garland McCormack of Katonah, NY.

+ 92 m VI. **Everett James Straube Jr.** was born in New Hartford, Pike County, Missouri, on April 13, 1920. He died in Louisiana, Pike County, Missouri, on November 19, 1972, at the age of 52. His cause of death was cerebral anoxia, carcinoma of stomach & esophagus. He was buried in Memorial Gardens Cemetery, Bowling Green, Pike County, Missouri, on November 21, 1972 (Find a Grave ID 68398423).

Everett James Straube Jr. was born on April 13, 1920, in Hartford Township of Pike County, Missouri. He was named after his father, Everett James Straube, and was fondly called by his initials, E.J. He attended the rural Pike County school of Vannoy through the eighth grade. E.J. graduated from Bowling Green High School in 1938. During high school there was no baseball team, but E.J. was on the basketball team and a charter member of the FFA (Future Farmers of America).

After graduation, E.J. was employed at Harbison-Walker Brick Plant in Vandalia, Missouri and after his discharge from service in the war; he worked at the Elder Garment Factory in Bowling Green and then worked for Hercules, Inc. in Louisiana, Missouri.

E.J. had a passion for baseball, both as a player and as a spectator. He had a strong throwing arm and once threw a baseball over the old Bowling Green water tower off the square. This was witnessed by several of the older townsmen and a good friend. He was a member of the Farmer baseball team and also played on the Bowling Green team. In the spring of 1941, E.J. tried out with the St. Louis Cardinals at the old Sportsman's Park. E.J. was privileged to be accepted and was with the Cardinals' minor league club in Albany, Georgia, that summer. At that time the minor league teams were referred to as "Farm Clubs." E.J. played centerfield, batted left and threw right.

It was also in 1941 that E.J. met his future wife, Lil. E.J.'s brother, Scott, was dating Ann, and they were going to a party given for Ike and Shirley Straube, and decided to invite Ann's sister, Lil. Even though Lil had plans with other friends, she changed her plans and accepted the invitation. It was not love at first sight for E.J. and Lil, but they dated that summer and over the course of six years it developed into a lasting romance.

E.J.'s call to military service dashed his hopes of being able to continue his baseball career. E.J. was inducted into the United States Army at Jefferson Barracks, St. Louis, Missouri, on December 3, 1941. He had been told to contact the club after his tour of duty. However, while stationed at Camp Campbell, Kentucky, E.J. was seriously injured on January 16, l942, by a fall on a footlocker resulting in the loss of his right kidney. His surgery was uncommon then and life expectancy was considered to be five years. After serving in the Army for four years and being injured, E.J. knew his opportunity to play professional ball was over. While on military bases though, E.J. made the base teams. Once he was playing against Lon Warneke's team. (Lon was a famous professional pitcher with the Cubs/Cardinals in the '30s and '40s. The younger generation should note that even major league players were drafted into service during the war.) As the story goes, E.J. was the only player to get a piece of the ball off Lon. E.J.'s daughter, Annice, recalls the story as E.J. flying out to center field. His son, Chris, recalls the story as E.J. getting a double.

In recent years, Coach Cotton Fitzsimmons of the Phoenix Suns basketball team was speaking at the local alumni banquet. He knew E.J. and Lil from ball team years and commented to Lil and Annice, "I have never seen a better centerfielder than E.J." Even Scott told Chris and Willis that their dad was a good player. Coming from Uncle Scott, who knew his baseball, they knew that was a big compliment. But E.J. was not the only talented family player. Scott and Ike, as well as the Willis cousins Bill, J. E., Dalton, Gene, Don and Jr., were all part of the well-respected Farmer ball team that Uncle Buford Willis coached. E.J. himself said that Ike was one of the smartest baseball men he knew. But despite being an avid baseball fan and for a short period, a farm team player, E.J. never complained about being called to serve his country. During his military career he was stationed at bases in Kentucky, Texas, West Virginia and Staten Island, New York. Annice recalls a story her dad told of seeing soldiers get off ships, and who were crying, and who got down and kissed the ground when they returned home to America.

On a historical note, the base in White Sulphur Springs, West Virginia, where E.J. was stationed, was located on a famous resort property where people came to "take the waters" to restore their health. It was called the Old White Hotel and later became known as The Greenbrier. During World War II, the Greenbrier was put to two different uses by the U. S. government. The State Department leased the hotel and used it to intern over 800 German, Japanese and Italian diplomatic personnel along with their families, until they could be exchanged for American diplomats stranded overseas. In the fall of 1942, the government purchased the Greenbrier and converted it into the 2,000-bed Ashford General Hospital. The government acquired the property because the Army believed new hospitals could not be built fast enough for future casualties. Over 24,000 soldiers were treated here in four years, and the hospital soon was referred to by journalists and many others as a "Shangri-La" for the sick and wounded. Six months after the hospital opened, the Army opened a 165-acre POW camp that had been constructed there.

The first Italian POWs, captured in Tunisia, were later replaced by German POWs who remained until May 1946. It was at this Army base that E.J. met and made friends with both the Italian and German prisoners. In fact, a POW made a large sketch of Georganna for E.J., which hung at Gladys' and which is now in Georganna's home. Lil saw The Greenbrier when she visited E.J. in 1944 at his base in White Sulphur Springs. Grandma Straube and Aunt Gladys also visited E.J. at this time, but Lil does not recall if they also visited the Greenbrier. After the war the Greenbrier, with its reputation as the Army's most beautiful hospital, was repurchased by the Chesapeake and Ohio Railway. It then once again became a resort.

While E.J. was home on leave in October of 1944 from Camp Barkeley, Texas, Hazel wrote that he, Lil, Scott and Ann attended the World Series game when the St. Louis Cardinals played the St. Louis Browns. Also, Gladys hosted a party for E.J. with friends and neighbors; they played party games and danced in the room where the store was. Hazel also wrote that E.J. surprised his parents on July 2, 1945, when he showed up at the front door for 12 days of leave. At that time, E.J. was a Tech. Sergeant and worked in the Payroll Department at Halloran General Hospital on Staten Island, New York.

Lil tells of another World Series game that she, E.J. and Scott attended. It was the seventh and deciding game of the 1946 World Series with the Boston Red Sox at old Sportsman's Park. Followers of baseball will remember that Enos Slaughter scored from first base on Harry Walker's game-winning single to left field when Red Sox shortstop Johnny Pesky took the throw from George Metkovich, but hesitated on the relay to home plate. In August 1971, E.J. and Lil attended the game at Busch Stadium when the Boston Red Sox and Cardinals held a 25th Anniversary reunion of the 1946 World Series teams. Players reunited for old timers' game and re-enactment of the eighth inning play from the '46 Series seventh game. The replay of that decisive '46 moment followed a two-inning game of the two teams. A regular game of the Cardinals vs. the Dodgers followed.

E.J.'s last assignment was with the Medical Detachment Halloran General Hospital, Staten Island, New York. He was honorably discharged December 20, 1945, having attained the rank of Master Sergeant, also that of Administrative NCO serving as Sergeant Major supervising personnel, civilian and enlisted men in the personnel department of the hospital.

Summers in Farmer were spent playing a lot of baseball. Games were played on Sunday afternoon but many of the boys gathered at the Farmer Store prior to the game, and usually during the morning. One warm sunny spring day, prior to the game, Gladys and Lil mentioned they were going to hunt mushrooms. The boys discouraged them, saying they had hunted everywhere and found none. That did not daunt Gladys and Lil and they went anyway. They did find "lots" and "lots" but as a straw pile was nearby they stuffed some straw in their gunny sacks and put the mushrooms on top to make the find even more impressive. Upon returning to the Store and showing the boys their harvest, the boys could hardly believe their eyes as to how many mushrooms they found!

On September 27, 1947, E.J. and Lil were married by Reverend G. O. Baxter of the Second Baptist Church at the parsonage at 215 West Locust in Bowling Green. Lillie (Lil) Mae Dieckmann was born April 1, 1925, near Silex in Lincoln County, Missouri, the youngest child of John Henry and Annie Neumann Dieckmann. To this union were born Annice Mae on December 18, 1947, Chris James on August 2, 1949, Stanley Willis on May 26, 1951, and Lucy Lynn on February 21, 1953.

Both E.J. and Lil were members of the Second Baptist Church of Bowling Green. E.J. was a deacon and Lil a Sunday school teacher of young children for many years. E.J. and Lil both loved gardening, Khoury League (E.J. helped at games when he was not working) and Cardinal games. Since the early '40s till E.J. passed away, he and Lil attended almost every World Series in St. Louis for at least one game. They also attended the 1959 World Series in Chicago when the White Sox faced the Los Angeles Dodgers. Lil was a Khoury League scorekeeper, and she was active in PTA. Later Lil was a member of the Cancer Society and the American Legion Auxiliary, and she is a member of the Association of Retired Missouri State Employees. She still enjoys her garden and still enjoys cooking. E.J. and Lil purchased the home at 1105 West Centennial in Bowling Green on June 20, 1967, following the death of Grandma Straube. This is the home where they lived years earlier and where their children were all born. It is also the last home of grandpa and grandma (Everett and Mary Anna) before they went to Uncle Scott and Aunt Ann's boarding home.

Having been diagnosed with cancer of the esophagus and stomach in 1971, E.J. retired from Hercules, Inc., Louisiana, Missouri, on April 1, 1972 completing 17 years of service. After a long battle with the disease, E.J. passed away at Pike County Memorial Hospital at 5:25 A.M. on Sunday, November 19, 1972 at the age of 52 years, 7 months and 6 days. Services were at the Second Baptist Church on November 21. The Rev. G. E. Rittenhouse, a special family friend of many years, officiated. Burial was at Memorial Gardens in Bowling Green, Missouri. Pallbearers were nephews: Ted Mummert, Duane Straube, Scott Straube Jr., Fred Smith, David Straube and Sam Hargadine IV.

Family of Luther Straube and Rosa Lewis

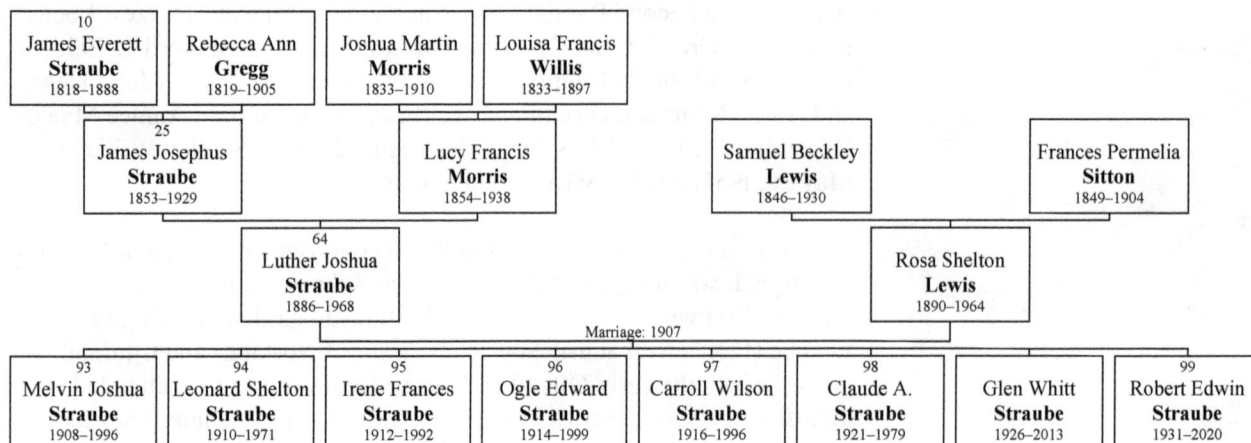

10 James Everett **Straube** 1818–1888	Rebecca Ann **Gregg** 1819–1905	Joshua Martin **Morris** 1833–1910	Louisa Francis **Willis** 1833–1897	

25 James Josephus **Straube** 1853–1929	Lucy Francis **Morris** 1854–1938	Samuel Beckley **Lewis** 1846–1930	Frances Permelia **Sitton** 1849–1904

64 Luther Joshua **Straube** 1886–1968	Rosa Shelton **Lewis** 1890–1964

Marriage: 1907

93 Melvin Joshua **Straube** 1908–1996	**94** Leonard Shelton **Straube** 1910–1971	**95** Irene Frances **Straube** 1912–1992	**96** Ogle Edward **Straube** 1914–1999	**97** Carroll Wilson **Straube** 1916–1996	**98** Claude A. **Straube** 1921–1979	**99** Glen Whitt **Straube** 1926–2013	Robert Edwin **Straube** 1931–2020

64. **Luther Joshua Straube** was born on Sunday, June 20, 1886, in New Hartford, Pike County, Missouri. He was the son of James Josephus Straube (25) and Lucy Francis Morris.

Luther Joshua died in Bowling Green, Pike County, Missouri, on December 14, 1968, at the age of 82. He was buried in Siloam Primitive Baptist Church Cemetery, Ashley, Pike County, Missouri, on December 17, 1968 (Find a Grave ID 69533077).

> Luther Joshua Straube was born near New Hartford, Missouri, on June 20, 1886. He is the son and 6th child of James Josephus Straube and Lucy Francis Morris.
>
> Luther's siblings are as follows and are on this site: Olie # 70940272, Anliza # 70941478, Ada May # 69238769, Bertha Lee # 69240088, Everett James # 68075841, Luther Joshua # 69533077, Grover Melvin # 70964070 and Lenard Sherman # 70964138.
>
> Luther married Rosa Shelton Lewis on December 1, 1907. To this union were born Melvin Joshua, Leonard Shelton, Irene Frances, Ogle Edward "Tutor," Carroll Wilson, Claude A., Glen Whitt and Bobby Edwin.

At the age of 21, Luther Joshua married **Rosa Shelton Lewis** on Sunday, December 01, 1907, when she was 17 years old. They had eight children.

Rosa Shelton was born in Missouri, USA, on Tuesday, January 07, 1890. She was the daughter of Samuel Beckley Lewis and Frances Permelia Sitton. She was also known as **Rosie**.

Rosa Shelton reached 74 years of age and died in Missouri, USA, on December 21, 1964. She was buried in Siloam Primitive Baptist Church Cemetery, Ashley, Pike County, Missouri (Find a Grave ID 69533612).

Children of Luther Joshua Straube and Rosa Shelton Lewis:

+ 93 m I. **Melvin Joshua Straube** was born in Gazette, Pike County, Missouri, on August 16, 1908. He was also known as **Pete**.

Melvin Joshua died in Vandalia, Audrain County, Missouri, on May 11, 1996, at the age of 87. He was buried in Fairmount Cemetery, Middletown, Montgomery County, Missouri (Find a Grave ID 84828021).

+ 94 m II. **Leonard Shelton Straube** was born in Pike County, Missouri, on February 11, 1910. He died in Fontana, San Bernardino County, California, on May 26, 1971, at the age of 61. Leonard Shelton was buried in Green Acres Memorial Park and Mortuary, Bloomington, San Bernardino County, California (Find a Grave ID 157391748).

+ 95 f III. **Irene Frances Straube** was born in Bowling Green, Pike County, Missouri, on March 26, 1912. She died in New Florence, Montgomery County, Missouri, on December 28, 1992, at the age of 80. Irene Frances was buried in Midway Cemetery, Montgomery County, Missouri (Find a Grave ID 49088094).

+ 96 m IV. **Ogle Edward Straube** was born in Gazette, Pike County, Missouri, on November 16, 1914. He was also known as **Tutor**.

Ogle Edward died in Montgomery City, Montgomery County, Missouri, on January 09, 1999, at the age of 84. He was buried in Bellflower Cemetery, Bellflower, Montgomery County, Missouri (Find a Grave ID 22785453).

On Dec 28, 1940 in New London, MO Ogle Edward "Tutor" Straube married Evelyn Begeman, the daughter of Hobart Lawrence Begeman, who is also buried in Bellflower Cemetery, and Floy Mae Woodson. Evelyn and Tutor were 5th cousins once removed.

The "Begemanns" immigrated from Germany in the late 1880s. They dropped the last N off their name in the late 1800s.

Gravesite Details:
Tutor was born in 1914 not 1913 as inscribed on monument.

+ 97 m V. **Carroll Wilson Straube** was born in Pike County, Missouri, on November 19, 1916.[62] He was also known as **Skeet**.

Carroll Wilson died in Wright City, Warren County, Missouri, on March 30, 1996, at the age of 79.[62] He was buried in Wright City Cemetery, Wright City, Warren County, Missouri (Find a Grave ID 101227293).[62]

---

62   Ancestry.com, Public Member Trees (Provo, UT, USA, Ancestry.com Operations, Inc., 2006), Ancestry.com, Record for Carroll Wilson "Skeet" Straube. https://search.ancestry.co.uk/cgi-bin/sse.dll?db=1030&h=392148224688&indiv=try.

+	98	m	VI.	**Claude A. Straube** was born in Missouri, USA, on December 08, 1921. He died in Montgomery County, Missouri, on March 09, 1979, at the age of 57. Claude A. was buried in Fairmount Cemetery, Middletown, Montgomery County, Missouri (Find a Grave ID 75961298).
		m	VII.	**Glen Whitt Straube** was born in Bellflower, Montgomery County, Missouri, on September 21, 1926. He died in Prescott, Yavapai County, Arizona, on November 18, 2013, at the age of 87. Glen Whitt's burial details are unknown (Find a Grave ID 233237531).
+	99	m	VIII.	**Robert Edwin Straube** was born in Missouri, USA, on December 05, 1931. He was also known as **Bobby**.

Robert Edwin died in Port Charlotte, Charlotte County, Florida, on June 26, 2020, at the age of 88. He was cremated.

Family of Arthur Straube and Elsie Miller

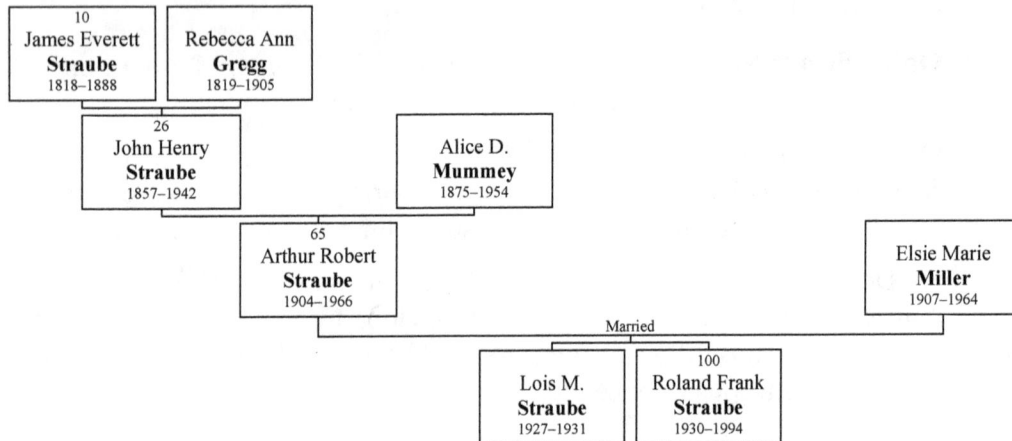

65.   **Arthur Robert Straube** was born on Wednesday, July 20, 1904, in Barry, Pike County, Illinois. He was the son of John Henry Straube (26) and Alice D. Mummey.

Arthur Robert died in Harvey, Cook County, Illinois, on October 03, 1966, at the age of 62. He was buried in Homewood Memorial Gardens, Homewood, Cook County, Illinois (Find a Grave ID 197513801).

He married **Elsie Marie Miller**. They had two children.

Elsie Marie was born in Harvey, Cook County, Illinois, on Saturday, March 02, 1907. She reached 56 years of age and died in Cook County, Illinois, on January 21, 1964. Elsie Marie was buried in Homewood Memorial Gardens, Homewood, Cook County, Illinois (Find a Grave ID 197514019).

Children of Arthur Robert Straube and Elsie Marie Miller:

      f   I.   **Lois M. Straube** was born in 1927. She died in 1931 at the age of 4. Lois M. was buried in Homewood Memorial Gardens, Homewood, Cook County, Illinois (Find a Grave ID 220097313).

+ 100   m   II. **Roland Frank Straube** was born in Harvey, Cook County, Illinois, on July 21, 1930. He died in Indianapolis, Marion County, Indiana, on September 07, 1994, at the age of 64. Roland Frank was buried in New Crown Cemetery and Mausoleum, Indianapolis, Marion County, Indiana (Find a Grave ID 197514294).

Family of Altha Straube and Frank Duncan

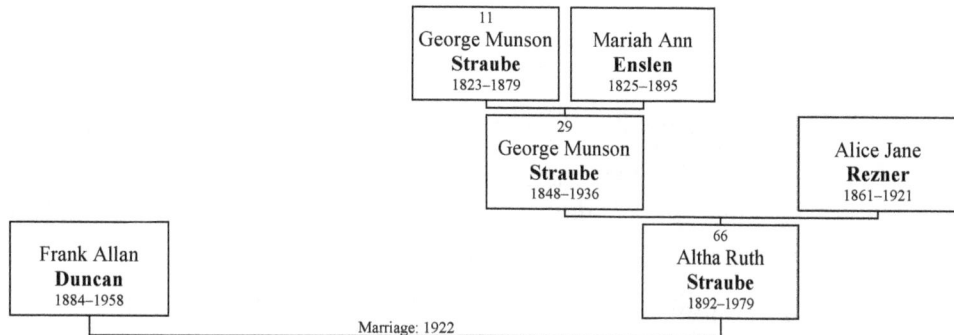

66.   **Altha Ruth Straube** was born on Wednesday, November 02, 1892, in Wellsville, Montgomery County, Missouri.[63] She was the daughter of George Munson Straube (29) and Alice Jane Rezner.

Altha Ruth died in Grand Haven, Ottawa County, Michigan, on August 15, 1979, at the age of 86.[63] She was buried in Saint Joseph Valley Memorial Park, Mishawaka, St. Joseph County, Indiana (Find a Grave ID 54901512).[63]

Altha Ruth married **Frank Allan Duncan** in 1922. Frank Allan was born in Saint Paul, Ramsey County, Minnesota, on Tuesday, March 11, 1884.

He reached 74 years of age and died in South Bend, St. Joseph County, Indiana, on July 26, 1958. His cause of death was coronary thrombosis. He was buried on July 28, 1958, in Saint Joseph Valley Memorial Park, Mishawaka, St. Joseph County, Indiana (Find a Grave ID 54901129).

---

63   Ancestry.com, Public Member Trees (Provo, UT, USA, Ancestry.com Operations, Inc., 2006), Ancestry.com, Record for Altha Ruth Straube. https://search.ancestry.co.uk/cgi-bin/sse.dll?db=1030&h=40424591245&indiv=try.

Family of Izola Straube and Raymond Alvey

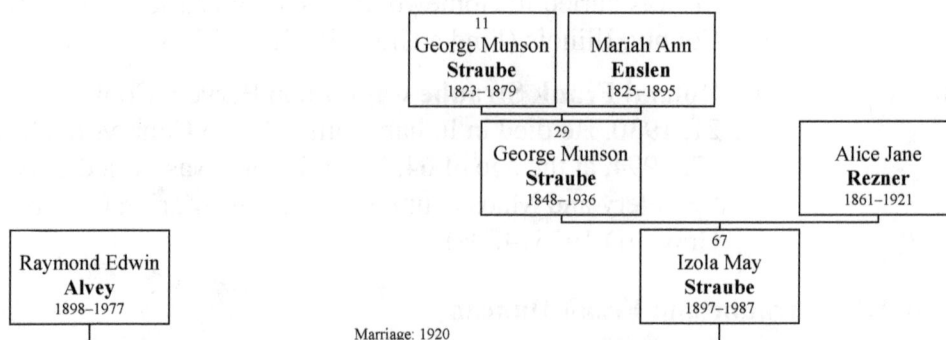

```
                              ┌──────────────┬──────────────┐
                              │      11      │              │
                              │George Munson │  Mariah Ann  │
                              │   Straube    │    Enslen    │
                              │  1823–1879   │  1825–1895   │
                              └──────────────┴──────────────┘
                                     ┌──────────────┐              ┌──────────────┐
                                     │      29      │              │              │
                                     │George Munson │              │  Alice Jane  │
                                     │   Straube    │              │    Rezner    │
                                     │  1848–1936   │              │  1861–1921   │
                                     └──────────────┘              └──────────────┘
       ┌──────────────┐                            ┌──────────────┐
       │              │                            │      67      │
       │Raymond Edwin │                            │  Izola May   │
       │    Alvey     │                            │   Straube    │
       │  1898–1977   │                            │  1897–1987   │
       └──────────────┘                            └──────────────┘
                        Marriage: 1920
```

67. **Izola May Straube** was born on Wednesday, May 12, 1897, in Missouri, USA.[64–69] She was the daughter of George Munson Straube (29) and Alice Jane Rezner.

Izola May died on June 25, 1987, at the age of 90.[66] Her burial details are unknown.

At the age of 22, Izola May married **Raymond Edwin Alvey** on Monday, April 12, 1920, in Saint Louis, Saint Louis County, Missouri, when he was 21 years old. Raymond Edwin was born in Sangamon County, Illinois, on Sunday, April 24, 1898.

He served in the military. U.S. Army, Corporal. Raymond Edwin reached 79 years of age and died in Memphis, Shelby County, Tennessee, on June 12, 1977. He was buried in Memphis National Cemetery, Memphis, Shelby County, Tennessee (Find a Grave ID 277835).

Raymond married several times and is buried with Inetha (last name unknown) who died in 1973.

64 FamilySearch.org, United States Census, 1940, FamilySearch, "United States Census, 1940", , <i>FamilySearch</i> (https://www.familysearch.org/ark:/61903/1:1:K7HN-43L : Tue Oct 03 09:55:28 UTC 2023), Entry for Emma L Brinkmann and I Zala Alvey, 1940.

65 FamilySearch.org, United States Census, 1930, FamilySearch, "United States Census, 1930", , <i>FamilySearch</i> (https://www.familysearch.org/ark:/61903/1:1:XHV6-2MM : Thu Oct 05 09:11:41 UTC 2023), Entry for Raymond Alvey and Izola Alvey, 1930.

66 FamilySearch.org, United States Social Security Death Index, FamilySearch, "United States Social Security Death Index," database, <i>FamilySearch</i> (https://familysearch.org/ark:/61903/1:1:JLPS-XY4 : 10 January 2021), Izola Alvey, Jun 1987; citing U.S. Social Security Administration, <i>Death Master File</i>, database (Alexandria, Virginia: National Technical Information Service, ongoing).

67 FamilySearch.org, United States Census, 1920, FamilySearch, "United States Census, 1920", , <i>FamilySearch</i> (https://www.familysearch.org/ark:/61903/1:1:M8CZ-8WH : Wed Oct 04 20:42:20 UTC 2023), Entry for T M Stroube and Alice Straube, 1920.

68 FamilySearch.org, United States Census, 1910, FamilySearch, "United States Census, 1910", , <i>FamilySearch</i> (https://www.familysearch.org/ark:/61903/1:1:M2B8-RGC : Thu Oct 05 19:55:14 UTC 2023), Entry for George M Straube and Alice J Straube, 1910.

69 FamilySearch.org, United States Census, 1900, FamilySearch, "United States Census, 1900", , <i>FamilySearch</i> (https://www.familysearch.org/ark:/61903/1:1:M3ZT-B7Q : Thu Oct 05 06:04:36 UTC 2023), Entry for Geo M Straube and Alice J Straube, 1900.

5th Generation

Family of Edna Dryden and Tracy Ferguson

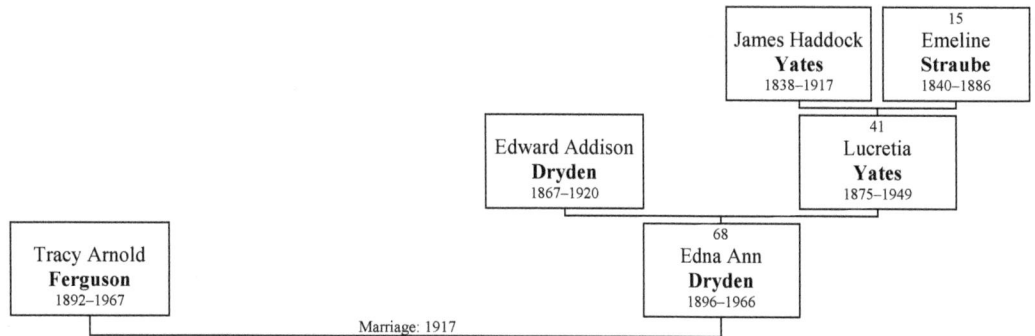

```
                                            ┌──────────────┐ ┌──────────────┐
                                            │ James Haddock│ │      15      │
                                            │    Yates     │ │   Emeline    │
                                            │  1838–1917   │ │   Straube    │
                                            │              │ │  1840–1886   │
                                            └──────────────┘ └──────────────┘
                              ┌──────────────┐ ┌──────────────┐
                              │Edward Addison│ │      41      │
                              │    Dryden    │ │   Lucretia   │
                              │  1867–1920   │ │    Yates     │
                              │              │ │  1875–1949   │
                              └──────────────┘ └──────────────┘
          ┌──────────────┐                   ┌──────────────┐
          │ Tracy Arnold │                   │      68      │
          │   Ferguson   │                   │   Edna Ann   │
          │  1892–1967   │                   │    Dryden    │
          │              │                   │  1896–1966   │
          └──────────────┘                   └──────────────┘
                              Marriage: 1917
```

68. **Edna Ann Dryden** was born on Sunday, October 11, 1896, in Winfield, Lincoln County, Missouri. She was the daughter of Edward Addison Dryden and Lucretia Yates (41).

Edna Ann died in Hannibal, Marion County, Missouri, on January 26, 1966, at the age of 69. She was buried in Mount Olivet Cemetery, Hannibal, Marion County, Missouri, on January 27, 1966 (Find a Grave ID 84028044).

At the age of 20, Edna Ann married **Tracy Arnold Ferguson** on Saturday, July 07, 1917, in Galesburg, Knox County, Illinois, when he was 25 years old. Tracy Arnold was born in Clarksville, Pike County, Missouri, on Friday, February 19, 1892.

He reached 75 years of age and died in Jefferson City, Cole County, Missouri, on December 04, 1967. Tracy Arnold was buried in Mount Olivet Cemetery, Hannibal, Marion County, Missouri (Find a Grave ID 152770331).

Family of Octavis Moore and Leona Chernault

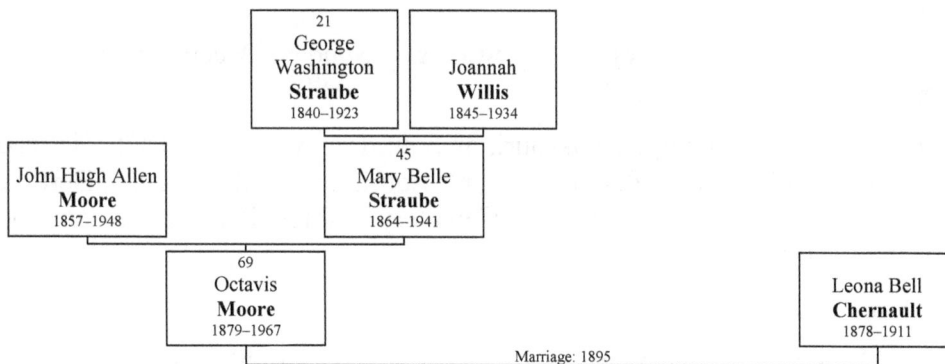

```
                        ┌──────────────┐ ┌──────────────┐
                        │      21      │ │              │
                        │    George    │ │   Joannah    │
                        │  Washington  │ │    Willis    │
                        │   Straube    │ │  1845–1934   │
                        │  1840–1923   │ │              │
                        └──────────────┘ └──────────────┘
          ┌──────────────┐ ┌──────────────┐
          │John Hugh Allen│ │     45       │
          │    Moore     │ │  Mary Belle  │
          │  1857–1948   │ │   Straube    │
          │              │ │  1864–1941   │
          └──────────────┘ └──────────────┘
          ┌──────────────┐                  ┌──────────────┐
          │      69      │                  │   Leona Bell │
          │   Octavis    │                  │   Chernault  │
          │    Moore     │                  │  1878–1911   │
          │  1879–1967   │                  │              │
          └──────────────┘                  └──────────────┘
                              Marriage: 1895
```

69. **Octavis Moore** was born on Saturday, July 12, 1879, in New Hartford, Pike County, Missouri. He was the son of John Hugh Allen Moore and Mary Belle Straube (45).

Octavis died in Chaplin, Saskatchewan, Canada, on November 04, 1967, at the age of 88. He was buried in Droxford Cemetery, Droxford, Moose Jaw Census Division, Saskatchewan, Canada (Find a Grave ID 21372903).

At the age of 16, Octavis married **Leona Bell Chernault** on Sunday, December 08, 1895, when she was 17 years old. Leona Bell was born in Pike County, Missouri, on Sunday, October 13, 1878.[70]

She reached 32 years of age and died in Pike County, Missouri, on March 22, 1911.[70] Leona Bell was buried on March 23, 1911, in Siloam Primitive Baptist Church Cemetery, Ashley, Pike County, Missouri (Find a Grave ID 83744451).[70]

Family of Audacia Moore and Bertie Stuart

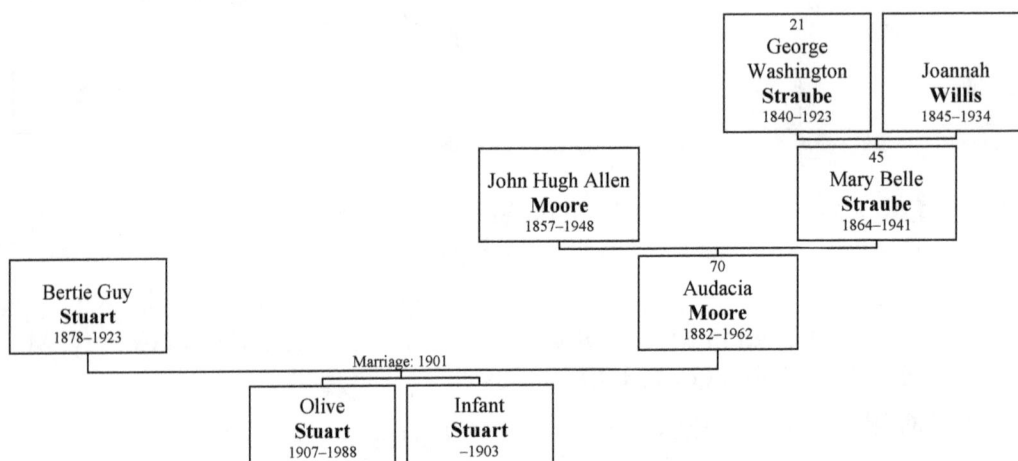

70. **Audacia Moore** was born on Monday, January 02, 1882, in New Hartford, Pike County, Missouri. She was the daughter of John Hugh Allen Moore and Mary Belle Straube (45). She was also known as **Audie**.

Audacia died in Louisiana, Pike County, Missouri, on May 05, 1962, at the age of 80. She was buried in Siloam Primitive Baptist Church Cemetery, Ashley, Pike County, Missouri (Find a Grave ID 83748464).

At the age of 19, Audacia married **Bertie Guy Stuart** on Sunday, December 01, 1901, when he was 23 years old. They had two children.

Bertie Guy was born in Bates County, Missouri, on Saturday, August 03, 1878. He reached 44 years of age and died in Ashley, Pike County, Missouri, on March 19, 1923. Bertie Guy was buried in Siloam Primitive Baptist Church Cemetery, Ashley, Pike County, Missouri (Find a Grave ID 83748625).

Children of Audacia Moore and Bertie Guy Stuart:

> f   I. **Olive Stuart** was born in New Hartford, Pike County, Missouri, on July 29, 1907. She died in Bowling Green, Pike County, Missouri, on May 17, 1988, at the age of 80. Olive was buried in Siloam Primitive Baptist Church Cemetery, Ashley, Pike County, Missouri (Find a Grave ID 83753246).

70   Ancestry.com, U.S., Find a Grave® Index, 1600s-Current (Lehi, UT, USA, Ancestry.com Operations, Inc., 2012), Ancestry.com, Record for Leona Bell Moore. https://search.ancestry.co.uk/cgi-bin/sse.dll?db=60525&h=55241096&indiv=try.

m   II. **Infant Stuart**. Infant died in Missouri, USA, on November 05, 1903. He was buried in Siloam Primitive Baptist Church Cemetery, Ashley, Pike County, Missouri (Find a Grave ID 83753112).

Family of Gilbert Moore and Anna Jeffries

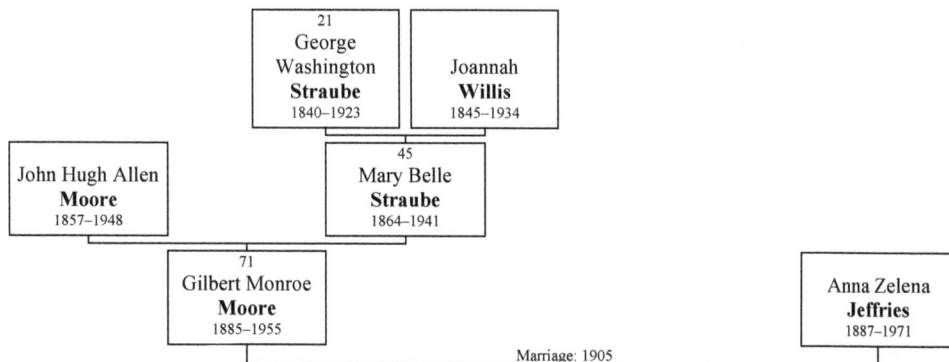

71.   **Gilbert Monroe Moore** was born on Tuesday, June 02, 1885, in New Hartford, Pike County, Missouri. He was the son of John Hugh Allen Moore and Mary Belle Straube (45).

Gilbert Monroe died in Hartford Township, Pike County, Missouri, on October 14, 1955, at the age of 70. He was buried in Bowling Green City Cemetery, Pike County, Missouri (Find a Grave ID 134950249).

At the age of 20, Gilbert Monroe married **Anna Zelena Jeffries** on Sunday, November 05, 1905, when she was 18 years old. Anna Zelena was born in Gazette, Pike County, Missouri, on Sunday, June 26, 1887. She was also known as **Lena**.

Anna Zelena reached 84 years of age and died in Bowling Green, Pike County, Missouri, on August 10, 1971. She was buried in Bowling Green City Cemetery, Pike County, Missouri (Find a Grave ID 141762735).

Family of Cecil Moore and Vera Flood

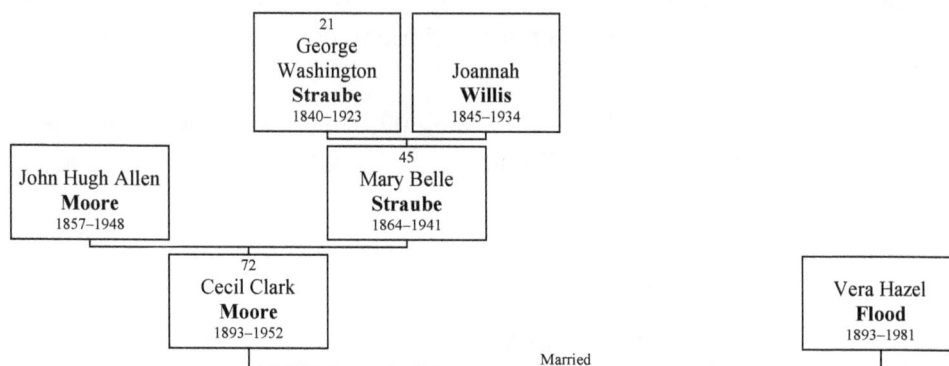

72.   **Cecil Clark Moore** was born on Saturday, August 05, 1893, in New Hartford, Pike County, Missouri. He was the son of John Hugh Allen Moore and Mary Belle Straube (45).

Cecil Clark died in Saskatchewan, Canada, on April 29, 1952, at the age of 58. He was buried in Droxford Cemetery, Droxford, Moose Jaw Census Division, Saskatchewan, Canada (Find a Grave ID 21400314).

He married **Vera Hazel Flood**. Vera Hazel was born in Missouri, USA, on Tuesday, January 24, 1893.

She reached 88 years of age and died in Chaplin, Moose Jaw Census Division, Saskatchewan, Canada, on July 07, 1981. Her cause of death was murdered in Canada. She was buried in Droxford Cemetery, Droxford, Moose Jaw Census Division, Saskatchewan, Canada (Find a Grave ID 21400349).

Daughter Marjorie Eileen Moore Turcott , born Feb 11, 1917, was the oldest child of Cecil and Vera Moore. She was murdered along with her mother, Vera , July 7, 1981. The murder occurred in Chaplin, Saskatchewan, Canada.

Family of Florence Straube and Herman Morris

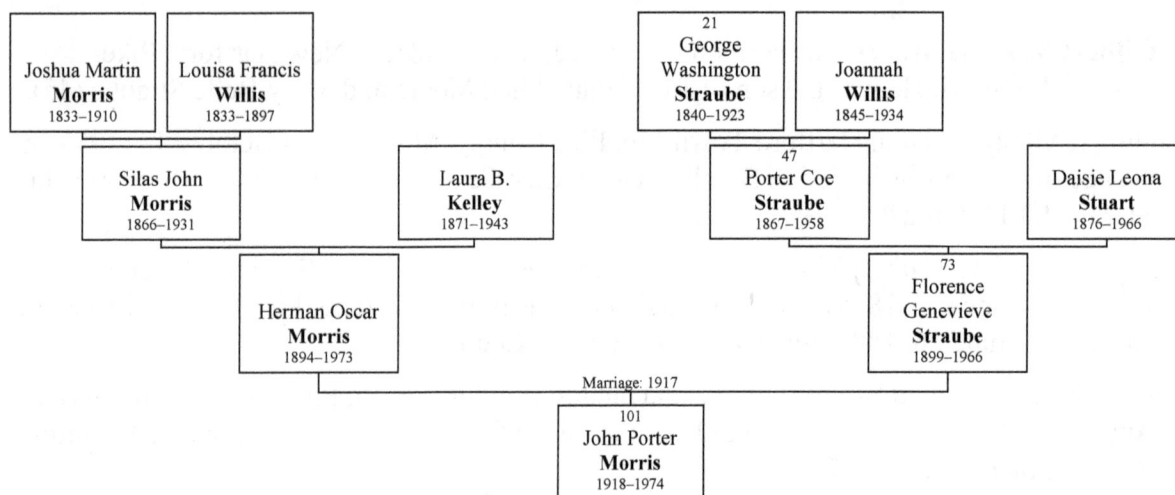

73.   **Florence Genevieve Straube** was born on Thursday, November 16, 1899, in Vandalia, Audrain County, Missouri. She was the daughter of Porter Coe Straube (47) and Daisie Leona Stuart.

Florence Genevieve died in Missouri, USA, on March 07, 1966, at the age of 66. She was buried in Siloam Primitive Baptist Church Cemetery, Ashley, Pike County, Missouri (Find a Grave ID 230052577).

At the age of 17, Florence Genevieve married **Herman Oscar Morris** on Sunday, June 03, 1917, when he was 23 years old. They had one son.

Herman Oscar was born in Pike County, Missouri, on Tuesday, May 15, 1894. He was the son of Silas John Morris and Laura B. Kelley.

Herman Oscar reached 78 years of age and died in Louisiana, Pike County, Missouri, on March 11, 1973. He was buried in Memorial Gardens Cemetery, Bowling Green, Pike County, Missouri (Find a Grave ID 216270222).

Son of Florence Genevieve Straube and Herman Oscar Morris:

+ 101   m   I. **John Porter Morris** was born in Pike County, Missouri, on May 29, 1918. He died in Mexico, Audrain County, Missouri, on January 30, 1974, at the age of 55. John Porter was buried in New Harmony Cemetery, Pike County, Missouri (Find a Grave ID 57890124).

Family of Grace Straube and Delbert Thompson

```
                        ┌──────────────┬──────────────┐
                        │      21      │              │
                        │    George    │              │
                        │  Washington  │   Joannah    │
                        │   Straube    │    Willis     │
                        │  1840–1923   │  1845–1934   │
                        └──────────────┴──────────────┘
                              ┌──────────────┐                ┌──────────────┐
                              │      47      │                │ Daisie Leona │
                              │  Porter Coe  │                │    Stuart    │
                              │   Straube    │                │  1876–1966   │
                              │  1867–1958   │                └──────────────┘
                              └──────────────┘
  ┌──────────────┐                         ┌──────────────┐
  │   Delbert    │                         │      74      │
  │   Thompson   │                         │    Grace     │
  │  1898–1975   │                         │   Straube    │
  └──────────────┘                         │  1902–1995   │
              Marriage: 1922               └──────────────┘
              ┌──────────────┬──────────────┐
              │Delbert Osborn│Charles Porter│
              │   Thompson   │   Thompson   │
              │  1923–2013   │  1925–2005   │
              └──────────────┴──────────────┘
```

74.   **Grace Straube** was born on Wednesday, April 02, 1902, in Farmer, Pike County, Missouri. She was the daughter of Porter Coe Straube (47) and Daisie Leona Stuart.

Grace died in Norwalk, Los Angeles County, California, on July 08, 1995, at the age of 93. She was buried in Park Lawn Memorial Park, Commerce, Los Angeles County, California (Find a Grave ID 184711343).

At the age of 20, Grace married **Delbert Thompson** on Saturday, August 12, 1922, when he was 24 years old. They had two sons.

Delbert was born in Marling, Montgomery County, Missouri, on Friday, May 20, 1898. He was also known as **Dutch**.

Delbert reached 76 years of age and died in Los Angeles County, California, on April 02, 1975. He was buried in Park Lawn Memorial Park, Commerce, Los Angeles County, California (Find a Grave ID 184995020).

Sons of Grace Straube and Delbert Thompson:

   m   I. **Delbert Osborn Thompson** was born on November 19, 1923. He was also known as **Jake**.

        Delbert Osborn died in March 2013 at the age of 89. His burial details are unknown (Find a Grave ID 232178965).

   m   II. **Charles Porter Thompson** was born on July 31, 1925. He died on May 30, 2005, at the age of 79. His burial details are unknown (Find a Grave ID 232178819).

Erma Straube

75. **Erma Straube** was born on Monday, April 30, 1906, in Pike County, Missouri.[71] She was the daughter of Porter Coe Straube (47) and Daisie Leona Stuart.

Erma died in Bowling Green, Pike County, Missouri, on August 15, 2000, at the age of 94.[71] She was buried in Curryville City Cemetery, Curryville, Pike County, Missouri (Find a Grave ID 100038977).[71]

Marriages with Raymond Paul Krigbaum and Orlan B. Kilby (Page 127) are known.

Family of Erma Straube and Raymond Krigbaum

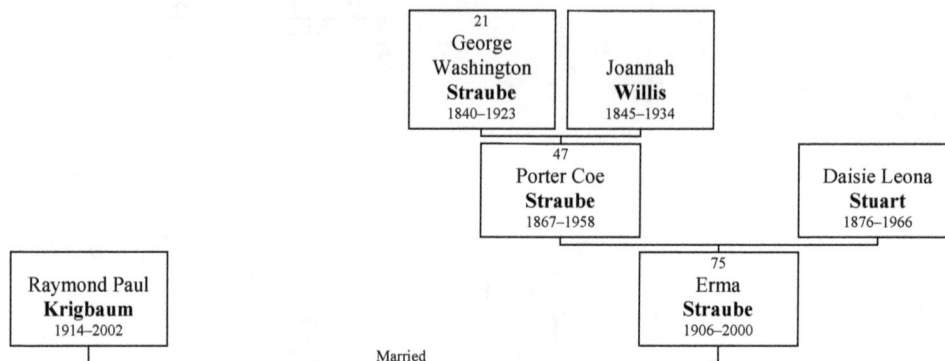

Here are the details about **Erma Straube's** first marriage, with Raymond Paul Krigbaum. You can read more about Erma on page 126.

Erma Straube married **Raymond Paul Krigbaum**. Raymond Paul was born on Friday, December 04, 1914.

He reached 87 years of age and died on June 11, 2002. Raymond Paul was buried in Curryville City Cemetery, Curryville, Pike County, Missouri (Find a Grave ID 19183146).

Family of Erma Straube and Orlan Kilby

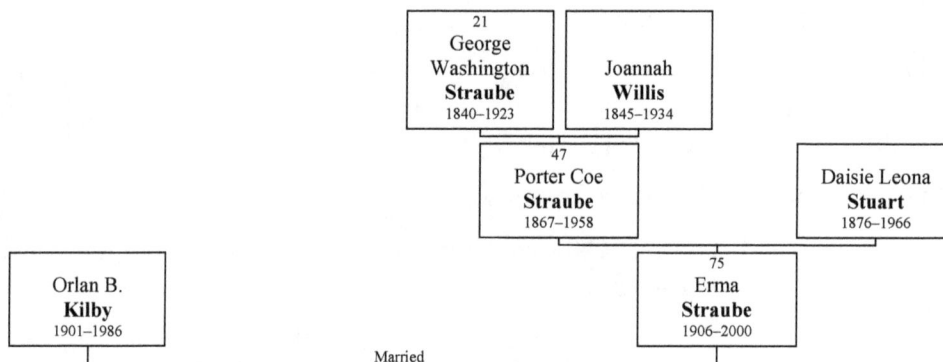

Here are the details about **Erma Straube's** second marriage, with Orlan B. Kilby. You can read more about Erma on page 126.

71 Ancestry.com, Public Member Trees (Provo, UT, USA, Ancestry.com Operations, Inc., 2006), Ancestry.com, Record for Erma L Straube. https://search.ancestry.co.uk/cgi-bin/sse.dll?db=1030&h=30514359916&indiv=try.

Erma Straube married **Orlan B. Kilby**. Orlan B. was born in Curryville, Pike County, Missouri, on Saturday, April 20, 1901.

He served in the U.S. Army during WWI. Orlan B. reached 84 years of age and died in California, USA, on February 07, 1986. He was buried in Kilby Cemetery, Curryville, Pike County, Missouri (Find a Grave ID 210196579).

Helen Straube

76.   **Helen Sue Straube** was born on Thursday, February 16, 1911, in Farmer, Pike County, Missouri. She was the daughter of Porter Coe Straube (47) and Daisie Leona Stuart.

Helen Sue died in Louisiana, Pike County, Missouri, on January 05, 1998, at the age of 86. She was buried in Curryville City Cemetery, Curryville, Pike County, Missouri (Find a Grave ID 125315606).

Marriages with Leslie Ray Henderson and Mason O Ogden (Page 129) are known.

Family of Helen Straube and Leslie Henderson

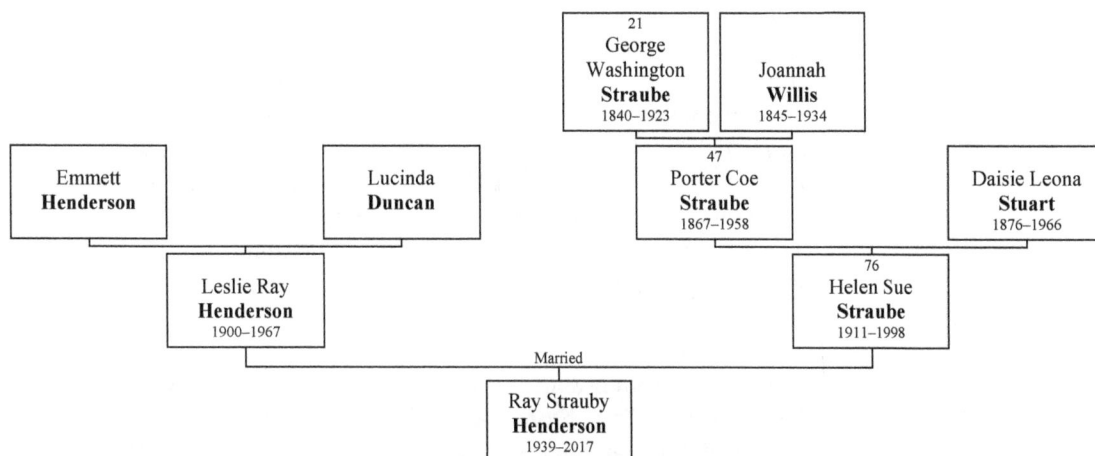

Here are the details about **Helen Sue Straube's** first marriage, with Leslie Ray Henderson. You can read more about Helen Sue on page 127.

Helen Sue Straube married **Leslie Ray Henderson**. They had one son.

Leslie Ray was born in Pike County, Missouri, on Wednesday, August 29, 1900. He was the son of Emmett Henderson and Lucinda Duncan. He was also known as **Les**.

Leslie Ray reached 67 years of age and died at St. Mary's Hospital in Richmond Heights, St. Louis County, Missouri, on November 30, 1967. He was buried on December 01, 1967, in Curryville City Cemetery, Curryville, Pike County, Missouri (Find a Grave ID 125315524).

Son of Helen Sue Straube and Leslie Ray Henderson:

m   I. **Ray Strauby Henderson** was born in Farmer, Pike County, Missouri, on February 02, 1939. He died in Grayson, Gwinnett County, Georgia, on February 23, 2017, at the age of 78. Ray Strauby was cremated- (Find a Grave ID 176856693).

Ray Strauby Henderson, 78, went home to be with Jesus on Thursday, February 23, 2017. Ray was born on February 2, 1939, in Farmer, MO, to Leslie Ray Henderson and Helen Sue Strauby Henderson. Ray was a loving and caring brother, husband, father, and grandfather who routinely placed the needs of others above the needs of his own. As Christ came to this world to serve and not be served, Ray followed this example to the fullest.

He began his education at Vannoy Country School, and attended high school at Bowling Green High School in Bowling Green, MO. He earned his B.S. at the University of Missouri, and his Masters at Webster College in St. Louis. His teaching career as a band director started in 1960 and spanned 37 years at 10 different high schools and one college. He attended Concord Country Church and remained active in many more churches serving as a music & youth minister and choir director. Later in his career, he also wrote music theory curriculum for Florida Baptist Seminary. Outside of work, he enjoyed fishing, hunting, and target practice. But his greatest joy was going to auctions and restoring antiques.

Survivors include wife of 56 1/2 years, Elizabeth Ann Pritchett Henderson; son, Kevin Henderson and daughter-in-law Bridgett and son, Seth of Colombia, MO; daughter, Crystal Elmore and son-in-law, Ed, of Tampa, FL; daughter, Kimberly Mayfield and son-in-law, Tom, and their son, Mitchell and daughter, Morgan of Grayson, GA., and niece Eldonna Steers Chestnut of Gardner, KS. Ray is preceded in death by his sister and brother-in-law, Betty & Eldon Steers and their son, John Leslie.

Visitation is from 6-8pm on Saturday, February 25, at Eternal Hills Funeral Home, 3594 Stone Mountain Hwy., Snellville, Ga. Funeral services will be held in the Chapel of Eternal Hills Funeral Home on Sunday, February 26, at 3pm with Pastor Doug Cox of Grace Fellowship Church officiating.

Family of Helen Straube and Mason Ogden

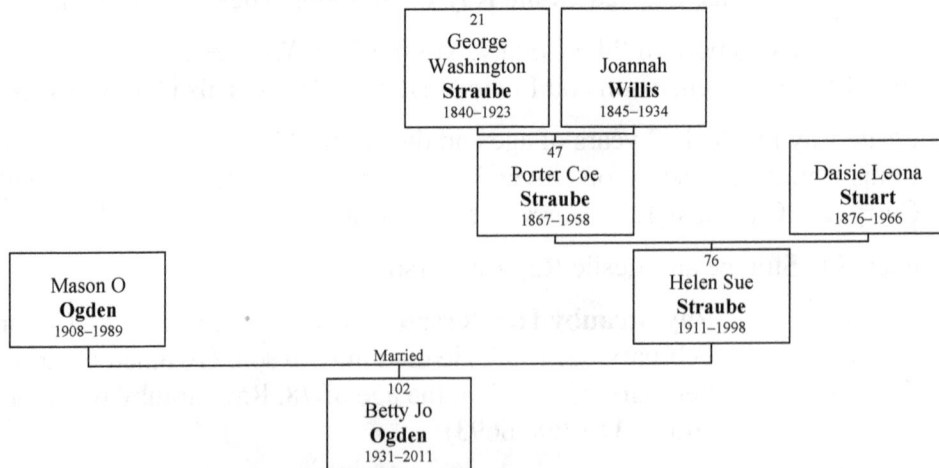

Here are the details about **Helen Sue Straube's** second marriage, with Mason O Ogden. You can read more about Helen Sue on page 127.

Helen Sue Straube married **Mason O Ogden**. They had one daughter.

Mason O was born in Bowling Green, Pike County, Missouri, on Wednesday, August 12, 1908. He reached 80 years of age and died in Louisiana, Pike County, Missouri, on January 21, 1989. Mason O was buried in Bowling Green City Cemetery, Pike County, Missouri (Find a Grave ID 180061481).

Daughter of Helen Sue Straube and Mason O Ogden:

+ 102   f   I. **Betty Jo Ogden** was born in Bowling Green, Pike County, Missouri, on January 07, 1931. She died in Olathe, Johnson County, Kansas, on October 09, 2011, at the age of 80. Betty Jo was buried in Louisiana Memorial Gardens, Louisiana, Pike County, Missouri (Find a Grave ID 125877469).

Family of Mayme Glascock and Murray Bunnell

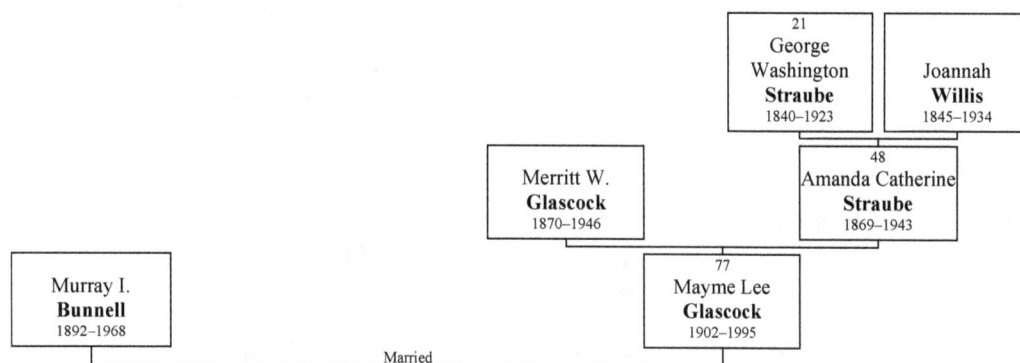

77.   **Mayme Lee Glascock** was born on Saturday, May 03, 1902, in Vandalia, Audrain County, Missouri. She was the daughter of Merritt W. Glascock and Amanda Catherine Straube (48).

Mayme Lee died in Scarborough, Toronto Municipality, Ontario, Canada, on February 05, 1995, at the age of 92. She was buried in Rosedale Cemetery, Moose Jaw, Moose Jaw Census Division, Saskatchewan, Canada (Find a Grave ID 178425272).

She married **Murray I. Bunnell**. Murray I. was born in 1892.

He reached 76 years of age and died in 1968. His burial details are unknown (Find a Grave ID 178425312).

Family of Iona Branstetter and Charles Peyton

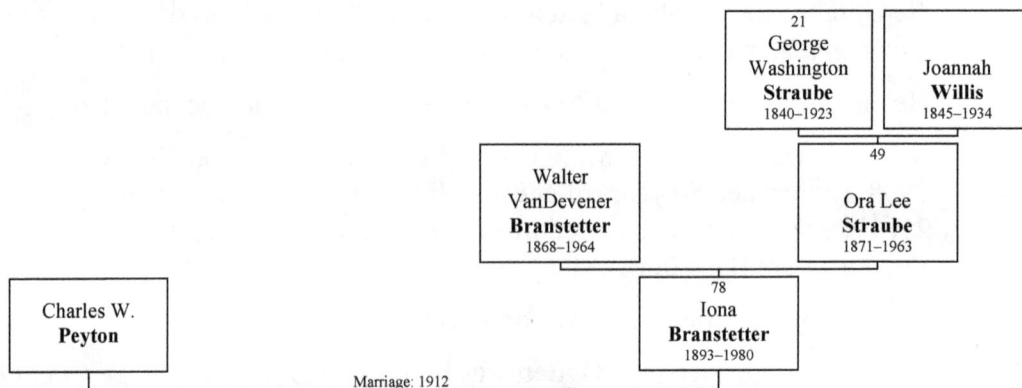

78. **Iona Branstetter** was born on Monday, September 11, 1893, in Audrain County, Missouri. She was the daughter of Walter VanDevener Branstetter and Ora Lee Straube (49).

Iona died in Saint Louis, Saint Louis County, Missouri, on August 20, 1980, at the age of 86. She was buried in Vandalia Cemetery, Vandalia, Ralls County, Missouri (Find a Grave ID 178435135).

Iona married **Charles W. Peyton** on Sunday, January 28, 1912.

Paul Branstetter

79. **Paul Branstetter** was born on Thursday, May 14, 1896, in Middletown, Montgomery County, Missouri. He was the son of Walter VanDevener Branstetter and Ora Lee Straube (49).

Paul died in Columbia, Boone County, Missouri, on September 28, 1972, at the age of 76. He was buried in Wellsville Cemetery, Wellsville, Montgomery County, Missouri (Find a Grave ID 163850826).

Marriages with Margaret Williams and Elizabeth Williams (Page 131) are known.

Family of Paul Branstetter and Margaret Williams

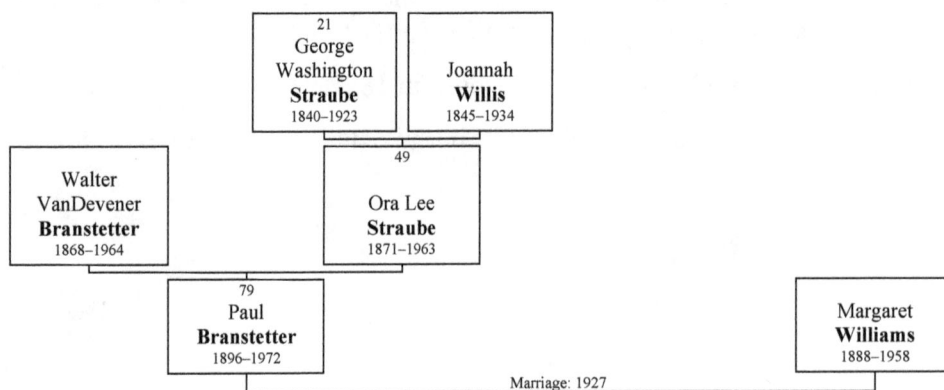

Here are the details about **Paul Branstetter's** first marriage, with Margaret Williams. You can read more about Paul on page 130.

At the age of 31, Paul Branstetter married **Margaret Williams** on Saturday, July 30, 1927, when she was 39 years old. Margaret was born in Vandalia, Audrain County, Missouri, on Friday, April 06, 1888.

She reached 70 years of age and died in Columbia, Boone County, Missouri, on May 02, 1958. Margaret was buried in Wellsville Cemetery, Wellsville, Montgomery County, Missouri (Find a Grave ID 163850838).

Family of Paul Branstetter and Elizabeth Williams

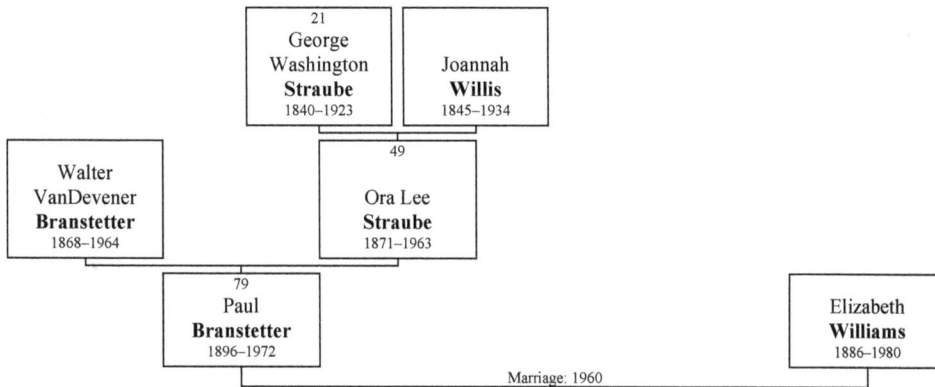

Here are the details about **Paul Branstetter's** second marriage, with Elizabeth Williams. You can read more about Paul on page 130.

At the age of 64, Paul Branstetter married **Elizabeth Williams** on Wednesday, December 28, 1960, when she was 74 years old. Elizabeth was born on Wednesday, February 03, 1886.

She reached 94 years of age and died on July 11, 1980. Elizabeth was buried in Wellsville Cemetery, Wellsville, Montgomery County, Missouri (Find a Grave ID 163850793).

Family of Lola Branstetter and Sanford Withers

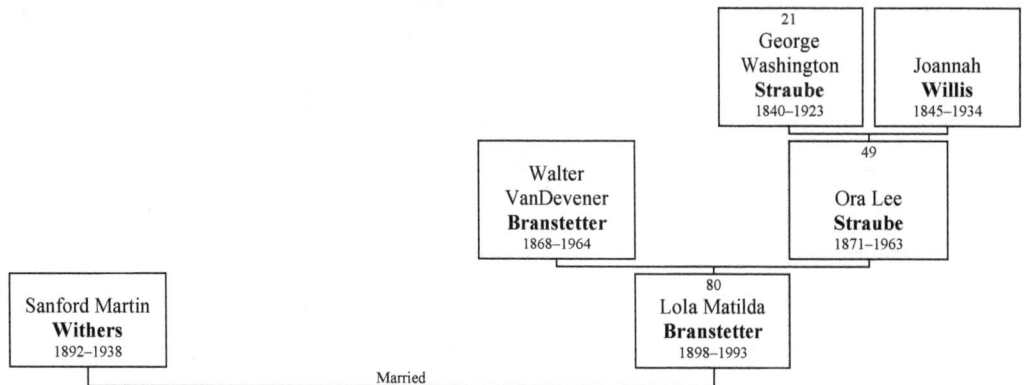

80. **Lola Matilda Branstetter** was born on Saturday, December 17, 1898, in Audrain County, Missouri. She was the daughter of Walter VanDevener Branstetter and Ora Lee Straube (49).

Lola Matilda died in Golden, Jefferson County, Colorado, on November 22, 1993, at the age of 94. Her burial details are unknown (Find a Grave ID 197788290).

She married **Sanford Martin Withers**. Sanford Martin was born in Clearwater, Ste. Genevieve County, Missouri, on Wednesday, November 23, 1892.

He reached 45 years of age and died in Denver, Denver County, Colorado, on March 08, 1938. Sanford Martin's burial details are unknown (Find a Grave ID 197788260).

Family of Walter Branstetter and Gladys Smart

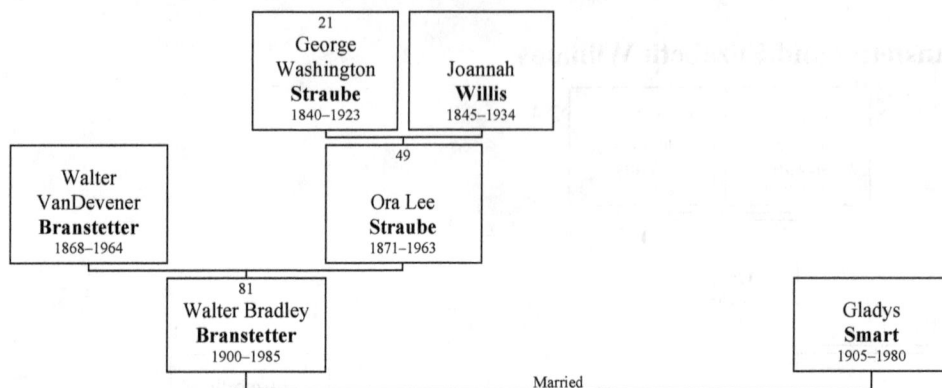

81.　　**Walter Bradley Branstetter** was born on Saturday, September 08, 1900, in Middletown, Montgomery County, Missouri. He was the son of Walter VanDevener Branstetter and Ora Lee Straube (49).

Walter Bradley died in Mexico, Audrain County, Missouri, on October 05, 1985, at the age of 85. He was buried in Callaway Memorial Gardens and Mausoleum, Fulton, Callaway County, Missouri (Find a Grave ID 94163544).

He married **Gladys Smart**. Gladys was born on Friday, October 20, 1905.

She reached 74 years of age and died on March 07, 1980. Gladys's burial details are unknown (Find a Grave ID 94163582).

Family of Porter Branstetter and Fern Gammel

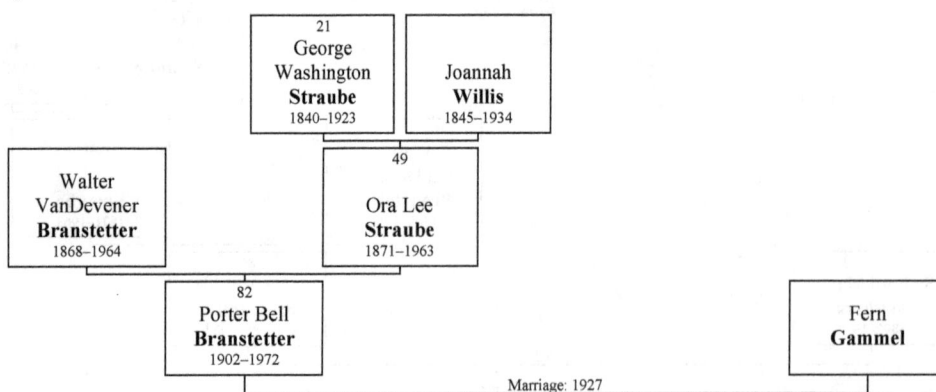

82.　　**Porter Bell Branstetter** was born on Saturday, June 28, 1902, in Audrain County, Missouri. He was the son of Walter VanDevener Branstetter and Ora Lee Straube (49).

Porter Bell died in San Bernardino, San Bernardino County, California, on September 21, 1972, at the age of 70. His burial details are unknown (Find a Grave ID 232330628).

Porter Bell married **Fern Gammel** on Monday, July 04, 1927.

Family of Esther Branstetter and Floyd Smith

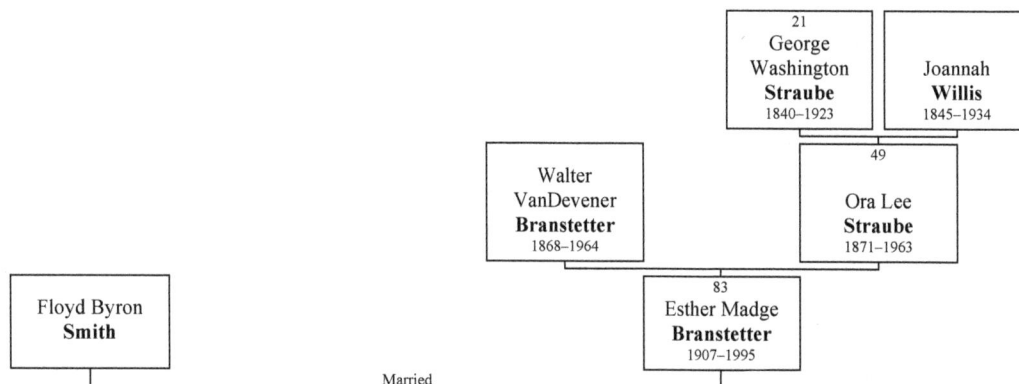

83.   **Esther Madge Branstetter** was born on Monday, July 22, 1907, in Wellsville, Montgomery County, Missouri. She was the daughter of Walter VanDevener Branstetter and Ora Lee Straube (49).

Esther Madge died in Jackson, Hinds County, Mississippi, on December 25, 1995, at the age of 88. She was cremated- (Find a Grave ID 232332133).

She married **Floyd Byron Smith**.

Family of Chester Wilhoit and Jewell Hellyer

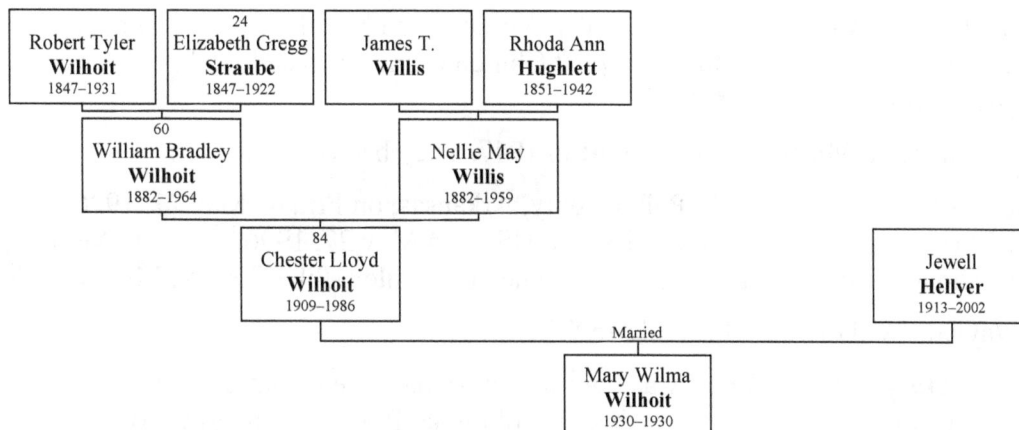

84.   **Chester Lloyd Wilhoit** was born on Monday, February 01, 1909, in Pike County, Missouri. He was the son of William Bradley Wilhoit (60) and Nellie May Willis.

Chester Lloyd died on February 13, 1986, at the age of 77. He was buried in Siloam Primitive Baptist Church Cemetery, Ashley, Pike County, Missouri (Find a Grave ID 84025318).

He married **Jewell Hellyer**. They had one daughter.

Jewell was born on Friday, November 07, 1913. She reached 89 years of age and died on November 20, 2002. Jewell was buried in Siloam Primitive Baptist Church Cemetery, Ashley, Pike County, Missouri (Find a Grave ID 100001491).

Daughter of Chester Lloyd Wilhoit and Jewell Hellyer:

f   I.   **Mary Wilma Wilhoit** was born in Pike County, Missouri, on August 16, 1930. She died in Pike County, Missouri, on August 20, 1930. Mary Wilma was buried in Siloam Primitive Baptist Church Cemetery, Ashley, Pike County, Missouri (Find a Grave ID 84025438).

Family of James Wilhoit and Molly Wilhoit

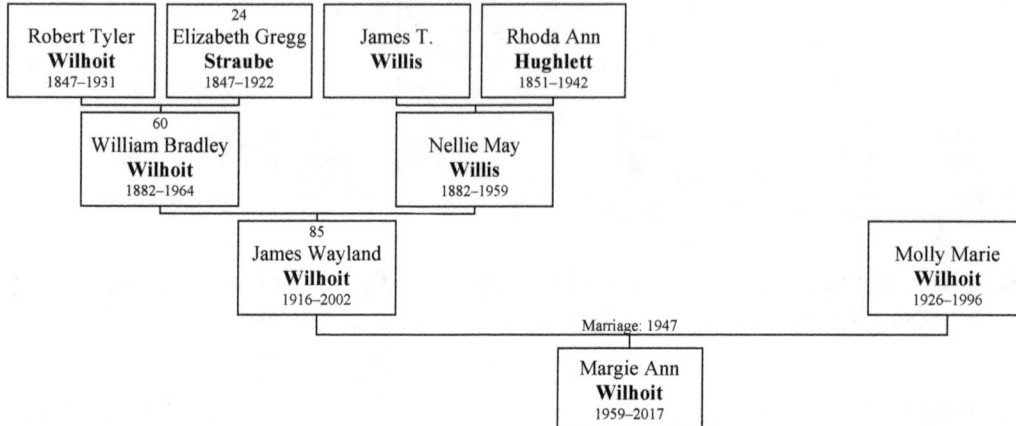

```
┌──────────────┬──────────────┐  ┌──────────────┬──────────────┐
│ Robert Tyler │ 24           │  │ James T.     │ Rhoda Ann    │
│   Wilhoit    │Elizabeth Gregg│  │   Willis     │  Hughlett    │
│  1847–1931   │   Straube    │  │              │  1851–1942   │
│              │  1847–1922   │  │              │              │
└──────────────┴──────────────┘  └──────────────┴──────────────┘
        ┌─────────────────┐         ┌─────────────────┐
        │ 60              │         │ Nellie May      │
        │ William Bradley │         │    Willis       │
        │    Wilhoit      │         │   1882–1959     │
        │   1882–1964     │         │                 │
        └─────────────────┘         └─────────────────┘
             ┌─────────────────┐              ┌──────────────┐
             │ 85              │              │ Molly Marie  │
             │ James Wayland   │              │   Wilhoit    │
             │    Wilhoit      │              │  1926–1996   │
             │   1916–2002     │              │              │
             └─────────────────┘              └──────────────┘
                   Marriage: 1947
                   ┌──────────────┐
                   │ Margie Ann   │
                   │   Wilhoit    │
                   │  1959–2017   │
                   └──────────────┘
```

85.   **James Wayland Wilhoit** was born on Sunday, July 16, 1916, in New Hartford, Pike County, Missouri.[72] He was the son of William Bradley Wilhoit (60) and Nellie May Willis.

James Wayland died in Mexico, Audrain County, Missouri, on March 06, 2002, at the age of 85.[72] He was buried in Siloam Primitive Baptist Church Cemetery, Ashley, Pike County, Missouri (Find a Grave ID 86162887).[72]

James Wayland married **Molly Marie Wilhoit** in 1947. They had one daughter.

Molly Marie was born in Cherry Hill, Polk County, Arkansas, on Friday, May 21, 1926.[72] She reached 70 years of age and died in Missouri, USA, on May 27, 1996.[72] Molly Marie was buried in Siloam Primitive Baptist Church Cemetery, Ashley, Pike County, Missouri.[72]

Daughter of James Wayland Wilhoit and Molly Marie Wilhoit:

f   I.   **Margie Ann Wilhoit** was born in Louisiana, Pike County, Missouri, on October 21, 1959.[72] She died in Columbia, Boone County, Missouri, on January 16, 2017, at the age of 57.[72] Margie Ann was buried in Siloam Primitive Baptist Church Cemetery, Ashley, Pike County, Missouri.[72]

Annie Wilhoit

86.   **Annie Katherine Wilhoit** was born on Saturday, December 12, 1925, in Pike County, Missouri. She was the daughter of William Bradley Wilhoit (60) and Nellie May Willis.

---

72   Ancestry.com, U.S., Find a Grave® Index, 1600s-Current (Lehi, UT, USA, Ancestry.com Operations, Inc., 2012), Ancestry.com, Record for James Wayland Wilhoit. https://search.ancestry.co.uk/cgi-bin/sse.dll?db=60525&h=53317179&indiv=try.

Annie Katherine died in Missouri, USA, on September 09, 2003, at the age of 77. She was buried in Siloam Primitive Baptist Church Cemetery, Ashley, Pike County, Missouri (Find a Grave ID 86166192).

Marriages with Willard Lee Lovelace and George Thomas Hummel (Page 135) are known.

Family of Annie Wilhoit and Willard Lovelace

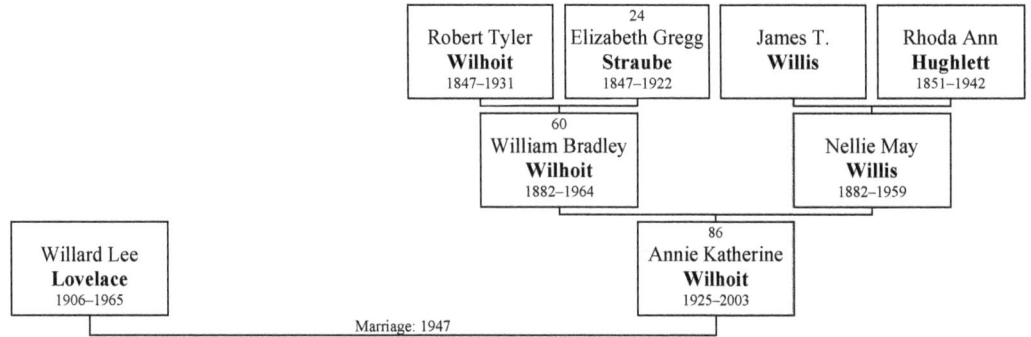

Here are the details about **Annie Katherine Wilhoit's** first marriage, with Willard Lee Lovelace. You can read more about Annie Katherine on page 134.

Annie Katherine Wilhoit married **Willard Lee Lovelace** in 1947. Willard Lee was born in Pike County, Missouri, on Wednesday, December 26, 1906.

He reached 58 years of age and died in St. Louis County, Missouri, on October 09, 1965. Willard Lee was buried in Indian Creek Cemetery, Pike County, Missouri (Find a Grave ID 55909520).

Family of Annie Wilhoit and George Hummel

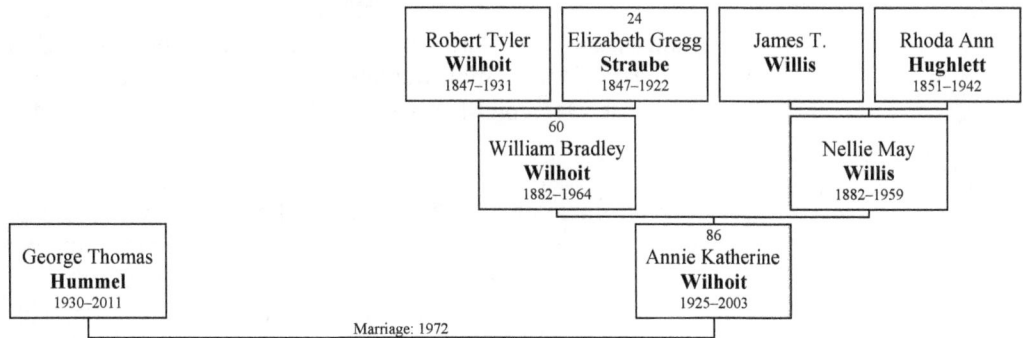

Here are the details about **Annie Katherine Wilhoit's** second marriage, with George Thomas Hummel. You can read more about Annie Katherine on page 134.

Annie Katherine Wilhoit married **George Thomas Hummel** in 1972. George Thomas was born on Tuesday, October 07, 1930.

He reached 81 years of age and died in Middletown, Montgomery County, Missouri, on December 12, 2011. George Thomas was buried in Siloam Primitive Baptist Church Cemetery, Ashley, Pike County, Missouri (Find a Grave ID 99693281).

Family of Tressa Straube and Floyd Chamberlain

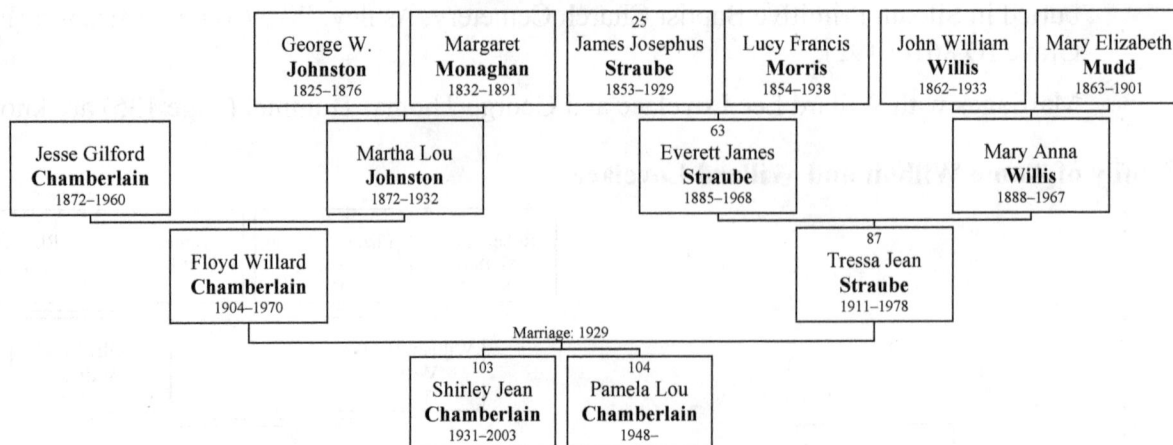

87.   **Tressa Jean Straube** was born on Saturday, July 01, 1911, in New Hartford, Pike County, Missouri.[73] She was the daughter of Everett James Straube (63) and Mary Anna Willis.

Tressa Jean died in Bowling Green, Pike County, Missouri, on May 20, 1978, at the age of 66. She was buried in Memorial Gardens Cemetery, Bowling Green, Pike County, Missouri, on May 23, 1978 (Find a Grave ID 68397409).

> Born Tressa Jean Straube on Saturday, July 1, 1911, in rural Pike County near New Harford, Missouri. She is the daughter of Everett James and Mary Anna (Willis) Straube.
>
> Tressa graduated from Bowling Green High School in 1929, attended Hannibal-LaGrange College and was a member of the Second Baptist Church in Bowling Green.
>
> Tressa married Floyd Willard Chamberlain on December 26, 1929, in Bowling Green. To this union were born at the family home in Curryville, Missouri, Shirley Jean on March 26, 1931, and Pamela Lou on July 16, 1948.
>
> Tressa was a woman of many talents of her time. After W.W. II and the Depression, she was active in Farmer Farmerette Extension Club where the women learned to cold pack foods, sew, cook new recipes and etch aluminum trays, just to name a few skills. She was a 4-H leader and loved to fish and dance. In her later years, she was a teacher's aide for 12 years in the Bowling Green School District, loved to talk politics with her friends and relatives and play bridge till the wee hours of the morning. She learned to drive the car in her 60s after Floyd died.
>
> Tressa passed away on Saturday, May 20, 1978, at the age of 66 years, 10 months and 19 days as a result of respiratory failure, cerebral hemorrhage and infraction of basal ganglia of the brain at the University of Missouri Medical Center in Columbia, Missouri. Funeral services were held on Tuesday, May 23, 1978, at the Second Baptist Church in Bowling Green,

---

73   SSDI.

with the Reverend G. E. Rittenhouse officiating. Burial was at Memorial Gardens in Bowling Green. Pallbearers were Mike, Willis and Jerry Straube, Fred Smith, R. J. Allensworth and John Hargadine.

Tressa is survived by two daughters, Mrs. Ted (Shirley) Mummert of Ennis, Texas, and Mrs. Wayne (Pam) Korte of Bowling Green, 10 grandchildren; a brother, Scott Straube, of Bowling Green; and two sisters, Gladys Myers of Columbia and Mrs. Garland (Hazel) Smith of Richmond Heights, Missouri.

At the age of 18, Tressa Jean married **Floyd Willard Chamberlain** on Thursday, December 26, 1929, in Bowling Green, Pike County, Missouri, when he was 25 years old. They had two daughters.

Floyd Willard was born in Curryville, Pike County, Missouri, on Sunday, December 11, 1904. He was the son of Jesse Gilford Chamberlain and Martha Lou Johnston.

Floyd Willard reached 65 years of age and died in Bowling Green, Pike County, Missouri, on August 15, 1970. He was buried in Memorial Gardens Cemetery, Bowling Green, Pike County, Missouri (Find a Grave ID 68398254).

> Floyd Willard Chamberlain was born on Sunday, December 11, 1904, in Curryville, Missouri, and was the son of Jesse Gilford and Martha Lou Johnston Chamberlain.
>
> Floyd was a witty and a jovial man who loved to hunt and fish, and he spent his early life on a farm near Farmer. He married Tressa Jean Straube on December 26, 1929, in Bowling Green. To this union were born at the family home in Curryville, Missouri, Shirley Jean on March 26, 1931, and Pamela Lou on July 16, 1948.
>
> Floyd staring working for Standard Oil in 1944. He traveled all over the state during the week checking pipelines. He later retired from Service Pipeline as an engineer and later worked part-time for Gentry-Bryant Ford in Bowling Green.
>
> He passed away suddenly at 11:30 AM of coronary thrombosis and Arteo-sclerosis on Saturday, August 15, 1970, at the age of 65 years, 8 months and 4 days while working at his part-time job. Funeral services were held on Monday, August 17, at the Second Baptist Church in Bowling Green, and burial was at Memorial Gardens in Bowling Green.
>
> He leaves behind his wife, two daughters, two sons-in law, six grandchildren: Paula Jean, Marsha Lynn and Susan Louann Henderson and Floyd James, Calvin Grant and Sharline Denise Mummert.

Daughters of Tressa Jean Straube and Floyd Willard Chamberlain:

+ 103 f I. **Shirley Jean Chamberlain** was born in Curryville, Pike County, Missouri, on March 26, 1931. She died in Ennis, Ellis County, Texas, on January 09, 2003, at the age of 71. Her cause of death was emphysema, COPD. She was buried in Myrtle Cemetery, Ennis, Ellis County, Texas, on January 13, 2003 (Find a Grave ID 70258741).

Born Shirley Jean Chamberlain on Thursday, March 26, 1931, on the family farm south of Curryville, Missouri. The eldest child and daughter of Floyd and Tressa Chamberlain and was named after her mother, Tressa Jean.

Shirley Jean loved growing up on the farm. She spent most of her younger days outdoors riding her horse "Lena" or a colt by the name of "Lady." Getting up early, packing a lunch, and taking off for the day was her usual schedule when she wasn't in school. Other activities she enjoyed was playing with her terrier dog, "Tony," or going fishing with her father and all the other men in the family. Floyd was always accused of turning Shirley Jean into a tomboy, which she really was because she was a substitute for a son.

"Shirley Jean was one of three 4-H girls chosen from Pike County to attend the American Royal Show in Kansas City," wrote her Aunt Hazel in a letter to her husband, Garland on October 12, 1944. She went on to write: "She left last night and will be back Saturday. They are having a banquet at the Muhlebach Hotel tonight so we can picture where she is. Shirley Jean has blossomed forth into a young lady in the past year. She very lady like now. In spite of her size, she looks neat in her clothes and carries herself well. She's outgrown the awkward stage. I'm real proud of her. She'll go to high school next year."

Shirley Jean attended Vannoy School until the family moved to Bowling Green, Missouri. While at Vannoy, Shirley Jean established a record of perfect attendance for 6 years and a perfect spelling record for 5 years. She was also a member of the 4-H Club, which kept her busy with projects and activities. Shirley Jean won the hardest of all contests at the time, a 1st place Blue ribbon at the District Contest for Judging Clothing.

While attending Bowling Green High School, Shirley Jean lettered 4 years as a member of the "Bobcat Band." She also was a member of the Glee Club, F. H. A., the concert band and Saxophone Quartet. A big surprise happened during this time as well. A baby sister, Pam, came along of who she was very tickled about.

Shirley Jean and her first cousin, Georganna, held rank on the rest of "to be" 23 cousins. The ones that were around in the early days knew that they had to be good when Shirley Jean and Georgie were baby-sitting them. Not only were they strict (wonder where they got that from), but they could tell some tales that would make you cover-up and not get out of bed at night.

Shirley Jean graduated from high school in 1949. An upcoming marriage only allowed Shirley Jean to attend one year of nursing school at DePaul School of Nursing in St. Louis, Missouri.

Shirley Jean was married to Randall Richard Henderson from July 28, 1951, until October of 1958. They were married in Pocahontas,

Arkansas, at which time Randall was in the United States Marine Corp. For seven years, they were stationed in many places. To this union were born Paula Jean on December 22, 1953, in Quantico, Virginia; Marsha Lynn on April 13, 1955, in the British West Indies; and Susan Luanne on June 21, 1957, in East St. Louis, Illinois, while Randall was stationed at Scott Air Force Base. From 1958 until 1960, Shirley Jean and the three daughters lived with her parents in Harrisonville, Missouri after she and Randall divorced.

On September 14, 1960, Shirley Jean married Ted J. Mummert in Miami, Oklahoma. Ted was born on April 10, 1931, in Fortuna, Missouri, and is the son of Calvin R. and Dora Mae Mummert. Shortly after their marriage, they moved to Dallas, Texas, to make their permanent home.

From this union were born a set of identical twins, Calvin Grant and Floyd James, on September 18, 1964, at Saint Paul Hospital, and Sharlene Denise on September 28, 1966, at Methodist Hospital. All were born in Dallas, Texas. Sharlene means "Little Shirley."

Ted was a Quality Control Inspector until his death from heart failure. He passed away at Methodist Hospital on March 12, 1994. Burial was at Myrtle Cemetery in Ennis, Texas.

After Sharlene was born, Shirley Jean went back to work at the Chief Admitting Officer at the Children's Medical Center in Dallas for three years, then as a medical secretary at the Physicians and Surgeons Clinic of Dallas until she retired in 1996.

Shirley Jean passed away on January 9, 2003, at the age of 71 years, 9 months and 14 days at Westchester Assisted Living Center, Fort Worth, Texas, from sever advanced emphysema, COPD. Burial was on January 13, 2003, at Myrtle Cemetery in Ennis, Texas.

+ 104 f II. **Pamela Lou Chamberlain** was born in Louisiana, Pike County, Missouri, on July 16, 1948.

Family of Bennett Straube and Shirley Livingston

```
┌──────────────┐ ┌──────────────┐ ┌──────────────┐ ┌──────────────┐
│      25      │ │ Lucy Francis │ │ John William │ │Mary Elizabeth│
│James Josephus│ │    Morris    │ │    Willis    │ │    Mudd      │
│   Straube    │ │  1854–1938   │ │  1862–1933   │ │  1863–1901   │
│  1853–1929   │ │              │ │              │ │              │
└──────────────┘ └──────────────┘ └──────────────┘ └──────────────┘
     ┌──────────────┐       ┌──────────────┐      ┌──────────────┐        ┌──────────────┐
     │      63      │       │  Mary Anna   │      │  Robert R.   │        │  Cora Bell   │
     │ Everett James│       │    Willis    │      │  Livingston  │        │   Bennett    │
     │   Straube    │       │  1888–1967   │      │  1879–1964   │        │  1884–1956   │
     │  1885–1968   │       │              │      │              │        │              │
     └──────────────┘       └──────────────┘      └──────────────┘        └──────────────┘
            ┌──────────────┐                              ┌──────────────┐
            │      88      │                              │Shirley Maxine│
            │Bennett Clark │                              │  Livingston  │
            │   Straube    │                              │  1917–1985   │
            │  1912–1970   │         Marriage: 1941        │              │
            └──────────────┘                              └──────────────┘
```

105	106	107	108	109	110
Tanya D'Arline **Straube** 1942–	Duane Bennett **Straube** 1943–2018	Elaine Rosemary **Straube** 1946–	Michael Dean **Straube** 1948–	Cheryl Denise **Straube** 1954–2020	Derwin Leon **Straube** 1956–

88. **Bennett Clark Straube** was born on Saturday, December 07, 1912, in New Hartford, Pike County, Missouri. He was the son of Everett James Straube (63) and Mary Anna Willis. He was also known as **Ike**.

Bennett Clark died in Hannibal, Marion County, Missouri, on August 14, 1970, at the age of 57. He was buried in Vandalia Cemetery, Vandalia, Audrain County, Missouri, on August 16, 1970 (Find a Grave ID 68885819).

> Born Bennett Clark Straube on Saturday, December 7, 1912, in Hartford Township of Pike County, Missouri. Named after James Beauchamp Clark, who is best known as Champ Clark, a prominent lawyer and politician from Bowling Green, Missouri. Clark was a member of the U.S. House of Representatives and was speaker from 1911 to 1919.
>
> Ike grew up on his parent's farm and attended Vannoy School. He enjoyed sports, especially baseball. Ike played on their small community Farmer team. At times, the team was made up of his brothers, Scott and E.J., and many of Ike's cousins. His Uncle Buford Willis was the team coach and manager.
>
> Ike loved to catch catfish by hand. The rare and painful fishing technique called "noodling" was a way of life for many country folks. Often Ike would go to Indian Creek in June and July when catfish are nesting, and he would lie on the bank and stick his arms down dark creek holes surrounded by craggily tree roots and wiggle his fingers around as bait hoping a catfish would latch on. Sometimes Ike hands would get scraped or bloody as a result of those catfish that were resistant to being caught. But that's part of the sport of "noodling."
>
> On March 1, 1941, Ike married Shirley Maxine Livingston. She was born Monday, March 19, 1917, in the home in rural route Curryville in Pike County and was the daughter of Robert and Cora Bennett Livingston. They lived on the Livingston 80 acres, and Ike farmed most of his life. Later he owned his own well drilling company. Ike was a member of the Farmer Methodist Church.
>
> To this union were born Tanya D'Arline on January 16, 1942; Duane Bennett on November 26, 1943; Elaine Rosemary on February 20, 1946; and Michael Dean on March 18, 1948 at the family home in rural route Curryville, Missouri. Cheryl

Denise was born on September 8, 1954, and Derwin Leon on October 11, 1956, at Saint Elizabeth's Hospital in Hannibal, Missouri.

Ike passed away at 4:35 PM on Friday, August 14, 1970, at the age of 57 years, 8 months and 7 days as a result of acute congestive heart failure, vague neuritis and a hemorrhaged gastric ulcer at Saint Elizabeth Hospital in Hannibal, Missouri. Funeral services were held on Sunday, August 16, 1970, at the First Baptist Church in Vandalia, Missouri, with the Reverend Walter Hinton officiating. Burial was at Vandalia City Cemetery in Vandalia, Missouri. Pallbearers were Ogle and Melvin Straube, Norbert Grawe, Raymond Dieckmann and J. W. Kohl.

Ike is survived by his wife, Shirley; three sons, Duane Straube of St. Louis, Michael Straube of Columbia and Derwin of the home; three daughters, Mrs. Tom (Tanya) Cunningham of Vandalia, Mrs. Clem (Elaine) Deters of St. Clement and Cheryl Straube of the home. He also leaves two brothers and three sisters, Scott Straube, Sr., E.J. Straube, Jr., Mrs. Floyd (Tressa) Chamberlain, Mrs. Gladys Myers of Bowling Green and Mrs. Garland (Hazel) Smith of St. Louis; and three grandchildren, Crystal Sue Straube of St. Louis and Robert and Terri Ann Cunningham of Vandalia.

At the age of 28, Bennett Clark married **Shirley Maxine Livingston** on Saturday, March 01, 1941, in Bowling Green, Pike County, Missouri, when she was 23 years old. They had six children.

Shirley Maxine was born in Curryville, Pike County, Missouri, on Monday, March 19, 1917. She was the daughter of Robert R. Livingston and Cora Bell Bennett.

Shirley Maxine reached 68 years of age and died in Hannibal, Ralls County, Missouri, on June 10, 1985. She was buried in Vandalia Cemetery, Vandalia, Audrain County, Missouri (Find a Grave ID 68886149).

Born Shirley Maxine Livingston on Monday, March 19, 1917, in the home in rural route Curryville in Pike County and was the daughter of Robert and Cora Bennett Livingston. She married Bennett Clark "Ike" Straube on March 1, 1941. They lived on the Livingston 80 acres, and Ike farmed most of his life. Later he owned his own well drilling company. Ike was a member of the Farmer Methodist Church.

To this union were born Tanya D'Arline on January 16, 1942; Duane Bennett on November 26, 1943; Elaine Rosemary on February 20, 1946; and Michael Dean on March 18, 1948 at the family home in rural route Curryville, Missouri. Cheryl Denise was born on September 8, 1954, and Derwin Leon on October 11, 1956, at Saint Elizabeth's Hospital in Hannibal, Missouri.

Shirley was an excellent seamstress and worked for Bobbie Brooks Garment Company in Vandalia, Missouri, where she retired after 35 years. Shirley was a member of the Estes Presbyterian Church.

Gladys, Shirley's sister-in-law, thought she was an "angel" and was a strong positive influence for her children. She had natural curly dark hair and always wore a smile on her face. Her girls, Tanya, Elaine and Sherry, wore hand-crocheted dresses and ringlet curls. Shirley attended every ballgame at home and away that her boys, Duane, Mike and Dewey, played.

Uncle Ike and Aunt Shirley wrote Georganna, their niece, lived on a farm near Vandalia after they were married. I remember going to their house as a child. Grandma and Grandpa Livingston lived there, too. There was always good food and a home baked cake, usually an angel food cake that looked 6 inches high (with farm eggs it probably was). Uncle Ike looked the most like Grandpa Straube as a young man. He had dark hair and a thin stature. He farmed. Aunt Shirley had dark natural curly hair that fell in ringlets. She was a seamstress as well as a master with knitting and crocket needles. Her girls, Tanya and Elaine, wore hand knitted dresses and coats. She had a jolly laugh and was a talker who liked to tell stories. The family was loyal by always attending family dinners and gatherings.

When I think of Aunt Shirley wrote her niece, Annice, I always see her smiling and laughing. I cannot remember any particular incident to cause that, but it is a nice memory. I also remember the homemade pie and pea salad when I would spend the night there. Of course, I always remember that Aunt Shirley and Tanya were both accomplished seamstresses, too. Uncle Ike brings to mind the men's discussions of sports. They kept up with the nephew's teams as well as the professional teams. How proud we all were of Duane's and Mike's athletic skills. (Dewey was too young for me to remember watching.) It was always fun when Vandalia was going to be playing Bowling Green. Uncle Ike also had an interesting job, I thought. I remember it as well drilling. Those were the days before rural water was available out in the country, and getting good water was so important. I never knew much about that job, but it always brings to mind the old-timers talking about men who could "witch water." Calvin Moore, a cousin of the family, was known to be able to do that. Now that is a real story the kids might like to hear about and try. A Y- or L-shaped twig or rod, called a witching rod, dowsing rod or divining rod is sometimes used in attempts to locate ground water without the use of scientific apparatus. Water witching is also known as dowsing or divining.

Shirley passed away at 1:06 AM on Monday, June 10, 1985, at the age of 68 years, 2 months and 22 days as a result of acute pulmonary embolism, hypercoagulable state and abdominal carcinoma at Saint Elizabeth Hospital in Hannibal, Missouri. Funeral services were held on Wednesday, June 12, 1985, at the Holt Funeral Home in Vandalia, Missouri, with the Reverend Jim Williams officiating. Burial was at Vandalia City Cemetery in Vandalia. Pallbearers were Guy, Gary and David Willis, Fred Smith, Chris Straube and Eugene Livingston.

Shirley is survived by three sons, Duane Straube of St. Louis, Michael Straube of Hannibal and Dewey Straube of Vandalia; three daughters, Mrs. Tom (Tanya) Cunningham of Vandalia, Mrs. Clem (Elaine) Deters of St. Clement and Mrs. Roger (Cheryl) Woodhurst of Perry; and 13 grandchildren. She also leaves a sister, Mrs. Isabell Willis of Curryville.

Children of Bennett Clark Straube and Shirley Maxine Livingston:

+   105   f   I. **Tanya D'Arline Straube** was born in Curryville, Pike County, Missouri, on January 16, 1942. She is also known as **Tannie**.

+   106   m   II. **Duane Bennett Straube** was born in Curryville, Pike County, Missouri, on November 26, 1943. He died in St. Lukes Hospital, Chesterfield, Saint Louis County Missouri, on June 04, 2018, at the age of 74. Duane Bennett was cremated- on June 07, 2018 (Find a Grave ID 190333630).

> Duane B. Straube, 74, of St. Ann died Monday, June 4, 2018 at St. Luke's Hospital in Chesterfield.
>
> Funeral services were Thursday at 6 p.m., at Collier's Funeral Home in St. Ann. Following the service the family invited everyone to the Straube home for a reception.
>
> He was born Nov. 26, 1943 the son of Bennett Clark and Shirley Maxine Livingston Straube. He married Kathee Meirink Straube. She survives.
>
> Other survivors include his children, Crystal Sadler and husband, Paul of Texas, Elizabeth Gallegos and husband, Al, St. Louis, Lance Straube and wife, Roj, Bangkok, Thailand; grandchildren, Lawson, Lukas, Ruby, Wells, Adam and Evan; siblings, Tanya Cunningham, Vandalia, Elaine Deters, Bowling Green, Mike Straube, Hannibal Cheryl Oligschlaeger, Perry, and Dewey Straube of Vandalia; brother-in-law, uncle, cousin and friend to many.
>
> Duane graduated from Van-Far High School in 1961 where he was recognized as the outstanding senior athlete. He attended University of Missouri-Columbia and graduated in 1965 with a BA degree in education. He later obtained his masters degree in education administration from UMSL.
>
> He taught physical education at Marvin Elementary School in the Ritenour School District in St. Louis for many years when he left to run Straube Painting Company.
>
> Duane was an avid Cardinals fan and loved all sports. He loved going to the track and to the boats. He played golf most of his life, bowled a few perfect games, and was loyal to his darts league. As a result, he made many friends in many walks of life who, in turn, enjoyed his sense of humor and camaraderie. He was loved for his dry wit and sarcasm and his willingness to give you the shirt off his back. He will be missed.
>
> Memorial contribution may be given to the American Cancer Society.

+ 107   f   III. **Elaine Rosemary Straube** was born in Curryville, Pike County, Missouri, on February 20, 1946.

+ 108   m   IV. **Michael Dean Straube** was born in Curryville, Pike County, Missouri, on March 18, 1948.

+ 109   f   V. **Cheryl Denise Straube** was born in Hannibal, Marion County, Missouri, on September 08, 1954. She died in Hannibal, Marion County, Missouri, on April 16, 2020, at the age of 65. Her cause of death was heart attack. She was buried in Lick Creek Cemetery, Perry, Ralls County, Missouri, on April 19, 2020 (Find a Grave ID 209173795).

> Private Family Graveside Services for Cheryl Denise Oligschlaeger, 65, of Perry, will be held Sunday, April 19, 2020 at Lick Creek Cemetery with Reverend Nancy Kellstrom officiating.
>
> Due to the public gathering restrictions caused by the COVID-19 pandemic, the funeral services for Cheryl were private. The family would like to extend their gratitude to the community for their support at this time.
>
> Cheryl passed away at 5:41 p.m. April 16, 2020 at Hannibal Regional Hospital. She was born in Hannibal, September 8, 1954, the daughter of Bennett Clark and Shirley Maxine Livingston Straube.
>
> She married Roger Woodhurst on May 21, 1971 and then she married Clyde Oligschlaeger on February 8, 1991 in Perry and he survives.
>
> Other survivors include: one son, Jerrid (Stacy) Woodhurst of Boonville; one daughter, Sherri (David) Bruce of Booneville; two brothers, Mike (Linda) Straube of Hannibal and Dewey (Barb) Straube of Vandalia; two sisters, Tanya (Tom) Cunningham of Vandalia and Elaine Deters of St. Clements; one sister-in-law, Kathee Straube of St. Ann; five grandchildren; and one great grandson.
>
> She was preceded in death by one brother, Duane Straube.
>
> Cheryl was a lifetime area resident and a member of the Perry Christian Church. She was a 1972 graduate of Van-Far High School and a 1990 graduate of Tarkio College with a Bachelor of Science degree in Business. She was a co-owner and Funeral Director for Bienhoff Funeral Home for over 29 years. Cheryl coached girls softball for 14 years and served as executive director and active member of both the Perry Chamber of Commerce and Mark Twain Lake Chamber of Commerce. She also served on the boards of Village Housing and Perry Ole Swimmin Hole. Cheryl was a member of Bass N Gals, Mark Twain Hookers Bass Club and very active in community affairs. She enjoyed fishing, playing golf and cards.
>
> Honorary pallbearers will be her nephews.
>
> Memorial contributions may be made to Lick Creek Cemetery, PO Box 430, Perry, MO 63462.

+   110   m   VI. **Derwin Leon Straube** was born in Hannibal, Marion County, Missouri, on October 11, 1956. He is also known as **Dewey**.

Family of Gladys Straube and William Myers

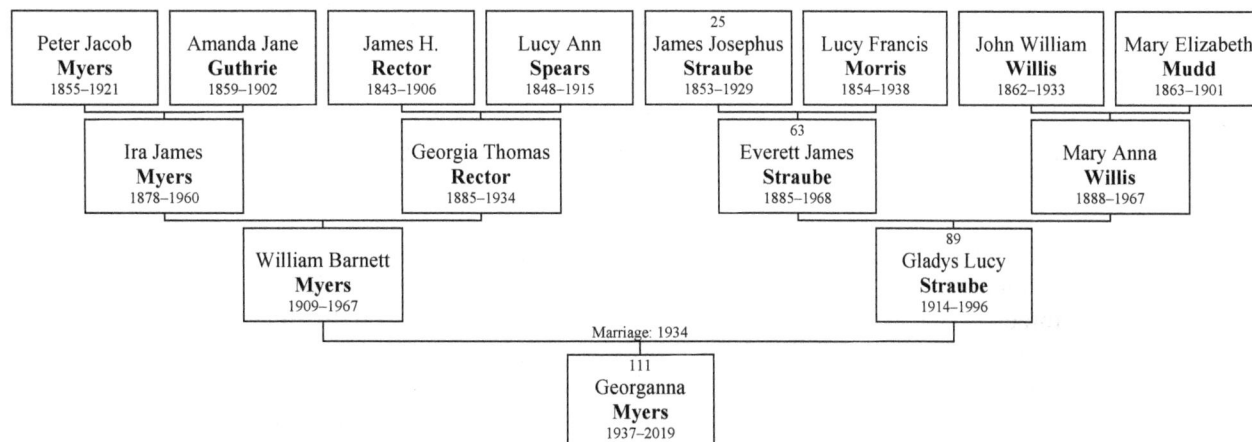

| Peter Jacob **Myers** 1855–1921 | Amanda Jane **Guthrie** 1859–1902 | James H. **Rector** 1843–1906 | Lucy Ann **Spears** 1848–1915 | 25 James Josephus **Straube** 1853–1929 | Lucy Francis **Morris** 1854–1938 | John William **Willis** 1862–1933 | Mary Elizabeth **Mudd** 1863–1901 |

Ira James **Myers** 1878–1960

Georgia Thomas **Rector** 1885–1934

63 Everett James **Straube** 1885–1968

Mary Anna **Willis** 1888–1967

William Barnett **Myers** 1909–1967

89 Gladys Lucy **Straube** 1914–1996

Marriage: 1934

111 Georganna **Myers** 1937–2019

89.   **Gladys Lucy Straube** was born on Thursday, September 17, 1914, in New Hartford, Pike County, Missouri. She was the daughter of Everett James Straube (63) and Mary Anna Willis. She was also known as **Tucky**.

Gladys Lucy died in Columbia, Boone County, Missouri, on August 19, 1996, at the age of 81. She was buried in Memorial Gardens Cemetery, Bowling Green, Pike County, Missouri, on August 22, 1996 (Find a Grave ID 68398299).

> Graduate of Hannibal-LaGrange College (Associate in Elementary Education) and the University of Missouri-Columbia (B.S. and M.S. in Elementary Education); Alpha Delta Kappa; Delta Pi Epsilon. She was a member of the First Baptist Church, Sneed Class for 25 years. Gladys was a principal at South School in Fulton, and the elementary schools in Frankford and Bowling Green. She taught public School for 37 years, retiring from West Boulevard Elementary School in Columbia. Gladys was a Life Master in American Contract Bridge League and Director of two duplicate contract bridge clubs in Columbia.
>
> Born Gladys Lucy Straube on Thursday, September 17, 1914, in rural Pike County near New Hartford, Missouri. She is the daughter of Everett James and Mary Anna Willis Straube. Gladys was named after her grandmother Lucy Francis Straube. Her nickname was "Tucky."
>
> Gladys married William Barnett Myers on April 28, 1934, in Bowling Green, Missouri. William Barnett was known by his nickname, "Sie," and was born on Sunday, April 5, 1909, in rural Pike County near New Hartford, Missouri. He was a farmer and the son of Ira James Myers and Georgia Thomas Rector. To this union was born Georganna Myers on December 30, 1937, at their home in Farmer, Missouri. Sie also broke horses, and Gladys had a fondness for them. One of her horses was named "Lady," who a beautiful five-gated mare. Gladys also liked to fish and enjoyed going to just about any lake, pond or steam.

Gladys started teaching in 1931 at Prairie View, a one-room rural school in Pike County, Missouri, where she taught all grades with 32 students. In 1941, she taught one year at Allison School, then two years at Vannoy School. Gladys started teaching with 12 hours of college credit and a teacher's examination.

Some of the extra duties teachers had to do were to build a fire in a big old coal stove, sweep and dust the building, cook lunch on many occasions, referee ball games and have the entertainment program for the entire community in the school building.

Like most teachers Gladys went back to college. She got an associate's degree in elementary education from Hannibal-LaGrange College after which she taught three years at Watson School and five years at Bowling Green. In 1955 she moved to Columbia, Missouri, while Georganna was attending the University of Missouri and taught for one year at the University Lab School. Gladys earned a Bachelor of Science and a Master of Science degree in elementary education from the University of Missouri in Columbia and was a member of Alpha Delta Kappa and Delta Pi Epsilon. She was the principal at South School in Fulton, Missouri, for two years. Then moved to Prince George's County in Maryland where she taught one year and also received the "Teacher of the Year" award.

Gladys moved to Bowling Green in 1963. She was the principal at Frankfort Elementary School for two years and Bowling Green Junior High School for seven years and was President of the Pike County Teacher's Association.

She returned to Columbia, Missouri and retired in 1975 from West Boulevard Elementary School where she was the principal. In 1964, Gladys was listed in "Who's Who West of the Mississippi" for education excellence.

When Gladys retired, she taught bridge twice a week-"Once a teacher always a teacher," she said. This was easy for her since she was also Life Master in Contract Bridge League and Director of two duplicate contract bridge clubs in Columbia.

Gladys passed away on Monday, August 19, 1996, at the age of 81 years, 11 months and 2 days at her residence, Candlelight Terrace Apartments, in Columbia, Missouri, from cerebra vascular accident and generalized arteriosclerosis. A funeral service was held at 10:00 AM on Thursday, August 22, 1996, at the First Baptist Church in Columbia, Missouri, with the Reverend Robert Russell officiating. At 2:00 PM a graveside service was held at Memorial Gardens Cemetery in Bowling Green, Missouri, with the Reverend Ed Engle officiating. She was buried alongside Sie. The inscription on the grave marker reads "Together Forever." Pallbearers were Duane, Chris, Jerry and Willis Straube, Wayne Korte and Bill Gates.

Survivors include one daughter, Georganna Beachboard of Jefferson City; two grandsons, Samuel E. Hargadine and John E. Hargadine, both of Columbia; and three great-grandsons.

At the age of 19, Gladys Lucy married **William Barnett Myers** on Saturday, April 28, 1934, in Bowling Green, Pike County, Missouri, when he was 25 years old. They had one daughter.

William Barnett was born in New Hartford, Pike County, Missouri, on Monday, April 05, 1909.[74] He was the son of Ira James Myers and Georgia Thomas Rector. He was also known as **Sie**.

William Barnett reached 58 years of age and died at Fulton State Hospital #1 in Fulton, Callaway County, Missouri, on June 08, 1967. He was buried on June 11, 1967, in Memorial Gardens Cemetery, Bowling Green, Pike County, Missouri (Find a Grave ID 68398340).

> Lived his adult life in the Fulton State Mental Hospital.
>
> William Barnett was known by his nickname, "Sie," and was born on Sunday, April 5, 1909, in rural Pike County near New Hartford, Missouri. He was a farmer and the son of Ira James Myers and Georgia Thomas Rector.
>
> Sie married Lucy Gladys Straube on April 28, 1934, in Bowling Green, Missouri. To this union was born Georganna Myers on December 30, 1937, at their home in Farmer, Missouri. Sie also broke horses, and Gladys had a fondness for them.
>
> Sie spent most of his adult life as a patient at State Hospital #1, Fulton, Missouri from February, 1943 until he he passed away on Thursday, June 8, 1967, at the age of 58 years, 2 months and 3 days as a result of a heart myocardial infarction. Funeral services were held on Sunday, June 11, at the Second Baptist Church in Bowling Green with the Reverend Joe Barbour officiating. Sie was buried at Memorial Gardens Cemetery in Bowling Green. Pallbearers were Floyd Chamberlain, Les Henderson, Jack Wilhoit, Duard Eastin, Virgil Myers and Ogle Straube.
>
> Sie is survived by his wife, Gladys Straube Myers, of Bowling Green; a daughter, Georganna Myers Hargadine of Alexandria, Va.; two grandsons, Samuel E. Hargadine and John E. Hargadine of Alexandria, Va.; five brothers, Otis and Herman Myers of Curryville, Burton Myers of Farmer, Billy Wayne Myers of California; two sisters, Mrs. Genevieve Thomason of Louisiana and Mrs. Mary Weber of St. Louis.

---

74   Death Certificate.

Daughter of Gladys Lucy Straube and William Barnett Myers:

+   111   f   I. **Georganna Myers** was born in Bowling Green, Pike County, Missouri, on December 30, 1937. She died in Jefferson City, Cole County, Missouri, on May 15, 2019, at the age of 81. Georganna was buried in Memorial Gardens Cemetery, Bowling Green, Pike County, Missouri, on May 20, 2019 (Find a Grave ID 199157394).

Graduate of University of Missouri-Columbia (B.S. and M.S. in Secondary Education). Inducted into Alpha Delta Kappa; Phi Delta Kappa; Delta Pi Epsilon and Pi Lambda Theta. Taught at Southern Boone county, Ashland, Missouri for eight years. Retired from the State of Missouri, Department of Elementary and Secondary Education.

Obituary

Georganna Myers Beachboard, age 81, of Jefferson City, Mo., went to be with her Lord Wednesday, May 15, 2019 at Capital Region Medical Center surrounded by her loving family.

She was born on December 30, 1937 in Bowling Green, Mo., the only child of William Barnett and Gladys (Straube) Myers. She was married on May 21, 1983 in Columbia, Mo. to Miles F. Beachboard.

After an experience abroad and in Washington D.C., Georganna was a lifelong resident of Central Missouri. Georganna graduated from Bowling Green High School in 1955. The Class of 1955 taught her many things, one of which was the class motto, "life is not a destination, but a journey." She went on to earn both a Bachelor of Science and a Master's degree in Education from the University of Missouri - Columbia.

Georganna worked as an administrative assistant for the United States Senator, Edward Long, in both the Missouri and Washington D.C. offices. She moved to central Missouri where she became a business education teacher for the Southern Boone School District in Ashland, Mo. for several years. During this time she authored the Missouri Title IX legislation, which prevents discrimination in education. From that experience, Georganna began her career with the State of Missouri - Department of Education for sixteen years and worked as the Director of Special Education Services. While there, her primary goal was to promote women in vocational education programs. These pioneering efforts led to her being recognized in many ways. The late Governor Carnahan presented her with the "Martin Luther King Diversity Award," First Lady, Melanie Blunt, recognized her with the "Award of Achievement in Education," and Governor Nixon presented her with the "Distinguished Service Award for Education by Missouri Council on Economic Development for Women."

Georganna was a member of First Christian Church and had previously been a member at Community Christian Church. Her faith was an integral part of her life and she was proud to be active with the Christian Women's Fellowship, Church Women United, and served as Elder and Deacon at both churches. She also enjoyed leading seniors in the "Learning in Retirement" program. She was a board member of the Community Concert Association and volunteered at Capital Region Medical Center.

Georganna spent many summers at the Lake of the Ozarks and enjoyed fishing. Her passions also included: golfing, being an avid bridge player, and a Master Gardener who enjoyed working with plants and flowers. Georganna cherished time with her husband, especially cruises to the Mediterranean, Vienna, Italy, Croatia, the Greek Isles, Isle of Capri, Athens, Rome, Alaska and the Holy Land.

Survivors include: her husband, Miles Beachboard; two sons, Samuel Hargadine V (wife Annette) of Hallsville, Mo. and John Hargadine (wife Mary) of St. Paul, Mo.; three grandchildren, Samuel Hargadine VI, Calvin Hargadine (wife Amber), and Mitchell Hargadine (wife Jenna); five great-grandchildren, Logan, Adam, Carter, Lucas and Mya Hargadine; sister-in-law, Juanita Dickerson (husband Lawrence) of Fayette, Mo.; her nephews, Doug Dickerson (wife Vicki) of Scottsdale, Arizona and Mitch Dickerson (Amie Ewigman) of Higbee, Mo.; as well as numerous cousins from the Straube family; and beloved friends.

Georganna was preceded in death by her parents, William and Gladys Myers.

Visitation will be held at Freeman Mortuary from 1:00 p.m. until 3:00 p.m. Sunday, May 19, 2019.

Funeral services will be conducted at 10:00 a.m. Monday, May 20, 2019 at First Christian Church in Jefferson City, Mo. with the Reverend Beau Underwood officiating. Graveside services and interment will be held at 2:00 p.m. Monday at Memorial Garden Cemetery in Bowling Green.

In lieu of flowers, memorial contributions are suggested to Dreams to Reality, 500 Jefferson Street, Jefferson City, Mo. 65101 or First Christian Church, 327 E. Capitol Avenue, Jefferson City, Mo. 65101.

Funeral arrangements are under the care of Freeman Mortuary.

Family of Walter Straube and Annie Dieckmann

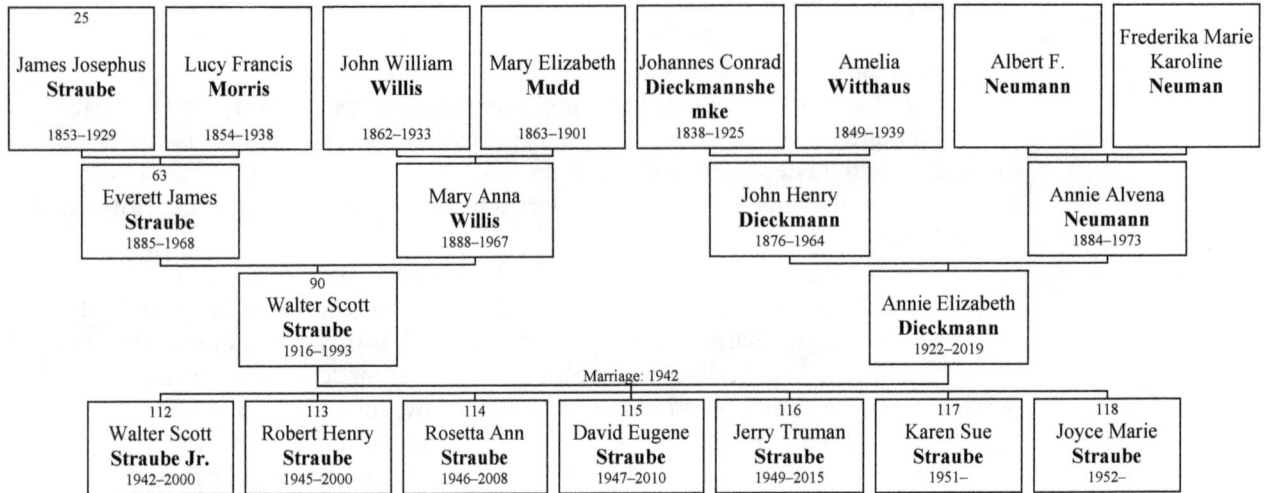

| 25 James Josephus **Straube** 1853–1929 | Lucy Francis **Morris** 1854–1938 | John William **Willis** 1862–1933 | Mary Elizabeth **Mudd** 1863–1901 | Johannes Conrad **Dieckmannshemke** 1838–1925 | Amelia **Witthaus** 1849–1939 | Albert F. **Neumann** | Frederika Marie Karoline **Neuman** |

| 63 Everett James **Straube** 1885–1968 | Mary Anna **Willis** 1888–1967 | John Henry **Dieckmann** 1876–1964 | Annie Alvena **Neumann** 1884–1973 |

| 90 Walter Scott **Straube** 1916–1993 | Annie Elizabeth **Dieckmann** 1922–2019 |

Marriage: 1942

| 112 Walter Scott **Straube Jr.** 1942–2000 | 113 Robert Henry **Straube** 1945–2000 | 114 Rosetta Ann **Straube** 1946–2008 | 115 David Eugene **Straube** 1947–2010 | 116 Jerry Truman **Straube** 1949–2015 | 117 Karen Sue **Straube** 1951– | 118 Joyce Marie **Straube** 1952– |

90. **Walter Scott Straube** was born on Tuesday, September 26, 1916, in New Hartford, Pike County, Missouri. He was the son of Everett James Straube (63) and Mary Anna Willis.

Walter Scott died in Bowling Green, Pike County, Missouri, on December 09, 1993, at the age of 77. He was buried in Memorial Gardens Cemetery, Bowling Green, Pike County, Missouri, on December 13, 1993 (Find a Grave ID 68398377).

> Born Walter Scott Straube on Tuesday, September 26, 1916, at the home in rural Pike County near New Hartford, Missouri. He is the son of Everett James and Mary Anna Willis Straube.
>
> Scott grew up on his parent's farm where he learned many skills that carried him throughout his life. During spring, summer and fall there were plenty of chores to do, fish to catch and animals to hunt. But the Christmas season was always special even during tough times. Christmas trees were cut from the nearby woods and decorated with paper ornaments and strings of homemade popcorn. His dad, Everett, sometimes sponsored a Molasses Pull around Christmas time followed by a square dance. Everett was the fiddler and his mother, Annie, accompanied on the piano.
>
> On Christmas Eve each child hung up a stocking or sock. It eventually had an orange in it plus one gift they requested from Santa. Christmas day dinner brought forth quail, turkey or goose, sweet potatoes, turnips, mincemeat pie and persimmons much of which came from their farm. In 1922 six-year-old Scott being the helpful and thoughtful boy, decided to practice "barbering" so he cut his four year old sister's hair a week before Christmas. Hazel was glad he did until she saw the results and was sure that Santa wouldn't recognize her. But Santa did and all was well!
>
> Scott attended Vannoy School in rural Pike County through the eighth grade. After graduating from Vannoy, he attended Bowling Green High School and graduated in 1934. During the school week, since the school was miles from his home he boarded with the Smith family. Of the things he did and accomplished in high school of which is history now, one still remains present. Scott signed the original

Future Farmers of America (FFA) Charter that hangs in the Ag building at Bowling Green High School today. After high school, Scott attended the University of Missouri in Columbia, Missouri then later went to work for Bridges Asphalt & Paving Company in Bowling Green.

On July 11, 1942, Scott married Annie Elizabeth Dieckmann. The marriage was performed by Rev-erend G. O. Baxter at the Second Baptist Church Parsonage at 215 West Locust in Bowling Green. Ann was born on Tuesday, November 7, 1922 near Silex, Missouri and is the fifth child of John Henry Dieckmann (100414395) and Annie Alvena Neumann (100414842). To this union the following seven children were born.

Ann.s early years were spent on a farm and in rural schools in Lincoln County. When her family moved to Pike County, Ann and her sister, Lillie, enrolled in the Butler School where there were only two other students, both girls. Ann worked for Confederate Cottage Hotel as a waitress. Jobs with Bridges Asphalt took Scott and Ann to St. Louis where they lived for a period of time. Then to Hillsboro, Illinois and then eventually back to Bowling Green.

Scott was an excellent baseball player in his own right and played on many ball teams including the Farmer baseball team. At times, players were his brothers, Ike and E.J., and many of Scott's cousins which made up the majority of the team. His Uncle Buford was the team coach and manager.

Scott also was employed by the Missouri Hatchery in Bowling Green for 24 years. After retiring from the hatchery, he drove a school bus for the Bowling Green School District for 14 years. Scott retired from bus driving in 1981. While Scott worked at the hatchery, Ann sometimes cared for elderly patients out of their home and also worked for the school district as a cook from 1958 to 1962. During this time, the family lived on a small five-acre farm with a pond. They had a large garden, cow, mean bull, ducks, chickens, hunting dogs and sometimes puppies. The girls were thrilled at Easter when they would find their baskets filled with baby chicks in a rainbow of colors.

Like his father, Scott had a talent for music and he could play the fiddle, but unlike his dad, he only played for recreational pleasure. After decades without the instrument, his daughter, Katie bought him a fiddle. After hours of painstaking practice, he amazed the family with "Turkey in the Straw" When traveling the county back roads with family, he would recount the adventures of his childhood and early adult days: riding horses (he had two), swimming in Indian Creek and later efforts to teach Ann to swim (she sank), hand-fishing with his brothers and hunting wild game.

In 1962 Scott and Ann purchased the Butler Pritchett Funeral Home and converted into the Straube Boarding Home. In addition to raising seven children, they ran a successful business boarding patients for over 25 years. Scott continued to hunt rabbits and quail and hook frogs; and until the kids were grown, outings focused on family-related gatherings, sports and fishing. Playing cards were kept within reach of the table-Pinochle, poker and Shanghai Rummy were his games of choice and he would lick his thumb and spin'em well into the night.

They sold the boarding home in 1987 and moved to 505 W. Lee Street. After Scott's death, Ann moved across the street to North High Street. After a couple of years, she moved to Wellsville where she became active as a senior volunteer. In 2000 she moved back to Bowling Green and resides at 509 West South Street. Ann is an accomplished cook, talented with needlework, quilting and china painting. She remains a member of the Second Baptist Church and enjoys playing cards and socializing with friends.

Scott passed away at their home on Thursday, December 9, 1993, at the age of 77 years, 2 months and 13 days as a result of progressive hypoxia and carcinoma of the lung. Services were held at the Second Baptist Church in Bowling Green on Monday, December 13, 1993, with Reverend Bill Peters officiating. Burial was at Memorial Gardens Cemetery in Bowling Green. Pallbearers were Chris, Willis, Jason and Dewey Straube and Sam and John Hargadine.

Scott is survived by his wife, Ann; four sons, Scott Straube, Jr. of Caruthersville, Robert "Bobby" Straube of Plant City, Florida; David Straube of Henderson, Kentucky and Jerry Straube of Bowling Green; three daughters, Rosetta Pagnella of Bowling Green; Karen Drennan and Joyce Roloff both of Juneau, Alaska; one sister, Gladys Myers of Columbia; 12 grandchildren and two great-grandchildren.

At the age of 25, Walter Scott married **Annie Elizabeth Dieckmann** on Saturday, July 11, 1942, in Bowling Green, Pike County, Missouri, when she was 19 years old. They had seven children.

Annie Elizabeth was born in Silex, Lincoln County, Missouri, on Tuesday, November 07, 1922. She was the daughter of John Henry Dieckmann and Annie Alvena Neumann.

Annie Elizabeth reached 96 years of age and died in Bowling Green, Pike County, Missouri, on April 29, 2019. She was buried in Memorial Gardens Cemetery, Bowling Green, Pike County, Missouri (Find a Grave ID 198729025).

> Annie Elizabeth Straube (1922-2019) Long time Bowling Green resident Annie Dieckmann Straube passed away on Monday, April 29th in Countryview Nursing Home in Bowling Green. Visitation will be Saturday May 11, 2019 from 9:30-11:00 at the Second Baptist Church in Bowling Green with the service immediately following. Interment will be at Memorial Gardens Cemetery next to her husband Scott in the family plot.
>
> Annie was born November 7, 1922 to John Henry and Annie Neumann Dieckmann. In her youth, her family moved to Pike County where she attended Butler School. She was a member of the Farmer Farmerette Club and enjoyed attending the local dances where she met Walter Scott Straube who played the fiddle. They married in 1942. One of her first jobs was a waitress for Confederate Cottage Hotel in Bowling Green. The couple briefly moved to St. Louis and Hillsboro, Illinois where Scott worked for the Bridges Asphalt Company. They returned to Bowling Green where they raised their 7 children.
> In June 1951-1958, she and Scott operated the Pike County Rest Home (later called Moore-Pike Nursing Home) before settling on a small farm on the outskirts of Bowling Green. During those years, she served as a cook with the Bowling Green School District. In 1962 Scott and Annie purchased the Butler Pritchett Funeral Home and converted it into the Straube Boarding Home, which

they ran until their retirement in 1987. After they retired, she and Scott enjoyed travelling to visit their children in Virginia, Kentucky, Wisconsin, and Alaska. One of the family's favorite gatherings was celebrating their golden 50th wedding anniversary in Kentucky in 1992.

Several years after her husband's passing in 1993, Annie moved to Wellsville but returned to Bowling Green a few years later where she remained until her passing. She was a gifted quilter and enjoyed needlework and porcelain china painting. Annie was an accomplished cook and baker and was a care-giver for many years operating the Boarding Home business and raising their seven children. In addition to spending time with her children and their families, her favorite past-times were playing cards and bingo with her friends, and trips to the casinos. She was a member of the Second Baptist Church in Bowling Green and remained strong in her faith throughout her life.

She was preceded in death by her husband Scott; her sons Scott Jr, Bob, David, and Jerry Straube; her daughter Rosetta Pagnella; son-in-law Chad Drennan; and grandson Troy Cashman; her brothers Ben, John, and Eli Dieckmann; and sister Hilda Evans. She is survived by her two daughters Karen (Bill) Corbus of Juneau, Alaska, and Joyce Roloff-Kroft (Doug) of Crested Butte, Colorado; Daughter-In-Law Barb Straube; Grandchildren Brian Pagnella, Nicole (Dave) Jensen, Laurie (Craig) Heckman, Neil Straube, Nathanial and Dylan (Gisele) Roloff, Booker Drennan, Dean and Scott Diddell; Great-grandchildren Kennedy Jensen, Aiden and Hailey Heckman; her sister Lillie Straube of Bowling Green, and numerous nieces, nephews and extended family. Serving as pallbearers will be Brian Pagnella, Dylan Roloff, Dean Diddell, Robert Evans, Jason and Seth Straube.

Children of Walter Scott Straube and Annie Elizabeth Dieckmann:

+ 112 m I. **Walter Scott Straube Jr.** was born in Bowling Green, Pike County, Missouri, on December 18, 1942. He died in Memphis, Shelby County, Tennessee, on February 04, 2000, at the age of 57. Walter Scott was buried in Memorial Gardens Cemetery, Bowling Green, Pike County, Missouri, on February 08, 2000 (Find a Grave ID 41791126).

> Scott Straube Jr.
> Caruthersville Dec. 18, 1942 - Feb. 4, 2000
>
> BOWLING GREEN - Scott Straube Jr., 57, of Caruthersville and formerly of Bowling Green, died Feb. 4, 2000, at Baptist Hospital East in Memphis, Tenn.
>
> Funeral services will be at 10 a.m. today at Smith Funeral Home in Caruthersville.
>
> A second funeral service will be at 1 p.m. Tuesday, Feb. 8, at Second Baptist Church in Bowling Green. The Rev. Jerry Gamm will officiate.

Burial will be at Memorial Gardens Cemetery in Bowling Green.

A memorial service for Mr. Straube and his brother, Robert (Bob) Straube, who died Jan. 29, will be at 11 a.m. Saturday, Feb. 12, at Second Baptist Church. The Rev. Jerry Gamm will officiate.

Visitation for Scott Straube Jr. will be from 11 a.m. until time of services Tuesday, Feb. 8, at Second Baptist Church.

Mudd-Veach Funeral Home in Bowling Green is in charge of local arrangements. Mr. Straube was born Dec. 18, 1942, in Bowling Green to Scott Straube Sr. and Annie Dieckmann Straube.

He was married to Sherrie Jo Sprunger on Oct. 17, 1992, in Louisiana. She survives.

Also surviving are his mother of Wellsville; five sons, Dean Diddell of Dallas, Scott Diddell of Houston, Texas, Josh Sprunger of Kingston, Tenn., Jason Sprunger of Caruthersville and Troy Cashman of Denver; eight grandchildren; two brothers, Dr. David Straube of Henderson, Ky., and Jerry Straube of Bowling Green; and three sisters, Rosetta Pagnella of Bowling Green, Karen Corbus of Juneau, Alaska, and Joyce Roloff of Sturgeon Bay, Wis.

He was preceded in death by his father.

Mr. Straube was a veteran of the U.S. Navy.

He was formerly administrator of Pike County Memorial Hospital in Louisiana.

He was currently employed by Pemiscot Memorial Health System in Hayti, where he was an assistant administrator and director of fiscal services.

Mr. Straube was a 1961 graduate of Bowling Green High School. He received a degree in business administration from the American University in Washington.

Memorials may be made to the American Cancer Society.

+   113   m   II. **Robert Henry Straube** was born in Bowling Green, Pike County, Missouri, on February 08, 1945. He was also known as **Bobby**.

Robert Henry died in Plant City, Hillsborough County, Florida, on January 29, 2000, at the age of 54. His cause of death was brain cancer. Robert Henry was buried in Memorial Gardens Cemetery, Bowling Green, Pike County, Missouri (Find a Grave ID 68398462).

> BOWLING GREEN – Robert (Bob) Straube, 54, of Plant City, Fla., and formerly of Bowling Green, died Jan. 29, 2000, at his home.
>
> Memorial services for Mr. Straube and his brother, Scott Straube Jr., who died Feb. 4, will be at 11 a.m. Saturday, Feb. 12, at Second Baptist Church in Bowling Green. The Rev. Jerry Gamm will officiate.
>
> Mudd-Veach Funeral Home in Bowling Green is in charge of arrangements.
>
> Robert Straube was born Feb. 8, 1945, in Bowling Green to Scott Straube Sr. and Ann Dieckmann Straube.
>
> He was married to Barbara Sloan on March 17, 1972, in Philadelphia, Pa. She survives.
>
> Also surviving are one daughter, Laurie Straube, a student at the University of South Florida; his mother of Wellsville; two brothers, Dr. David Straube of Henderson, Ky., and Jerry Straube of Bowling Green; and three sisters, Rosetta Pagnella of Bowling Green, Karen Corbus of Juneau, Alaska, and Joyce Roloff of Sturgeon Bay, Wis.
>
> He was preceded in death by his father.
>
> Mr. Straube was a U.S. Navy veteran during the Vietnam war. He served aboard the USS BonHomme Richard.
>
> After his discharge from the Navy in 1971, Mr. Straube began a career in the insurance field, which he continued for more than 25 years.
>
> He was a graduate of Bowling Green High School. He attended Hannibal-LaGrange College and Strayer College in Washington, D.C. While in Washington he worked for Senator Stuart Symington.
>
> Memorials may be made to the H.L. Moffitt Cancer Center, 12902 Magnolia Drive, Tampa, Fla. 33612, The Bowling Green Alumni Association or Second Baptist Church in Bowling Green.

+   114   f   III. **Rosetta Ann Straube** was born in Bowling Green, Pike County, Missouri, on May 05, 1946. She was also known as **Rosie**.

Rosetta Ann died in Saint Charles, St. Charles County, Missouri, on February 12, 2008, at the age of 61. She was buried in Memorial Gardens Cemetery, Bowling Green, Pike County, Missouri (Find a Grave ID 68398501).

+   115   m   IV. **David Eugene Straube** was born in Bowling Green, Pike County, Missouri, on August 03, 1947. He was also known as **Doc**.

David Eugene died in Tampa, Hillsborough County, Florida, on June 25, 2010, at the age of 62. He was buried in Memorial Gardens Cemetery, Bowling Green, Pike County, Missouri (Find a Grave ID 68398611).

> David Eugene Straube was born on Sunday, August 3, 1947, in Bowling Green, Missouri. The son of Scott and Ann Straube. He was affectionately called "Doc" by many of his colleagues, clients, and friends.
>
> David grew up in Bowling Green, worked for Bankhead's Restaurant and Pollards minnow ponds during high school. He took an active interest in the veterinarian clinic, perhaps influenced by his father, Scott, who had an interest in veterinary medicine. David was active in athletics including baseball and basketball. He graduated from Bowling Green High School in 1965, attended Northeast Missouri State at Kirksville from 1965-67 and then attended the University of Missouri in Columbia. In 1973, David graduated from the University of Missouri School of Veterinary Medicine with a degree in veterinary medicine and sciences (DVM). He subsequently became licensed in Missouri, Illinois, Maryland, Washington, D.C., Kentucky, and Florida.
>
> David moved to McLean, Virginia, in 1973 to join most of his family members who resided in the area and worked for a small animal clinic until 1974. He moved to West Virginia where he continued to practice before taking a position in Lexington Kentucky for Dr. Holbrook and Dr. Gentry who were searching for an Equine Clinic. He also served as a Kentucky Commission Veterinarian in 1974 and 1989. He was offered a job with Dr. Joe Burch in Miami for a position in his Equine Thoroughbred Racetrack Practice and obtained a license to work for Dr. Burch. In 1976, David established his own Thoroughbred racing and breeding clinic in Odessa, Florida and began a solo medical practice specializing in equine medicine. His true passion was equines and while living in Florida he began a long career working on racehorses.
>
> David married Ginny Ann Henely on October 14, 1978, in Bowling Green. They had one son, Walter Neil Straube, born February 4, 1981, in Tampa, Florida.

David began spending summers working the racetrack circuit in Kentucky that included Churchill Downs, Kentucky Downs and Ellis Park. In the late 1990s, he purchased a farm called Hidden Acres in Henderson, Kentucky, and lived there for several years. His family enjoyed numerous reunions and gatherings at the farm. It was a wonderful vintage farmhouse with livestock, barns, ponds and acres to explore. One of his fondest memories was celebrating his parent's 50th wedding anniversary July 1992 in Henderson and spending the day at the racetrack with one of his horses winning, the family photo taken with the jockey and horse, and then returning to celebrate at the farm. It was the last family vacation before his father's passing in December 1993. Unfortunately, the farm was destroyed by fire and sold in 2001.

In 2008, David shifted from private practice to working as a State Veterinarian Inspector for Tampa Bay Downs. In the summer of 2009, he worked as a Commission Veterinarian for the Presque Isle Downs racetrack in Eerie, Pennsylvania.

Throughout his career David continued to make his home in Florida during the winter months and traveled to other tracks during the summer. But shortly after David completed his 35th year at Tampa Bay Downs he became ill and was admitted to Town and Country Hospital in Tampa on May 23, 2010.

David passed away on June 25, 2010, at the Town and Country Hospital in Tampa, Florida at the age of 62 years, 10 months and 22 days as a result of renal failure. A memorial service for was held on Friday, July 9 at the Second Baptist Church in Bowling Green. Brother Don Amelung, Pastor, officiated. Parts of his ashes were buried at Memorial Gardens in Bowling Green.

A Celebration of Life service is to be at the December 2010 reopening of Tampa Bay Downs Racetrack. He will be honored in the "Winners Circle" and parts of his ashes will be scattered by horseback while making a memorial lap.

David is survived by his mother, Ann Straube of Bowling Green; his son, Neil Straube of Fayetteville, N.C.; one brother, Jerry Straube of Bowling Green; two sisters, Karen Corbus of Juneau, Alaska and Joyce Roloff of Crested Butte, Colorado; many nephews and nieces.

David was a proud father, an avid St. Louis Cardinals baseball fan, and as an alumnus of the University of Missouri, he remained a true Mizzou Tiger fan.

+   116   m   V.   **Jerry Truman Straube** was born in Bowling Green, Pike County, Missouri, on March 03, 1949. He was also known as **Jake**.

Jerry Truman died in Bowling Green, Pike County, Missouri, on February 03, 2015, at the age of 65. He was buried in Memorial Gardens Cemetery, Bowling Green, Pike County, Missouri (Find a Grave ID 143001000).

The Vandalia Leader April 29, 2015

Bowling Green resident Jerry Truman Straube, age 65, passed away from lung cancer on Feb. 3 2015 at the Moore Pike Nursing Home in Bowling Green. He was born March 3, 1949 to Scott and Annie Straube at the former BB Springs in Bowling Green. He was the fifth of seven children and was named after President Harry S. Truman. Memorial services were held at 11 a.m., Tuesday, Feb. 10, at the Bibb-Veach Funeral Home in Bowling Green with Rev. Don Amelung officiating. Memorial visitation was held at 9:30 a.m. until time of service at the funeral home. Jerry was raised in Bowling Green, where he attended local schools and graduated in 1967 from BGHS. In January 1968, he enlisted in the US Navy and spent his first year on the USS BobHomme Richard, serving alongside his brother Bob. In 1969, he commenced an overseas tour and served active duty in Vietnam. He was honorably discharged in January 1974 and settled in the Washington, D.C. suburbs near his siblings. After moving back to Missouri, he married Pamela Fischer in 1979 and divorced in 1980.

Jerry developed an interest in traveling and for a couple of years he accompanied cross country truck drivers as a loading assistant. He also worked on a variety of construction projects and was an accomplished carpenter with Gary Wendel's Carpeting service in Bowling Green for several years. He was artistic and enjoyed numerous hobbies including drawing, woodworking, and playing billiards. His favorite pastime was collecting a wide variety of music and movies, building an impressive collection over 30 years.

In addition to his military travels abroad, he managed to see a majority of the US through his early cross country drives and visits with his brother David in Florida and Kentucky, family road trips to Wisconsin to visit his sister Joyce, and flying to Alaska, where he spent several summers with his sister Karen.

Jerry was preceded in death by his father Walter Scott Straube, Sr., brothers, Scott, Jr., Bob, and David Straube, sister Rosetta Pagnella, and brother-in-law Chad Drennan. He is survived by his mother, Annie Straube of Bowling Green, sisters Karen "Katie" (Bill) Corbus of Juneau, Ala., Joyce Roloff (Doug Kroft) of Crested Butte, Colo., as well as several nieces, nephews, and extended family.

In lieu of flowers, his family suggest memorial donations be made to Home Care and Hospice (#1 Health Care Place, Bowling Green, Mo 63334), Second Baptist Church (319 W. Church, Bowling Green, Mo. 63334), or to VFW Post 5553 (505 VFW Road, Bowling Green, Mo. 63334).

+ 117 f VI. **Karen Sue Straube** was born in Bowling Green, Pike County, Missouri, on January 04, 1951. She is also known as **Katie**.

+ 118 f VII. **Joyce Marie Straube** was born in Bowling Green, Pike County, Missouri, on November 08, 1952.

Family of Hazel Straube and Garland Smith

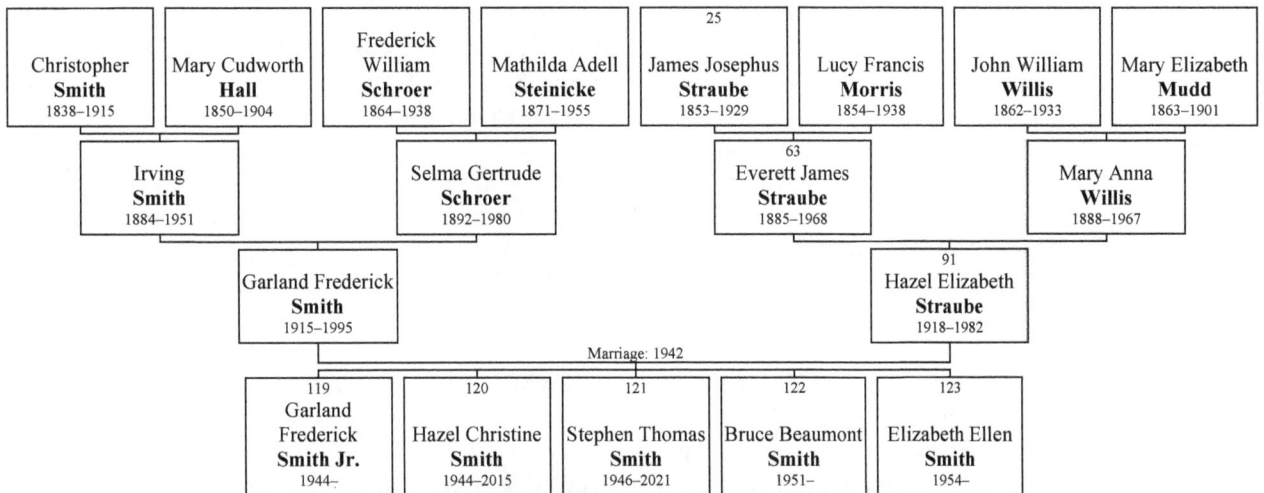

Christopher **Smith** 1838–1915	Mary Cudworth **Hall** 1850–1904	Frederick William **Schroer** 1864–1938

Relationships chart:

- Christopher **Smith** (1838–1915) & Mary Cudworth **Hall** (1850–1904)
- Frederick William **Schroer** (1864–1938) & Mathilda Adell **Steinicke** (1871–1955)
- 25 James Josephus **Straube** (1853–1929) & Lucy Francis **Morris** (1854–1938)
- John William **Willis** (1862–1933) & Mary Elizabeth **Mudd** (1863–1901)
- Irving **Smith** (1884–1951)
- Selma Gertrude **Schroer** (1892–1980)
- 63 Everett James **Straube** (1885–1968)
- Mary Anna **Willis** (1888–1967)
- Garland Frederick **Smith** (1915–1995)
- 91 Hazel Elizabeth **Straube** (1918–1982)
- Marriage: 1942

Children:
- 119 Garland Frederick **Smith Jr.** 1944–
- 120 Hazel Christine **Smith** 1944–2015
- 121 Stephen Thomas **Smith** 1946–2021
- 122 Bruce Beaumont **Smith** 1951–
- 123 Elizabeth Ellen **Smith** 1954–

91. **Hazel Elizabeth Straube** was born on Sunday, October 13, 1918, in New Hartford, Pike County, Missouri. She was the daughter of Everett James Straube (63) and Mary Anna Willis.

Hazel Elizabeth died in Saint Louis, Saint Louis County, Missouri, on April 21, 1982, at the age of 63. She was buried in Oak Hill Cemetery, Kirkwood, St. Louis County, Missouri (Find a Grave ID 68614261).

Born Hazel Elizabeth Straube on Sunday, October 13, 1918, in Hartford Township in rural Pike County, Missouri. She is the daughter of Everett James and Mary Anna Willis Straube.

After graduation from Bowling Green High School in 1935, Hazel taught at Allison School, a one-room schoolhouse, for two years. After two years of teaching, Hazel saved enough money to put herself through Brown Business and Secretarial School in St. Louis to become a stenographer. On April 21, 1939, Hazel graduated and became secretary at Washington University School of Medicine.

Hazel married Garland F. Smith, M. D. on April 17, 1942, at Central Presbyterian Church in Clayton, Missouri. They were married by the Revered Dr. Benjamin Franklin Hall.

To this union were born Garland Frederick (Fred) Jr. on February 4, 1944, at St. Patrick's Hospital, Lake Charles, Louisiana; Hazel Christine on December 4, 1944, at St. Luke's Hospital; Stephen Thomas on November 17, 1946, at DePaul Hospital; Bruce Beaumont on June 30, 1951, at St. Luke's Hospital; and Elizabeth Ellen on September 22, 1954, at St. John's Hospital. All were born in St. Louis except Fred.

Hazel was a member of Central Presbyterian Church in Clayton loved to garden, collect antiques and do volunteer work. She was active in many organizations and clubs including the National Society of the Daughters of the American Revolution (DAR) national number 658345; President of St. Louis Presbytery, 1967-68; Southeast Missouri Presbytery, 1970-71; St. John's Mercy Women's Auxiliary, 1969-71; 9th District of Church Women United, 1973-75 and Central Branch of the American Cancer Society, 1975-76. Hazel also received Honorary Life Membership Awards from Central Presbyterian Women of the Church, 1967; Clayton Garden Club Group I, 1973 and St. John's Mercy Medical Center Auxiliary, 1971. She received Auxilian of the Year Award for St. John's Mercy Auxiliary in 1975 and State Auxiliary Woman of the Year Award for the Missouri Hospital Association in 1975. She also was the recipient of the Mercy Award given by St. John's Mercy Medical Center in 1980.

In October of 1978 Hazel was diagnosed with cancer and had a radical mastectomy followed by chemotherapy treatments. Later the disease spread to the lymphatic area and she passed away on Wednesday, April 21, 1982, at St. John's Mercy Medical Center in Creve Coeur at the age of 63 years, 6 months and 8 days. The cause of death was listed as metastatic cancer of the breast. A funeral service was conducted on Friday, April 23, at the Lupton Chapel, and burial was at Oak Hill Cemetery, Kirkwood, Missouri. The Reverend Dr. Andrew Jumper and Reverend Donald M. Megahan officiated.

Hazel is survived by her husband, Garland F. Smith, M.D.; three sons, Garland F. (Fred) (Karen) Jr. of Florissant, Stephen Thomas (Karen) of Westwood, N.J. and Bruce Beaumont (Ruth) of Annapolis, MD; two daughters, Hazel Christine Smith (Jacques) McCormack of Katonah, NY and Elizabeth Ellen Smith of Chicago; one sister, Gladys Straube Myers of Columbia, MO and one brother, Scott Straube, Sr. of Bowling Green, MO; and two grandchildren, Christiane Elizabeth Smith of Florissant and John Garland McCormack of Katonah, NY.

At the age of 23, Hazel Elizabeth married **Dr. Garland Frederick Smith** on Friday, April 17, 1942, in Saint Louis, Saint Louis County, Missouri, when he was 26 years old. They had five children.

Garland Frederick was born in Saint Louis, Saint Louis County, Missouri, on Sunday, May 23, 1915. He was the son of Irving Smith and Selma Gertrude Schroer.

Garland Frederick reached 80 years of age and died in Saint Louis, Saint Louis County, Missouri, on July 28, 1995. He was buried in Oak Hill Cemetery, Kirkwood, St. Louis County, Missouri (Find a Grave ID 68614507).

Born Garland Frederick Smith on Sunday, May 23, 1915, in Saint Louis, Missouri, the only child of Irving and Selma Gertrude Schroer Smith.

Garland graduated from Soldan High School in St. Louis in 1933; from Westminster College, Fulton, Missouri June 1937 with a bachelor's degree; and from Washington University Medical School, St. Louis, Missouri June 1941 with a M.D. degree. He interned at St. Luke's Hospital in St. Louis from July 1, 1941, to June 30, 1942.

Garland served in the United States Army Medical Corps with the highest rank of major and duties of Platoon Commander, Company Commander and Ward Surgeon during World War II from June 29, 1942, to March 31, 1946. He was honorably discharged on April 1, 1953. Decorations received were Asiatic-Pacific Theater Campaign Ribbon, American Theatre Campaign Ribbon and Victory Medal. During his service, he attended the Medical Field Service School at Carlisle Barracks, Carlisle, Pennsylvania from June 29, 1942, to July 31, 1942; 9th Armored Division Medical Field Service School at Fort Riley, Junction City, Kansas July 24, 1942, to January 1944. While stationed at Fort Riley, Garland attended Chemical Warfare School at Edgewood Arsenal, Maryland, from November 29, 1942, to December 26, 1942, and trained at the Desert Training Center at Camp Ibis, Needles, California. While Garland was away Hazel resided in Manhattan, Kansas. In late January 1944, Garland was transferred to Camp Polk, Leesville, Louisiana, until late February 1944. In March 1944, Garland was transferred to Camp Rucker, Enterprise, Alabama then to Fort Lawton Staging Area, Fort Lawton, Washington, on April 16, 1944. He was sent overseas for duty to Kauai, Hawaii, seven miles south of the town of Lawai from May 1944 until September 1945 serving in administrative capacities. On September 18, 1945 Garland, was transferred to The 219th General Hospital at Schofield Barracks, Oahu, Hawaii to practice orthopedic surgery until December 1945. After completing his duty on the islands, he was sent through the Port of Los Angles to Riverside, California, for transportation to Jefferson Barracks at St. Louis, Missouri.

Garland was on the staffs at St. John's, De Paul, St. Anthony's and Deaconess Hospitals in the city. Later Garland joined the staff at St. Joseph's Hospital in Kirkwood. In 1963, St. John's Hospital moved from the Euclid Avenue location to a new large state-of-the-art facility in Creve Coeur. He eventually practiced only at St. John's which became known as St. John's Mercy Medical Center.

Garland was Chairman of Orthopedic Surgery at St. John's from 1964 to 1975, President of the St. Louis Orthopedic Society in 1980, and he won the Mercy Award given by St. John's Mercy Medical Center in 1985. He retired from full practice in 1985 but continued as a consultant for two years.

Garland married Hazel Elizabeth Straube on April 17, 1942, at Central Presbyterian Church, Clayton, Missouri. They were married by the Revered Dr. Benjamin Franklin Hall.

To this union were born Garland Frederick (Fred) Jr. on February 4, 1944, at St. Patrick's Hospital, Lake Charles, Louisiana; Hazel Christine on December 4, 1944, at St. Luke's Hospital; Stephen Thomas on November 17, 1946, at DePaul Hospital; Bruce Beaumont on June 30, 1951, at St. Luke's Hospital; and Elizabeth Ellen on September 22, 1954, at St. John's Hospital. All were born in St. Louis except Fred.

Garland had several hobbies he enjoyed. As a boy he made tables, lamps and many wooden items including model sailboats, a skill he leaned from his grandfather, Frederick Schroer. Garland along with his dad, Irving Smith, and grandfather, would take the sailboats Garland made to Forest Park and launch them on a lake. The men would spread out around the lake and catch them and sail them back and forth. At 12 years old he entered the Fisher Body Contest and from scratch made a model replica Napoleonic Coach, the logo of General Motors. He won his age group and was awarded a prize and scholarship money. Garland also was very artistic and sketched with pin and ink. Another hobby was photography. But most of all he loved model shipbuilding. He built from scratch five major scale models. The Sea Witch was the first he completed in 1940. The next four were The Flying Cloud completed in 1953 after 5,000 hours of work, Mayflower II completed in 1986 after 5,050 hours of work, Pride of Baltimore completed in 1988, Ranger completed in 1990 and the H. M. S. Halifax completed in 1993 after 2,115 hours of work. Between ships he collected and painted in minute detail cast lead Scottish miniature military figures. Each taking several months to research and finish. The steadiness of his hands in later years was incredible. All in all he completed about 100 miniatures before he passed away.

Garland passed away at 10:57 AM on Friday, July 28, 1995, at the age of 80 years, 2 months and 5 days of congestive heart failure, following a myocardial infarction 9 months prior and 8 years of atherosclerotic, benign prostatic hypertrophy and Dressler's Syndrome at St. John's Mercy Skilled Nursing Center in Creve Coeur, Missouri. He was a member of Central Presbyterian Church in Clayton. Funeral services were held on Monday, July 31, at Lupton Chapel and burial at Oak Hill Cemetery in Kirkwood, Missouri. The Reverend Donald M. Megahan officiated. Sister Mary Marthalene Joines, RSM, a long time colleague of Garland's, gave a eulogy sharing many memories of the years they worked together at St. John's.

Garland is survived by three sons, Garland F. (Fred) (Karen) Jr. of Florissant, Stephen Thomas of San Jose, CA and Bruce Beaumont (Ruth) of Severn, MD; two daughters, Hazel Christine Smith (Jacques) McCormack of Columbia, SC and Elizabeth Ellen Smith (Ron) Kolman of Chicago; and five grandchildren, Christiane Elizabeth Smith Hamai of Florissant, John Garland McCormack and Andrew Malcolm McCormack of Columbia, SC, Ian Christopher Smith and Matthew Brendan Smith of Severn, MD.

Children of Hazel Elizabeth Straube and Garland Frederick Smith:

+ 119 m I. **Garland Frederick Smith Jr.** was born in Lake Charles, Calcasieu Parish, Louisianna, on February 04, 1944.

+ 120 f II. **Hazel Christine Smith** was born in Saint Louis, Saint Louis County, Missouri, on December 04, 1944. She was also known as **Christy**.

Hazel Christine died in Columbia, Richland County, South Carolina, on April 11, 2015, at the age of 70. She was buried in Elmwood Memorial Gardens, Columbia, Richland County, South Carolina, on April 18, 2015 (Find a Grave ID 144881059).

+ 121 m III. **Stephen Thomas Smith** was born in Saint Louis, Saint Louis County, Missouri, on November 17, 1946. He died in San Jose, Santa Clara County, California, on February 25, 2021, at the age of 74. Stephen Thomas was buried in Jefferson Barracks National Cemetery, Lemay, St. Louis County, Missouri (Find a Grave ID 223492939).

On February 25, 2021, Stephen Thomas "Steve" Smith passed away surrounded by family and friends after a short battle with cancer at the age of 74 at his home in San Jose, CA.

Steve was born on November 17, 1946 in St. Louis, MO to the late Dr. Garland F. and Hazel E. (Straube) Smith.

Steve grew up in Richmond Heights, MO and graduated from Maplewood-Richmond Heights High School in 1965 with achievements in football, track and student affairs. He attended the University of Missouri-Columbia, enlisted in the United States Marine Corps becoming a U.S. Marine Corps Photographer. His assignments included photographing anything from "grip and grins" and luncheons to parades, officer portraits, award ceremonies, and forensics. The Corporal was as a 3-star general's favorite and "go to photographer." He also was a photographer for the Quantico Sentry. In 1970, Steve enrolled at the Rochester Institute of Technology studying Film Making, Photojournalism, and World and Art History. A Dean's List honoree and editor of the school magazine "The Genesean" graduating in 1973.

In August 1973, Steve began his professional career with E. Leitz Inc. manufacturers of Leica Cameras as a sales representative in the Midwest. In 1976 Steve became national sales manager for the company and resided in Rockleigh, NJ. Steve became Vice President of the Photographic Division in January 1982 responsible for all sales of Leica cameras and accessories in the U.S. market.

For a short time Steve returned to St. Louis starting his own corporate outplacement firm. In 1993 Olympus Camera County hired Steve as a regional manager and later sale manager for the Western U.S. Region and Hawaii being based in San Jose, CA.

Downsizing forced Steve to make a career change. He became a licensed real estate agent and joined Coldwell Banker Realty San Jose-Willow Glen Office in 2009 and remained with the firm until his death.

Steve had many hobbies over the years – photography, woodworking, automotive restorations and playing golf. He coached golf for many years at Piedmont Hills High School in San Jose.

Steve was preceded in death by his father, mother and sister Hazel Christine Smith (Jacques T.) McCormack. He is survived by his brothers Garland F. "Fred" (Karen) Smith, Jr., O'Fallon, MO and Bruce B. (Ruth) Smith, Severn, MD and sister Elizabeth E. Smith, Chicago, IL. Uncle to Christiane E. Smith (John) Hamai, St. Paul, MO; John G. McCormack, Columbia, SC; Andrew M. McCormack, San Francisco, CA; Ian C. Smith, Havre de Grace, MD; Matthew B. Smith, Severn, MD. Great-uncle to Noah J. Hamai, Mallory E. Hamai, Reagan C. Hamai, Jonah C. Hamai, St. Paul, MO; Alannah F. Smith, Lillian M. Smith, Havre de Grace, MD. Former wife Karen Lee (Osterman) Smith, nice and nephews, Marguerite, Mark and Chris Basso as well as his "adopted" children, Elizabeth and Khang Nyugen. Numerous cousins.

Services: Committal service with military honors will be held at 11:00 a.m. on Thursday, June 3, 2021 at the Jefferson Barracks National Cemetery. Donations may be made to American Cancer Society. Please share memories at https://www.dignitymemorial.com/obituaries/san-jose-ca/stephen-smith-10075770

+   122   m   **IV. Bruce Beaumont Smith** was born in Saint Louis, Saint Louis County, Missouri, on June 30, 1951.

+   123   f   **V. Elizabeth Ellen Smith** was born in Saint Louis, Saint Louis County, Missouri, on September 22, 1954.

Family of Everett Straube and Lillie Dieckmann

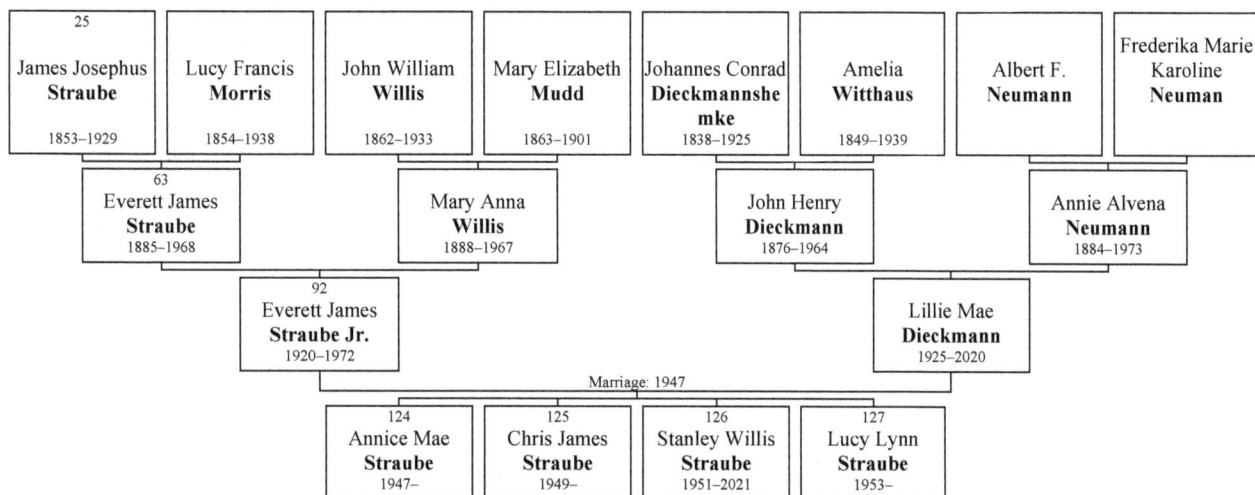

25 James Josephus **Straube** 1853–1929	Lucy Francis **Morris** 1854–1938	John William **Willis** 1862–1933	Mary Elizabeth **Mudd** 1863–1901	Johannes Conrad **Dieckmannshe mke** 1838–1925	Amelia **Witthaus** 1849–1939	Albert F. **Neumann**	Frederika Marie Karoline **Neuman**

63
Everett James **Straube** 1885–1968 — Mary Anna **Willis** 1888–1967

John Henry **Dieckmann** 1876–1964 — Annie Alvena **Neumann** 1884–1973

92
Everett James **Straube Jr.** 1920–1972

Lillie Mae **Dieckmann** 1925–2020

Marriage: 1947

124 Annice Mae **Straube** 1947–	125 Chris James **Straube** 1949–	126 Stanley Willis **Straube** 1951–2021	127 Lucy Lynn **Straube** 1953–

92. **Everett James Straube Jr.** was born on Tuesday, April 13, 1920, in New Hartford, Pike County, Missouri. He was the son of Everett James Straube (63) and Mary Anna Willis.

Everett James died at Pike County Memorial Hospital in Louisiana, Pike County, Missouri, on November 19, 1972, at the age of 52. His cause of death was cerebral anoxia, carcinoma of stomach & esophagus. Everett James was buried in Memorial Gardens Cemetery, Bowling Green, Pike County, Missouri, on November 21, 1972 (Find a Grave ID 68398423).

> Everett James Straube Jr. was born on April 13, 1920, in Hartford Township of Pike County, Missouri. He was named after his father, Everett James Straube, and was fondly called by his initials, E.J. He attended the rural Pike County school of Vannoy through the eighth grade. E.J. graduated from Bowling Green High School in 1938. During high school there was no baseball team, but E.J. was on the basketball team and a charter member of the FFA (Future Farmers of America).
>
> After graduation, E.J. was employed at Harbison-Walker Brick Plant in Vandalia, Missouri and after his discharge from service in the war; he worked at the Elder Garment Factory in Bowling Green and then worked for Hercules, Inc. in Louisiana, Missouri.
>
> On September 27, 1947, E.J. and Lil were married by Reverend G. O. Baxter of the Second Baptist Church at the parsonage at 215 West Locust in Bowling Green. Lillie (Lil) Mae Dieckmann was born April 1, 1925, near Silex in Lincoln County, Missouri, the youngest child of John Henry and Annie Neumann Dieckmann. To this union were born Annice Mae on December 18, 1947, Chris James on August 2, 1949, Stanley Willis on May 26, 1951, and Lucy Lynn on February 21, 1953.
>
> Both E.J. and Lil were members of the Second Baptist Church of Bowling Green. E.J. was a deacon and Lil a Sunday school teacher of young children for many years. E.J. and Lil both loved gardening, Khoury League (E.J. helped at games when he was not working) and Cardinal games. Since the early '40s till E.J. passed away, he and Lil attended almost every World Series in St. Louis for at least one game. They also attended the 1959 World

Series in Chicago when the White Sox faced the Los Angeles Dodgers. Lil was a Khoury League scorekeeper, and she was active in PTA. Later Lil was a member of the Cancer Society and the American Legion Auxiliary, and she is a member of the Association of Retired Missouri State Employees. She still enjoys her garden and still enjoys cooking. E.J. and Lil purchased the home at 1105 West Centennial in Bowling Green on June 20, 1967, following the death of Grandma Straube. This is the home where they lived years earlier and where their children were all born. It is also the last home of grandpa and grandma (Everett and Mary Anna) before they went to Uncle Scott and Aunt Ann's boarding home.

Having been diagnosed with cancer of the esophagus and stomach in 1971, E.J. retired from Hercules, Inc., Louisiana, Missouri, on April 1, 1972 completing 17 years of service. After a long battle with the disease, E.J. passed away at Pike County Memorial Hospital at 5:25 A.M. on Sunday, November 19, 1972 at the age of 52 years, 7 months and 6 days. Services were at the Second Baptist Church on November 21. The Rev. G. E. Rittenhouse, a special family friend of many years, officiated. Burial was at Memorial Gardens in Bowling Green, Missouri. Pallbearers were nephews: Ted Mummert, Duane Straube, Scott Straube Jr., Fred Smith, David Straube and Sam Hargadine IV.

At the age of 27, Everett James married **Lillie Mae Dieckmann** on Saturday, September 27, 1947, in Bowling Green, Pike County, Missouri, when she was 22 years old. They had four children.

Lillie Mae was born in Silex, Lincoln County, Missouri, on Wednesday, April 01, 1925. She was the daughter of John Henry Dieckmann and Annie Alvena Neumann.

Lillie Mae reached 95 years of age and died in Bowling Green, Pike County, Missouri, on December 11, 2020. She was buried on December 19, 2020, in Memorial Gardens Cemetery, Bowling Green, Pike County, Missouri (Find a Grave ID 218043956).

Obituary for Lillie Mae Straube:

Lillie Mae (Dieckmann) Straube, age 95, passed away at her home in Bowling Green, MO, Friday, December 11, 2020. Funeral services will be December 19th, 2020, at Second Baptist Church, Bowling Green, with visitation from 9 to 11 a.m. followed by the service at 11:00. Rev. Jerry Gamm will officiate, assisted by Pastor Mark West. Burial will be in Bowling Green Memorial Garden Cemetery.

Lil, the youngest child of John Henry and Annie Alvena (Neumann) Dieckmann, was born April 1, 1925, in Lincoln County, MO, near Silex. Throughout her life she cherished the happy memories of her early years spent with her parents and siblings.

Lil's early education was in rural one-room schools in Lincoln and Pike counties. After the family's move to Pike County, she attended Bowling Green schools, graduating with the class of 1943. Soon after graduation, she accepted a clerical position with the Social Security Administration in Bowling Green where she continued to be employed until her marriage.

She married Everett James (E.J.) Straube Jr., and they established their first home in Bowling Green on Centennial Street, where their children were all born. After the birth of their children, Lil was a stay-at-home mom. She and her husband were actively involved in church and the activities of their children: church, sports, band and PTA.

In 1966, she returned to full-time employment with the Division of Social Services, formerly the Social Security Administration. She retired from the position of caseworker in 1996 after 34 years of service. Her husband preceded her in death on November 19, 1972.

Lil enjoyed the simple pleasures of life such as tending a large garden and sharing its abundance with others. The many family get togethers in her home were highlighted with her special homemade rolls and burnt caramel cake. Activities included mushroom hunting, picking blackberries, crossword puzzles, playing cards and documenting family history. She was an avid Cardinal baseball fan and enjoyed attending games and several World Series with family. She enjoyed Sunday rides, reminiscing, and visiting with relatives near and far. She also felt blessed by friendships of church, family and friends.

She was a member of Second Baptist Church, where she had taught Sunday school for younger children, Training Union, was a home-bound visitor and kitchen volunteer. Her strong Christian faith was an example to her family. She was a member of the Association of Retired Missouri State Employees, and a former member of the American Legion Auxiliary and Pike County Cancer Unit.

Survivors include two sons: Chris (Vickie Ruth) Straube, Center; Willis Straube, Bowling Green; two daughters: Annice (R.J.) Allensworth, Bowling Green; Lucy Scherder of Warrenton. Grandchildren: Trent Straube, Christina (Randy) Hays, Aaron (Kelly) Straube, Jason Straube, Eric (Kayla) Scherder, Ricky (Malarie) Allensworth, Carmen (Johnny) Charlton, Curtis (Christina) Scherder, Matthew (Mary Ann) Scherder, Seth (Jeni) Straube, great grandchildren, nieces, nephews and close friends Betty and Ake Takahashi.

She was preceded in death by her parents, siblings: Eli, Ben and John Penn Dieckmann, Hilda Evans, Ann Straube, granddaughter Sara (Straube) Anders, and daughter-in-law Vicki Ann (Willis) Straube.

Pallbearers are: Aaron, Jason and Seth Straube, Ricky Allensworth, Curtis and Matthew Scherder.

Honorary pallbearers were Trent Straube, Eric Scherder, Randy Hays, Johnny Charlton, Brian Anders and Ake Takahashi.

Memorials may be made to the Sara Straube Anders Teaching Scholarship Fund, Child Evangelism Fellowship (Warrenton, MO) or Second Baptist Church funeral dinners.

Children of Everett James Straube Jr. and Lillie Mae Dieckmann:

+   124   f   I. **Annice Mae Straube** was born in Bowling Green, Pike County, Missouri, on December 18, 1947.

+   125   m   II. **Chris James Straube** was born in Bowling Green, Pike County, Missouri, on August 02, 1949.

+   126   m   III. **Stanley Willis Straube** was born in Bowling Green, Pike County, Missouri, on May 26, 1951. He died on January 21, 2021, at the age of 69. Stanley Willis was buried in Edgewood Cemetery, Edgewood, Pike County, Missouri, on January 30, 2021 (Find a Grave ID 221636104).

Stanley "Willis" Straube, 69, of Bowling Green, passed away January 21, 2021 at his home. Funeral services for Willis will be held Saturday, January 30, 2021 at 11:30 a.m. at Second Baptist Church in Bowling Green with Rev. Jerry Gamm and Pastor Mark West officiating. Burial will be in Edgewood Cemetery. Visitation will be from 9:00 to 11:30 a.m. at Second Baptist Church. Online streaming of the service will be available on Bibb-Veach Funeral Home's Facebook page.

Willis was born May 26, 1951 in Bowling Green, Missouri to Everett James Straube Jr. and Lillie Mae Dieckmann Straube. He was united in marriage to Vicki Ann Burnett on June 20, 1976. She preceded him in death on January 6, 2006.
Willis lived in Bowling Green his entire life. He graduated from Bowling Green High School in 1969. Immediately after graduation, he enlisted in the United States Marine Corps. During Vietnam, he served as a Corporal in Futenma, Okinawa. After discharging from active duty, Willis served in the United States Marine Corp Reserves from 1969 - 1972. He is a lifetime member of the VFW Post #5553 in Bowling Green.

Willis worked as a laborer for several construction companies over the years and enjoyed the many friendships he made during that time. When he wasn't working, he liked to spend his time hunting, fishing, gardening, and playing golf or baseball. He once played on an all-star team at Sportsman's Park. He also enjoyed playing his guitar and studied the history of music. He was a fan of blues and country music. He enjoyed barbequing and playing cards, but his favorite pastime was spending time with his family and grandchildren.

Willis is survived by sons, Jason Straube (Wendy Summers) of Bowling Green and Seth Straube (Jeni) of Bowling Green; daughter, Carmen Charlton (John) of Bowling Green; grandchildren: Kinley and Kaylyn Charlton, Kyle and Jayce Straube, Steven Bryant, Everli Straube, Carly Ledford, and Jaymeson Portwood; brother, Chris Straube (Vickie Ruth) of Center, Missouri; sisters, Annice Allensworth (R.J.) of Bowling

Green and Lucy Scherder of Warrenton, Missouri; and many nieces, nephews, and cousins. He was preceded in death by his parents and wife, Vicki.

Pallbearers will be Ricky Allensworth, Aaron Straube, Shawn Burnett, John Charlton, Randy Hays, and Curtis Scherder. Memorials may be made to the donor's choice.

+   127   f   IV. **Lucy Lynn Straube** was born in Bowling Green, Pike County, Missouri, on February 21, 1953.

Family of Melvin Straube and Leta McCoy

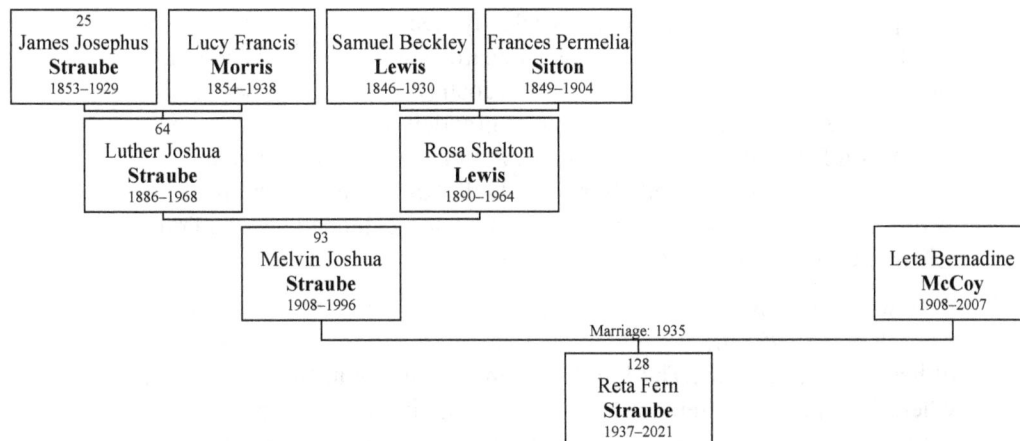

93.   **Melvin Joshua Straube** was born on Sunday, August 16, 1908, in Gazette, Pike County, Missouri. He was the son of Luther Joshua Straube (64) and Rosa Shelton Lewis. He was also known as **Pete**.

Melvin Joshua died in Vandalia, Audrain County, Missouri, on May 11, 1996, at the age of 87. He was buried in Fairmount Cemetery, Middletown, Montgomery County, Missouri (Find a Grave ID 84828021).

At the age of 27, Melvin Joshua married **Leta Bernadine McCoy** on Wednesday, September 18, 1935, in Vandalia, Audrain County, Missouri, when she was 26 years old. They had one daughter.

Leta Bernadine was born in Middletown, Montgomery County, Missouri, on Tuesday, September 29, 1908. She reached 98 years of age and died in Mexico, Audrain County, Missouri, on January 06, 2007. Leta Bernadine was buried in Fairmount Cemetery, Middletown, Montgomery County, Missouri (Find a Grave ID 100195467).

Daughter of Melvin Joshua Straube and Leta Bernadine McCoy:

+   128   f   I. **Reta Fern Straube** was born in Middletown, Montgomery County, Missouri, on February 14, 1937. She died in Vandalia, Audrain County, Missouri, on March 27, 2021, at the age of 84. Reta Fern was buried in Fairmount Cemetery, Middletown, Montgomery County, Missouri (Find a Grave ID 225033682).

Services for Reta Fern Dempsey, 84, of Vandalia, will be held 12:00 p.m. Monday, March 29, 2021 at Bienhoff Funeral Home in Vandalia with Reverend Jamie Franke officiating. Burial will be in Fairmount Cemetery in Middletown. Visitation will be from 10:00 until the time of service on Monday at the funeral home. She passed away at 4:35 a.m. March 27, 2021 at Tri-County Care Center in Vandalia.

Reta was born at home in Middletown on February 14, 1937, the only child of Melvin "Pete" and Leta McCoy Straube. She was married to Leon Dempsey from 1956 through 1970 and was blessed with three sons.

Survivors include: three sons, Melvin Dempsey of Hannibal, Mike (Jan) Dempsey of Kansas City, and Larry (Sandy) Dempsey of Rapid City, SD; seven grandchildren, Beth (Chad) Blanchard, Sarah (James) Waddell, Becky (Shea) Williams, Brad Dempsey, Josh (Ashton) Dempsey, and Jacob and Zach Dempsey; sixteen great grandchildren, Jacob, Annabel, and Aaron Blanchard, Madisyn, Mathew and Mara, Bennet, Brennah, Grant, Makenna, Elliot, and Quinn Waddell, Kaeden and Kyndal Williams, and Dax and Channing Dempsey; and extended special family – Mike, Charla and Emily Smith of Vandalia.

Reta was a lifetime area resident, member of the Vandalia First Christian Church and a 1955 graduate of Wellsville High School and Valedictorian of her graduating class. The family began their home in Bowling Green where she worked in Senator Ed Long's office in Pike County. They moved to Vandalia in 1964 and she started babysitting and working for the city pool. This was followed by a 25-year adventure working as night manager for the Vandalia Dairy Queen. Her relationships with all the kids she worked with through the years were so very special and remains in touch with several still to this day. Her church family were all so good to her through the years and she loved to attend all the services and special events. Reta had been living at Tri County Care Center for the past five years and she was blessed with faithful friends who visited and called and wrote. Maza Carnes wrote her weekly notes filled with wonderful stories, Carla Thompson called her multiple times a day, those calls Reta counted on, weekly visitors Juanita Lynn, Pat Miller, Dwight Galloway and Lana Terry plus many others stopping by. Reta loved her visits, calls and letters. She also loved her DQ treats, those always brought on the smiles. She always wanted to know "when are you coming to see me again" or "when are you going to call again." Covid made the past year extremely challenging for Reta. With limited outside personal contact, she relied on the friends and Staff at Tri-County as well as her faith to see her through. She endured and beat Covid, and held on until family could once again be by her side. As the end became near, the close contact again with family, brought smiles, hugs, kisses, and comfort.

Pallbearers: Brad Dempsey, Josh Dempsey, Jake Dempsey, Zach Dempsey, Chad Blanchard, James Waddell, Shea Williams
In lieu of flowers the family asks memorials be given to the First Christian Church, Vandalia, MO In Care of Bienhoff Funeral Home, PO Box 54, Vandalia, MO 63382.

Descendants of Johann Stroube and Francis Feagen

Family of Leonard Straube and Alta Snarr

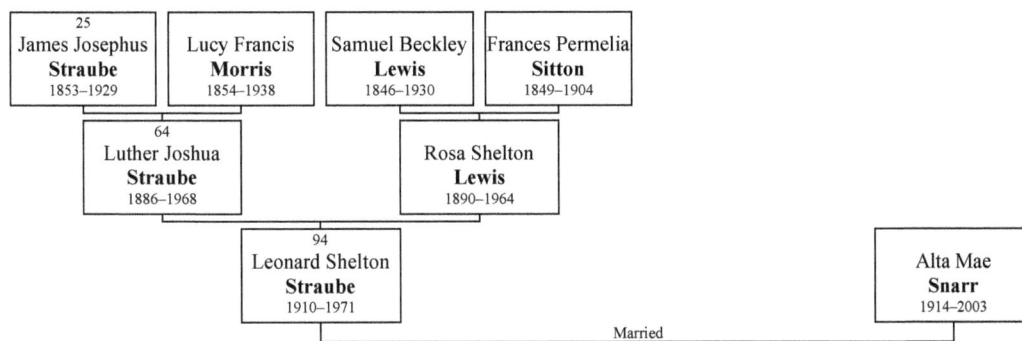

94. **Leonard Shelton Straube** was born on Friday, February 11, 1910, in Pike County, Missouri. He was the son of Luther Joshua Straube (64) and Rosa Shelton Lewis.

Leonard Shelton died in Fontana, San Bernardino County, California, on May 26, 1971, at the age of 61. He was buried in Green Acres Memorial Park and Mortuary, Bloomington, San Bernardino County, California (Find a Grave ID 157391748).

He married **Alta Mae Snarr**. Alta Mae was born in Missouri, USA, on Wednesday, January 21, 1914.

She reached 89 years of age and died in California, USA, on May 22, 2003. Alta Mae was buried in Green Acres Memorial Park and Mortuary, Bloomington, San Bernardino County, California (Find a Grave ID 157391749).

Family of Irene Straube and William Baugh

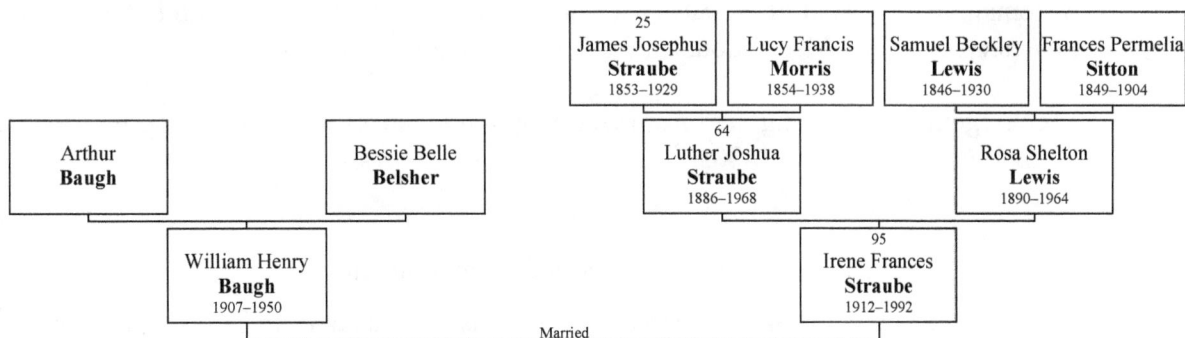

95. **Irene Frances Straube** was born on Tuesday, March 26, 1912, at 28 Dec 1992 in Bowling Green, Pike County, Missouri. She was the daughter of Luther Joshua Straube (64) and Rosa Shelton Lewis.

Irene Frances died in New Florence, Montgomery County, Missouri, on December 28, 1992, at the age of 80. She was buried in Midway Cemetery, Montgomery County, Missouri (Find a Grave ID 49088094).

She married **William Henry Baugh**. William Henry was born in Wellsville, Montgomery County, Missouri, on Friday, March 15, 1907. He was the son of Arthur Baugh and Bessie Belle Belsher.

William Henry reached 43 years of age and died in Wellsville, Montgomery County, Missouri, on May 10, 1950. He was buried in Midway Cemetery, Montgomery County, Missouri (Find a Grave ID 49088012).

Family of Ogle Straube and Evelyn Begeman

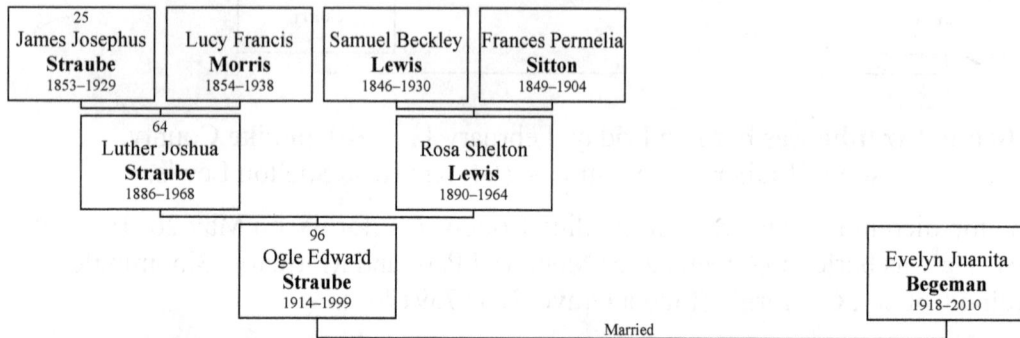

```
┌──────────────┐ ┌──────────────┐ ┌──────────────┐ ┌──────────────┐
│      25      │ │              │ │              │ │              │
│James Josephus│ │ Lucy Francis │ │Samuel Beckley│ │Frances Permelia│
│   Straube    │ │   Morris     │ │   Lewis      │ │   Sitton     │
│  1853–1929   │ │  1854–1938   │ │  1846–1930   │ │  1849–1904   │
└──────────────┘ └──────────────┘ └──────────────┘ └──────────────┘
        ┌──────────────┐            ┌──────────────┐
        │      64      │            │              │
        │Luther Joshua │            │ Rosa Shelton │
        │   Straube    │            │    Lewis     │
        │  1886–1968   │            │  1890–1964   │
        └──────────────┘            └──────────────┘
               ┌──────────────┐                        ┌──────────────┐
               │      96      │                        │              │
               │ Ogle Edward  │                        │Evelyn Juanita│
               │   Straube    │                        │   Begeman    │
               │  1914–1999   │                        │  1918–2010   │
               └──────────────┘        Married         └──────────────┘
```

96. **Ogle Edward Straube** was born on Monday, November 16, 1914, in Gazette, Pike County, Missouri. He was the son of Luther Joshua Straube (64) and Rosa Shelton Lewis. He was also known as **Tutor**.

Ogle Edward died in Montgomery City, Montgomery County, Missouri, on January 09, 1999, at the age of 84. He was buried in Bellflower Cemetery, Bellflower, Montgomery County, Missouri (Find a Grave ID 22785453).

On Dec 28, 1940 in New London, MO Ogle Edward "Tutor" Straube married Evelyn Begeman, the daughter of Hobart Lawrence Begeman, who is also buried in Bellflower Cemetery, and Floy Mae Woodson. Evelyn and "Tutor" were 5th cousins once removed.

The "Begemann's" immigrated from Germany in the late 1880's. They dropped the last N off their name in the late 1800s.

Gravesite Details
Tutor was born in 1914 not 1913 as inscribed on monument.

He married **Evelyn Juanita Begeman**. Evelyn Juanita was born in Truxton, Lincoln County, Missouri, on Sunday, August 25, 1918.

She reached 92 years of age and died in Mount Pleasant, Henry County, Iowa, on December 20, 2010. Evelyn Juanita was buried in Bellflower Cemetery, Bellflower, Montgomery County, Missouri (Find a Grave ID 108848854).

Evelyn is the daughter of Hobart Lawrence Begeman, who is also buried in Bellflower Cemetery, and Floy Mae Woodson. She married Ogle Edward "Tutor" Straube. Evelyn and "Tutor" were 5th cousins once removed.

Carroll Straube

97. **Carroll Wilson Straube** was born on Sunday, November 19, 1916, in Pike County, Missouri.[75] He was the son of Luther Joshua Straube (64) and Rosa Shelton Lewis. He was also known as **Skeet**.

Carroll Wilson served in the U.S. Army during WWII, SSgt in Camp Dodge, Herrold, Iowa, on March 10, 1943.[75] He died in Wright City, Warren County, Missouri, on March 30, 1996, at the age of 79.[75] Carroll Wilson was buried in Wright City Cemetery, Wright City, Warren County, Missouri (Find a Grave ID 101227293).[75]

Marriages with Frankie Francine Mills and Helen Marie Lange (Page 174) are known.

Family of Carroll Straube and Frankie Mills

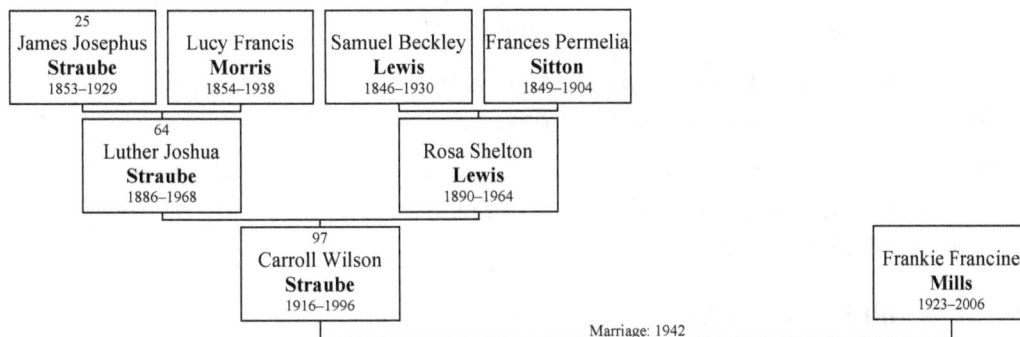

```
25                                Samuel Beckley   Frances Permelia
James Josephus   Lucy Francis     Lewis            Sitton
Straube          Morris           1846–1930        1849–1904
1853–1929        1854–1938

        64
    Luther Joshua                      Rosa Shelton
    Straube                            Lewis
    1886–1968                          1890–1964

            97                                    Frankie Francine
        Carroll Wilson                            Mills
        Straube                                   1923–2006
        1916–1996
                        Marriage: 1942
```

Here are the details about **Carroll Wilson Straube's** first marriage, with Frankie Francine Mills. You can read more about Carroll Wilson on page 173.

Carroll Wilson Straube married **Frankie Francine Mills** in 1942. Frankie Francine was born in Winterset, Madison County, Iowa, on Saturday, October 13, 1923.

She reached 82 years of age and died in Adair County, Iowa, on February 21, 2006. Frankie Francine was buried in Oakwood Cemetery, Walnut Township, Adair County, Iowa (Find a Grave ID 53476456).

75   Ancestry.com, Public Member Trees (Provo, UT, USA, Ancestry.com Operations, Inc., 2006), Ancestry.com, Record for Carroll Wilson "Skeet" Straube. https://search.ancestry.co.uk/cgi-bin/sse.dll?db=1030&h=392148224688&indiv=try.

Family of Carroll Straube and Helen Lange

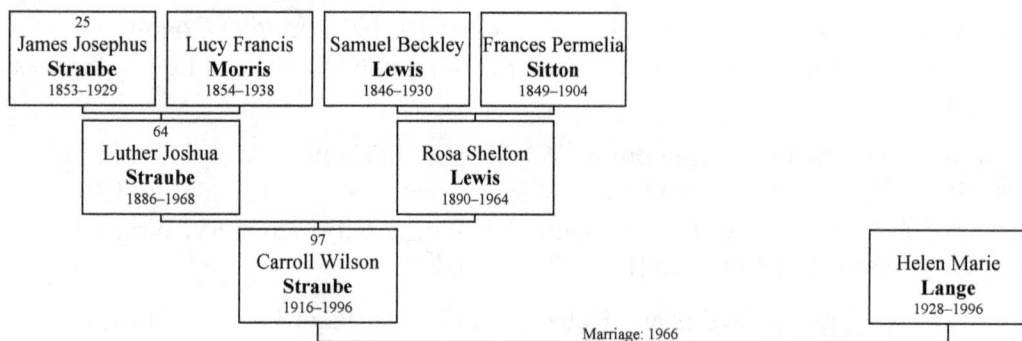

```
┌─────────────┐ ┌─────────────┐ ┌─────────────┐ ┌─────────────┐
│ 25          │ │ Lucy Francis│ │Samuel Beckley│ │Frances Permelia│
│James Josephus│ │   Morris    │ │    Lewis    │ │    Sitton   │
│   Straube   │ │  1854–1938  │ │  1846–1930  │ │  1849–1904  │
│  1853–1929  │ └─────────────┘ └─────────────┘ └─────────────┘
└─────────────┘
      ┌─────────────┐           ┌─────────────┐
      │ 64          │           │ Rosa Shelton│
      │Luther Joshua│           │    Lewis    │
      │   Straube   │           │  1890–1964  │
      │  1886–1968  │           └─────────────┘
      └─────────────┘
            ┌─────────────┐                      ┌─────────────┐
            │ 97          │                      │ Helen Marie │
            │Carroll Wilson│                     │    Lange    │
            │   Straube   │                      │  1928–1996  │
            │  1916–1996  │                      └─────────────┘
            └─────────────┘
                     Marriage: 1966
```

Here are the details about **Carroll Wilson Straube's** second marriage, with Helen Marie Lange. You can read more about Carroll Wilson on page 173.

Carroll Wilson Straube married **Helen Marie Lange** in 1966. Helen Marie was born in Wright City, Warren County, Missouri, on Thursday, January 19, 1928.

She reached 68 years of age and died in Jonesburg, Montgomery County, Missouri, on November 29, 1996. Helen Marie was buried in Wright City Cemetery, Wright City, Warren County, Missouri (Find a Grave ID 101227298).

Family of Claude Straube and Beatrice Chandler

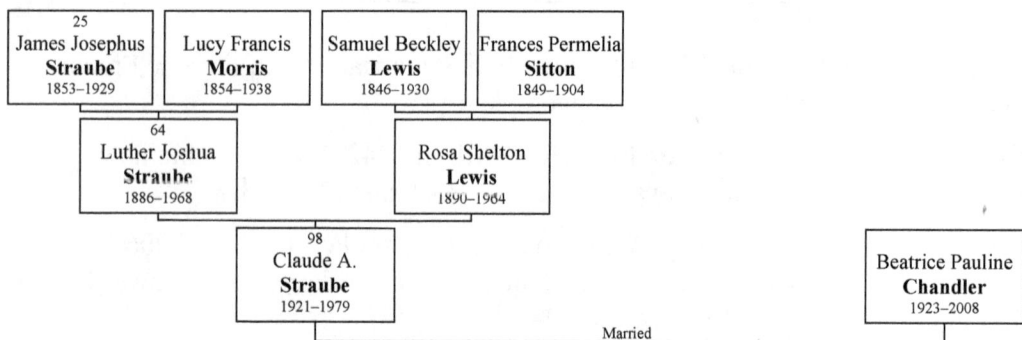

```
┌─────────────┐ ┌─────────────┐ ┌─────────────┐ ┌─────────────┐
│ 25          │ │ Lucy Francis│ │Samuel Beckley│ │Frances Permelia│
│James Josephus│ │   Morris    │ │    Lewis    │ │    Sitton   │
│   Straube   │ │  1854–1938  │ │  1846–1930  │ │  1849–1904  │
│  1853–1929  │ └─────────────┘ └─────────────┘ └─────────────┘
└─────────────┘
      ┌─────────────┐           ┌─────────────┐
      │ 64          │           │ Rosa Shelton│
      │Luther Joshua│           │    Lewis    │
      │   Straube   │           │  1890–1964  │
      │  1886–1968  │           └─────────────┘
      └─────────────┘
            ┌─────────────┐                      ┌─────────────┐
            │ 98          │                      │Beatrice Pauline│
            │  Claude A.  │                      │   Chandler  │
            │   Straube   │                      │  1923–2008  │
            │  1921–1979  │                      └─────────────┘
            └─────────────┘
                       Married
```

98. **Claude A. Straube** was born on Thursday, December 08, 1921, in Missouri, USA. He was the son of Luther Joshua Straube (64) and Rosa Shelton Lewis.

Claude A. served in the military between 1942 and 1946. Army Air Force, SSgt. He died in Montgomery County, Missouri, on March 09, 1979, at the age of 57. Claude A. was buried in Fairmount Cemetery, Middletown, Montgomery County, Missouri (Find a Grave ID 75961298).

He married **Beatrice Pauline Chandler**. Beatrice Pauline was born in Missouri, USA, on Friday, December 28, 1923.

She reached 84 years of age and died in Missouri, USA, on November 23, 2008. Beatrice Pauline was buried in Fairmount Cemetery, Middletown, Montgomery County, Missouri (Find a Grave ID 171653178).

Family of Robert Straube and Wanda Conrad

```
┌──────────────┐ ┌──────────────┐ ┌──────────────┐ ┌──────────────┐
│      25      │ │              │ │              │ │              │
│James Josephus│ │ Lucy Francis │ │Samuel Beckley│ │Frances Permelia│
│   Straube    │ │    Morris    │ │    Lewis     │ │    Sitton    │
│  1853–1929   │ │  1854–1938   │ │  1846–1930   │ │  1849–1904   │
└──────────────┘ └──────────────┘ └──────────────┘ └──────────────┘
         ┌──────────────┐         ┌──────────────┐
         │      64      │         │              │
         │Luther Joshua │         │ Rosa Shelton │
         │   Straube    │         │    Lewis     │
         │  1886–1968   │         │  1890–1964   │
         └──────────────┘         └──────────────┘
              ┌──────────────┐              ┌──────────────┐
              │      99      │              │              │
              │ Robert Edwin │              │  Wanda Jean  │
              │   Straube    │              │    Conrad    │
              │  1931–2020   │              │              │
              └──────────────┘              └──────────────┘
                         Marriage: 1956
```

99.   **Robert Edwin Straube** was born on Saturday, December 05, 1931, in Missouri, USA. He was the son of Luther Joshua Straube (64) and Rosa Shelton Lewis. He was also known as **Bobby**.

Robert Edwin died in Port Charlotte, Charlotte County, Florida, on June 26, 2020, at the age of 88. He was cremated.

Robert Edwin married **Wanda Jean Conrad** in 1956.

Family of Roland Straube and Nancy Lund

```
┌──────────────┐ ┌──────────────┐
│      26      │ │              │
│ John Henry   │ │   Alice D.   │
│   Straube    │ │   Mummey     │
│  1857–1942   │ │  1875–1954   │
└──────────────┘ └──────────────┘
      ┌──────────────┐         ┌──────────────┐
      │      65      │         │              │
      │Arthur Robert │         │ Elsie Marie  │
      │   Straube    │         │    Miller    │
      │  1904–1966   │         │  1907–1964   │
      └──────────────┘         └──────────────┘
           ┌──────────────┐              ┌──────────────┐
           │     100      │              │              │
           │ Roland Frank │              │  Nancy Lee   │
           │   Straube    │              │     Lund     │
           │  1930–1994   │              │              │
           └──────────────┘              └──────────────┘
                          Married
              ┌──────────────┐
              │ Roland Frank │
              │  Straube Jr. │
              │  1953–2016   │
              └──────────────┘
```

100.   **Roland Frank Straube** was born on Monday, July 21, 1930, in Harvey, Cook County, Illinois. He was the son of Arthur Robert Straube (65) and Elsie Marie Miller.

Roland Frank died in Indianapolis, Marion County, Indiana, on September 07, 1994, at the age of 64. He was buried in New Crown Cemetery and Mausoleum, Indianapolis, Marion County, Indiana (Find a Grave ID 197514294).

He married **Nancy Lee Lund**. They had one son.

Unknown if Nancy and Roland Sr. were married but she is the mother of Roland Jr.

Son of Roland Frank Straube and Nancy Lee Lund:

m I. **Roland Frank Straube Jr.** was born in Harvey, Cook County, Illinois, on July 13, 1953. He served in the military. U.S. Air Force, Vietnam.

Roland Frank died in Eureka Springs, Carroll County, Arkansas, on May 21, 2016, at the age of 62. He was cremated- (Find a Grave ID 163318469).

6th Generation

John Morris

101.   **John Porter Morris** was born on Wednesday, May 29, 1918, in Pike County, Missouri. He was the son of Herman Oscar Morris and Florence Genevieve Straube (73).

John Porter died in Mexico, Audrain County, Missouri, on January 30, 1974, at the age of 55. He was buried in New Harmony Cemetery, Pike County, Missouri (Find a Grave ID 57890124).

Marriages with Stella Mae Adams and Mary Mildred Clifton (Page 178) are known.

Family of John Morris and Stella Adams

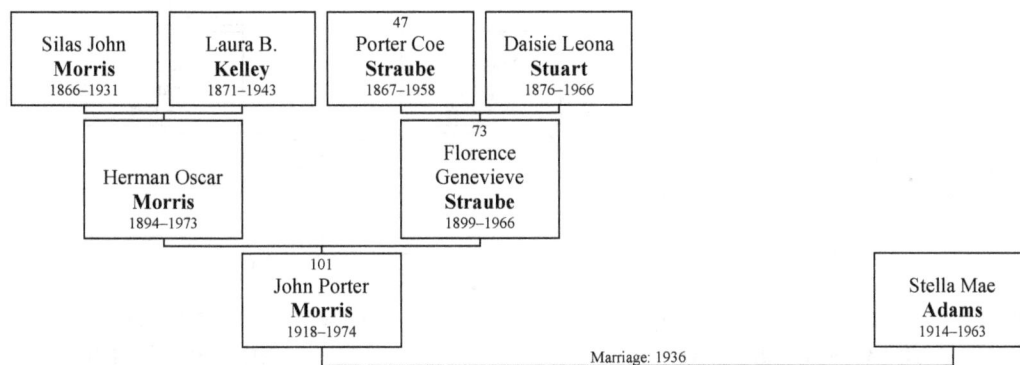

Here are the details about **John Porter Morris's** first marriage, with Stella Mae Adams. You can read more about John Porter on page 177.

At the age of 18, John Porter Morris married **Stella Mae Adams** on Wednesday, November 25, 1936, when she was 22 years old. Stella Mae was born in Oakwood, Clay County, Missouri, on Wednesday, March 04, 1914.

She reached 49 years of age and died in Mexico, Audrain County, Missouri, on September 24, 1963. Stella Mae was buried in Evergreen Memorial Gardens Cemetery, Vandalia, Audrain County, Missouri (Find a Grave ID 125567118).

Family of John Morris and Mary Clifton

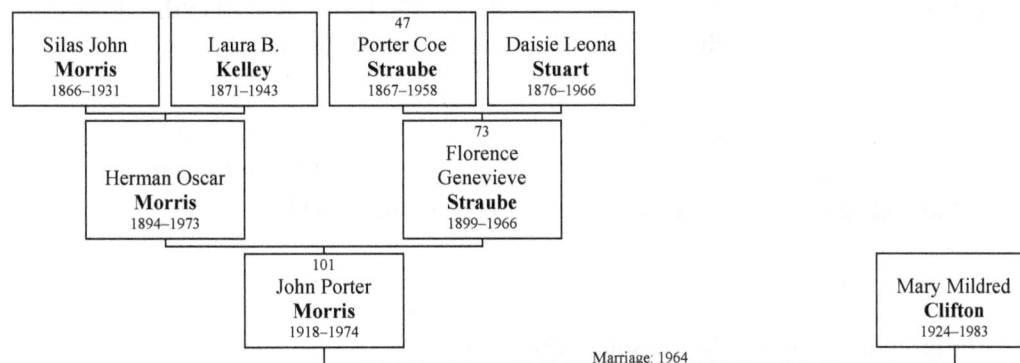

Here are the details about **John Porter Morris's** second marriage, with Mary Mildred Clifton. You can read more about John Porter on page 177.

At the age of 45, John Porter Morris married **Mary Mildred Clifton** on Sunday, March 29, 1964, when she was 39 years old. Mary Mildred was born in Pike County, Missouri, on Saturday, July 19, 1924.

She reached 58 years of age and died in Missouri, USA, in May 1983. Mary Mildred was buried in New Harmony Cemetery, Pike County, Missouri (Find a Grave ID 57890087).

Family of Betty Ogden and Eldon Steers

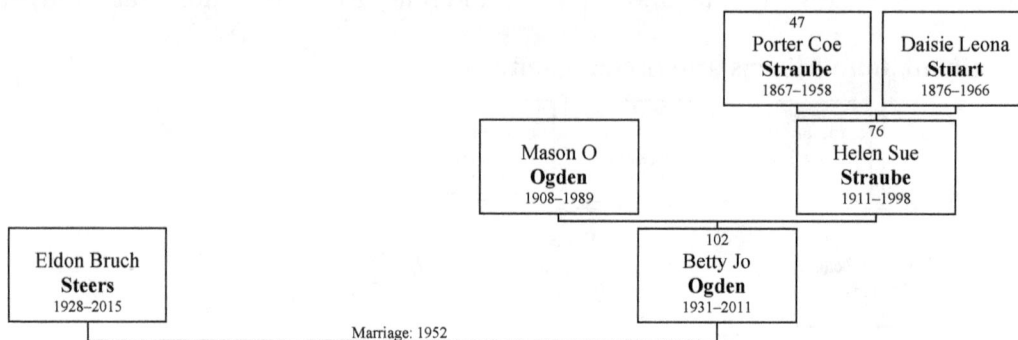

102. **Betty Jo Ogden** was born on Wednesday, January 07, 1931, in Bowling Green, Pike County, Missouri. She was the daughter of Mason O Ogden and Helen Sue Straube (76).

Betty Jo died in Olathe, Johnson County, Kansas, on October 09, 2011, at the age of 80. She was buried in Louisiana Memorial Gardens, Louisiana, Pike County, Missouri (Find a Grave ID 125877469).

At the age of 21, Betty Jo married **Eldon Bruch Steers** on Saturday, February 16, 1952, when he was 23 years old. Eldon Bruch was born on Saturday, June 16, 1928.

He reached 86 years of age and died on April 11, 2015. Eldon Bruch was buried in Louisiana Memorial Gardens, Louisiana, Pike County, Missouri (Find a Grave ID 145010603).

Shirley Chamberlain

103. **Shirley Jean Chamberlain** was born on Thursday, March 26, 1931, in Curryville, Pike County, Missouri. She was the daughter of Floyd Willard Chamberlain and Tressa Jean Straube (87).

Shirley Jean died in Ennis, Ellis County, Texas, on January 09, 2003, at the age of 71. Her cause of death was emphysema, COPD. Shirley Jean was buried in Myrtle Cemetery, Ennis, Ellis County, Texas, on January 13, 2003 (Find a Grave ID 70258741).

> Born Shirley Jean Chamberlain on Thursday, March 26, 1931, on the family farm south of Curryville, Missouri. The eldest child and daughter of Floyd and Tressa Chamberlain and was named after her mother, Tressa Jean.

Shirley Jean loved growing up on the farm. She spent most of her younger days outdoors riding her horse "Lena" or a colt by the name of "Lady." Getting up early, packing a lunch, and taking off for the day was her usually schedule when she wasn't in school. Other activities she enjoyed was playing with her terrier dog, "Tony," or going fishing with her father and all the other men in the family. Floyd was always accused of turning Shirley Jean into a tomboy, which she really was because she was a substitute for a son.

"Shirley Jean was one of three 4-H girls chosen from Pike County to attend the American Royal Show in Kansas City," wrote her Aunt Hazel in a letter to her husband, Garland on October 12, 1944. She went on to write: "She left last night and will be back Saturday. They are having a banquet at the Muhlebach Hotel tonight so we can picture where she is. Shirley Jean has blossomed forth into a young lady in the past year. She's very lady like now. In spite of her size, she looks neat in her clothes and carries herself well. She's outgrown the awkward stage. I'm really proud of her. She'll go to high school next year."

Shirley Jean attended Vannoy School until the family moved to Bowling Green, Missouri. While at Vannoy, Shirley Jean established a record of perfect attendance for 6 years and a perfect spelling record for 5 years. She was also a member of the 4-H Club, which kept her busy with projects and activities. Shirley Jean won the hardest of all contests at the time, a 1st place Blue ribbon at the District Contest for Judging Clothing.

While attending Bowling Green High School, Shirley Jean lettered 4 years as a member of the "Bobcat Band." She also was a member of the Glee Club, F. H. A., the concert band and Saxophone Quartet. A big surprise happened during this time as well. A baby sister, Pam, came along of who she was very tickled about.

Shirley Jean and her first cousin, Georganna, held rank on the rest of "to be" 23 cousins. The ones that were around in the early days knew that they had to be good when Shirley Jean and Georgie were baby-sitting them. Not only were they strict (wonder where they got that from), but they could tell some tales that would make you cover-up and not get out of bed at night.

Shirley Jean graduated from high school in 1949. An upcoming marriage only allowed Shirley Jean to attend one year of nursing school at DePaul School of Nursing in St. Louis, Missouri.

Shirley Jean was married to Randall Richard Henderson from July 28, 1951, until October of 1958. They were married in Pocahontas, Arkansas, at which time Randall was in the United States Marine Corp. For seven years, they were stationed in many places. To this union were born Paula Jean on December 22, 1953, in Quantico, Virginia; Marsha Lynn on April 13, 1955, in the British West Indies; and Susan Luanne on June 21, 1957, in East St. Louis, Illinois, while Randall was stationed at Scott Air Force Base. From 1958 until 1960, Shirley Jean and the three daughters lived with her parents in Harrisonville, Missouri after she and Randall divorced.

On September 14, 1960, Shirley Jean married Ted J. Mummert in Miami, Oklahoma. Ted was born on April 10, 1931, in Fortuna, Missouri, and is the son of Calvin R. and Dora Mae Mummert. Shortly after their marriage, they moved to Dallas, Texas, to make their permanent home.

From this union were born a set of identical twins, Calvin Grant and Floyd James, on September 18, 1964, at Saint Paul Hospital, and Sharlene Denise on September 28, 1966, at Methodist Hospital. All were born in Dallas, Texas. Sharlene means "Little Shirley."

Ted was a Quality Control Inspector until his death from heart failure. He passed away at Methodist Hospital on March 12, 1994. Burial was at Myrtle Cemetery in Ennis, Texas.

After Sharlene was born, Shirley Jean went back to work at the Chief Admitting Officer at the Children's Medical Center in Dallas for three years, then as a medical secretary at the Physicians and Surgeons Clinic of Dallas until she retired in 1996.

Shirley Jean passed away on January 9, 2003, at the age of 71 years, 9 months and 14 days at Westchester Assisted Living Center, Fort Worth, Texas, from severe advanced emphysema, COPD. Burial was on January 13, 2003, at Myrtle Cemetery in Ennis, Texas.

Marriages with Randal Richard Henderson and Teddy Junior Mummert (Page 181) are known.

Family of Shirley Chamberlain and Randal Henderson

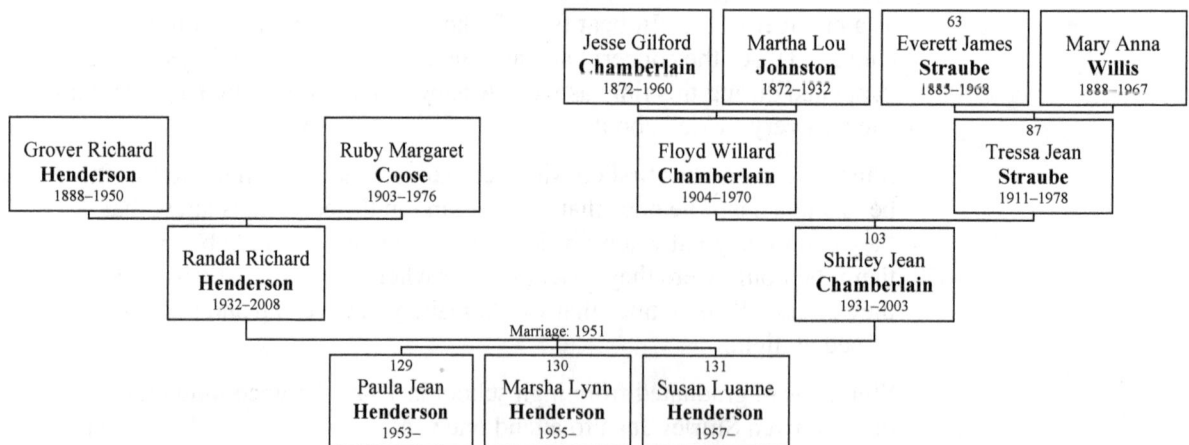

Here are the details about **Shirley Jean Chamberlain's** first marriage, with Randal Richard Henderson. You can read more about Shirley Jean on page 178.

At the age of 20, Shirley Jean Chamberlain married **Randal Richard Henderson** on Saturday, July 28, 1951, in Pocahontas, Randolph County, Arkansas, when he was 18 years old. They had three daughters.

Randal Richard was born in Pike County, Missouri, on Thursday, October 13, 1932. He was the son of Grover Richard Henderson and Ruby Margaret Coose.

He served in the USMC during the Korean War. SSGT. Randal Richard reached 75 years of age and died in Texas, USA, on January 06, 2008. He was buried in Houston National Cemetery, Houston, Harris County, Texas (Find a Grave ID 71057633).

Daughters of Shirley Jean Chamberlain and Randal Richard Henderson:

+ 129 f I. **Paula Jean Henderson** was born in Quantico, Prince William County, Virginia, on December 22, 1953.

+ 130 f II. **Marsha Lynn Henderson** was born in British West Indies on April 13, 1955.

+ 131 f III. **Susan Luanne Henderson** was born in East St. Louis, Illinois, on June 21, 1957.

Family of Shirley Chamberlain and Teddy Mummert

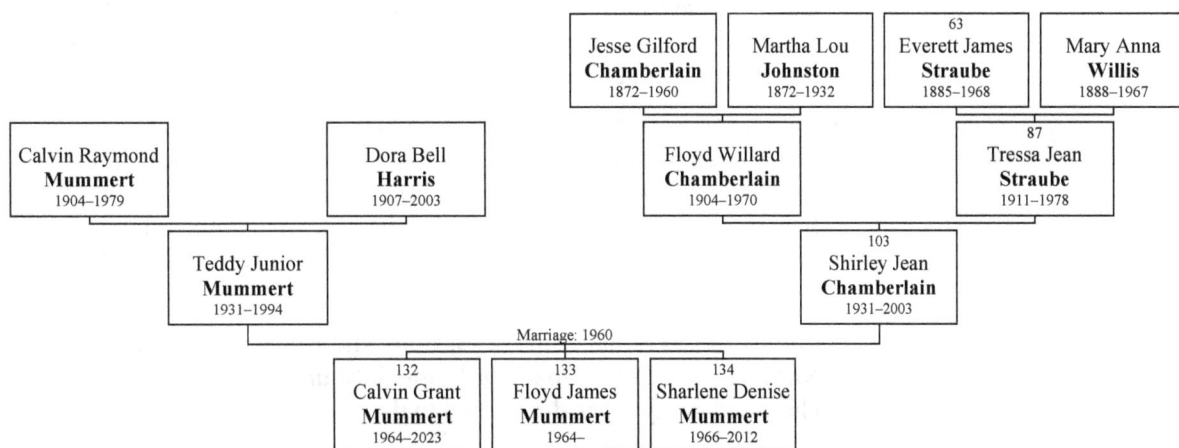

Here are the details about **Shirley Jean Chamberlain's** second marriage, with Teddy Junior Mummert. You can read more about Shirley Jean on page 178.

At the age of 29, Shirley Jean Chamberlain married **Teddy Junior Mummert** on Wednesday, September 14, 1960, in Miami, Ottawa County, Oklahoma, when he was 29 years old. They had three children.

Teddy Junior was born in Fortuna, Moniteau County, Missouri, on Friday, April 10, 1931. He was the son of Calvin Raymond Mummert and Dora Bell Harris. He was also known as **Ted**.

Teddy Junior reached 62 years of age and died in Ennis, Ellis County, Texas, on March 12, 1994. He was buried in Myrtle Cemetery, Ennis, Ellis County, Texas (Find a Grave ID 70259023).

Ted was born on April 10, 1931, in Fortuna, Missouri, and is the son of Calvin R. and Dora Mae Mummert. Ted served in the U.S. Army and was a Korean War Veteran. On September 14, 1960, Ted married Shirley Jean Chamberlain Henderson in Miami, Oklahoma. Shortly after their marriage, they moved to Dallas, Texas, to make their permanent home.

From this union were born a set of identical twins, Calvin Grant and Floyd James, on September 18, 1964, at Saint Paul Hospital, and Sharlene Denise on September 28, 1966, at Methodist Hospital. All were born in Dallas, Texas. Sharlene means "Little Shirley."

Ted was a Quality Control Inspector until his death from heart failure. He passed away at Methodist Hospital on March 12, 1994. Burial was at Myrtle Cemetery in Ennis, Texas.

Children of Shirley Jean Chamberlain and Teddy Junior Mummert:

+ 132 m I. **Calvin Grant Mummert** was born in Dallas, Dallas County, Texas, on September 18, 1964. He died in Dallas, Dallas County, Texas, on December 22, 2023, at the age of 59. Calvin Grant was buried in Myrtle Cemetery, Ennis, Ellis County, Texas (Find a Grave ID 262460835).

Twin brother to Floyd James Mummert

Obituary

Calvin Grant Mummert, 59, was surrounded by loved ones as he journeyed home to experience the fullness of Christmas in Heaven, December 22, 2023 in Dallas, Texas.

Calvin was born in Dallas, Texas on September 18, 1964, to Ted and Shirley (Chamberlain) Mummert. He grew up in Oak Cliff and moved to Ennis in 1976. He graduated from St. John's Catholic School in 1983. In 1985, he married the love of his life, Tammy Watson. He worked for DCI as a driver and was a member of The Avenue Church.

Calvin was so proud of his boys, Cody and Brice and grandson Kace. He was "Pops" to his little angel, Brandie Erynn and cherished doing what she wanted to do.

In all the things Calvin enjoyed, being outside, hunting, working on projects, building things, spending time with family, he never met a stranger and was always so generous with his time, wit and wisdom.

He will be greatly missed but we know his legacy will be carried on by his wife of 37 years, Tammy Watson Mummert, Sons: Cody Grant Mummert, and wife Danielle Ashford, Brice Wade Mummert and girlfriend Bailey Armstrong, Granddaughter, Brandie Erynn Mummert and Grandson, Kace Lane McDaniel. He is also survived by his brother, Floyd Mummert and wife Stephanie and Phil Mummert and wife Debbie, sisters, Paula Doyle and husband John, Marsha Dunn, Susie Saling and husband Dennis, Pam King and husband Jerry, and Mary Podraza, Mother-in-Law, Trixi McManus, and numerous niece and nephews.

He goes home to join his parents, Ted and Shirley Mummert, two brothers, Bruce Mummert and Michael Ted Mummert, Sister, Sharlene Mummert, Brother-in-Law, Troy Dunn, Good Friend, Wes Hammond, several grandparents, aunts and uncles.

Calvin's generosity extends past his life by giving the beautiful gift of life to many others this Christmas, as he was a registered organ donor.

Visitation will be held at J. E. Keever Mortuary in Ennis, TX on Friday, December 29th, from 6:00 p.m. to 8:00 p.m.

A celebration of life will be held on Saturday, December 30th at 10:00 a.m. at J. E. Keever Mortuary, with interment following at Myrtle Cemetery, Ennis, TX.

In lieu of flowers, the family suggests making a donation to the American Heart Association, www.heart.org or to the Texas Parks and Wildlife, https://tpwd.texas.gov/business/donations to celebrate Calvin's life and legacy.

Pallbearers are sons, Cody Mummert, Brice Mummert, brother, Floyd Mummert, grandson, Kace McDaniel, nephews: Chris Mummert and Clayton Mummert and good friend, Lance Ueberroth.

"I will lie down and sleep in peace for you alone, O Lord make me dwell in safety." Psalm 4:8

+ 133 m II. **Floyd James Mummert** was born in Dallas, Dallas County, Texas, on September 18, 1964.

Twin brother to Calvin Grant Mummert.

+ 134 f III. **Sharlene Denise Mummert** was born in Dallas, Dallas County, Texas, on September 28, 1966. She died in Dallas, Dallas County, Texas, on February 24, 2012, at the age of 45. Sharlene Denise was cremated- on March 03, 2012 (Find a Grave ID 100197165).

Sharlene died of a stroke, heart condition, high blood pressure. [1] Common law married to Norman Manuere [2] Met Willie Hernandez [3] On Dec 15, 2001 in Garland, TX married Mike Imuzeze. Child of Sharlene and [1] Norman Manuere: Norman Ted "Junior"; b. 11-18-1991, Fort Worth, TX. Child of Sharlene and [2] Willie Hernandez: Savannah Denise Hernandez; b. 5-11-1999, Euless, TX

Family of Pamela Chamberlain and Wayne Korte

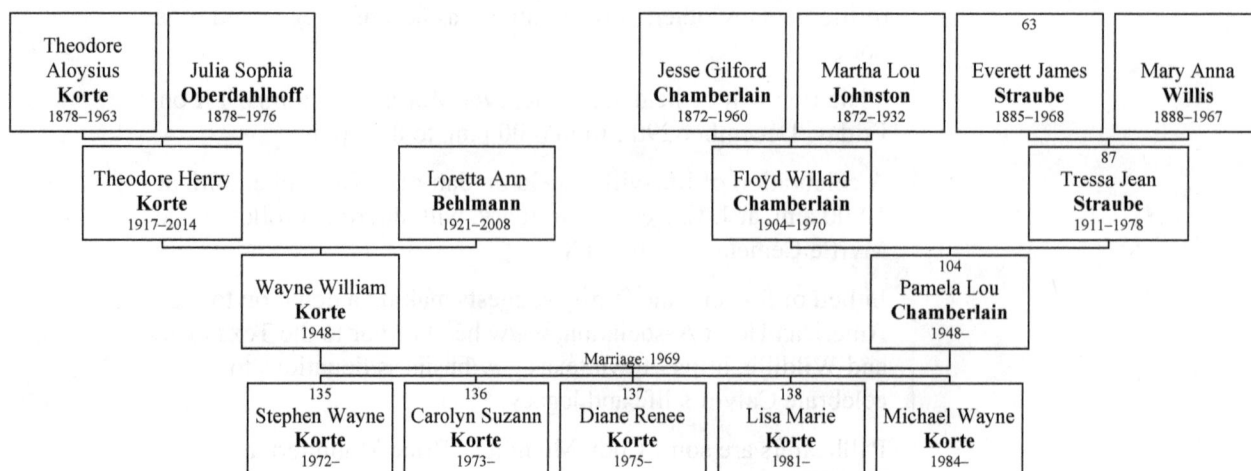

```
┌─────────────┐ ┌─────────────┐                    ┌─────────────┐ ┌─────────────┐ ┌────63───────┐ ┌─────────────┐
│  Theodore   │ │             │                    │             │ │             │ │             │ │             │
│  Aloysius   │ │Julia Sophia │                    │Jesse Gilford│ │ Martha Lou  │ │Everett James│ │ Mary Anna   │
│   Korte     │ │Oberdahlhoff │                    │Chamberlain  │ │  Johnston   │ │  Straube    │ │   Willis    │
│  1878–1963  │ │  1878–1976  │                    │  1872–1960  │ │  1872–1932  │ │  1885–1968  │ │  1888–1967  │
└─────────────┘ └─────────────┘                    └─────────────┘ └─────────────┘ └─────────────┘ └─────────────┘
     ┌──────────────┐           ┌──────────────┐          ┌──────────────┐              ┌────87────────┐
     │Theodore Henry│           │ Loretta Ann  │          │Floyd Willard │              │ Tressa Jean  │
     │    Korte     │           │  Behlmann    │          │ Chamberlain  │              │   Straube    │
     │  1917–2014   │           │  1921–2008   │          │  1904–1970   │              │  1911–1978   │
     └──────────────┘           └──────────────┘          └──────────────┘              └──────────────┘
            ┌──────────────┐                                     ┌────104───────┐
            │Wayne William │                                     │  Pamela Lou  │
            │    Korte     │                                     │ Chamberlain  │
            │    1948–     │                                     │    1948–     │
            └──────────────┘                                     └──────────────┘
                               Marriage: 1969
   ┌────135────┐ ┌────136────┐ ┌────137────┐ ┌────138────┐ ┌──────────────┐
   │Stephen    │ │Carolyn    │ │Diane Renee│ │Lisa Marie │ │Michael Wayne │
   │Wayne Korte│ │Suzann Korte│ │  Korte   │ │  Korte    │ │    Korte     │
   │  1972–    │ │  1973–    │ │  1975–    │ │  1981–    │ │    1984–     │
   └───────────┘ └───────────┘ └───────────┘ └───────────┘ └──────────────┘
```

104. **Pamela Lou Chamberlain** was born on Friday, July 16, 1948, in Louisiana, Pike County, Missouri. She is the daughter of Floyd Willard Chamberlain and Tressa Jean Straube (87).

At the age of 21, Pamela Lou married **Wayne William Korte** on Saturday, September 13, 1969, in St. Clement, Pike County, Missouri, when he was 21 years old. They have five children.

Wayne William was born in Louisiana, Pike County, Missouri, on Wednesday, March 10, 1948. He is the son of Theodore Henry Korte and Loretta Ann Behlmann.

Children of Pamela Lou Chamberlain and Wayne William Korte:

+   135   m   I. **Stephen Wayne Korte** was born in Louisiana, Pike County, Missouri, on May 10, 1972.

+   136   f   II. **Carolyn Suzann Korte** was born in Louisiana, Pike County, Missouri, on November 25, 1973.

+   137   f   III. **Diane Renee Korte** was born in Louisiana, Pike County, Missouri, on December 11, 1975.

+   138   f   IV. **Lisa Marie Korte** was born in Louisiana, Pike County, Missouri, on April 09, 1981.

            m   V. **Michael Wayne Korte** was born in Louisiana, Pike County, Missouri, on January 31, 1984.

Family of Tanya Straube and Tom Cunningham

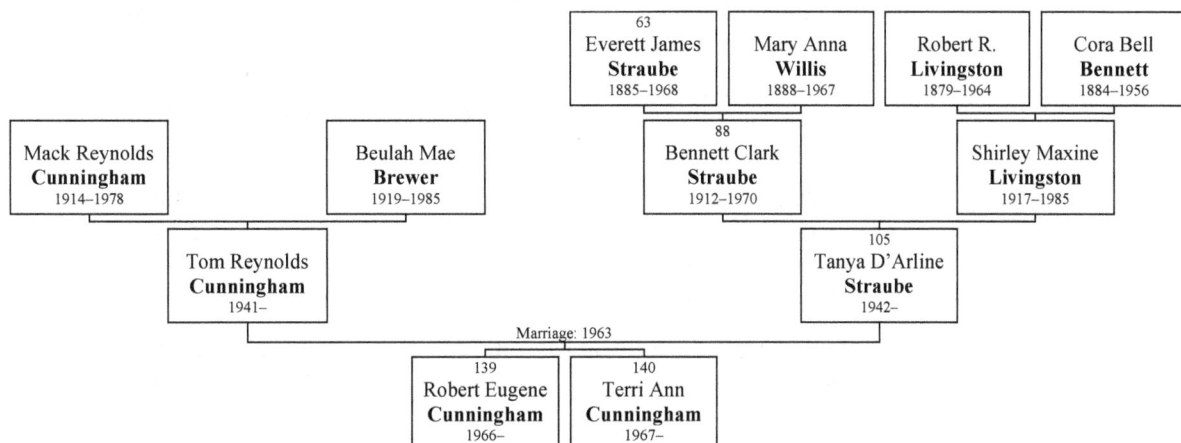

```
                                    ┌──────────────┐ ┌──────────────┐ ┌──────────────┐ ┌──────────────┐
                                    │      63      │ │  Mary Anna   │ │  Robert R.   │ │  Cora Bell   │
                                    │ Everett James│ │    Willis    │ │  Livingston  │ │   Bennett    │
                                    │   Straube    │ │  1888–1967   │ │  1879–1964   │ │  1884–1956   │
                                    │  1885–1968   │ └──────────────┘ └──────────────┘ └──────────────┘
                                    └──────────────┘
┌──────────────┐ ┌──────────────┐       ┌──────────────┐         ┌──────────────┐
│ Mack Reynolds│ │  Beulah Mae  │       │      88      │         │Shirley Maxine│
│  Cunningham  │ │    Brewer    │       │ Bennett Clark│         │  Livingston  │
│  1914–1978   │ │  1919–1985   │       │   Straube    │         │  1917–1985   │
└──────────────┘ └──────────────┘       │  1912–1970   │         └──────────────┘
        ┌──────────────┐                └──────────────┘              ┌──────────────┐
        │ Tom Reynolds │                                              │     105      │
        │  Cunningham  │                                              │ Tanya D'Arline│
        │    1941–     │          Marriage: 1963                      │   Straube    │
        └──────────────┘                                              │    1942–     │
                            ┌──────────────┐ ┌──────────────┐        └──────────────┘
                            │     139      │ │     140      │
                            │Robert Eugene │ │  Terri Ann   │
                            │  Cunningham  │ │  Cunningham  │
                            │    1966–     │ │    1967–     │
                            └──────────────┘ └──────────────┘
```

105.   **Tanya D'Arline Straube** was born on Friday, January 16, 1942, in Curryville, Pike County, Missouri. She is the daughter of Bennett Clark Straube (88) and Shirley Maxine Livingston. She is also known as **Tannie**.

At the age of 21, Tanya D'Arline married **Tom Reynolds Cunningham** on Saturday, October 19, 1963, in Vandalia, Audrain County, Missouri, when he was 22 years old. They have two children.

Tom Reynolds was born in Bowling Green, Pike County, Missouri, on Sunday, October 19, 1941. He is the son of Mack Reynolds Cunningham and Beulah Mae Brewer.

Children of Tanya D'Arline Straube and Tom Reynolds Cunningham:

+   139   m   I. **Robert Eugene Cunningham** was born in Hannibal, Marion County, Missouri, on May 24, 1966. He is also known as **Bobby**.

+   140   f   II. **Terri Ann Cunningham** was born in Hannibal, Marion County, Missouri, on September 06, 1967.

Duane Straube

106.   **Duane Bennett Straube** was born on Friday, November 26, 1943, in Curryville, Pike County, Missouri. He was the son of Bennett Clark Straube (88) and Shirley Maxine Livingston.

Duane Bennett died in St. Lukes Hospital, Chesterfield, Saint Louis County Missouri, on June 04, 2018, at the age of 74. He was cremated on June 07, 2018 (Find a Grave ID 190333630).

> Duane B. Straube, 74, of St. Ann died Monday, June 4, 2018 at St. Luke's Hospital in Chesterfield.
>
> Funeral services were Thursday at 6 p.m., at Collier's Funeral Home in St. Ann. Following the service the family invited everyone to the Straube home for a reception.
>
> He was born Nov. 26, 1943 the son of Bennett Clark and Shirley Maxine Livingston Straube. He married Kathee Meirink Straube. She survives.

Other survivors include his children, Crystal Sadler and husband, Paul of Texas, Elizabeth Gallegos and husband, Al, St. Louis, Lance Straube and wife, Roj, Bangkok, Thailand; grandchildren, Lawson, Lukas, Ruby, Wells, Adam and Evan; siblings, Tanya Cunningham, Vandalia, Elaine Deters, Bowling Green, Mike Straube, Hannibal Cheryl Oligschlaeger, Perry, and Dewey Straube of Vandalia; brother-in-law, uncle, cousin, and friend to many.

Duane graduated from Van-Far High School in 1961 where he was recognized as the outstanding senior athlete. He attended University of Missouri-Columbia and graduated in 1965 with a BA degree in education. He later obtained his masters degree in education administration from UMSL.

He taught physical education at Marvin Elementary School in the Ritenour School District in St. Louis for many years when he left to run Straube Painting Company.

Duane was an avid Cardinals fan and loved all sports. He loved going to the track and to the boats. He played golf most of his life, bowled a few perfect games, and was loyal to his darts league. As a result, he made many friends in many walks of life who, in turn, enjoyed his sense of humor and camaraderie. He was loved for his dry wit and sarcasm and his willingness to give you the shirt off his back. He will be missed.

Memorial contribution may be given to the American Cancer Society.

Marriages with Mary Katherine Lawson and Kathleen Meirink (Page 187) are known.

Family of Duane Straube and Mary Lawson

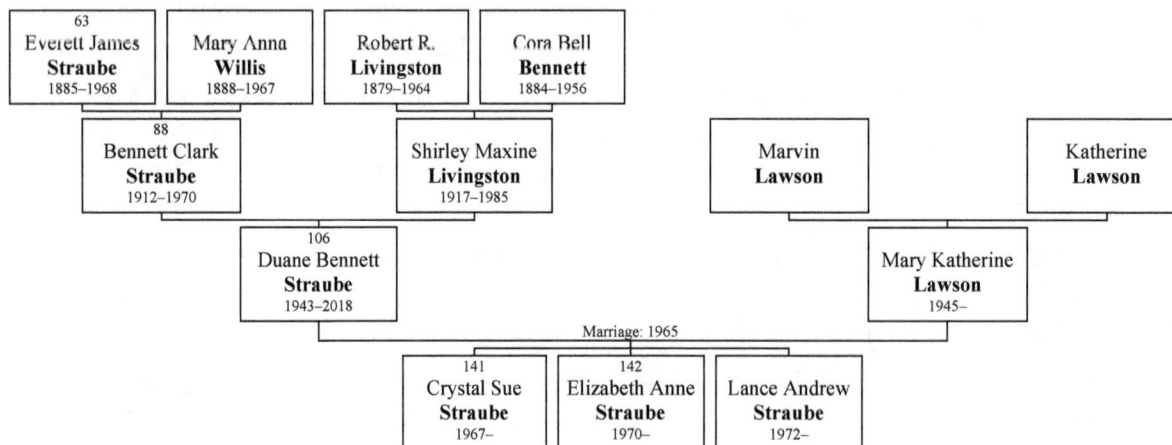

Here are the details about **Duane Bennett Straube's** first marriage, with Mary Katherine Lawson. You can read more about Duane Bennett on page 185.

At the age of 22, Duane Bennett Straube married **Mary Katherine Lawson** on Saturday, December 18, 1965, in Bowling Green, Pike County, Missouri, when she was 20 years old. They had three daughters.

Mary Katherine was born in Louisiana, Pike County, Missouri, on Wednesday, February 28, 1945. She is the daughter of Marvin Lawson and Katherine Lawson.

Daughters of Duane Bennett Straube and Mary Katherine Lawson:

+ 141   f   I. **Crystal Sue Straube** was born in Saint Louis, Saint Louis County, Missouri, on April 16, 1967.

+ 142   f   II. **Elizabeth Anne Straube** was born in Saint Louis, Saint Louis County, Missouri, on September 25, 1970.

           f   III. **Lance Andrew Straube** was born on February 04, 1972.

Family of Duane Straube and Kathleen Meirink

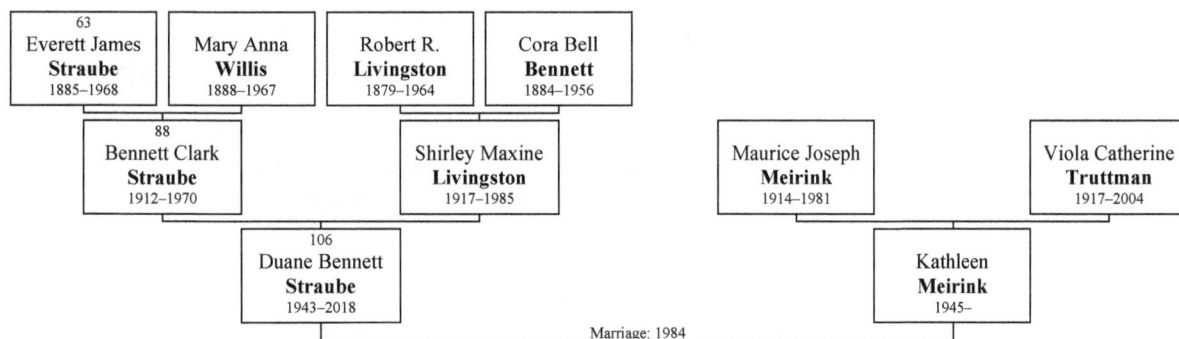

63 Everett James **Straube** 1885–1968	Mary Anna **Willis** 1888–1967	Robert R. **Livingston** 1879–1964	Cora Bell **Bennett** 1884–1956	Maurice Joseph **Meirink** 1914–1981	Viola Catherine **Truttman** 1917–2004
88 Bennett Clark **Straube** 1912–1970		Shirley Maxine **Livingston** 1917–1985			
106 Duane Bennett **Straube** 1943–2018				Kathleen **Meirink** 1945–	

Marriage: 1984

Here are the details about **Duane Bennett Straube's** second marriage, with Kathleen Meirink. You can read more about Duane Bennett on page 185.

At the age of 40, Duane Bennett Straube married **Kathleen Meirink** on Friday, November 02, 1984, in Clayton, St. Louis County, Missouri, when she was 38 years old. Kathleen was born in Belleville, St. Clair County, Illinois, on Thursday, December 27, 1945. She is the daughter of Maurice Joseph Meirink and Viola Catherine Truttman.

Family of Elaine Straube and Clemens Deters

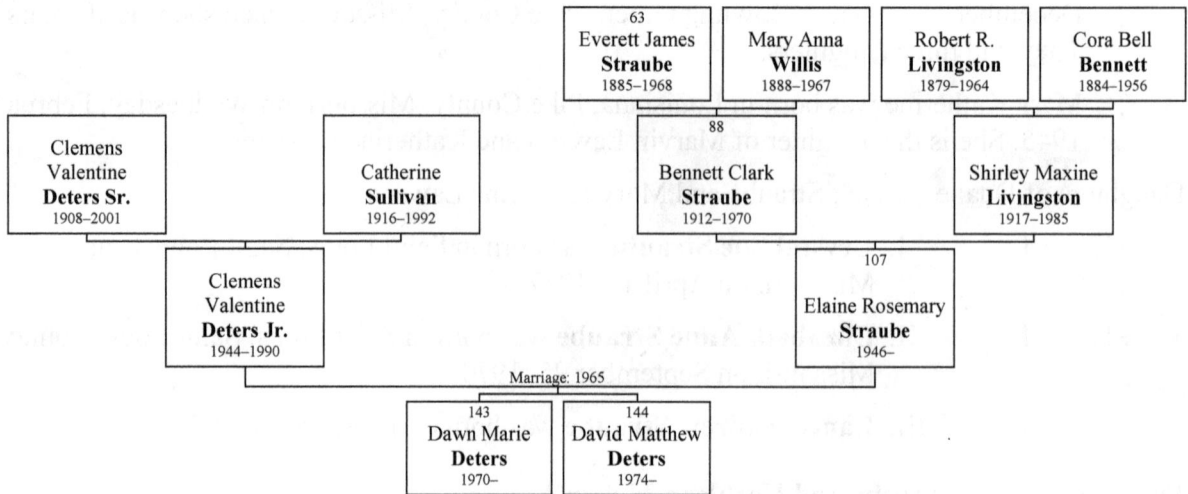

| | | 63 Everett James **Straube** 1885–1968 | Mary Anna **Willis** 1888–1967 | Robert R. **Livingston** 1879–1964 | Cora Bell **Bennett** 1884–1956 |

| Clemens Valentine **Deters Sr.** 1908–2001 | Catherine **Sullivan** 1916–1992 | 88 Bennett Clark **Straube** 1912–1970 | Shirley Maxine **Livingston** 1917–1985 |

| Clemens Valentine **Deters Jr.** 1944–1990 | 107 Elaine Rosemary **Straube** 1946– |

Marriage: 1965

| 143 Dawn Marie **Deters** 1970– | 144 David Matthew **Deters** 1974– |

107. **Elaine Rosemary Straube** was born on Wednesday, February 20, 1946, in Curryville, Pike County, Missouri. She is the daughter of Bennett Clark Straube (88) and Shirley Maxine Livingston.

At the age of 19, Elaine Rosemary married **Clemens Valentine Deters Jr.** on Saturday, November 13, 1965, in St. Clement, Pike County, Missouri, when he was 21 years old. They had two children.

Clemens Valentine was born in Louisiana, Pike County, Missouri, on Friday, February 25, 1944. He was the son of Clemens Valentine Deters Sr. and Catherine Sullivan. He was also known as **Clem**.

Clemens Valentine reached 46 years of age and died in Bowling Green, Pike County, Missouri, on July 25, 1990. His cause of death was malignant brain tumor. Clemens Valentine was buried in Saint Clement Cemetery, Saint Clement, Pike County, Missouri (Find a Grave ID 46954605).

> Clemens Valentine Deters, Jr. was called Clem all of his life was born on February 25, 1944, at Pike County Hospital in Louisiana, Missouri, and is the son of Clem V. Deters, Sr. and Catherine Sullivan Deters.
>
> Clem married Elaine Rosemary Straube on November 13, 1965 at Saint Clement Catholic Church. Clem and Elaine adopted Dawn Marie Deters who was born November 29, 1970 and adopted David Matthew Deters who was born on August 13, 1974.
>
> The family lived at St. Clement where Clem was engaged in farming with his dad, and Elaine did bookkeeping over the years for several companies.
>
> In March 1989, Clem was diagnosed with a malignant brain tumor and had surgery at Missouri Baptist Hospital in St. Louis in March 1989. He had daily radiation for eight weeks and chemo monthly but to no avail. The final try was an experimental heat treatment being used on brain tumors at the time. Clem only agreed to this treatment hoping to help someone else because he knew it was too late for him.

Clem passed away on July 25, 1990 at the Moore Pike Nursing Home in Bowling Green, Missouri. He didn't complain and only worried that he wouldn't be there for the kids and get to see them as adults.

Dawn Marie Deters married Bradley John Niemeyer on September 17, 2002, at St. Clement Catholic Church. Brad was born on August 29, 1974, and is the son of Leonard Niemeyer and Judy Twellman. To this union Andrew Clemens was born on June 29, 2004, and Lydia Catherine on September 29, 2008.

David Matthew Deters married Amy Levi Holtsman on July 13, 1996, at St. Clement Catholic Church. Amy was born Mary 13, 1976, and is the daughter of Clifford Holtsman and Pam Dempsey. To this union Gabrielle Levi was born on August 29, 2000, Gavin Clemens on January 21, 2002, and Gracie Rose on February 3, 2005.

Children of Elaine Rosemary Straube and Clemens Valentine Deters Jr.:

+ 143   f   I. **Dawn Marie Deters** was born on November 29, 1970.

+ 144   m   II. **David Matthew Deters** was born in Hannibal, Marion County, Missouri, on August 13, 1974.

Family of Michael Straube and Linda Hodgson

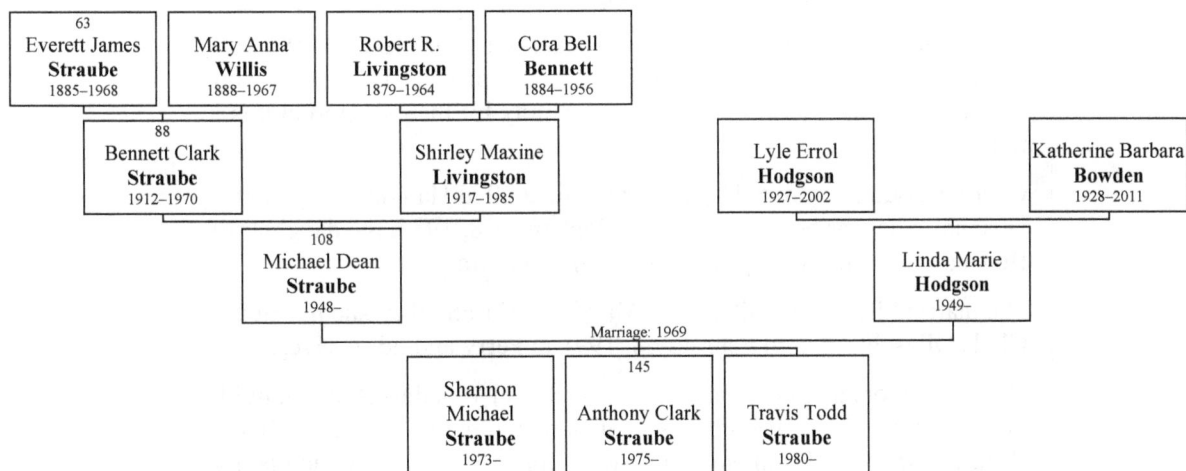

108.   **Michael Dean Straube** was born on Thursday, March 18, 1948, in Curryville, Pike County, Missouri. He is the son of Bennett Clark Straube (88) and Shirley Maxine Livingston.

At the age of 21, Michael Dean married **Linda Marie Hodgson** on Sunday, June 08, 1969, in Vandalia, Audrain County, Missouri, when she was 19 years old. They have three children.

Linda Marie was born in Hannibal, Marion County, Missouri, on Friday, July 15, 1949. She is the daughter of Lyle Errol Hodgson and Katherine Barbara Bowden.

Children of Michael Dean Straube and Linda Marie Hodgson:

m   I. **Shannon Michael Straube** was born in Mexico, Audrain County, Missouri, on February 21, 1973.

+   145   f   II. **Anthony Clark Straube** was born in Mexico, Audrain County, Missouri, on April 02, 1975. She is also known as **Andy**.

m   III. **Travis Todd Straube** was born in Mexico, Audrain County, Missouri, on June 08, 1980.

Cheryl Straube

109. **Cheryl Denise Straube** was born on Wednesday, September 08, 1954, at St. Elizabeth's Hospital in Hannibal, Marion County, Missouri. She was the daughter of Bennett Clark Straube (88) and Shirley Maxine Livingston.

Cheryl Denise died at Hannibal Regional Hospital in Hannibal, Marion County, Missouri, on April 16, 2020, at the age of 65. Her cause of death was heart attack. Cheryl Denise was buried in Lick Creek Cemetery, Perry, Ralls County, Missouri, on April 19, 2020 (Find a Grave ID 209173795).

Private Family Graveside Services for Cheryl Denise Oligschlaeger, 65, of Perry, will be held Sunday, April 19, 2020 at Lick Creek Cemetery with Reverend Nancy Kellstrom officiating.

Due to the public gathering restrictions caused by the COVID-19 pandemic, the funeral services for Cheryl were private. The family would like to extend their gratitude to the community for their support at this time.

Cheryl passed away at 5:41 p.m. April 16, 2020 at Hannibal Regional Hospital. She was born in Hannibal, September 8, 1954, the daughter of Bennett Clark and Shirley Maxine Livingston Straube.

She married Roger Woodhurst on May 21, 1971 and then she married Clyde Oligschlaeger on February 8, 1991 in Perry and he survives.

Other survivors include: one son, Jerrid (Stacy) Woodhurst of Boonville; one daughter, Sherri (David) Bruce of Booneville; two brothers, Mike (Linda) Straube of Hannibal and Dewey (Barb) Straube of Vandalia; two sisters, Tanya (Tom) Cunningham of Vandalia and Elaine Deters of St. Clements; one sister-in-law, Kathee Straube of St. Ann; five grandchildren; and one great grandson.

She was preceded in death by one brother, Duane Straube.

Cheryl was a lifetime area resident and a member of the Perry Christian Church. She was a 1972 graduate of Van-Far High School and a 1990 graduate of Tarkio College with a Bachelor of Science degree in Business. She was a co-owner and Funeral Director for Bienhoff Funeral Home for over 29 years. Cheryl coached girls softball for 14 years and served as executive director and active member of both the Perry Chamber of Commerce and Mark Twain Lake Chamber of Commerce. She also served on the boards of Village Housing and Perry Ole Swimmin' Hole. Cheryl was a member of Bass N Gals, Mark Twain Hookers Bass Club and very active in community affairs. She enjoyed fishing, playing golf and cards.

Honorary pallbearers will be her nephews.

Memorial contributions may be made to Lick Creek Cemetery, PO Box 430, Perry, MO 63462.

Marriages with Roger Lee Woodhurst and Clyde Leo Oligschlaeger (Page 192) are known.

Family of Cheryl Straube and Roger Woodhurst

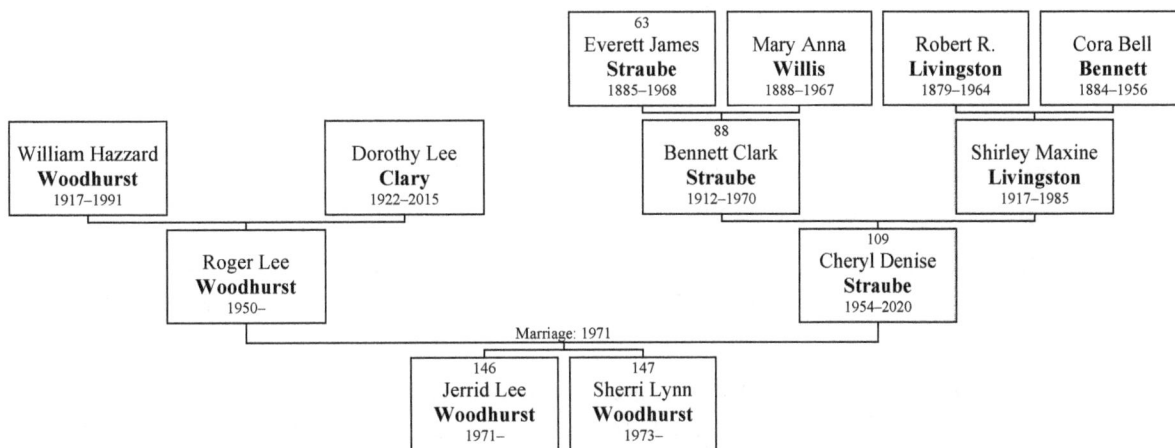

Here are the details about **Cheryl Denise Straube's** first marriage, with Roger Lee Woodhurst. You can read more about Cheryl Denise on page 190.

At the age of 16, Cheryl Denise Straube married **Roger Lee Woodhurst** on Friday, May 21, 1971, in Vandalia, Audrain County, Missouri, when he was 20 years old. They had two children.

Roger Lee was born in Hannibal, Marion County, Missouri, on Saturday, June 10, 1950. He is the son of William Hazzard Woodhurst and Dorothy Lee Clary.

Children of Cheryl Denise Straube and Roger Lee Woodhurst:

+ 146 m I. **Jerrid Lee Woodhurst** was born in Hannibal, Marion County, Missouri, on December 11, 1971.

+ 147 f II. **Sherri Lynn Woodhurst** was born in Hannibal, Marion County, Missouri, on September 07, 1973.

Family of Cheryl Straube and Clyde Oligschlaeger

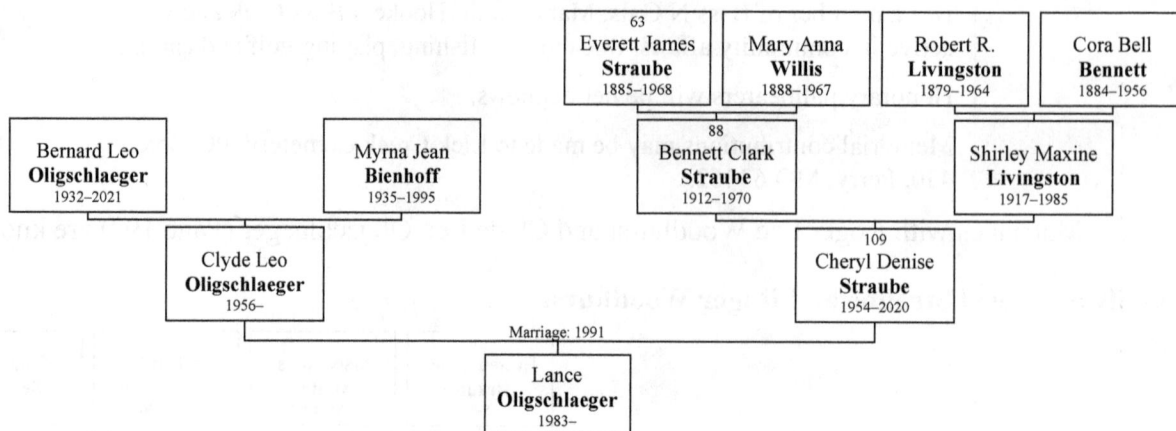

Here are the details about **Cheryl Denise Straube's** second marriage, with Clyde Leo Oligschlaeger. You can read more about Cheryl Denise on page 190.

At the age of 36, Cheryl Denise Straube married **Clyde Leo Oligschlaeger** on Friday, February 08, 1991, in Perry, Ralls County, Missouri, when he was 34 years old. They had one son.

Clyde Leo was born at Audrain Medical Center in Mexico, Audrain County, Missouri, on Monday, September 24, 1956. He is the son of Bernard Leo Oligschlaeger and Myrna Jean Bienhoff.

Son of Cheryl Denise Straube and Clyde Leo Oligschlaeger:

m   I. **Lance Oligschlaeger** was born on September 29, 1983.

Family of Derwin Straube and Barbara Nilges

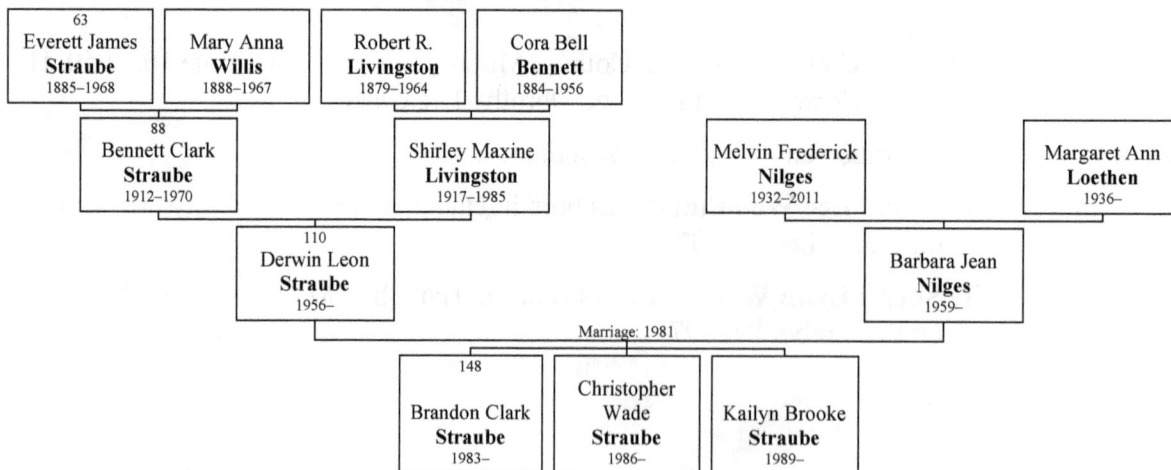

110.   **Derwin Leon Straube** was born on Thursday, October 11, 1956, in Hannibal, Marion County, Missouri. He is the son of Bennett Clark Straube (88) and Shirley Maxine Livingston. He is also known as **Dewey**.

At the age of 25, Derwin Leon married **Barbara Jean Nilges** on Saturday, October 17, 1981, in Martinsburg, Audrain County, Missouri, when she was 22 years old. They have three children.

Barbara Jean was born in Latham Sanatorium, California, Moniteau County, Missouri, on Monday, February 02, 1959. She is the daughter of Melvin Frederick Nilges and Margaret Ann Loethen.

Children of Derwin Leon Straube and Barbara Jean Nilges:

+ 148 m I. **Brandon Clark Straube** was born in Hannibal, Marion County, Missouri, on October 16, 1983.

     m II. **Christopher Wade Straube** was born at Audrain Medical Center in Mexico, Audrain County, Missouri, on April 28, 1986.

     f III. **Kailyn Brooke Straube** was born at Audrain Medical Center in Mexico, Audrain County, Missouri, on January 06, 1989.

Georganna Myers

111. **Georganna Myers** was born on Thursday, December 30, 1937, in Bowling Green, Pike County, Missouri. She was the daughter of William Barnett Myers and Gladys Lucy Straube (89).

Georganna died at Capitol Region Hospital in Jefferson City, Cole County, Missouri, on May 15, 2019, at the age of 81. She was buried in Memorial Gardens Cemetery, Bowling Green, Pike County, Missouri, on May 20, 2019 (Find a Grave ID 199157394).

> Graduate of University of Missouri-Columbia (B.S. and M.S. in Secondary Education). Inducted into Alpha Delta Kappa; Phi Delta Kappa; Delta Pi Epsilon and Pi Lambda Theta. Taught at Southern Boone county, Ashland, Missouri for eight years. Retired from the State of Missouri, Department of Elementary and Secondary Education.

Obituary

> Georganna Myers Beachboard, age 81, of Jefferson City, Mo., went to be with her Lord Wednesday, May 15, 2019 at Capital Region Medical Center surrounded by her loving family.

> She was born on December 30, 1937 in Bowling Green, Mo., the only child of William Barnett and Gladys (Straube) Myers. She was married on May 21, 1983 in Columbia, Mo. to Miles F. Beachboard.

> After an experience abroad and in Washington D.C., Georganna was a lifelong resident of Central Missouri. Georganna graduated from Bowling Green High School in 1955. The Class of 1955 taught her many things, one of which was the class motto, "life is not a destination, but a journey." She went on to earn both a Bachelor of Science and a Master's degree in Education from the University of Missouri - Columbia.

> Georganna worked as an administrative assistant for the United States Senator, Edward Long, in both the Missouri and Washington D.C. offices. She moved to central Missouri where she became a business education teacher for the Southern

Boone School District in Ashland, Mo. for several years. During this time, she authored the Missouri Title IX legislation, which prevents discrimination in education. From that experience, Georganna began her career with the State of Missouri - Department of Education for sixteen years and worked as the Director of Special Education Services. While there, her primary goal was to promote women in vocational education programs. These pioneering efforts led to her being recognized in many ways. The late Governor Carnahan presented her with the "Martin Luther King Diversity Award," First Lady, Melanie Blunt, recognized her with the "Award of Achievement in Education," and Governor Nixon presented her with the "Distinguished Service Award for Education by Missouri Council on Economic Development for Women."

Georganna was a member of First Christian Church and had previously been a member at Community Christian Church. Her faith was an integral part of her life and she was proud to be active with the Christian Women's Fellowship, Church Women United, and served as Elder and Deacon at both churches. She also enjoyed leading seniors in the "Learning in Retirement" program. She was a board member of the Community Concert Association and volunteered at Capital Region Medical Center.

Georganna spent many summers at the Lake of the Ozarks and enjoyed fishing. Her passions also included: golfing, being an avid bridge player, and a Master Gardener who enjoyed working with plants and flowers. Georganna cherished time with her husband, especially cruises to the Mediterranean, Vienna, Italy, Croatia, the Greek Isles, Isle of Capri, Athens, Rome, Alaska and the Holy Land.

Survivors include: her husband, Miles Beachboard; two sons, Samuel Hargadine V (wife Annette) of Hallsville, Mo. and John Hargadine (wife Mary) of St. Paul, Mo.; three grandchildren, Samuel Hargadine VI, Calvin Hargadine (wife Amber), and Mitchell Hargadine (wife Jenna); five great-grandchildren, Logan, Adam, Carter, Lucas and Mya Hargadine; sister-in-law, Juanita Dickerson (husband Lawrence) of Fayette, Mo.; her nephews, Doug Dickerson (wife Vicki) of Scottsdale, Arizona and Mitch Dickerson (Amie Ewigman) of Higbee, Mo.; as well as numerous cousins from the Straube family; and beloved friends.

Georganna was preceded in death by her parents, William and Gladys Myers.

Visitation will be held at Freeman Mortuary from 1:00 p.m. until 3:00 p.m. Sunday, May 19, 2019.

Funeral services will be conducted at 10:00 a.m. Monday, May 20, 2019 at First Christian Church in Jefferson City, Mo. with the Reverend Beau Underwood officiating. Graveside services and interment will be held at 2:00 p.m. Monday at Memorial Garden Cemetery in Bowling Green.

In lieu of flowers, memorial contributions are suggested to Dreams to Reality, 500 Jefferson Street, Jefferson City, Mo. 65101 or First Christian Church, 327 E. Capitol Avenue, Jefferson City, Mo. 65101.

Funeral arrangements are under the care of Freeman Mortuary.

Marriages with Samuel Emmett Hargadine IV, Robert Leonard Turner (Page 197) and Miles Franklin Beachboard (Page 198) are known.

Family of Georganna Myers and Samuel Hargadine

```
┌──────────────┐ ┌──────────────┐ ┌──────────────┐ ┌──────────────┐ ┌──────────────┐ ┌──────────────┐ ┌─────63───────┐ ┌──────────────┐
│Samuel Emmett │ │ Caroline Mae │ │  Charles B.  │ │  Donna Lee   │ │  Ira James   │ │Georgia Thomas│ │Everett James │ │  Mary Anna   │
│Hargadine II  │ │    Smith     │ │     Cox      │ │   Griffin    │ │    Myers     │ │    Rector    │ │   Straube    │ │    Willis    │
│  1864–1921   │ │  1870–1960   │ │  1863–1944   │ │  1866–1941   │ │  1878–1960   │ │  1885–1934   │ │  1885–1968   │ │  1888–1967   │
└──────────────┘ └──────────────┘ └──────────────┘ └──────────────┘ └──────────────┘ └──────────────┘ └──────────────┘ └──────────────┘
     ┌──────────────┐            ┌──────────────┐             ┌──────────────┐            ┌─────89───────┐
     │Samuel Emmett │            │ Viola Belle  │             │William Barnett│            │ Gladys Lucy  │
     │Hargadine III │            │     Cox      │             │    Myers     │            │   Straube    │
     │  1897–1979   │            │  1902–1976   │             │  1909–1967   │            │  1914–1996   │
     └──────────────┘            └──────────────┘             └──────────────┘            └──────────────┘
            ┌──────────────┐                              ┌─────111──────┐
            │Samuel Emmett │                              │  Georganna   │
            │Hargadine IV  │                              │    Myers     │
            │  1930–2020   │                              │  1937–2019   │
            └──────────────┘                              └──────────────┘
                          Marriage: 1957, Divorce: 1965
                    ┌─────149──────┐ ┌─────150──────┐
                    │Samuel Emmett │ │John Everett  │
                    │Hargadine V   │ │  Hargadine   │
                    │   1958–      │ │   1962–      │
                    └──────────────┘ └──────────────┘
```

Here are the details about **Georganna Myers's** first marriage, with Samuel Emmett Hargadine IV. You can read more about Georganna on page 193.

At the age of 19, Georganna Myers married **Samuel Emmett Hargadine IV** on Sunday, August 25, 1957, in Bowling Green, Pike County, Missouri, when he was 27 years old. They were divorced in Fairfax, Fairfax County, Virginia, on October 03, 1965. They had two sons.

Samuel Emmett was born in Bowling Green, Pike County, Missouri, on Thursday, June 05, 1930. He was the son of Samuel Emmett Hargadine III and Viola Belle Cox.

He served in the U.S. Army on April 21, 1953 during the Korean War Conflict, Corporal. Samuel Emmett reached 90 years of age and died in Saint Louis, Saint Louis County, Missouri, on June 27, 2020. He was buried on October 23, 2021, in Memorial Gardens Cemetery, Bowling Green, Pike County, Missouri (Find a Grave ID 211927637).

> Honorably Discharged from U.S. Army on April 29, 1961 at the rank of Corporal.

> Samuel Emmett Hargadine IV

> On June 27, 2020, Samuel Emmett Hargadine IV died at home with his loving wife, Regina at his side in Saint Louis Missouri. He was born on June 5th, 1930 to Samuel E. Hargadine III and Viola Bell Cox Hargadine at Pike County Hospital, Louisiana, Missouri. He graduated from Bowling Green High School Class of 1948 and went on to the University of Missouri at Columbia where he graduated in 1953 with a major in Psychology. He served honorably in the U.S. Army in the Intelligence Division during the Korean War. After the war, he returned to the University of Missouri where he obtained a degree in Electrical Engineering. He married Georganna Myers, August 25, 1957, and had two sons Samuel E. Hargadine V and John E. Hargadine. While impossible to convey in a brief tribute, know he was a true renaissance man and experienced a distinguished career in government service where he lived all over the world throughout his career.

> He married Regina Mandour, February 11, 1994, in Bisbee, Arizona. He then taught computer science courses for the Cochise Community College in Sierra Vista, Arizona.

Sam was an avid pilot for most of his adult life achieving commercial, instrument, and multi-engine ratings. He was raised in a musical home and instructed by his mother who was a concert pianist and instructor. During his lifelong love of swing and jazz, he mastered the clarinet and saxophone. Sam played in and organized jazz bands in the St. Louis area up until his later years. For a brief period, he was also a DJ in St. Louis after college which was his true passion. In addition to his love of music, Sam loved the game of Bridge and earned the Life Master designation for tournament play.

Survived by his wife Regina, sons Samuel and daughter-in-law Annette of Hallsville, Missouri, and John and daughter-in-law Mary of Saint Paul, Missouri. Three Grandchildren, Calvin Hargadine (Amber) of Honolulu, Hawaii, Samuel Hargadine VI of Grand Baie, Mauritius, and Mitchell (Jenna) of Charlotte, North Carolina. Five Great Grandchildren, Logan, Adam, Carter, Lucas, and Mya Hargadine.

Sam was a diehard fan of the Washington Redskins and a lifelong fan of the St. Louis Cardinals. Regina and Sam divided their time living in Tempe, Arizona, Puerto Penasco, Mexico, and St. Louis where they enjoyed socializing with their many dear friends and family.

Due to Coronavirus, private services pending at a later date.

More facts and events for Samuel Emmett Hargadine IV:

Individual Note: March 10, 1969   Received Medal for Civilian Service in Vietnam

Sons of Georganna Myers and Samuel Emmett Hargadine IV:

+ 149   m   I. **Samuel Emmett Hargadine V** was born in Columbia, Boone County, Missouri, on August 10, 1958.

+ 150   m   II. **John Everett Hargadine** was born in Washington D.C. on March 21, 1962.

Named after John W. Willis and Everett James Straube. This book is dedicated to John.

Family of Georganna Myers and Robert Turner

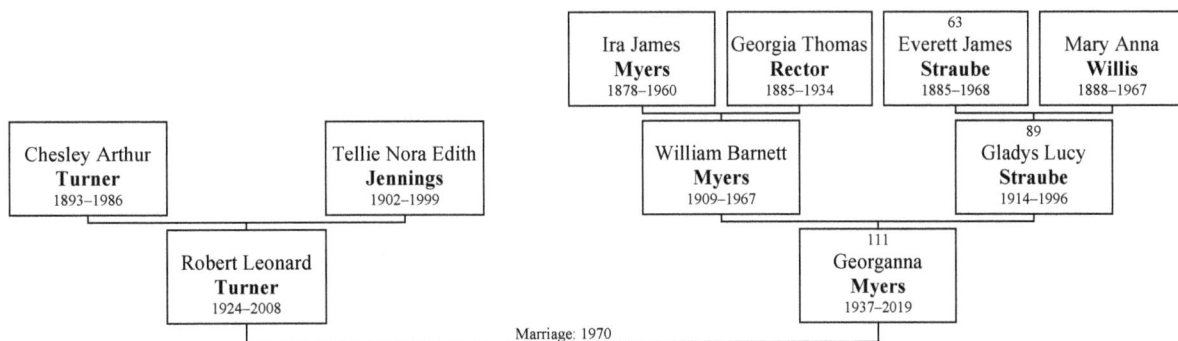

Ira James **Myers** 1878–1960	Georgia Thomas **Rector** 1885–1934	63 Everett James **Straube** 1885–1968	Mary Anna **Willis** 1888–1967

Chesley Arthur **Turner** 1893–1986	Tellie Nora Edith **Jennings** 1902–1999	William Barnett **Myers** 1909–1967	89 Gladys Lucy **Straube** 1914–1996

Robert Leonard **Turner** 1924–2008

111 Georganna **Myers** 1937–2019

Marriage: 1970

Here are the details about **Georganna Myers's** second marriage, with Robert Leonard Turner. You can read more about Georganna on page 193.

Georganna Myers married **Robert Leonard Turner** in 1970 in Columbia, Boone County, Missouri. Robert Leonard was born in Noble, Ozark County, Missouri, on Wednesday, December 03, 1924. He was the son of Chesley Arthur Turner and Tellie Nora Edith Jennings.

He served in the military at U.S Army, WWII in China, Burma, and India. Robert Leonard reached 83 years of age and died in Columbia, Boone County, Missouri, on February 24, 2008. He was buried in Ava Cemetery, Ava, Douglas County, Missouri (Find a Grave ID 26104844).

Robert, 83, Columbia, died at University Hospital, Columbia MO. A Masonic service was held at the Wright-Baker-Hill Funeral Home, Brookfield MO. Also, funeral services at VFW Hall, Ava led by VFW Post 5993. Burial with military honors rendered by VFW Post 5993 in Ava Cemetery.

Bob, son of Chesley A. and Nora (Jennings) Turner was born in Noble, Ozark County MO. He graduated Thornfield High Sch in 1943, and from Missouri State University, Springfield MO in 1953, with a Bachelor of Science Degree in Agriculture. He served in US Army in WW II with the Mars Task Force in China, Burma, and in India.

Married Bobbie Renee Jones, who died in 1955. He then married in 1977, Dr. Ann Wilson, who died 1989. Survivors includes 4 daughters, Carol Moore, Knoxville TN; Nancy Turner, Albuquerque, NM; Linda Turner, High Ridge MO; and Lori Fletcher, Brookfield MO; 4 Grandchildren, Rob Moore, Asheville, NC; Jodi Fletcher, Kansas City MO; Duane Turner, High Ridge MO; and Jill Fletcher, Brookfield MO; a great grandson, Trevor Peyton Turner, High Ridge MO; and a brother, Clinton C. Turner, Ontario OR.

Preceded by parents, one daughter Judy Renee Turner; and 2 brothers, Orville M. Turner and Kenneth R. Turner.

Family of Georganna Myers and Miles Beachboard

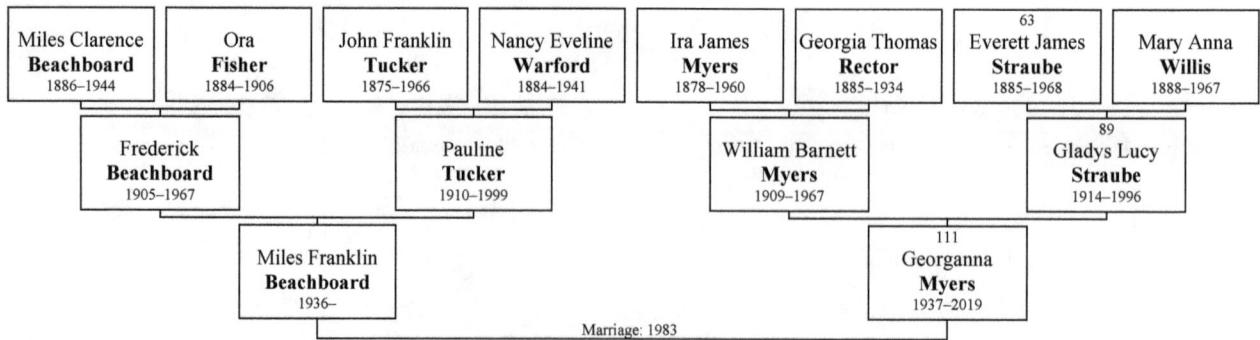

```
┌──────────────┐ ┌──────────────┐ ┌──────────────┐ ┌──────────────┐   ┌──────────────┐ ┌──────────────┐   ┌──────63──────┐ ┌──────────────┐
│Miles Clarence│ │     Ora      │ │John Franklin │ │Nancy Eveline │   │  Ira James   │ │Georgia Thomas│   │Everett James │ │  Mary Anna   │
│  Beachboard  │ │    Fisher    │ │    Tucker    │ │   Warford    │   │    Myers     │ │    Rector    │   │   Straube    │ │    Willis    │
│  1886–1944   │ │  1884–1906   │ │  1875–1966   │ │  1884–1941   │   │  1878–1960   │ │  1885–1934   │   │  1885–1968   │ │  1888–1967   │
└──────────────┘ └──────────────┘ └──────────────┘ └──────────────┘   └──────────────┘ └──────────────┘   └──────────────┘ └──────────────┘
```

Frederick **Beachboard** 1905–1967	Pauline **Tucker** 1910–1999	William Barnett **Myers** 1909–1967	89 Gladys Lucy **Straube** 1914–1996

Miles Franklin **Beachboard** 1936–	111 Georganna **Myers** 1937–2019

Marriage: 1983

Here are the details about **Georganna Myers's** third marriage, with Miles Franklin Beachboard. You can read more about Georganna on page 193.

At the age of 45, Georganna Myers married **Miles Franklin Beachboard** on Saturday, May 21, 1983, in Columbia, Boone County, Missouri, when he was 46 years old. Miles Franklin was born in Bethel, Wyandotte County, Kansas, on Saturday, June 20, 1936. Married at Parkade Baptist Church by Rev. William Camp. He is the son of Frederick Beachboard and Pauline Tucker.

Walter Straube

112.   **Walter Scott Straube Jr.** was born on Friday, December 18, 1942, in Bowling Green, Pike County, Missouri. He was the son of Walter Scott Straube (90) and Annie Elizabeth Dieckmann.

Walter Scott died in Memphis, Shelby County, Tennessee, on February 04, 2000, at the age of 57. He was buried in Memorial Gardens Cemetery, Bowling Green, Pike County, Missouri, on February 08, 2000 (Find a Grave ID 41791126).

> Caruthersville Dec. 18, 1942 - Feb. 4, 2000
>
> BOWLING GREEN - Scott Straube Jr., 57, of Caruthersville and formerly of Bowling Green, died Feb. 4, 2000, at Baptist Hospital East in Memphis, Tenn.
>
> Funeral services will be at 10 a.m. today at Smith Funeral Home in Caruthersville.
>
> A second funeral service will be at 1 p.m. Tuesday, Feb. 8, at Second Baptist Church in Bowling Green. The Rev. Jerry Gamm will officiate. Burial will be at Memorial Gardens Cemetery in Bowling Green.
>
> A memorial service for Mr. Straube and his brother, Robert (Bob) Straube, who died Jan. 29, will be at 11 a.m. Saturday, Feb. 12, at Second Baptist Church. The Rev. Jerry Gamm will officiate.
>
> Visitation for Scott Straube Jr. will be from 11 a.m. until time of services Tuesday, Feb. 8, at Second Baptist Church.
>
> Mudd-Veach Funeral Home in Bowling Green is in charge of local arrangements. Mr. Straube was born Dec. 18, 1942, in Bowling Green to Scott Straube Sr. and Annie Dieckmann Straube.

He was married to Sherrie Jo Sprunger on Oct. 17, 1992, in Louisiana. She survives.

Also surviving are his mother of Wellsville; five sons, Dean Diddell of Dallas, Scott Diddell of Houston, Texas, Josh Sprunger of Kingston, Tenn., Jason Sprunger of Caruthersville and Troy Cashman of Denver; eight grandchildren; two brothers, Dr. David Straube of Henderson, Ky., and Jerry Straube of Bowling Green; and three sisters, Rosetta Pagnella of Bowling Green, Karen Corbus of Juneau, Alaska, and Joyce Roloff of Sturgeon Bay, Wis.

He was preceded in death by his father.

Mr. Straube was a veteran of the U.S. Navy.

He was formerly administrator of Pike County Memorial Hospital in Louisiana.

He was currently employed by Pemiscot Memorial Health System in Hayti, where he was an assistant administrator and director of fiscal services.

Mr. Straube was a 1961 graduate of Bowling Green High School. He received a degree in business administration from the American University in Washington.

Memorials may be made to the American Cancer Society.

Marriages with Karen Louise Green, Doni Nadine Allred (Page 200) and Sherrie Jo Sprunger (Page 200) are known.

Family of Walter Straube and Karen Green

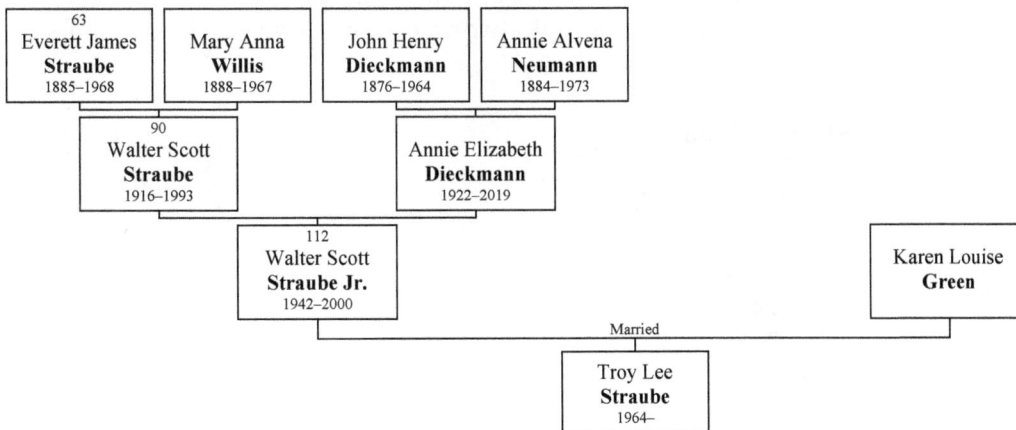

Here are the details about **Walter Scott Straube Jr.'s** first marriage, with Karen Louise Green. You can read more about Walter Scott on page 198.

Walter Scott Straube Jr. married **Karen Louise Green**. They had one son.

Son of Walter Scott Straube Jr. and Karen Louise Green:

m   I. **Troy Lee Straube** was born on February 15, 1964. He is also known as **Troy Lee Cashman**. Troy Lee was adopted. Last name now Cashman.

Last name is Cashman, last known to be living in Denver, Colorado.

Family of Walter Straube and Doni Allred

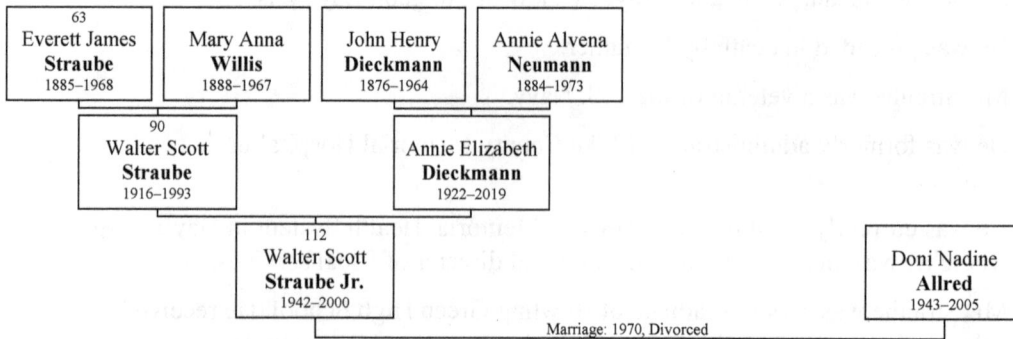

Here are the details about **Walter Scott Straube Jr.'s** second marriage, with Doni Nadine Allred. You can read more about Walter Scott on page 198.

At the age of 27, Walter Scott Straube Jr. married **Doni Nadine Allred** on Saturday, May 16, 1970, in Folkston City, Charlton County, Georgia, when she was 27 years old. They are divorced. Unknown.

Doni Nadine was born in Brunswick, Glynn County, Georgia, on Sunday, April 18, 1943. She reached 62 years of age and died in Missouri, USA, on August 16, 2005. Doni Nadine was buried in Greenwood Cemetery, Mobridge, Walworth County, South Dakota (Find a Grave ID 88998154).

Family of Walter Straube and Sherrie Sprunger

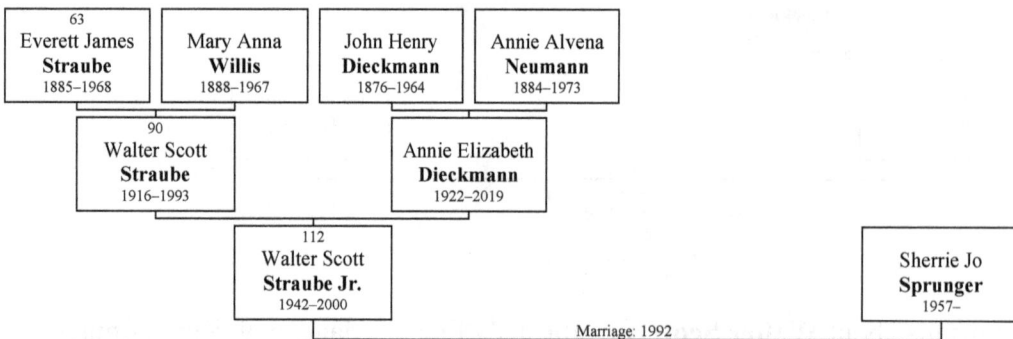

Here are the details about **Walter Scott Straube Jr.'s** third marriage, with Sherrie Jo Sprunger. You can read more about Walter Scott on page 198.

At the age of 49, Walter Scott Straube Jr. married **Sherrie Jo Sprunger** on Saturday, October 17, 1992, in Louisiana, Pike County, Missouri, when she was 34 years old. Sherrie Jo was born on Tuesday, November 12, 1957.

Family of Robert Straube and Barbara Sloan

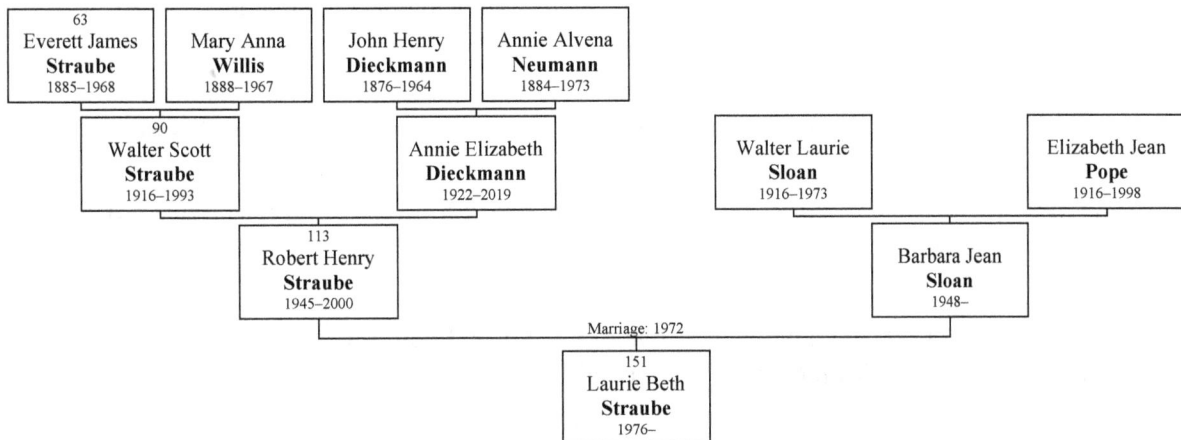

| 63
Everett James
Straube
1885–1968 | Mary Anna
Willis
1888–1967 | John Henry
Dieckmann
1876–1964 | Annie Alvena
Neumann
1884–1973 | | | Walter Laurie
Sloan
1916–1973 | | Elizabeth Jean
Pope
1916–1998 |

90
Walter Scott
Straube
1916–1993

Annie Elizabeth
Dieckmann
1922–2019

113
Robert Henry
Straube
1945–2000

Barbara Jean
Sloan
1948–

Marriage: 1972

151
Laurie Beth
Straube
1976–

113. **Robert Henry Straube** was born on Thursday, February 08, 1945, in Bowling Green, Pike County, Missouri. He was the son of Walter Scott Straube (90) and Annie Elizabeth Dieckmann. He was also known as **Bobby**.

Robert Henry served in the US Navy during the Vietnam War. He died in Plant City, Hillsborough County, Florida, on January 29, 2000, at the age of 54. His cause of death was brain cancer. His body was cremated in Plant City, Hillsborough County, Florida. Robert Henry was buried in Memorial Gardens Cemetery, Bowling Green, Pike County, Missouri (Find a Grave ID 68398462).

BOWLING GREEN - Robert (Bob) Straube, 54, of Plant City, Fla., and formerly of Bowling Green, died Jan. 29, 2000, at his home.

Memorial services for Mr. Straube and his brother, Scott Straube Jr., who died Feb. 4, will be at 11 a.m. Saturday, Feb. 12, at Second Baptist Church in Bowling Green. The Rev. Jerry Gamm will officiate.

Mudd-Veach Funeral Home in Bowling Green is in charge of arrangements.

Robert Straube was born Feb. 8, 1945, in Bowling Green to Scott Straube Sr. and Ann Dieckmann Straube.

He was married to Barbara Sloan on March 17, 1972, in Philadelphia, Pa. She survives.

Also surviving are one daughter, Laurie Straube, a student at the University of South Florida; his mother of Wellsville; two brothers, Dr. David Straube of Henderson, Ky., and Jerry Straube of Bowling Green; and three sisters, Rosetta Pagnella of Bowling Green, Karen Corbus of Juneau, Alaska, and Joyce Roloff of Sturgeon Bay, Wis.

He was preceded in death by his father.

Mr. Straube was a U.S. Navy veteran of the Vietnam war. He served aboard the USS *BonHomme Richard*.

After his discharge from the Navy in 1971, Mr. Straube began a career in the insurance field, which he continued for more than 25 years.

He was a graduate of Bowling Green High School. He attended Hannibal-LaGrange College and Strayer College in Washington, D.C. While in Washington he worked for Sen. Stuart Symington.

Memorials may be made to the H.L. Moffitt Cancer Center, 12902 Magnolia Drive, Tampa, Fla. 33612, The Bowling Green Alumni Association or Second Baptist Church in Bowling Green.

At the age of 27, Robert Henry married **Barbara Jean Sloan** on Friday, March 17, 1972, in Worcester, Montgomery County, Pennsylvania, when she was 23 years old. They had one daughter.

Barbara Jean was born in Cleveland, Cuyahoga County, Ohio, on Friday, August 27, 1948. She is the daughter of Walter Laurie Sloan and Elizabeth Jean Pope.

Daughter of Robert Henry Straube and Barbara Jean Sloan:

+ 151 f I. **Laurie Beth Straube** was born in Annandale, Fairfax County, Virginia, on August 02, 1976.

Family of Rosetta Straube and William Pagnella

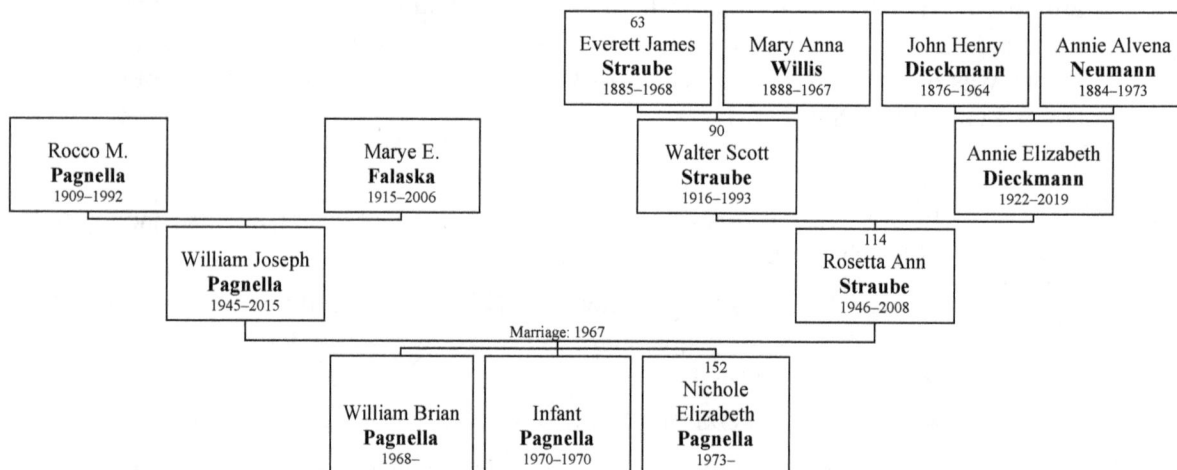

114. Rosetta Ann Straube was born on Sunday, May 05, 1946, in Bowling Green, Pike County, Missouri. She was the daughter of Walter Scott Straube (90) and Annie Elizabeth Dieckmann. She was also known as **Rosie**.

Rosetta Ann died in Saint Charles, St. Charles County, Missouri, on February 12, 2008, at the age of 61. She was buried in Memorial Gardens Cemetery, Bowling Green, Pike County, Missouri (Find a Grave ID 68398501).

At the age of 21, Rosetta Ann married **William Joseph Pagnella** on Saturday, September 02, 1967, in Bowling Green, Pike County, Missouri, when he was 22 years old. They had three children.

William Joseph was born in Rochester, Monroe County, New York, on Sunday, July 01, 1945. He was the son of Rocco M. Pagnella and Marye E. Falaska.

William Joseph reached 70 years of age and died in Alexandria, Alexandria City, Virginia, on November 11, 2015. He was cremated- (Find a Grave ID 155054259).

> William Joseph Pagnella died peacefully at home surrounded by loved ones on November 11, 2015. He is survived by his wife, Mary Beth Pagnella; sons, Brian Pagnella, Patrick Chambers and Joey Pagnella; daughter, Nicole Jensen and son-in-law, Dave; as well as his granddaughter, Kennedy Jensen. Family and friends may gather on Sunday, November 15, 2015 from 5 to 8 p.m. at Everly-Wheatley Funeral Home, 1500 W. Braddock Rd., Alexandria, VA 22302.
>
> A Memorial Mass will be held on Monday, November 16, 2015 at 10 a.m. at St. Mary's Catholic Church, 310 S. Royal St., Alexandria, VA 22314. In lieu of flowers, please donate in honor of Bill to the American Red Cross. A guest register may be found at: www.everlywheatley.com

Children of Rosetta Ann Straube and William Joseph Pagnella:

m   I. **William Brian Pagnella** was born in Alexandria, Virginia, on September 16, 1968.

       II. **Infant Pagnella** was born in Alexandria City, Virginia, on September 11, 1970. He or she died in Alexandria City, Virginia, on September 11, 1970. Infant was buried (Find a Grave ID 241514071).

       Donated to Medical Science

+ 152   f   III. **Nichole Elizabeth Pagnella** was born in Alexandria, Virginia, on February 19, 1973. She is also known as **Nicki**.

Family of David Straube and Ginny Henely

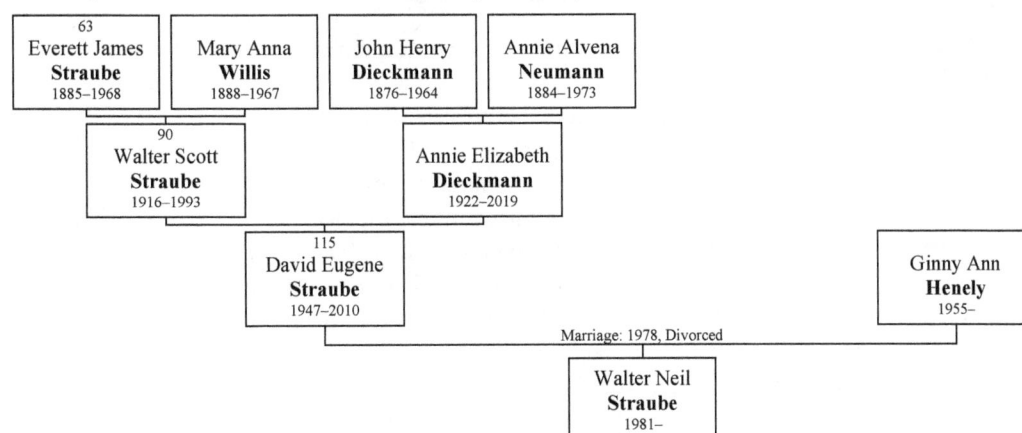

115. **David Eugene Straube** was born on Sunday, August 03, 1947, in Bowling Green, Pike County, Missouri. He was the son of Walter Scott Straube (90) and Annie Elizabeth Dieckmann. He was also known as **Doc**.

David Eugene died in Tampa, Hillsborough County, Florida, on June 25, 2010, at the age of 62. He was buried in Memorial Gardens Cemetery, Bowling Green, Pike County, Missouri (Find a Grave ID 68398611).

David Eugene Straube was born on Sunday, August 3, 1947, in Bowling Green, Missouri. The son of Scott and Ann Straube. He was affectionately called "Doc" by many of his colleagues, clients and friends.

David grew up in Bowling Green, worked for Bankhead's Restaurant and Pollards minnow ponds during high school. He took an active interest in the veterinarian clinic, perhaps influenced by his father, Scott, who had an interest in veterinary medicine. David was active in athletics including baseball and basketball. He graduated from Bowling Green High School in 1965, attended Northeast Missouri State at Kirksville from 1965-67 and then attended the University of Missouri in Columbia. In 1973, David graduated from the University of Missouri School of Veterinary Medicine with a degree in veterinary medicine and sciences (DVM). He subsequently became licensed in Missouri, Illinois, Maryland, Washington, D.C., Kentucky and Florida.

David moved to McLean, Virginia, in 1973 to join most of his family members who resided in the area and worked for a small animal clinic until 1974. He moved to West Virginia where he continued to practice before taking a position in Lexington Kentucky for Dr. Holbrook and Dr. Gentry who were searching for an Equine Clinic. He also served as a Kentucky Commission Veterinarian in 1974 and 1989. He was offered a job with Dr. Joe Burch in Miami for a position in his Equine Thoroughbred Racetrack Practice and obtained a license to work for Dr. Burch. In 1976, David established his own Thoroughbred racing and breeding clinic in Odessa, Florida and began a solo medical practice specializing in equine medicine. His true passion was equines and while living in Florida he began a long career working on racehorses.

David married Ginny Ann Henely on October 14, 1978, in Bowling Green. They had one son, Walter Neil Straube, born February 4, 1981, in Tampa, Florida.

David began spending summers working the racetrack circuit in Kentucky that included Churchill Downs, Kentucky Downs and Ellis Park. In the late 1990s, he purchased a farm called Hidden Acres in Henderson, Kentucky, and lived there for several years. His family enjoyed numerous reunions and gatherings at the farm. It was a wonderful vintage farmhouse with livestock, barns, ponds and acres to explore. One of his fondest memories was celebrating his parent's 50th wedding anniversary July 1992 in Henderson and spending the day at the racetrack with one of his horses winning, the family photo taken with the jockey and horse, and then returning to celebrate at the farm. It was the last family vacation before his father's passing in December 1993. Unfortunately, the farm was destroyed by fire and sold in 2001.

In 2008, David shifted from private practice to working as a State Veterinarian Inspector for Tampa Bay Downs. In the summer of 2009, he worked as a Commission Veterinarian for the Presque Isle Downs racetrack in Eerie, Pennsylvania.

Throughout his career David continued to make his home in Florida during the winter months and traveled to other tracks during the summer. But shortly after David completed his 35th year at Tampa Bay Downs he became ill and was admitted to Town and Country Hospital in Tampa on May 23, 2010.

David passed away on June 25, 2010, at the Town and Country Hospital in Tampa, Florida at the age of 62 years, 10 months and 22 days as a result of renal failure. A memorial service for was held on Friday, July 9 at the Second Baptist Church in Bowling Green. Brother Don Amelung, Pastor, officiated. Parts of his ashes were buried at Memorial Gardens in Bowling Green.

A Celebration of Life service is to be at the December 2010 reopening of Tampa Bay Downs Racetrack. He will be honored in the "Winners Circle" and parts of his ashes will be scattered by horseback while making a memorial lap.

David is survived by his mother, Ann Straube of Bowling Green; his son, Neil Straube of Fayetteville, N.C.; one brother, Jerry Straube of Bowling Green; two sisters, Karen Corbus of Juneau, Alaska and Joyce Roloff of Crested Butte, Colorado; many nephews and nieces.

David was a proud father, an avid St. Louis Cardinals baseball fan, and as an alumnus of the University of Missouri, he remained a true Mizzou Tiger fan.

More facts and events for David Eugene Straube:

Individual Note: 1973   Doctor of Veterinary Medicine

At the age of 31, David Eugene married **Ginny Ann Henely** on Saturday, October 14, 1978, in Bowling Green, Pike County, Missouri, when she was 23 years old. They are divorced. They had one son.

Ginny Ann was born in Chicago, Cook County, Illinois, on Tuesday, January 18, 1955.

Son of David Eugene Straube and Ginny Ann Henely:

m   I. **Walter Neil Straube** was born in Tampa, Hillsborough County, Florida, on February 04, 1981.

Family of Jerry Straube and Pamela Fisher

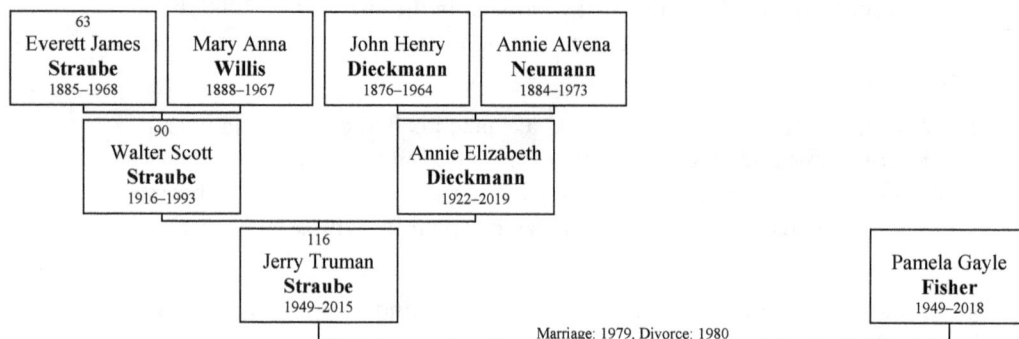

```
┌─────────────┐ ┌─────────────┐ ┌─────────────┐ ┌─────────────┐
│     63      │ │             │ │             │ │             │
│Everett James│ │ Mary Anna   │ │ John Henry  │ │Annie Alvena │
│  Straube    │ │   Willis    │ │  Dieckmann  │ │  Neumann    │
│  1885–1968  │ │  1888–1967  │ │  1876–1964  │ │  1884–1973  │
└─────────────┘ └─────────────┘ └─────────────┘ └─────────────┘
      ┌─────────────┐               ┌─────────────┐
      │     90      │               │             │
      │Walter Scott │               │Annie Elizabeth│
      │  Straube    │               │  Dieckmann  │
      │  1916–1993  │               │  1922–2019  │
      └─────────────┘               └─────────────┘
            ┌─────────────┐                        ┌─────────────┐
            │    116      │                        │             │
            │Jerry Truman │                        │Pamela Gayle │
            │  Straube    │                        │  Fisher     │
            │  1949–2015  │                        │  1949–2018  │
            └─────────────┘                        └─────────────┘
                    Marriage: 1979, Divorce: 1980
```

116. **Jerry Truman Straube** was born on Thursday, March 03, 1949, in Bowling Green, Pike County, Missouri. He was the son of Walter Scott Straube (90) and Annie Elizabeth Dieckmann. He was also known as **Jake**.

Jerry Truman served in the U.S. Navy during the Vietnam War. He died in Bowling Green, Pike County, Missouri, on February 03, 2015, at the age of 65. Jerry Truman was buried in Memorial Gardens Cemetery, Bowling Green, Pike County, Missouri (Find a Grave ID 143001000).

The Vandalia Leader April 29, 2015

> Bowling Green resident Jerry Truman Straube, age 65, passed away from lung cancer on Feb. 3 2015 at the Moore Pike Nursing Home in Bowling Green. He was born March 3, 1949 to Scott and Annie Straube at the former BB Springs in Bowling Green. He was the fifth of seven children and was named after President Harry S. Truman. Memorial services were held at 11 a.m., Tuesday, Feb. 10, at the Bibb-Veach Funeral Home in Bowling Green with Rev. Don Amelung officiating. Memorial visitation was held at 9:30 a.m. until time of service at the funeral home. Jerry was raised in Bowling Green, where he attended local schools and graduated in 1967 from BGHS. In January 1968, he enlisted in the US Navy and spent his first year on the USS Bonhomme Richard, serving alongside his brother Bob. In 1969, he commenced an overseas tour and served active duty in Vietnam. He was honorably discharged in January 1974 and settled in the Washington, D.C. suburbs near his siblings. After moving back to Missouri, he married Pamela Fischer in 1979 and divorced in 1980.
>
> Jerry developed an interest in traveling and for a couple of years he accompanied cross country truck drivers as a loading assistant. He also worked on a variety of construction projects and was an accomplished carpenter with Gary Wendel's Carpeting service in Bowling Green for several years. He was artistic and enjoyed numerous hobbies including drawing, woodworking, and playing billiards. His favorite pastime was collecting a wide variety of music and movies, building an impressive collection over 30 years.
>
> In addition to his military travels abroad, he managed to see a majority of the US through his early cross country drives and visits with his brother David in Florida and Kentucky, family road trips to Wisconsin to visit his sister Joyce, and flying to Alaska, where he spent several summers with his sister Karen.

Jerry was preceded in death by his father Walter Scott Straube, Sr., brothers, Scott, Jr., Bob, and David Straube, sister Rosetta Pagnella, and brother-in-law Chad Drennan. He is survived by his mother, Annie Straube of Bowling Green, sisters Karen "Katie" (Bill) Corbus of Juneau, Ala., Joyce Roloff (Doug Kroft) of Crested Butte, Colo., as well as several nieces, nephews, and extended family.

In lieu of flowers, his family suggest memorial donations be made to Home Care and Hospice (#1 Health Care Place, Bowling Green, Mo 63334), Second Baptist Church (319 W. Church, Bowling Green, Mo. 63334), or to VFW Post 5553 (505 VFW Road, Bowling Green, Mo. 63334).

At the age of 30, Jerry Truman married **Pamela Gayle Fisher** on Friday, August 03, 1979, in Frankford, Pike County, Missouri, when she was 30 years old. They were divorced in 1980.

Pamela Gayle was born in Hannibal, Marion County, Missouri, on Wednesday, March 23, 1949. She was also known as **Pam**.

Pamela Gayle reached 69 years of age and died in Bridgeton, St. Louis County, Missouri, on December 05, 2018. She was buried in Grand View Burial Park, Hannibal, Ralls County, Missouri (Find a Grave ID 195194419).

Pam Williams age 69, of Bowling Green passed away December 5, 2018 at the DePaul Hospital in Bridgetown surrounded by love.

Funeral services will be 5:00 p.m. Sunday, December 9, 2018 at the First Christian Church in Frankford with Rev. Gail Aurand officiating. Visitation will be held 2:00 - 5:00 p.m. Sunday, December 9, 2018 at the church.
A Memorial Graveside will be held at a later date in Grandview Cemetery.

Pam was born March 23, 1949 in Hannibal the daughter of Dawson and Pauline Griffin Fisher. On August 4, 1990 in Bowling Green she married Tom Williams. He preceded her in death on May 6, 2016. She was also preceded in death by her parents and cousin Beverly Jane Andrews.

Pam was raised in Frankford and lived in Bowling Green most of her life. She graduated from Bowling Green High School in 1966, achieved her Bachelors of Science and Education Degree in 1971 and a Master's Degree in Education from the University of Missouri in 1976. Pam was a member in the Frankford Christian Church with an unwavering faith in God, the Eastern Star Organization, DAR and numerous organizations. Pam taught kindergarten for 31 years, was the pianist for her church and was an amazing cook. She was involved and helped anyone she could. Pam loved crafting, quilting, sewing, scrapbooking, crocheting and was "Spunky". Her most cherished possessions were her family, friends, and her church. She taught us to never give up, never stop learning or exploring. Pam was a treasured gift and blessing to everyone she knew.

Serving as pallbearers will be Brad Darnell, Scott Baumgartner, Brad Tennensen, Harry Benn, Elmo Shaw and Steve Spegal.

Memorials may be made to the First Christian Church in Frankford.

Karen Straube

117. **Karen Sue Straube** was born on Thursday, January 04, 1951, in Bowling Green, Pike County, Missouri. She is the daughter of Walter Scott Straube (90) and Annie Elizabeth Dieckmann. She is also known as **Katie**.

Marriages with Charles Norman Drennan and William Ashley Corbus (Page 209) are known.

Family of Karen Straube and Charles Drennan

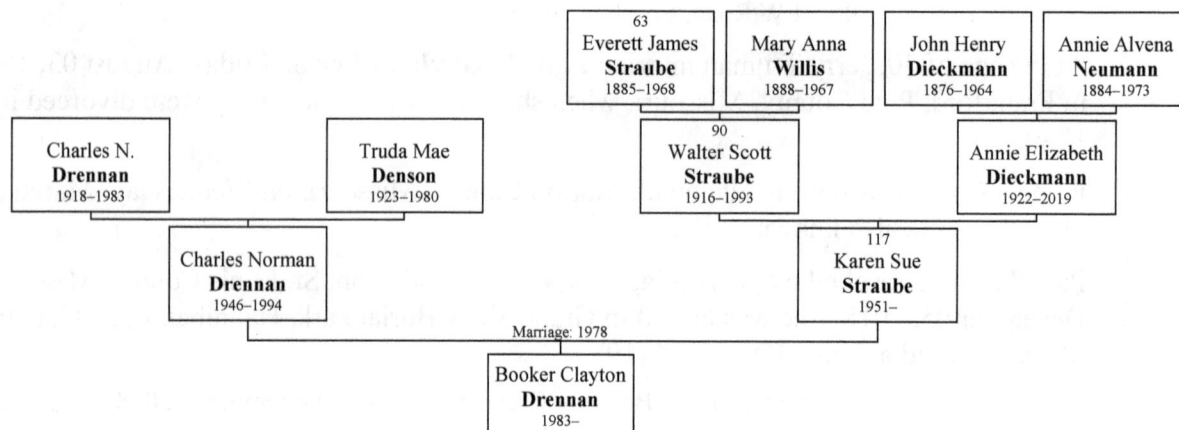

Here are the details about **Karen Sue Straube's** first marriage, with Charles Norman Drennan. You can read more about Karen Sue on page 208.

At the age of 27, Karen Sue Straube married **Charles Norman Drennan** on Saturday, November 25, 1978, in Bowling Green, Pike County, Missouri, when he was 32 years old. They had one son.

Charles Norman was born in Gideon, New Madrid County, Missouri, on Tuesday, November 19, 1946.[76] He was the son of Charles N. Drennan and Truda Mae Denson. He was also known as **Chad**.

Charles Norman reached 47 years of age and died in Juneau, Borough of Juneau, Alaska, on August 06, 1994.[76] He was buried in Alaskan Memorial Park, Juneau, Juneau Borough, Alaska (Find a Grave ID 86912776).[76]

Son of Karen Sue Straube and Charles Norman Drennan:

m   I. **Booker Clayton Drennan** was born at Bartlett Memorial Hospital in Juneau, Borough of Juneau, Alaska, on June 30, 1983.

---

76   Ancestry.com, U.S., Find a Grave® Index, 1600s-Current (Lehi, UT, USA, Ancestry.com Operations, Inc., 2012), Ancestry.com, Record for Truda Mae Drennan. https://search.ancestry.co.uk/cgi-bin/sse.dll?db=60525&h=95596773&indiv=try.

Family of Karen Straube and William Corbus

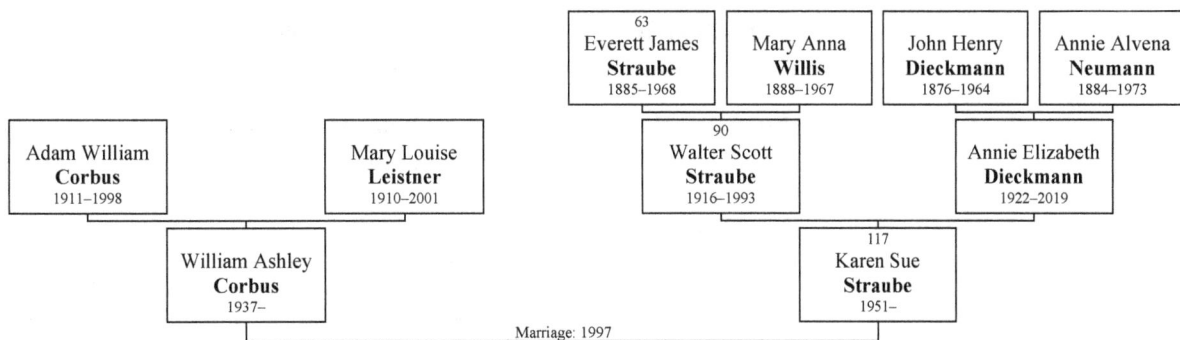

	63 Everett James **Straube** 1885–1968	Mary Anna **Willis** 1888–1967	John Henry **Dieckmann** 1876–1964	Annie Alvena **Neumann** 1884–1973

Adam William **Corbus** 1911–1998	Mary Louise **Leistner** 1910–2001	90 Walter Scott **Straube** 1916–1993	Annie Elizabeth **Dieckmann** 1922–2019

William Ashley **Corbus** 1937–

117 Karen Sue **Straube** 1951–

Marriage: 1997

Here are the details about **Karen Sue Straube's** second marriage, with William Ashley Corbus. You can read more about Karen Sue on page 208.

At the age of 46, Karen Sue Straube married **William Ashley Corbus** on Saturday, April 05, 1997, in Menlo Park, San Mateo County, California, when he was 59 years old. William Ashley was born in San Francisco, San Francisco County, California, on Wednesday, August 18, 1937. He is the son of Adam William Corbus and Mary Louise Leistner.

Joyce Straube

118. **Joyce Marie Straube** was born on Saturday, November 08, 1952, in Bowling Green, Pike County, Missouri. She is the daughter of Walter Scott Straube (90) and Annie Elizabeth Dieckmann.

Marriages with Kip Cary Roloff and Douglas Verle Kroft (Page 210) are known.

Family of Joyce Straube and Kip Roloff

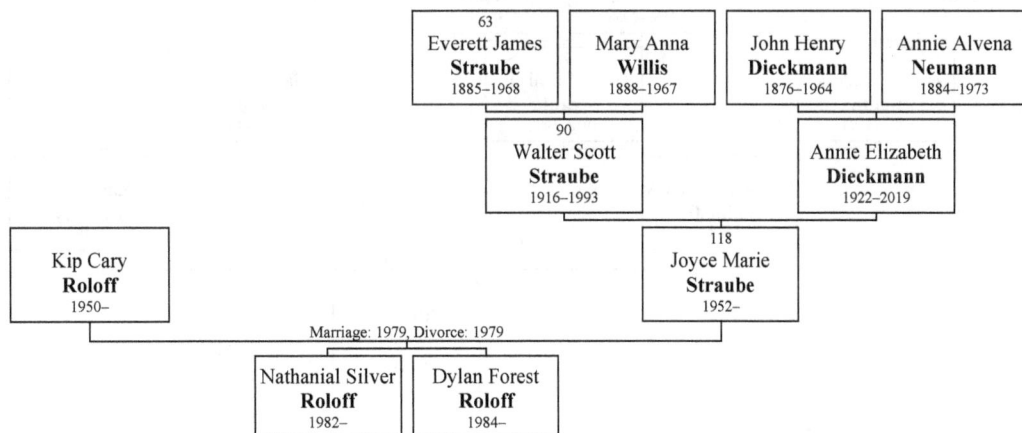

63 Everett James **Straube** 1885–1968	Mary Anna **Willis** 1888–1967	John Henry **Dieckmann** 1876–1964	Annie Alvena **Neumann** 1884–1973

90 Walter Scott **Straube** 1916–1993	Annie Elizabeth **Dieckmann** 1922–2019

Kip Cary **Roloff** 1950–	118 Joyce Marie **Straube** 1952–

Marriage: 1979, Divorce: 1979

Nathanial Silver **Roloff** 1982–	Dylan Forest **Roloff** 1984–

Here are the details about **Joyce Marie Straube's** first marriage, with Kip Cary Roloff. You can read more about Joyce Marie on page 209.

At the age of 26, Joyce Marie Straube married **Kip Cary Roloff** on Saturday, June 30, 1979, in Auk Bay, Juneau Borough County, Alaska, when he was 28 years old. They were divorced on June 30, 1979. They have two sons.

Kip Cary was born in Red River, Kewaunee, Wisconsin, on Wednesday, July 12, 1950.

Sons of Joyce Marie Straube and Kip Cary Roloff:

m   I. **Nathanial Silver Roloff** was born at Bartlett Memorial Hospital in Juneau, Borough of Juneau, Alaska, on December 13, 1982.

m   II. **Dylan Forest Roloff** was born at Shawano County Hospital in Shawano, Shawano County, Wisconsin, on October 12, 1984.

Family of Joyce Straube and Douglas Kroft

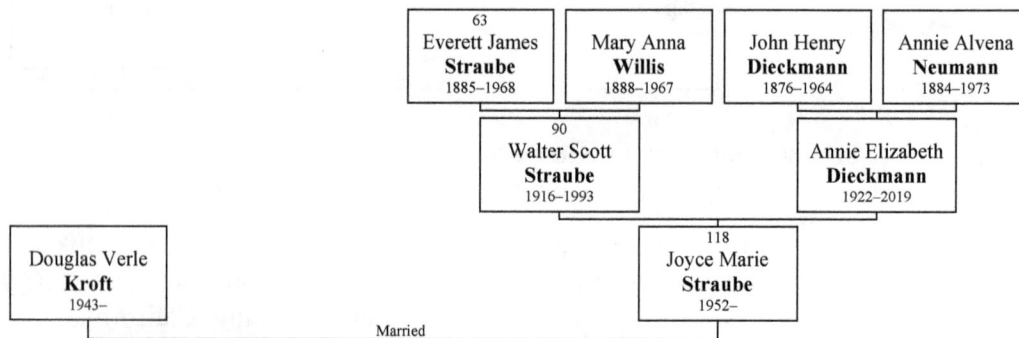

Here are the details about **Joyce Marie Straube's** second marriage, with Douglas Verle Kroft. You can read more about Joyce Marie on page 209.

Joyce Marie Straube married **Douglas Verle Kroft**. Douglas Verle was born on Wednesday, August 11, 1943.

Family of Garland Smith and Karen Langley

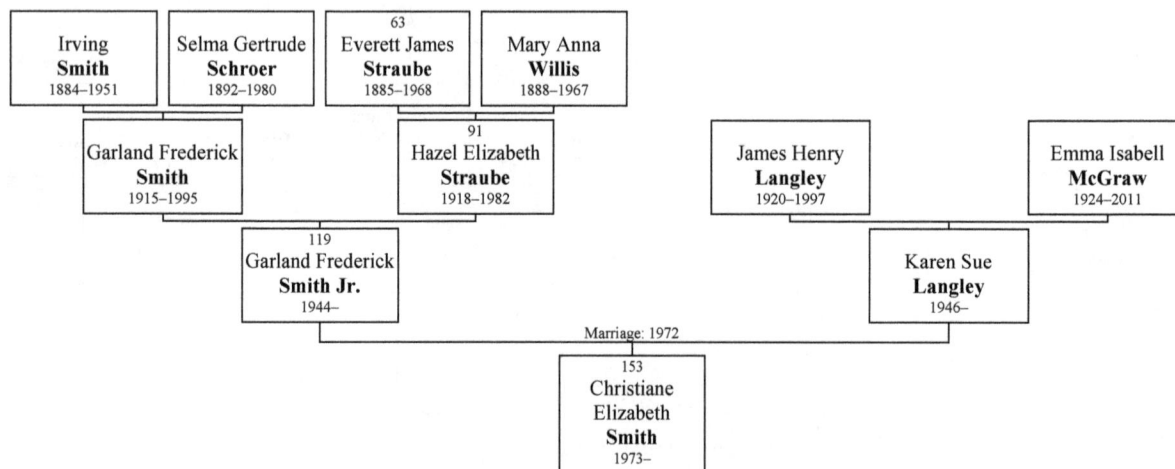

119.   **Garland Frederick Smith Jr.** was born on Friday, February 04, 1944, in Lake Charles, Calcasieu Parish, Louisianna. He is the son of Garland Frederick Smith and Hazel Elizabeth Straube (91).

At the age of 28, Garland Frederick married **Karen Sue Langley** on Saturday, February 19, 1972, in Florissant, Saint Louis County, Missouri, when she was 25 years old. They have one daughter.

Karen Sue was born in Saint Louis, Saint Louis County, Missouri, on Sunday, October 20, 1946. She is the daughter of James Henry Langley and Emma Isabell McGraw.

Daughter of Garland Frederick Smith Jr. and Karen Sue Langley:

+ 153   f   I. **Christiane Elizabeth Smith** was born in City of Creve Coeur, Saint Louis County, Missouri, on June 29, 1973.

Family of Hazel Smith and Jacques McCormack

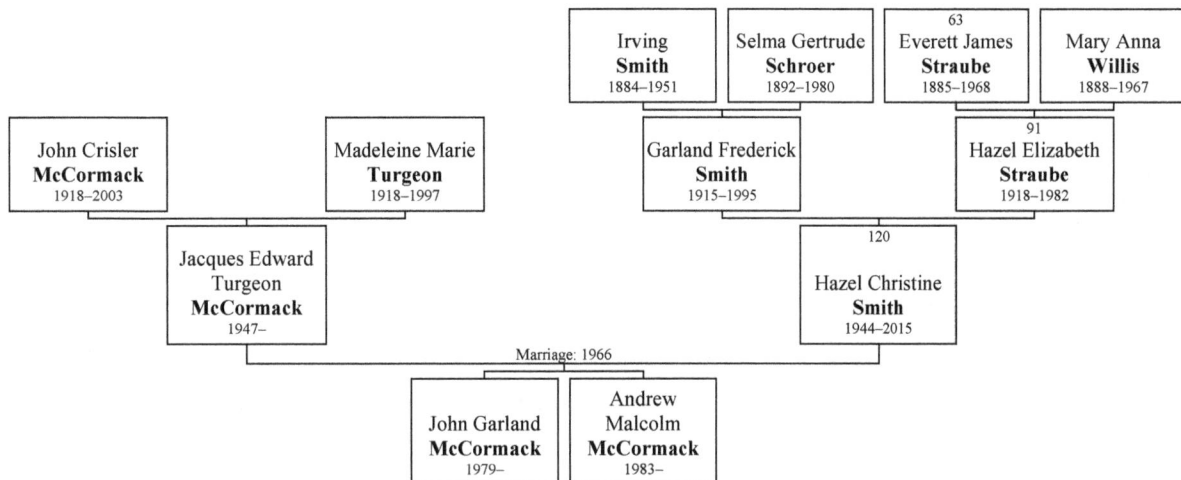

120.   **Hazel Christine Smith** was born on Monday, December 04, 1944, in Saint Louis, Saint Louis County, Missouri. She was the daughter of Garland Frederick Smith and Hazel Elizabeth Straube (91). She was also known as **Christy**.

Hazel Christine died in Columbia, Richland County, South Carolina, on April 11, 2015, at the age of 70. She was buried in Elmwood Memorial Gardens, Columbia, Richland County, South Carolina, on April 18, 2015 (Find a Grave ID 144881059).

At the age of 21, Hazel Christine married **Jacques Edward Turgeon McCormack** on Saturday, October 15, 1966, in Dillon, Dillon County, South Carolina, when he was 18 years old. They had two children.

Jacques Edward Turgeon was born in Memphis, Shelby County, Tennessee, on Sunday, October 26, 1947. He is the son of John Crisler McCormack and Madeleine Marie Turgeon.

Children of Hazel Christine Smith and Jacques Edward Turgeon McCormack:

     f   I. **John Garland McCormack** was born in Paris, France, on May 06, 1979.

     m   II. **Andrew Malcolm McCormack** was born in Katona, Westchester County, New York, on April 07, 1983. He is also known as **Andy**.

Family of Stephen Smith and Karen Sedan

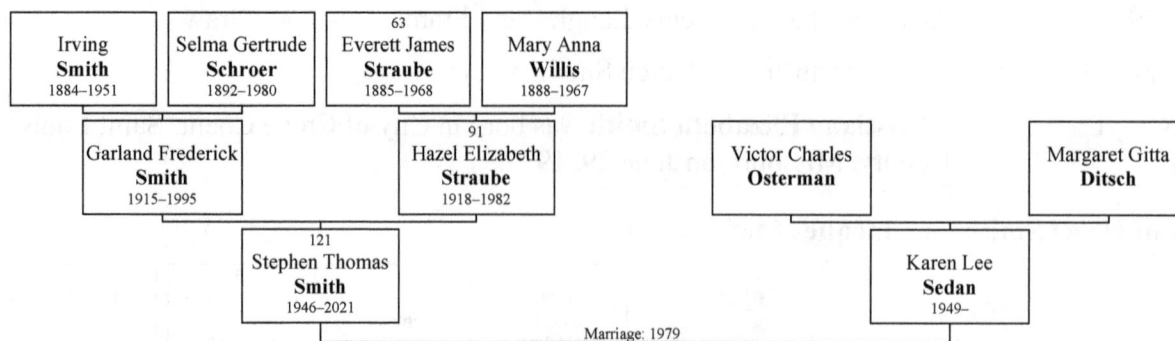

		63			
Irving **Smith** 1884–1951	Selma Gertrude **Schroer** 1892–1980	Everett James **Straube** 1885–1968	Mary Anna **Willis** 1888–1967		

Garland Frederick **Smith** 1915–1995	91 Hazel Elizabeth **Straube** 1918–1982	Victor Charles **Osterman**	Margaret Gitta **Ditsch**

121 Stephen Thomas **Smith** 1946–2021	Karen Lee **Sedan** 1949–

Marriage: 1979

---

121. **Stephen Thomas Smith** was born on Sunday, November 17, 1946, in Saint Louis, Saint Louis County, Missouri. He was the son of Garland Frederick Smith and Hazel Elizabeth Straube (91).

Stephen Thomas died in San Jose, Santa Clara County, California, on February 25, 2021, at the age of 74. He was buried in Jefferson Barracks National Cemetery, Lemay, St. Louis County, Missouri (Find a Grave ID 223492939).

> On February 25, 2021, Stephen Thomas "Steve" Smith passed away surrounded by family and friends after a short battle with cancer at the age of 74 at his home in San Jose, CA.
>
> Steve was born on November 17, 1946 in St. Louis, MO to the late Dr. Garland F. and Hazel E. (Straube) Smith.
>
> Steve grew up in Richmond Heights, MO and graduated from Maplewood-Richmond Heights High School in 1965 with achievements in football, track and student affairs. He attended the University of Missouri-Columbia, enlisted in the United States Marine Corps becoming a U.S. Marine Corps Photographer. His assignments included photographing anything from "grip and grins" and luncheons to parades, officer portraits, award ceremonies, and forensics. The Corporal was as a 3-star general's favorite and "go to photographer." He also was a photographer for the Quantico Sentry. In 1970, Steve enrolled at the Rochester Institute of Technology studying Film Making, Photojournalism, and World and Art History. A Dean's List honoree and editor of the school magazine "The Genesean" graduating in 1973.
>
> In August 1973, Steve began his professional career with E. Leitz Inc. manufacturers of Leica Cameras as a sales representative in the Midwest. In 1976 Steve became national sales manager for the company and resided in Rockleigh, NJ. Steve became Vice President of the Photographic Division in January 1982 responsible for all sales of Leica cameras and accessories in the U.S. market.
>
> For a short time Steve returned to St. Louis starting his own corporate outplacement firm. In 1993 Olympus Camera County hired Steve as a regional manager and later sale manager for the Western U.S. Region and Hawaii being based in San Jose, CA. Downsizing forced Steve to make a career change. He became a licensed real estate agent and joined Coldwell Banker Realty San Jose-Willow Glen Office in 2009 and remained with the firm until his death.

Steve had many hobbies over the years - photography, woodworking, automotive restorations and playing golf. He coached golf for many years at Piedmont Hills High School in San Jose.

Steve was preceded in death by his father, mother and sister Hazel Christine Smith (Jacques T.) McCormack. He is survived by his brothers Garland F. "Fred" (Karen) Smith, Jr., O'Fallon, MO and Bruce B. (Ruth) Smith, Severn, MD and sister Elizabeth E. Smith, Chicago, IL. Uncle to Christiane E. Smith (John) Hamai, St. Paul, MO; John G. McCormack, Columbia, SC; Andrew M. McCormack, San Francisco, CA; Ian C. Smith, Havre de Grace, MD; Matthew B. Smith, Severn, MD. Great-uncle to Noah J. Hamai, Mallory E. Hamai, Reagan C. Hamai, Jonah C. Hamai, St. Paul, MO; Alannah F. Smith, Lillian M. Smith, Havre de Grace, MD. Former wife Karen Lee (Osterman) Smith, nice and nephews, Marguerite, Mark and Chris Basso as well as his "adopted" children, Elizabeth and Khang Nyugen. Numerous cousins.

Services: Committal service with military honors will be held at 11:00 a.m. on Thursday, June 3, 2021 at the Jefferson Barracks National Cemetery. Donations may be made to American Cancer Society. Please share memories at https://www.dignitymemorial.com/obituaries/san-jose-ca/stephen-smith-10075770

At the age of 33, Stephen Thomas married **Karen Lee Sedan** on Monday, December 24, 1979, in Saint Louis, Saint Louis County, Missouri, when she was 30 years old. Karen Lee was born in Pittsburgh, Allegheny County, Pennsylvania, on Thursday, August 25, 1949. She is the daughter of Victor Charles Osterman and Margaret Gitta Ditsch.

Family of Bruce Smith and Ruth Gettis

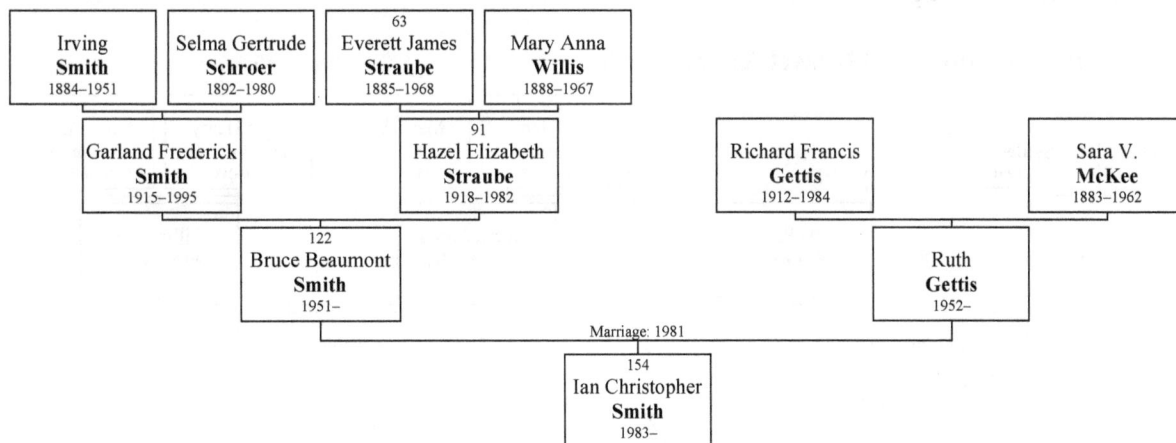

122. **Bruce Beaumont Smith** was born on Saturday, June 30, 1951, at Saint Lukes Hospital in Saint Louis, Saint Louis County, Missouri. He is the son of Garland Frederick Smith and Hazel Elizabeth Straube (91).

At the age of 29, Bruce Beaumont married **Ruth Gettis** on Saturday, June 20, 1981, in Edgewater, Anne Arundel County, Maryland, when she was 29 years old. They have one son.

Ruth was born in Philadelphia, Philadelphia County, Pennsylvania, on Thursday, April 10, 1952. She is the daughter of Richard Francis Gettis and Sara V. McKee.

Son of Bruce Beaumont Smith and Ruth Gettis:

+ 154 m I. **Ian Christopher Smith** was born in Annapolis, Anne Arundel County, Maryland, on August 09, 1983.

Family of Elizabeth Smith and Ronald Schussler

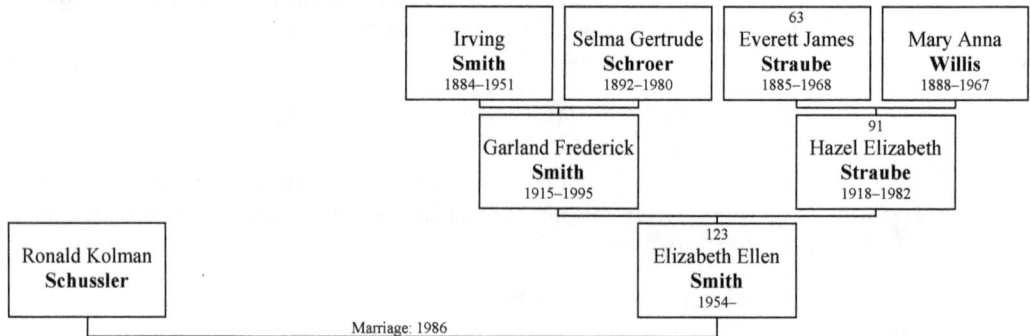

123. **Elizabeth Ellen Smith** was born on Wednesday, September 22, 1954, at St. John's Mercy Hospital in Saint Louis, Saint Louis County, Missouri. She is the daughter of Garland Frederick Smith and Hazel Elizabeth Straube (91).

Elizabeth Ellen married **Ronald Kolman Schussler** on Saturday, September 27, 1986, in Warrenville, DuPage County, Illinois.

Family of Annice Straube and Russel Allensworth

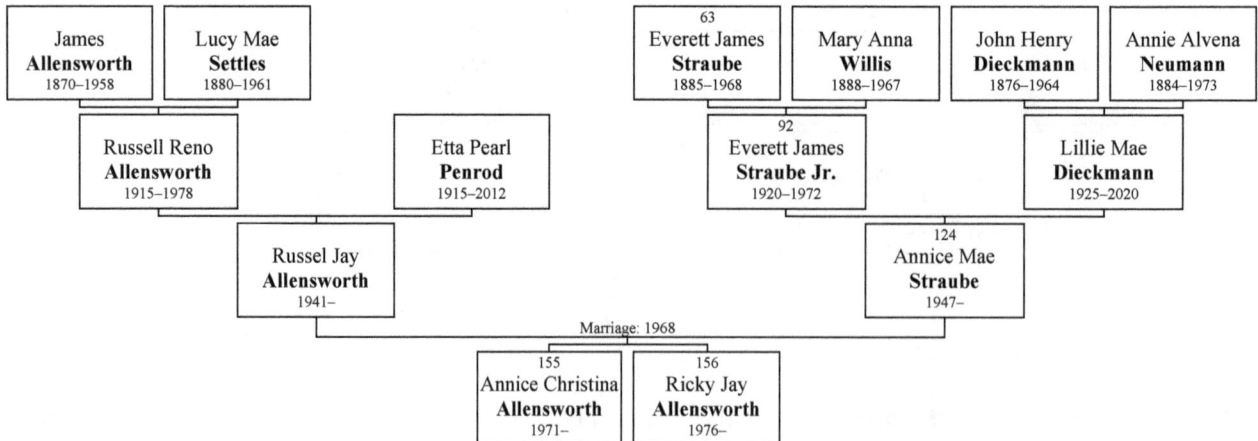

124. **Annice Mae Straube** was born on Thursday, December 18, 1947, in Bowling Green, Pike County, Missouri. She is the daughter of Everett James Straube Jr. (92) and Lillie Mae Dieckmann.

At the age of 20, Annice Mae married **Russel Jay Allensworth** on Friday, June 14, 1968, in Bowling Green, Pike County, Missouri, when he was 26 years old. They have two children.

Russel Jay was born in Louisiana, Pike County, Missouri, on Thursday, December 11, 1941. He is the son of Russell Reno Allensworth and Etta Pearl Penrod. He is also known as **R.J.**.

Children of Annice Mae Straube and Russel Jay Allensworth:

+ 155   f   I. **Annice Christina Allensworth** was born in Hannibal, Marion County, Missouri, on December 27, 1971. She is also known as **Tina**.

+ 156   m   II. **Ricky Jay Allensworth** was born in Hannibal, Marion County, Missouri, on February 04, 1976.

Family of Chris Straube and Vickie Turner

63 Everett James **Straube** 1885–1968	Mary Anna **Willis** 1888–1967	John Henry **Dieckmann** 1876–1964	Annie Alvena **Neumann** 1884–1973

92 Everett James **Straube Jr.** 1920–1972	Lillie Mae **Dieckmann** 1925–2020	Earl Elsworth **Turner** 1914–1961	Lula Elizabeth **Callon**

125 Chris James **Straube** 1949–

Vickie Ruth **Turner** 1950–

Marriage: 1968

Trenton James **Straube** 1969–	157 Aaron Willis **Straube** 1973–	158 Sara Beth **Straube** 1981–2003

125.   **Chris James Straube** was born on Tuesday, August 02, 1949, in Bowling Green, Pike County, Missouri. He is the son of Everett James Straube Jr. (92) and Lillie Mae Dieckmann.

Chris James served in the military. U.S. Marine Corps.

At the age of 19, Chris James married **Vickie Ruth Turner** on Sunday, August 04, 1968, in Frankford, Pike County, Missouri, when she was 17 years old. They had three children.

Vickie Ruth was born in Hannibal, Marion County, Missouri, on Saturday, October 07, 1950. She is the daughter of Earl Elsworth Turner and Lula Elizabeth Callon.

Children of Chris James Straube and Vickie Ruth Turner:

       m   I. **Trenton James Straube** was born in Hannibal, Marion County, Missouri, on January 06, 1969.

+ 157   m   II. **Aaron Willis Straube** was born in Hannibal, Marion County, Missouri, on June 14, 1973.

+ 158   f   III. **Sara Beth Straube** was born in Hannibal, Marion County, Missouri, on January 06, 1981. She died in Saint Louis, Saint Louis County, Missouri, on August 14, 2003, at the age of 22. Her cause of death was leukemia.

She was buried in Memorial Gardens Cemetery, Bowling Green, Pike County, Missouri, on August 17, 2003 (Find a Grave ID 68398672).

Born Sara Beth Straube on January 6, 1981. She is the daughter of Chris James Straube and Vickie Ruth Turner.

Sara got a degree in elementary education from Missouri Baptist. She married Brian Anders in 2002 and was just beginning her teaching career when diagnosed with acute leukemia. She passed away on August 14, 2003, at the age of 22 at the Siteman Cancer Center of Barnes-Jewish Hospital in St. Louis, Missouri. Services for Sara were conducted on August 17, 2003, at the Second Baptist Church, and burial was at Memorial Gardens in Bowling Green.

A fund to award an elementary teaching scholarship annually in Sara's memory was set up.

Sara is survived by her husband, Brian Anders; her parents, Chris and Vickie Straube; two brothers, Trent Straube of New York and Aaron Straube of Bowling Green; her sister-in-law, Kelly Straube; her grandmother, Mrs. E.J. (Lil) Straube, Jr. of Bowling Green and a host of relatives and friends.

Family of Stanley Straube and Vicki Burnett

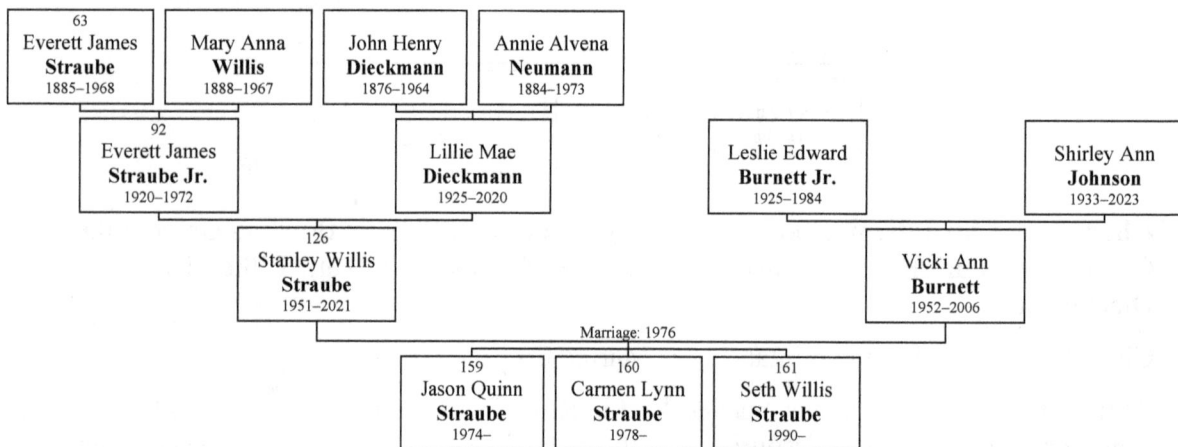

63 Everett James **Straube** 1885–1968	Mary Anna **Willis** 1888–1967	John Henry **Dieckmann** 1876–1964	Annie Alvena **Neumann** 1884–1973

92 Everett James **Straube Jr.** 1920–1972	Lillie Mae **Dieckmann** 1925–2020

Leslie Edward **Burnett Jr.** 1925–1984	Shirley Ann **Johnson** 1933–2023

126
Stanley Willis **Straube** 1951–2021

Vicki Ann **Burnett** 1952–2006

Marriage: 1976

159 Jason Quinn **Straube** 1974–	160 Carmen Lynn **Straube** 1978–	161 Seth Willis **Straube** 1990–

126. **Stanley Willis Straube** was born on Saturday, May 26, 1951, in Bowling Green, Pike County, Missouri. He was the son of Everett James Straube Jr. (92) and Lillie Mae Dieckmann.

Stanley Willis served in the military at U.S. Marine Corps in Futema, Okinawa; Vietnam era. He died on January 21, 2021, at the age of 69. Stanley Willis was buried in Edgewood Cemetery, Edgewood, Pike County, Missouri, on January 30, 2021 (Find a Grave ID 221636104).

Stanley "Willis" Straube, 69, of Bowling Green, passed away January 21, 2021 at his home. Funeral services for Willis will be held Saturday, January 30, 2021 at 11:30 a.m. at Second Baptist Church in Bowling Green with Rev. Jerry Gamm and Pastor Mark West officiating. Burial will be in Edgewood Cemetery. Visitation will be from 9:00 to 11:30 a.m. at Second Baptist Church. Online streaming of the service will be available on Bibb-Veach Funeral Home's Facebook page.

Willis was born May 26, 1951 in Bowling Green, Missouri to Everett James Straube Jr. and Lillie Mae Dieckmann Straube. He was united in marriage to Vicki Ann Burnett on June 20, 1976. She preceded him in death on January 6, 2006. Willis lived in Bowling Green his entire life. He graduated from Bowling Green High School in 1969. Immediately after graduation, he enlisted in the United States Marine Corps. During Vietnam, he served as a Corporal in Futenma, Okinawa. After discharging from active duty, Willis served in the United States Marine Corp Reserves from 1969 - 1972. He is a lifetime member of the VFW Post #5553 in Bowling Green.

Willis worked as a laborer for several construction companies over the years and enjoyed the many friendships he made during that time. When he wasn't working, he liked to spend his time hunting, fishing, gardening, and playing golf or baseball. He once played on an all-star team at Sportsman's Park. He also enjoyed playing his guitar and studied the history of music. He was a fan of blues and country music. He enjoyed barbequing and playing cards, but his favorite pastime was spending time with his family and grandchildren.

Willis is survived by sons, Jason Straube (Wendy Summers) of Bowling Green and Seth Straube (Jeni) of Bowling Green; daughter, Carmen Charlton (John) of Bowling Green; grandchildren: Kinley and Kaylyn Charlton, Kyle and Jayce Straube, Steven Bryant, Everli Straube, Carly Ledford, and Jaymeson Portwood; brother, Chris Straube (Vickie Ruth) of Center, Missouri; sisters, Annice Allensworth (R.J.) of Bowling Green and Lucy Scherder of Warrenton, Missouri; and many nieces, nephews, and cousins. He was preceded in death by his parents and wife, Vicki.

Pallbearers will be Ricky Allensworth, Aaron Straube, Shawn Burnett, John Charlton, Randy Hays, and Curtis Scherder. Memorials may be made to the donor's choice.

At the age of 25, Stanley Willis married **Vicki Ann Burnett** on Sunday, June 20, 1976, in Bowling Green, Pike County, Missouri, when she was 23 years old. They had three children.

Vicki Ann was born in Louisiana, Pike County, Missouri, on Thursday, September 04, 1952. She was the daughter of Leslie Edward Burnett Jr. and Shirley Ann Johnson.

Vicki Ann reached 53 years of age and died in Bowling Green, Pike County, Missouri, on January 06, 2006. She was buried on January 11, 2006, in Edgewood Cemetery, Edgewood, Pike County, Missouri (Find a Grave ID 75956624).

Vicki was the oldest child of Leslie and Shirley Burnett and was born September 4, 1952. Vicki graduated from Bowling Green High School in 1970. In June 1976, Vicki married Stanley Willis Straube. She died unexpectedly of a massive heart attack on January 6, 2006. To this union were born Jason Quinn on February 23, 1974; Carmen Lynn on August 5, 1978; and Seth Willis on July 14, 1990. Jason married Christie Lynn Gosnell on April 26, 2003. Their three children are: Steven Alexander Bryant born on January 3, 1995; Kyle Lane born on September 30, 2003; and Jayce Lynn born on November 18, 2005. Carmen married John William Charlton II on September 18, 1999. They have two daughters: Kinley Nicole born on June 26, 2002, and Kaylyn Paige born on August 9, 2005.

Children of Stanley Willis Straube and Vicki Ann Burnett:

+ 159 m **I. Jason Quinn Straube** was born in Hannibal, Marion County, Missouri, on February 23, 1974.

+ 160 f **II. Carmen Lynn Straube** was born in Hannibal, Marion County, Missouri, on August 05, 1978.

+ 161 m **III. Seth Willis Straube** was born in Hannibal, Marion County, Missouri, on July 14, 1990.

Family of Lucy Straube and Stephen Scherder

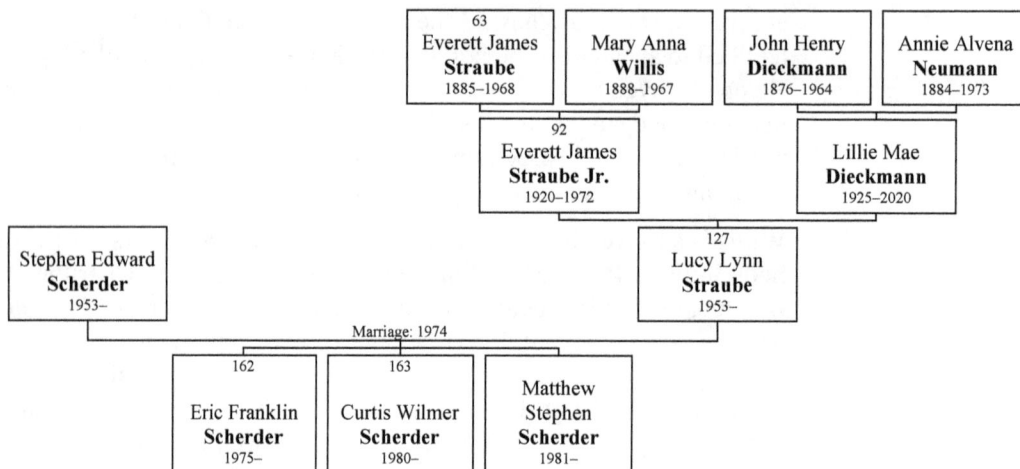

```
                                  ┌──────────┬──────────┬──────────┬──────────┐
                                  │    63    │          │          │          │
                                  │ Everett  │ Mary     │ John     │ Annie    │
                                  │ James    │ Anna     │ Henry    │ Alvena   │
                                  │ Straube  │ Willis   │ Dieckmann│ Neumann  │
                                  │1885-1968 │1888-1967 │1876-1964 │1884-1973 │
                                  └──────────┴──────────┴──────────┴──────────┘
                                        │                    │
                                  ┌──────────┐         ┌──────────┐
                                  │    92    │         │          │
                                  │ Everett  │         │ Lillie   │
                                  │ James    │         │ Mae      │
                                  │ Straube  │         │ Dieckmann│
                                  │  Jr.     │         │1925-2020 │
                                  │1920-1972 │         └──────────┘
                                  └──────────┘
                                        │                    │
        ┌──────────┐               ┌──────────┐
        │ Stephen  │               │   127    │
        │ Edward   │               │ Lucy     │
        │ Scherder │               │ Lynn     │
        │  1953-   │               │ Straube  │
        └──────────┘               │  1953-   │
                    Marriage: 1974 └──────────┘
        ┌──────────┬──────────┬──────────┐
        │   162    │   163    │          │
        │ Eric     │ Curtis   │ Matthew  │
        │ Franklin │ Wilmer   │ Stephen  │
        │ Scherder │ Scherder │ Scherder │
        │  1975-   │  1980-   │  1981-   │
        └──────────┴──────────┴──────────┘
```

127. **Lucy Lynn Straube** was born on Saturday, February 21, 1953, in Bowling Green, Pike County, Missouri. She is the daughter of Everett James Straube Jr. (92) and Lillie Mae Dieckmann.

At the age of 20, Lucy Lynn married **Stephen Edward Scherder** on Saturday, February 09, 1974, in Bowling Green, Pike County, Missouri, when he was 20 years old. They have three sons.

Stephen Edward was born in Mexico, Audrain County, Missouri, on Sunday, May 24, 1953.

Sons of Lucy Lynn Straube and Stephen Edward Scherder:

+ 162 m **I. Eric Franklin Scherder** was born in Hannibal, Marion County, Missouri, on December 30, 1975.

+ 163 m **II. Curtis Wilmer Scherder** was born in Mexico, Audrain County, Missouri, on February 20, 1980.

  m **III. Matthew Stephen Scherder** was born in Mexico, Audrain County, Missouri, on June 10, 1981.

Family of Reta Straube and Leon Dempsey

```
                        ┌─────────────────┬─────────────────┐
                        │       64        │                 │
                        │ Luther Joshua   │  Rosa Shelton   │
                        │   Straube       │    Lewis        │
                        │  1886–1968      │   1890–1964     │
                        └─────────────────┴─────────────────┘
                              ┌──────────────────┐        ┌──────────────────┐
                              │       93         │        │ Leta Bernadine   │
                              │ Melvin Joshua    │        │    McCoy         │
                              │   Straube        │        │  1908–2007       │
                              │  1908–1996       │        └──────────────────┘
                              └──────────────────┘
  ┌──────────────────┐                   ┌──────────────────┐
  │                  │                   │      128         │
  │     Leon         │                   │   Reta Fern      │
  │   Dempsey        │                   │    Straube       │
  │                  │                   │   1937–2021      │
  └──────────────────┘                   └──────────────────┘
                        Marriage: 1956
```

128.   **Reta Fern Straube** was born on Sunday, February 14, 1937, in Middletown, Montgomery County, Missouri. She was the daughter of Melvin Joshua Straube (93) and Leta Bernadine McCoy.

Reta Fern died in Vandalia, Audrain County, Missouri, on March 27, 2021, at the age of 84. She was buried in Fairmount Cemetery, Middletown, Montgomery County, Missouri (Find a Grave ID 225033682).

> Services for Reta Fern Dempsey, 84, of Vandalia, will be held 12:00 p.m. Monday, March 29, 2021 at Bienhoff Funeral Home in Vandalia with Reverend Jamie Franke officiating. Burial will be in Fairmount Cemetery in Middletown. Visitation will be from 10:00 until the time of service on Monday at the funeral home. She passed away at 4:35 a.m. March 27, 2021 at Tri-County Care Center in Vandalia.
>
> Reta was born at home in Middletown on February 14, 1937, the only child of Melvin "Pete" and Leta McCoy Straube. She was married to Leon Dempsey from 1956 through 1970 and was blessed with three sons.
>
> Survivors include: three sons, Melvin Dempsey of Hannibal, Mike (Jan) Dempsey of Kansas City, and Larry (Sandy) Dempsey of Rapid City, SD; seven grandchildren, Beth (Chad) Blanchard, Sarah (James) Waddell, Becky (Shea) Williams, Brad Dempsey, Josh (Ashton) Dempsey, and Jacob and Zach Dempsey; sixteen great grandchildren, Jacob, Annabel, and Aaron Blanchard, Madisyn, Mathew and Mara, Bennet, Brennah, Grant, Makenna, Elliot, and Quinn Waddell, Kaeden and Kyndal Williams, and Dax and Channing Dempsey; and extended special family - Mike, Charla and Emily Smith of Vandalia.
>
> Reta was a lifetime area resident, member of the Vandalia First Christian Church and a 1955 graduate of Wellsville High School and Valedictorian of her graduating class. The family began their home in Bowling Green where she worked in Senator Ed Long's office in Pike County. They moved to Vandalia in 1964 and she started babysitting and working for the city pool. This was followed by a 25-year adventure working as night manager for the Vandalia Dairy Queen. Her relationships with all the kids she worked with through the years were so very special and keeps in touch with several still to this day. Her church family were all so good to her through the years and she loved to attend all the services and special events. Reta had been living at Tri County Care Center for the past five years and she was blessed with faithful friends who visited and called and wrote. Maza Carnes wrote her weekly

notes filled with wonderful stories, Carla Thompson called her multiple times a day, those calls Reta counted on, weekly visitors Juanita Lynn, Pat Miller, Dwight Galloway and Lana Terry plus many others stopping by. Reta loved her visits, calls and letters. She also loved her DQ treats, those always brought on the smiles. She always wanted to know "when are you coming to see me again" or "when are you going to call again." Covid made the past year extremely challenging for Reta. With limited outside personal contact, she relied on the friends and Staff at Tri-County as well as her faith to see her through. She endured and beat Covid, and held on until family could once again be by her side. As the end became near, the close contact again with family, brought smiles, hugs, kisses, and comfort.

Pallbearers: Brad Dempsey, Josh Dempsey, Jake Dempsey, Zach Dempsey, Chad Blanchard, James Waddell, Shea Williams
In lieu of flowers the family asks memorials be given to the First Christian Church, Vandalia, MO In Care of Bienhoff Funeral Home, PO Box 54, Vandalia, MO 63382.

Reta Fern married **Leon Dempsey** in 1956.

7th Generation

Family of Paula Henderson and John Doyle

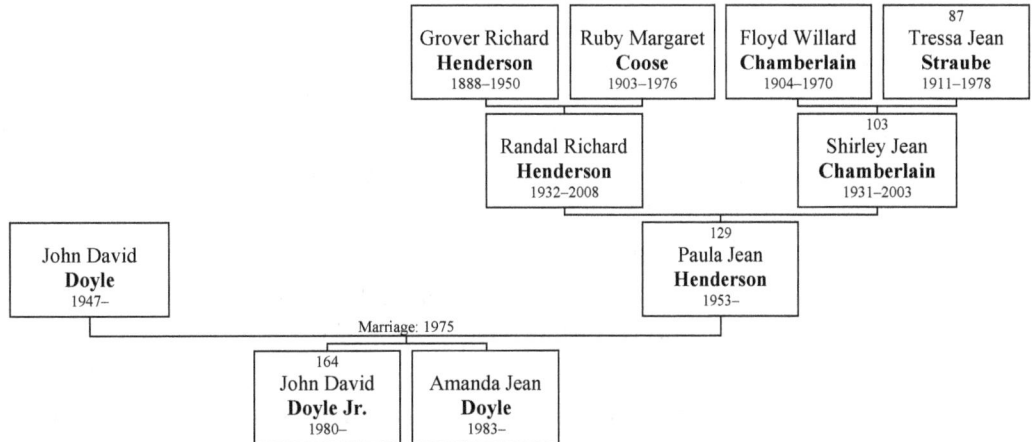

			87
Grover Richard **Henderson** 1888–1950	Ruby Margaret **Coose** 1903–1976	Floyd Willard **Chamberlain** 1904–1970	Tressa Jean **Straube** 1911–1978

Randal Richard **Henderson** 1932–2008	103 Shirley Jean **Chamberlain** 1931–2003

John David **Doyle** 1947–	129 Paula Jean **Henderson** 1953–

Marriage: 1975

164 John David **Doyle Jr.** 1980–	Amanda Jean **Doyle** 1983–

129. **Paula Jean Henderson** was born on Tuesday, December 22, 1953, in Quantico, Prince William County, Virginia. She is the daughter of Randal Richard Henderson and Shirley Jean Chamberlain (103).

At the age of 21, Paula Jean married **John David Doyle** on Saturday, August 16, 1975, in Dallas, Dallas County, Texas, when he was 27 years old. They have two children.

John David was born in Joplin, Jasper County, Missouri, on Saturday, December 13, 1947.

Children of Paula Jean Henderson and John David Doyle:

+ 164   m   I. **John David Doyle Jr.** was born in Dallas, Dallas County, Texas, on August 12, 1980.

       f   II. **Amanda Jean Doyle** was born on May 07, 1983.

Family of Marsha Henderson and Troy Dunn

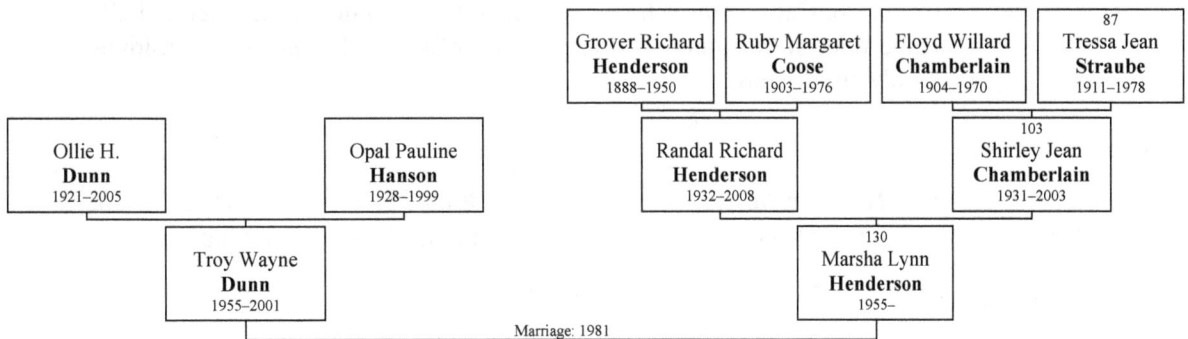

			87
Grover Richard **Henderson** 1888–1950	Ruby Margaret **Coose** 1903–1976	Floyd Willard **Chamberlain** 1904–1970	Tressa Jean **Straube** 1911–1978

Ollie H. **Dunn** 1921–2005	Opal Pauline **Hanson** 1928–1999	Randal Richard **Henderson** 1932–2008	103 Shirley Jean **Chamberlain** 1931–2003

Troy Wayne **Dunn** 1955–2001	130 Marsha Lynn **Henderson** 1955–

Marriage: 1981

130. **Marsha Lynn Henderson** was born on Wednesday, April 13, 1955, in British West Indies. She is the daughter of Randal Richard Henderson and Shirley Jean Chamberlain (103).

At the age of 25, Marsha Lynn married **Troy Wayne Dunn** on Saturday, January 03, 1981, in Dallas, Dallas County, Texas, when he was 25 years old. Troy Wayne was born in Fort

Worth, Tarrant County, Texas, on Friday, April 22, 1955. He was the son of Ollie H. Dunn and Opal Pauline Hanson.

Troy Wayne reached 45 years of age and died in Dallas, Dallas County, Texas, on March 31, 2001. He was cremated on April 04, 2001, his ashes were entombed East Breaks, Gulf of Mexico off the coast of Port Aransas, Texas (Find a Grave ID 7120673).

Ft. Worth Star-Telegram Monday, April 02, 2001-Troy Wayne Dunn

> NORTH RICHLAND HILLS-Troy Wayne Dunn, 45, peacefully completed his lifelong health battle and went to glory with God on Saturday, March 31, 2001, at a Dallas hospital.
>
> Funeral: 2 p.m. Wednesday at North Richland Hills Baptist Church, 4001 Vance Road, North Richland Hills.
>
> Visitation: There will be an open visitation 8 a.m. to 8 p.m. Tuesday at the funeral home; the family will receive friends 2:30 to 4 and 6:30 to 8 p.m.
>
> Memorials: Should you desire, memorials may be made to the National Kidney Foundation or the Southwest Organ Donor Program, but if you would truly like to honor Troy, please be an organ and tissue donor.
>
> Troy Wayne Dunn was born April 22, 1955, in Fort Worth. Troy was many things to many people: husband, son, brother, brother-in-law, uncle, nephew, cousin, friend, buddy and inspiration. His love of life and all that life has to offer made him a man for all seasons. Through his many health struggles, he was human and experienced all the highs and lows but handled them with a unique outlook and grace. After many years in his beloved marine industry, Troy was disabled and was able for a short time to pursue his love of all things outside-fishing, boating, gardening and tinkering. Troy was very fortunate to receive the most wonderful gift of life of a new kidney and pancreas transplant after diabetes destroyed his own organs. His new lease on life was great to see and very inspiring. Troy was preceded in death by his mother, Opal Jolly. Survivors: Wife, Marsha Dunn of North Richland Hills; daughter, Springer Hood of Denton; father, Ollie Dunn of Hurst; sisters, Dolores Rudick of Coronado, Calif., Pam Schnepp of Coppell, Rae Simmons of Wichita Falls, Anne Wier of McKinney and Jean Kraft of Colleyville; and a host of loving family and friends.

Susan Henderson

131.   **Susan Luanne Henderson** was born on Friday, June 21, 1957, in East St. Louis, Illinois. She is the daughter of Randal Richard Henderson and Shirley Jean Chamberlain (103).

Marriages with Jeffery Wayne McDill and Dennis Dean Saling (Page 223) are known.

Family of Susan Henderson and Jeffery McDill

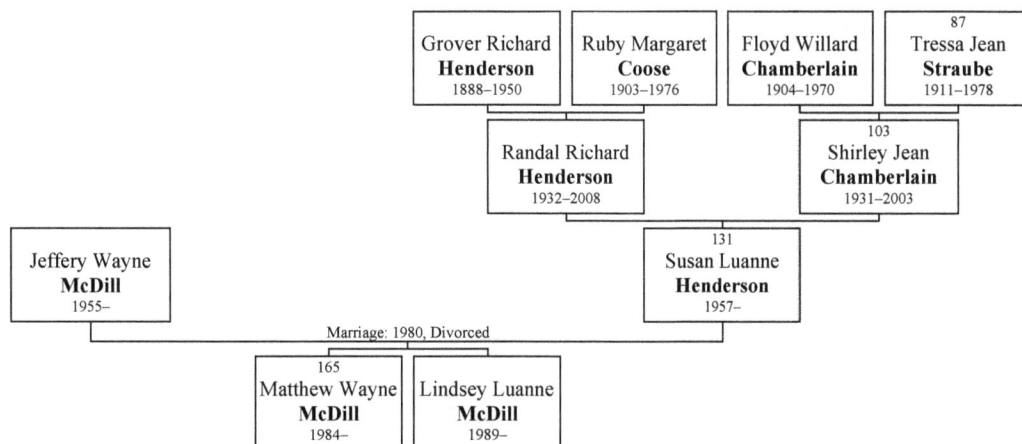

```
┌──────────────┐ ┌──────────────┐ ┌──────────────┐ ┌──────87──────┐
│Grover Richard│ │Ruby Margaret │ │Floyd Willard │ │ Tressa Jean  │
│  Henderson   │ │    Coose     │ │ Chamberlain  │ │   Straube    │
│  1888–1950   │ │  1903–1976   │ │  1904–1970   │ │  1911–1978   │
└──────────────┘ └──────────────┘ └──────────────┘ └──────────────┘
         ┌──────────────┐          ┌──────103──────┐
         │Randal Richard│          │ Shirley Jean  │
         │  Henderson   │          │  Chamberlain  │
         │  1932–2008   │          │  1931–2003    │
         └──────────────┘          └───────────────┘
                      ┌──────131──────┐
                      │ Susan Luanne  │
                      │  Henderson    │
┌──────────────┐      │    1957–      │
│Jeffery Wayne │      └───────────────┘
│   McDill     │
│   1955–      │
└──────────────┘
      Marriage: 1980, Divorced
         ┌──────165──────┐┌──────────────┐
         │Matthew Wayne  ││Lindsey Luanne│
         │   McDill      ││   McDill     │
         │   1984–       ││   1989–      │
         └───────────────┘└──────────────┘
```

Here are the details about **Susan Luanne Henderson's** first marriage, with Jeffery Wayne McDill. You can read more about Susan Luanne on page 222.

At the age of 22, Susan Luanne Henderson married **Jeffery Wayne McDill** on Saturday, March 15, 1980, in Dallas, Dallas County, Texas, when he was 24 years old. They were divorced in Texas, USA. They have two children.

Jeffery Wayne was born in Columbus, Franklin County, Ohio, on Wednesday, October 12, 1955.

Children of Susan Luanne Henderson and Jeffery Wayne McDill:

+ 165 m I. **Matthew Wayne McDill** was born in Plano, Collin County, Texas, on September 21, 1984.

       f II. **Lindsey Luanne McDill** was born in Plano, Collin County, Texas, on June 13, 1989.

Family of Susan Henderson and Dennis Saling

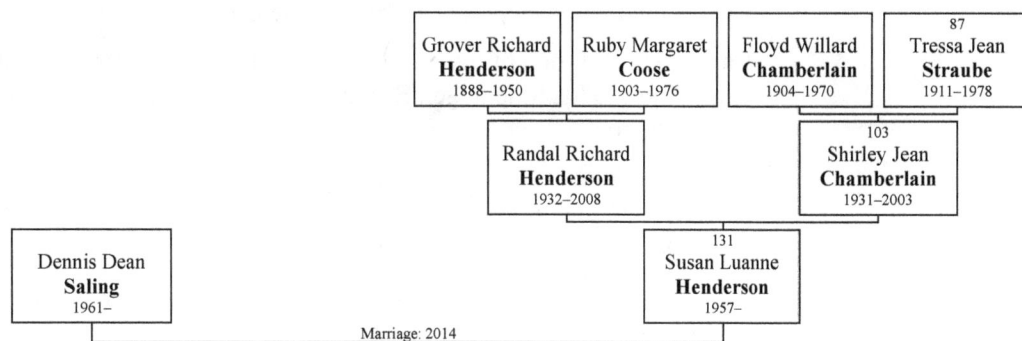

```
┌──────────────┐ ┌──────────────┐ ┌──────────────┐ ┌──────87──────┐
│Grover Richard│ │Ruby Margaret │ │Floyd Willard │ │ Tressa Jean  │
│  Henderson   │ │    Coose     │ │ Chamberlain  │ │   Straube    │
│  1888–1950   │ │  1903–1976   │ │  1904–1970   │ │  1911–1978   │
└──────────────┘ └──────────────┘ └──────────────┘ └──────────────┘
         ┌──────────────┐          ┌──────103──────┐
         │Randal Richard│          │ Shirley Jean  │
         │  Henderson   │          │  Chamberlain  │
         │  1932–2008   │          │  1931–2003    │
         └──────────────┘          └───────────────┘
                      ┌──────131──────┐
                      │ Susan Luanne  │
┌──────────────┐      │  Henderson    │
│ Dennis Dean  │      │    1957–      │
│   Saling     │      └───────────────┘
│   1961–      │
└──────────────┘
          Marriage: 2014
```

Here are the details about **Susan Luanne Henderson's** second marriage, with Dennis Dean Saling. You can read more about Susan Luanne on page 222.

Susan Luanne Henderson married **Dennis Dean Saling** on Saturday, September 13, 2014, in Port Aransas, Texas. Dennis Dean was born in June 1961.

Family of Calvin Mummert and Tamara Watson

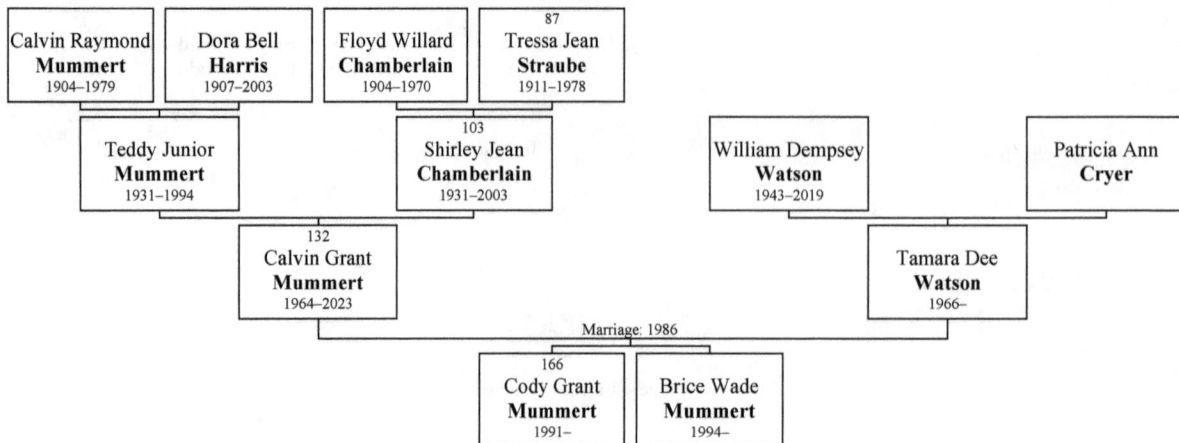

```
Calvin Raymond        Dora Bell        Floyd Willard      87
  Mummert             Harris          Chamberlain     Tressa Jean
  1904–1979          1907–2003         1904–1970         Straube
                                                         1911–1978

         Teddy Junior                    103
           Mummert                  Shirley Jean
          1931–1994                 Chamberlain       William Dempsey        Patricia Ann
                                     1931–2003            Watson                Cryer
                 132                                      1943–2019
           Calvin Grant
            Mummert                                           Tamara Dee
            1964–2023                                           Watson
                                Marriage: 1986                  1966–

                      166
                 Cody Grant        Brice Wade
                  Mummert          Mummert
                   1991–            1994–
```

132. **Calvin Grant Mummert** was born on Friday, September 18, 1964, in Dallas, Dallas County, Texas. He was the son of Teddy Junior Mummert and Shirley Jean Chamberlain (103).

Calvin Grant died at Baylor Hospital Center in Dallas, Dallas County, Texas, on December 22, 2023, at the age of 59. He was buried in Myrtle Cemetery, Ennis, Ellis County, Texas (Find a Grave ID 262460835).

Twin brother to Floyd James Mummert

Obituary

Calvin Grant Mummert, 59, was surrounded by loved ones as he journeyed home to experience the fullness of Christmas in Heaven, December 22, 2023 in Dallas, Texas.

Calvin was born in Dallas, Texas on September 18, 1964, to Ted and Shirley (Chamberlain) Mummert. He grew up in Oak Cliff and moved to Ennis in 1976. He graduated from St. John's Catholic School in 1983. In 1985, he married the love of his life, Tammy Watson. He worked for DCI as a driver and was a member of The Avenue Church.

Calvin was so proud of his boys, Cody and Brice and grandson Kace. He was "Pops" to his little angel, Brandie Erynn and cherished doing what she wanted to do.

In all the things Calvin enjoyed, being outside, hunting, working on projects, building things, spending time with family, he never met a stranger and was always so generous with his time, wit and wisdom.

He will be greatly missed but we know his legacy will be carried on by his wife of 37 years, Tammy Watson Mummert, Sons: Cody Grant Mummert, and wife Danielle Ashford, Brice Wade Mummert and girlfriend Bailey Armstrong, Granddaughter, Brandie Erynn Mummert and Grandson, Kace Lane McDaniel. He is also survived by his brother, Floyd Mummert and wife Stephanie and Phil Mummert and wife Debbie, sisters, Paula Doyle and husband John, Marsha Dunn, Susie Saling and husband Dennis, Pam King and husband Jerry, and Mary Podraza, Mother-in-Law, Trixi McManus, and numerous niece and nephews.

He goes home to join his parents, Ted and Shirley Mummert, two brothers, Bruce Mummert and Michael Ted Mummert, Sister, Sharlene Mummert, Brother-in-Law, Troy Dunn, Good Friend, Wes Hammond, several grandparents, aunts and uncles.

Calvin's generosity extends past his life by giving the beautiful gift of life to many others this Christmas, as he was a registered organ donor.

Visitation will be held at J. E. Keever Mortuary in Ennis, TX on Friday, December 29th, from 6:00 p.m. to 8:00 p.m.

A celebration of life will be held on Saturday, December 30th at 10:00 a.m. at J. E. Keever Mortuary, with interment following at Myrtle Cemetery, Ennis, TX.

In lieu of flowers, the family suggests making a donation to the American Heart Association, www.heart.org or to the Texas Parks and Wildlife, https://tpwd.texas.gov/business/donations to celebrate Calvin's life and legacy.

Pallbearers are sons, Cody Mummert, Brice Mummert, brother, Floyd Mummert, grandson, Kace McDaniel, nephews: Chris Mummert and Clayton Mummert and good friend, Lance Ueberroth.

"I will lie down and sleep in peace for you alone, O Lord make me dwell in safety." Psalm 4:8

At the age of 22, Calvin Grant married **Tamara Dee Watson** on Saturday, October 25, 1986, in Ellis County, Texas, when she was 19 years old. They had two sons.

Tamara Dee was born in Navarro, Navarro County, Texas, on Thursday, December 01, 1966. She is the daughter of William Dempsey Watson and Patricia Ann Cryer.

Sons of Calvin Grant Mummert and Tamara Dee Watson:

+   166   m   I. **Cody Grant Mummert** was born in Corsicana, Navarro County, Texas, on January 21, 1991.

          m   II. **Brice Wade Mummert** was born in Corsicana, Navarro County, Texas, on July 07, 1994.

Family of Floyd Mummert and Stephanie Rickert

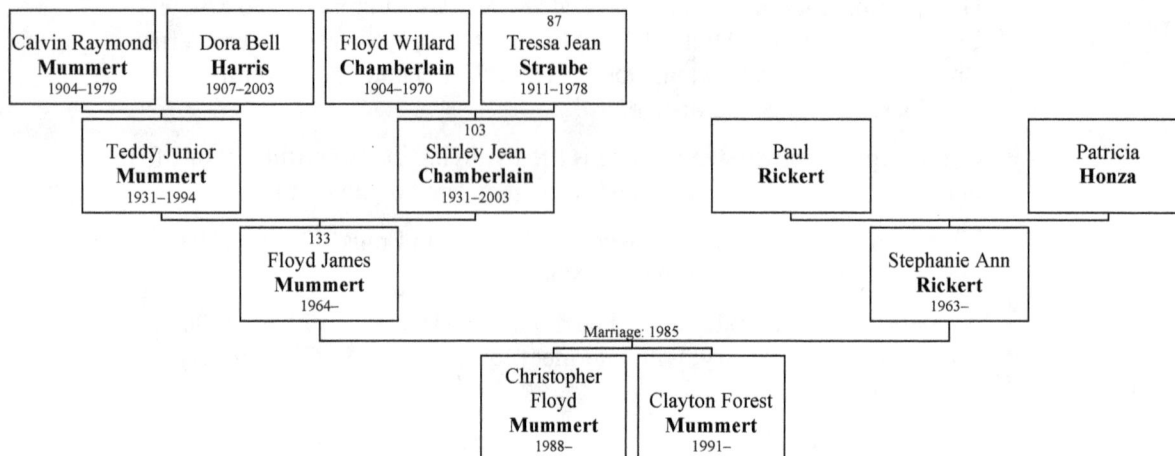

133.   **Floyd James Mummert** was born on Friday, September 18, 1964, in Dallas, Dallas County, Texas. He is the son of Teddy Junior Mummert and Shirley Jean Chamberlain (103).

Twin brother to Calvin Grant Mummert.

At the age of 20, Floyd James married **Stephanie Ann Rickert** on Friday, August 09, 1985, in Ennis, Ellis County, Texas, when she was 21 years old. They have two sons.

Stephanie Ann was born in Corsicana, Navarro County, Texas, on Monday, October 14, 1963. Married in St. John's Catholic Church She is the daughter of Paul Rickert and Patricia Honza.

Sons of Floyd James Mummert and Stephanie Ann Rickert:

m   I. **Christopher Floyd Mummert** was born in Ennis, Ellis County, Texas, on April 27, 1988.

> Eagle Scout Honor: Chris Mummert of St. John Boy Scout Troop 203 in Ennis, Texas recently earned the rank of Eagle Scout. He will receive the actual award in a special Eagle Scout Court of Honor Ceremony held Sunday May 16, 2004 at the Knights of Columbus Hall. Chris has been active in Scouting for over a decade and has earned every rank possible in the organization. He started in first grade as a Tiger Cub and progressed through the Cub Scout program earning Wolf, Bear, Webelos, and the Arrow of Light ranks. Transferring into the Boy Scout Program he went on to earn Scout, Tenderfoot, Second Class, First Class, Star, Life and finally Eagle Scout rank. He was also elected by his peers into the Order of the Arrow which is a honor camping organization dedicated to service.
>
> As part of his Eagle rank requirements, Chris completed a project which helped to provide St. John's Life Teen Group, Edge Program, Spanish Ministries along with the entire Parish and students of St. John School and Catholic Church a recreational volleyball court. The court will provide the members of these groups a safe and fun activity area that can be used daily. Chris has earned over 21 merit badges including Photography, Soil & Water Conservation, Railroad, Woodcarving, BSA Lifeguard Certification and many other diverse areas. He has served the troop as a Patrol leader,

Assistant Senior Patrol Leader and Senior Patrol Leader. He currently serves as Troop Guide.

Chris is a sophomore at Ennis High School. He is also a member of Life Press, Life Teen, His Hands, Interact, Pan American Student Forum, The Passion of Jesus Christ Play, Life Teen Skit team, Altar Server, Lector, Reader, Usher and Ennis Lions Football. He has also received the award of Outstanding work in Integrated Physics and Chemistry his freshman year and the Sera Altar Serving Award.

He is the son of Floyd and Stephanie Mummert and the brother of Clayton Mummert of Ennis. He is also the grandson of Patsy Rickert and the late Paul Rickert as well as the late Ted and Shirley Mummert.

More facts and events for Christopher Floyd Mummert:

Individual Note: February 2004   Received Eagle Scout honor

m   II. **Clayton Forest Mummert** was born in Waxahachie, Ellis County, Texas, on July 06, 1991.

Sharlene Mummert

134.   **Sharlene Denise Mummert** was born on Wednesday, September 28, 1966, in Dallas, Dallas County, Texas. She was the daughter of Teddy Junior Mummert and Shirley Jean Chamberlain (103).

Sharlene Denise died in Dallas, Dallas County, Texas, on February 24, 2012, at the age of 45. She was cremated- on March 03, 2012 (Find a Grave ID 100197165).

Sharlene died of a stroke, heart condition, high blood pressure. [1] Common law married to Norman Manuere [2] Met Willie Hernandez [3] On Dec 15, 2001 in Garland, TX married Mike Imuzeze. Child of Sharlene and [1] Norman Manuere: Norman Ted "Junior"; b. 11-18-1991, Fort Worth, TX. Child of Sharlene and [2] Willie Hernandez: Savannah Denise Hernandez; b. 5-11-1999, Euless, TX

Marriages with Norman Ikemo Manuere and Michael Imuzeze (Page 228) are known.

Family of Sharlene Mummert and Norman Manuere

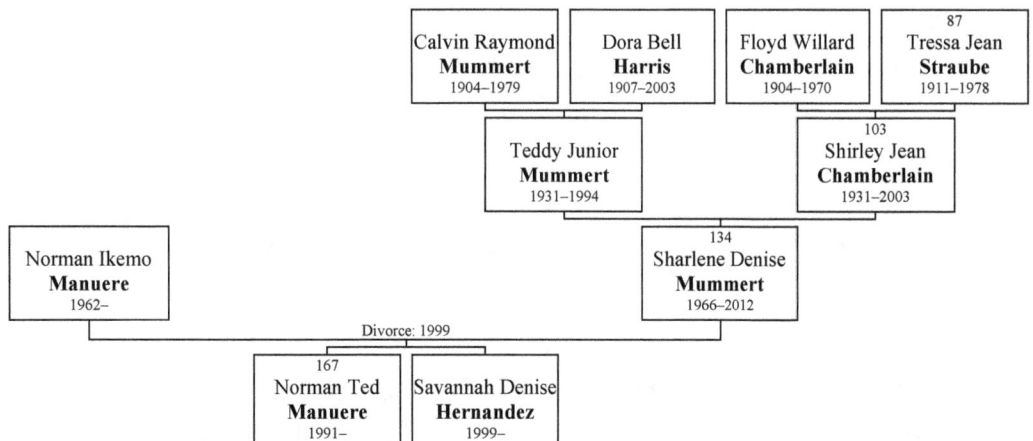

Here are the details about **Sharlene Denise Mummert's** first marriage, with Norman Ikemo Manuere. You can read more about Sharlene Denise on page 227.

Sharlene Denise Mummert married **Norman Ikemo Manuere**. Common law. They were divorced in Tarrant County, Texas, on April 05, 1999. They had two children.

Norman Ikemo was born in November 1962.

Children of Sharlene Denise Mummert and Norman Ikemo Manuere:

+ 167   m   I. **Norman Ted Manuere** was born in Fort Worth, Tarrant County, Texas, on November 18, 1991.

          f   II. **Savannah Denise Hernandez** was born in Euless, Tarrant County, Texas, on May 11, 1999.

Family of Sharlene Mummert and Michael Imuzeze

Here are the details about **Sharlene Denise Mummert's** second marriage, with Michael Imuzeze. You can read more about Sharlene Denise on page 227.

Sharlene Denise Mummert married **Michael Imuzeze** on Saturday, December 15, 2001, in Dallas, Dallas County, Texas. Michael was born in January 1970.

Family of Stephen Korte and Angela Ray

135. **Stephen Wayne Korte** was born on Wednesday, May 10, 1972, in Louisiana, Pike County, Missouri. He is the son of Wayne William Korte and Pamela Lou Chamberlain (104).

Stephen Wayne worked as an elected Sheriff of Pike County Missouri on January 01, 2009.

At the age of 23, Stephen Wayne married **Angela Ray** on Saturday, October 21, 1995, in St. Clement, Pike County, Missouri, when she was 21 years old. They have five children.

Angela was born in Cincinnati, Hamilton County, Ohio, on Monday, June 24, 1974. She is the daughter of Loran Paul Ray and Cynthia Jo Rosey. She is also known as **Angi**.

Children of Stephen Wayne Korte and Angela Ray:

f I. **Samantha Jean Korte** was born in Troy, Lincoln County, Missouri, on August 08, 1994.

f II. **Devin Elizabeth Korte** was born in Louisiana, Pike County, Missouri, on November 21, 1997.

m III. **Luke Michael Korte** was born in Lake St. Louis, Saint Charles County, Missouri, on July 10, 2006.

f IV. **Lorna Rae Korte** was born in Lake St. Louis, Saint Charles County, Missouri, on January 08, 2009.

f V. **Stevie Ann Korte** was born in Lake St. Louis, Saint Charles County, Missouri, on November 14, 2009.

Family of Carolyn Korte and Michael Mullins

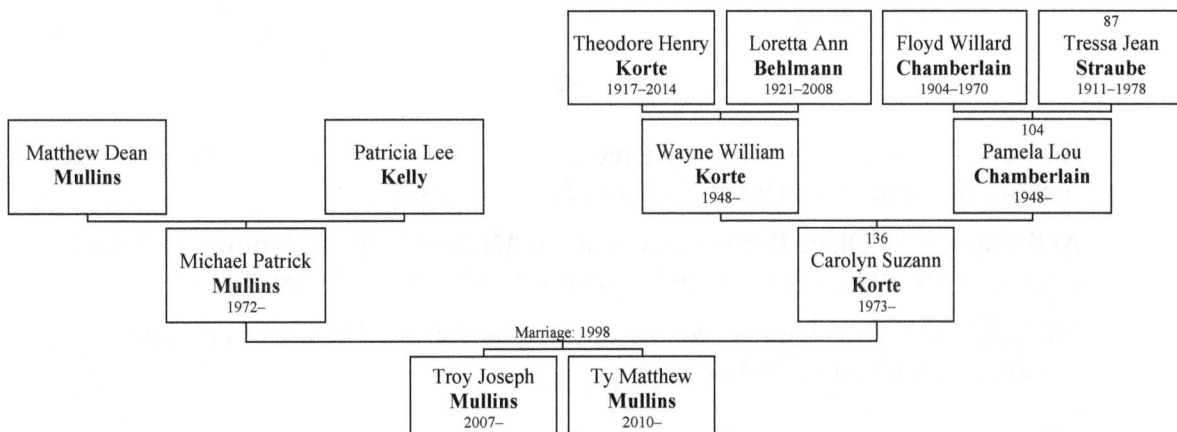

136. **Carolyn Suzann Korte** was born on Sunday, November 25, 1973, in Louisiana, Pike County, Missouri. She is the daughter of Wayne William Korte and Pamela Lou Chamberlain (104).

At the age of 24, Carolyn Suzann married **Michael Patrick Mullins** on Saturday, September 12, 1998, in St. Clement, Pike County, Missouri, when he was 25 years old. They have two sons.

Michael Patrick was born in Warrensburg, Johnson County, Missouri, on Tuesday, October 10, 1972. He is the son of Matthew Dean Mullins and Patricia Lee Kelly.

Sons of Carolyn Suzann Korte and Michael Patrick Mullins:

> m   I. **Troy Joseph Mullins** was born in Jefferson City, Cole County, Missouri, on July 22, 2007.

> m   II. **Ty Matthew Mullins** was born in Jefferson City, Cole County, Missouri, on September 08, 2010.

Diane Korte

137.   **Diane Renee Korte** was born on Thursday, December 11, 1975, in Louisiana, Pike County, Missouri. She is the daughter of Wayne William Korte and Pamela Lou Chamberlain (104).

Marriages with Michael Eugene Jenkins, Jason Kieth Burns (Page 231) and Jon Michael Silvis (Page 231) are known.

Family of Diane Korte and Michael Jenkins

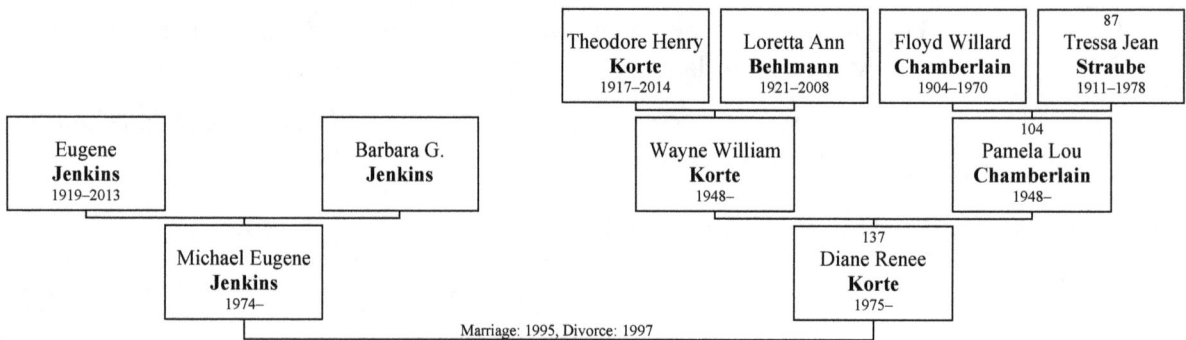

Here are the details about **Diane Renee Korte's** first marriage, with Michael Eugene Jenkins. You can read more about Diane Renee on page 230.

At the age of 20, Diane Renee Korte married **Michael Eugene Jenkins** on Saturday, December 30, 1995, when he was 21 years old. They were divorced in 1997.

Michael Eugene was born on Wednesday, September 25, 1974. He is the son of Eugene Jenkins and Barbara G. Jenkins.

Family of Diane Korte and Jason Burns

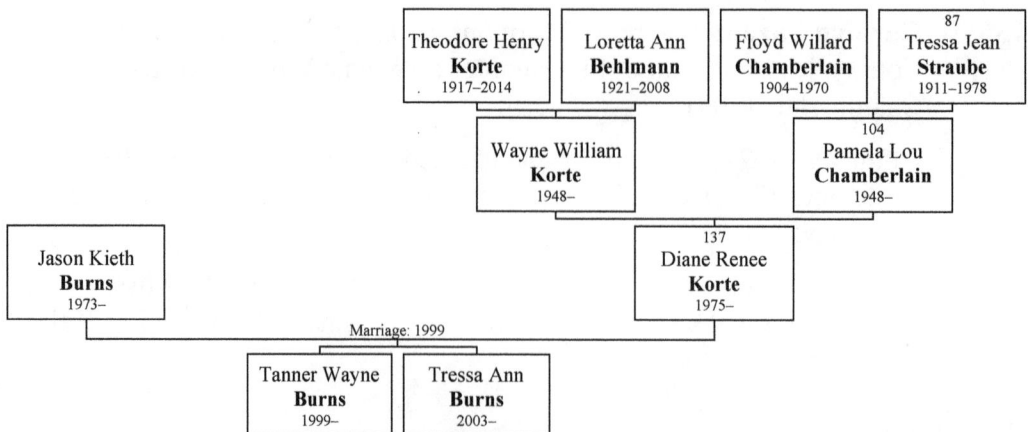

Here are the details about **Diane Renee Korte's** second marriage, with Jason Kieth Burns. You can read more about Diane Renee on page 230.

At the age of 23, Diane Renee Korte married **Jason Kieth Burns** on Wednesday, February 24, 1999, in Sarasota County, Florida, when he was 25 years old. They have two children.

Jason Kieth was born on Tuesday, July 31, 1973.

Children of Diane Renee Korte and Jason Kieth Burns:

> m   I. **Tanner Wayne Burns** was born in Sarasota, Sarasota County, Florida, on January 17, 1999.

> f   II. **Tressa Ann Burns** was born in Kinston, Lenoir County, North Carolina, on December 06, 2003.

Family of Diane Korte and Jon Silvis

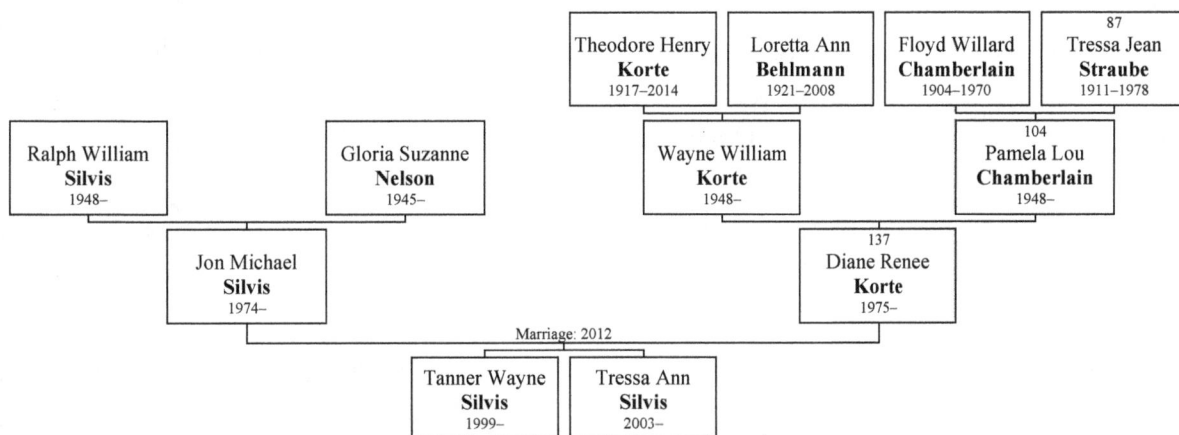

Here are the details about **Diane Renee Korte's** third marriage, with Jon Michael Silvis. You can read more about Diane Renee on page 230.

At the age of 36, Diane Renee Korte married **Jon Michael Silvis** on Monday, February 13, 2012, in Las Vegas, Clark County, Nevada, when he was 37 years old. They have two children.

Jon Michael was born in Erie, Erie County, Pennsylvania, on Wednesday, July 03, 1974. He is the son of Ralph William Silvis and Gloria Suzanne Nelson.

Children of Diane Renee Korte and Jon Michael Silvis:

> m   I. **Tanner Wayne Silvis** was born in Sarasota, Sarasota County, Florida, on January 17, 1999.

> f   II. **Tressa Ann Silvis** was born in Kinston, Lenoir County, North Carolina, on December 06, 2003.

Family of Lisa Korte and Ryan Wieberg

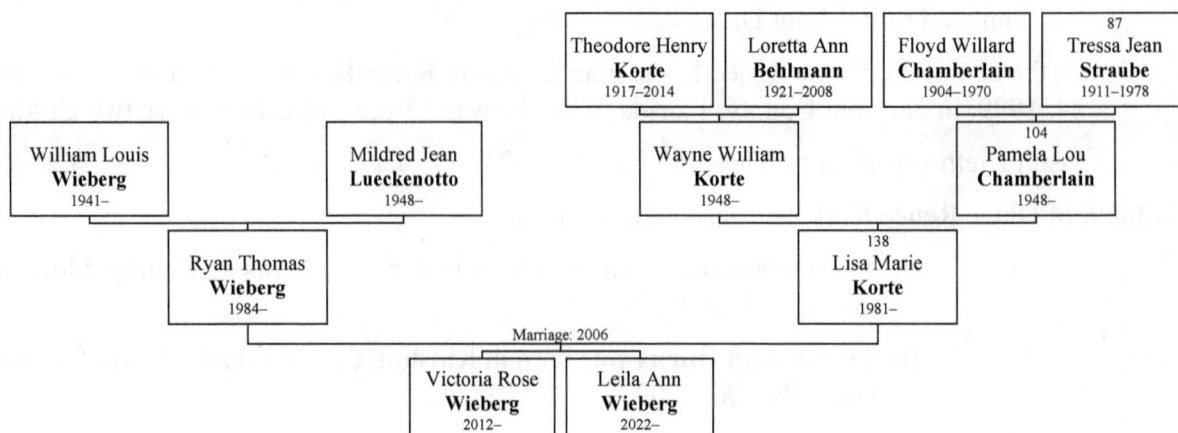

138. **Lisa Marie Korte** was born on Thursday, April 09, 1981, in Louisiana, Pike County, Missouri. She is the daughter of Wayne William Korte and Pamela Lou Chamberlain (104).

At the age of 25, Lisa Marie married **Ryan Thomas Wieberg** on Saturday, November 11, 2006, in St. Thomas, Cole County, Missouri, when he was 22 years old. They have two daughters.

Ryan Thomas was born in Jefferson City, Cole County, Missouri, on Wednesday, January 04, 1984. He is the son of William Louis Wieberg and Mildred Jean Lueckenotto.

Daughters of Lisa Marie Korte and Ryan Thomas Wieberg:

> f   I. **Victoria Rose Wieberg** was born in Jefferson City, Cole County, Missouri, on May 04, 2012.

> f   II. **Leila Ann Wieberg** was born on April 02, 2022.

Robert Cunningham

139. **Robert Eugene Cunningham** was born on Tuesday, May 24, 1966, in Hannibal, Marion County, Missouri. He is the son of Tom Reynolds Cunningham and Tanya D'Arline Straube (105). He is also known as **Bobby**.

Marriages with Amy Ann Jones and Linda Owen (Page 234) are known.

Family of Robert Cunningham and Amy Jones

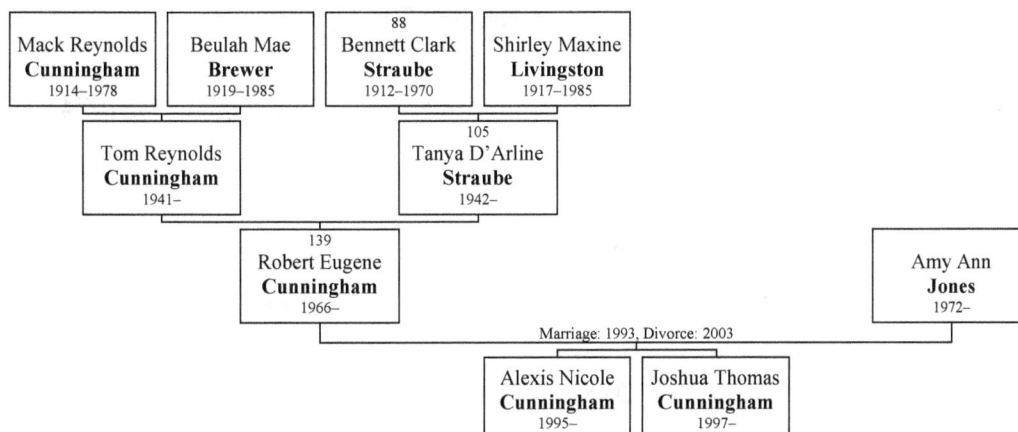

Mack Reynolds **Cunningham** 1914–1978	Beulah Mae **Brewer** 1919–1985	88 Bennett Clark **Straube** 1912–1970	Shirley Maxine **Livingston** 1917–1985

Tom Reynolds **Cunningham** 1941–

105 Tanya D'Arline **Straube** 1942–

139 Robert Eugene **Cunningham** 1966–

Amy Ann **Jones** 1972–

Marriage: 1993, Divorce: 2003

Alexis Nicole **Cunningham** 1995–	Joshua Thomas **Cunningham** 1997–

Here are the details about **Robert Eugene Cunningham's** first marriage, with Amy Ann Jones. You can read more about Robert Eugene on page 232.

At the age of 27, Robert Eugene Cunningham married **Amy Ann Jones** on Saturday, November 06, 1993, in Mexico, Audrain County, Missouri, when she was 20 years old. They were divorced in Mexico, Audrain County, Missouri, on September 29, 2003. They have two children.

Amy Ann was born on Tuesday, November 28, 1972.

Children of Robert Eugene Cunningham and Amy Ann Jones:

f   I. **Alexis Nicole Cunningham** was born in Mexico, Audrain County, Missouri, on July 29, 1995.

m   II. **Joshua Thomas Cunningham** was born in Mexico, Audrain County, Missouri, on April 07, 1997.

Family of Robert Cunningham and Linda Owen

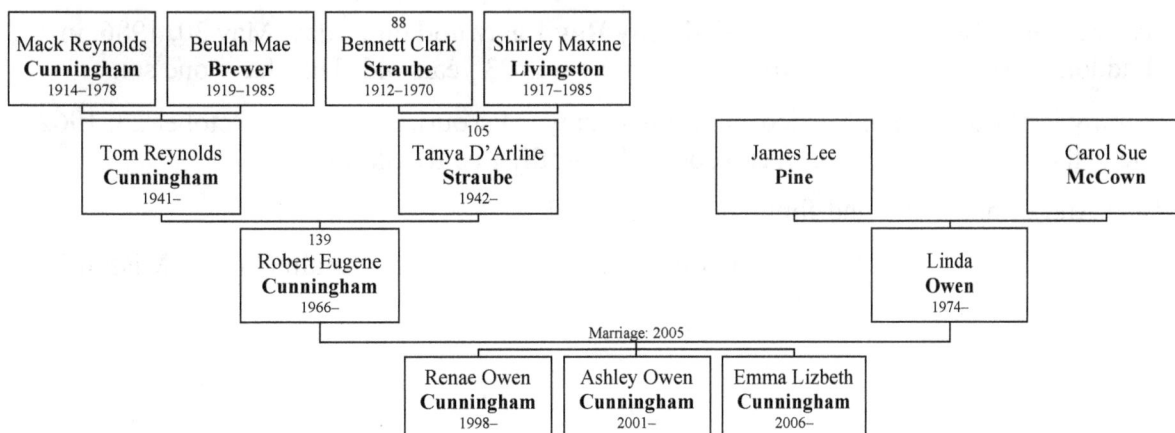

Mack Reynolds **Cunningham** 1914–1978	Beulah Mae **Brewer** 1919–1985	88 Bennett Clark **Straube** 1912–1970	Shirley Maxine **Livingston** 1917–1985

Tom Reynolds **Cunningham** 1941–

105 Tanya D'Arline **Straube** 1942–

James Lee **Pine**

Carol Sue **McCown**

139 Robert Eugene **Cunningham** 1966–

Linda **Owen** 1974–

Marriage: 2005

Renae Owen **Cunningham** 1998–	Ashley Owen **Cunningham** 2001–	Emma Lizbeth **Cunningham** 2006–

Here are the details about **Robert Eugene Cunningham's** second marriage, with Linda Owen. You can read more about Robert Eugene on page 232.

At the age of 39, Robert Eugene Cunningham married **Linda Owen** on Saturday, May 28, 2005, in Mexico, Audrain County, Missouri, when she was 30 years old. They have three daughters.

Linda was born in Mexico, Audrain County, Missouri, on Saturday, November 23, 1974. She is the daughter of James Lee Pine and Carol Sue McCown.

Daughters of Robert Eugene Cunningham and Linda Owen:

> f   I. **Renae Owen Cunningham** was born on December 10, 1998.

> f   II. **Ashley Owen Cunningham** was born on June 13, 2001.

> f   III. **Emma Lizbeth Cunningham** was born in Columbia, Boone County, Missouri, on January 03, 2006.

Family of Terri Cunningham and Jimmy Eastwood

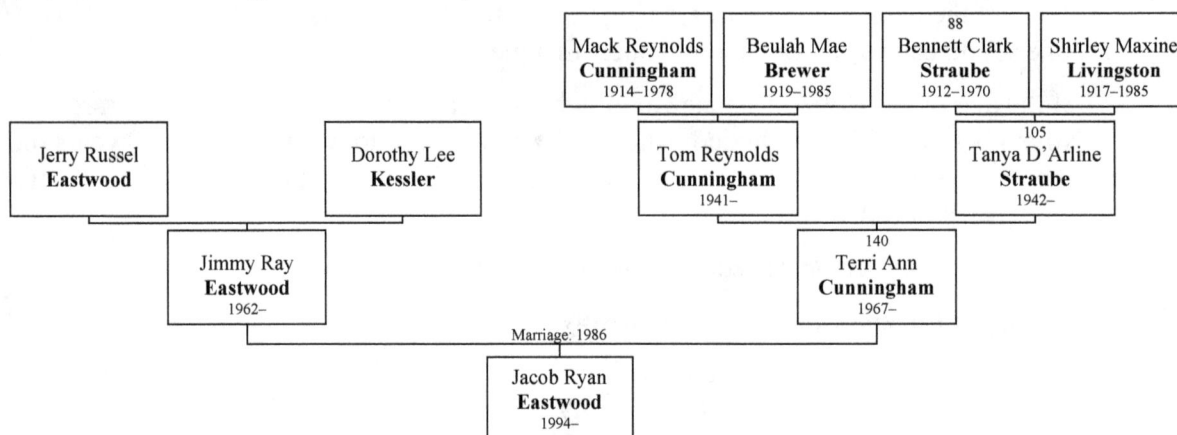

140.   **Terri Ann Cunningham** was born on Wednesday, September 06, 1967, in Hannibal, Marion County, Missouri. She is the daughter of Tom Reynolds Cunningham and Tanya D'Arline Straube (105).

At the age of 18, Terri Ann married **Jimmy Ray Eastwood** on Friday, May 30, 1986, in Laddonia, Audrain County, Missouri, when he was 23 years old. They have one son.

Jimmy Ray was born in Mexico, Audrain County, Missouri, on Sunday, October 28, 1962. He is the son of Jerry Russel Eastwood and Dorothy Lee Kessler.

Son of Terri Ann Cunningham and Jimmy Ray Eastwood:

> m   I. **Jacob Ryan Eastwood** was born in Mexico, Audrain County, Missouri, on August 04, 1994.

Family of Crystal Straube and John Stump

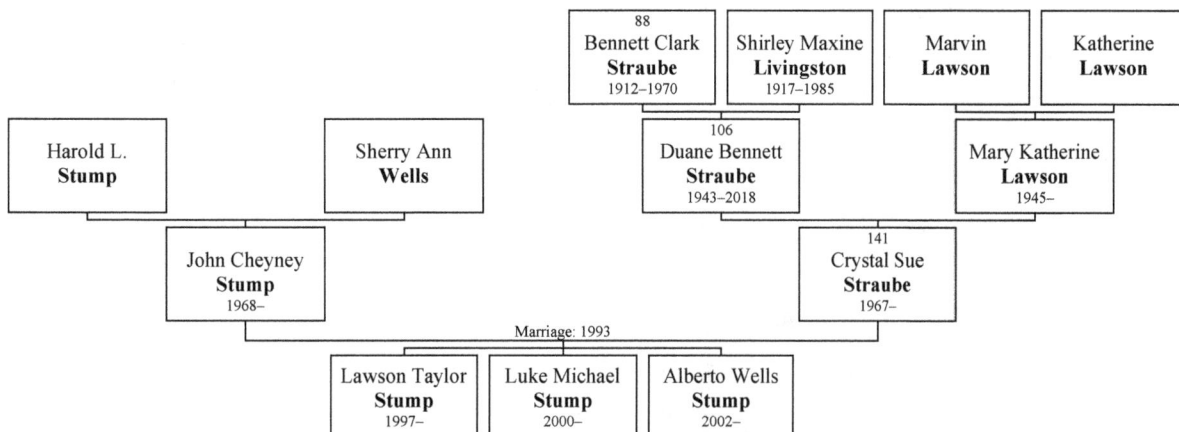

Harold L. **Stump** — Sherry Ann **Wells**

88
Bennett Clark **Straube** 1912–1970 — Shirley Maxine **Livingston** 1917–1985

Marvin **Lawson** — Katherine **Lawson**

106
Duane Bennett **Straube** 1943–2018

Mary Katherine **Lawson** 1945–

John Cheyney **Stump** 1968–

141
Crystal Sue **Straube** 1967–

Marriage: 1993

Lawson Taylor **Stump** 1997–

Luke Michael **Stump** 2000–

Alberto Wells **Stump** 2002–

141. **Crystal Sue Straube** was born on Sunday, April 16, 1967, in Saint Louis, Saint Louis County, Missouri. She is the daughter of Duane Bennett Straube (106) and Mary Katherine Lawson.

At the age of 26, Crystal Sue married **John Cheyney Stump** on Saturday, August 07, 1993, in Charleston, West Virginia, when he was 25 years old. They have three sons.

John Cheyney was born in Charleston, Kanawha County, West Virginia, on Wednesday, July 31, 1968. He is the son of Harold L. Stump and Sherry Ann Wells.

Sons of Crystal Sue Straube and John Cheyney Stump:

m   I. **Lawson Taylor Stump** was born in Charleston, Kanawha County, West Virginia, on August 29, 1997.

m   II. **Luke Michael Stump** was born in Guatemala on August 31, 2000. He was adopted in Guatemala.

m   III. **Alberto Wells Stump** was born in Guatemala on June 16, 2002. He was adopted in Guatemala.

Family of Elizabeth Straube and Alfonso Gallegos

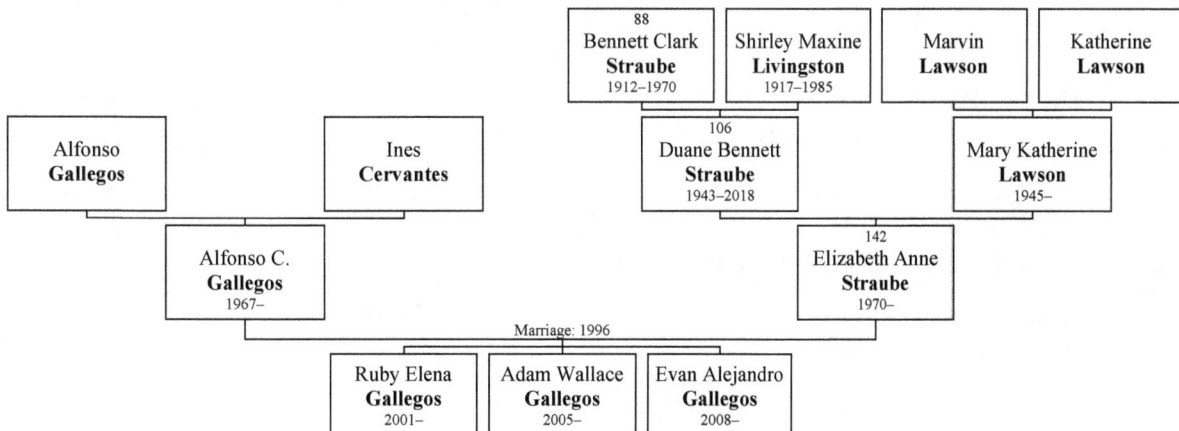

Alfonso **Gallegos** — Ines **Cervantes**

88
Bennett Clark **Straube** 1912–1970 — Shirley Maxine **Livingston** 1917–1985

Marvin **Lawson** — Katherine **Lawson**

106
Duane Bennett **Straube** 1943–2018

Mary Katherine **Lawson** 1945–

Alfonso C. **Gallegos** 1967–

142
Elizabeth Anne **Straube** 1970–

Marriage: 1996

Ruby Elena **Gallegos** 2001–

Adam Wallace **Gallegos** 2005–

Evan Alejandro **Gallegos** 2008–

142. **Elizabeth Anne Straube** was born on Friday, September 25, 1970, in Saint Louis, Saint Louis County, Missouri. She is the daughter of Duane Bennett Straube (106) and Mary Katherine Lawson.

At the age of 25, Elizabeth Anne married **Alfonso C. Gallegos** on Saturday, August 24, 1996, in Forest Park, Saint Louis County, Missouri, when he was 28 years old. They have three children.

Alfonso C. was born in Chicago, Cook County, Illinois, on Friday, September 15, 1967. He is the son of Alfonso Gallegos and Ines Cervantes. He is also known as **Al**.

Children of Elizabeth Anne Straube and Alfonso C. Gallegos:

f   I. **Ruby Elena Gallegos** was born at St. John's Mercy Medical Center, St. Louis, Missouri in City of Creve Coeur, Saint Louis County, Missouri, on October 09, 2001.

m   II. **Adam Wallace Gallegos** was born in City of Town & Country, Saint Louis County, Missouri, on November 22, 2005.

m   III. **Evan Alejandro Gallegos** was born in City of Town & Country, Saint Louis County, Missouri, on December 08, 2008.

Family of Dawn Deters and Bradly Niemeyer

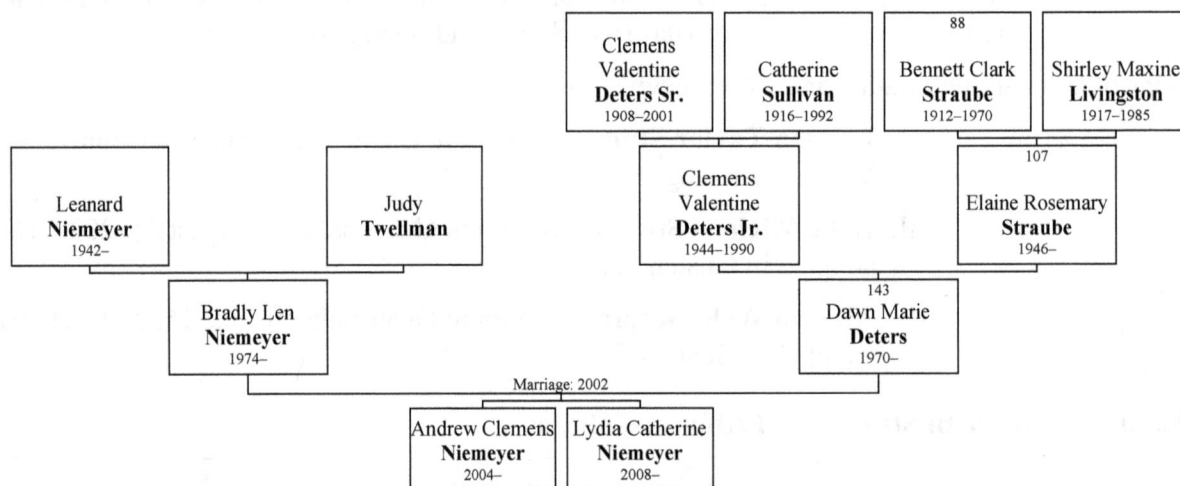

143. **Dawn Marie Deters** was born on Sunday, November 29, 1970. She is the daughter of Clemens Valentine Deters Jr. and Elaine Rosemary Straube (107).

At the age of 31, Dawn Marie married **Bradly Len Niemeyer** on Tuesday, September 17, 2002, in Saint Clement Catholic Church, Saint Clement, Pike County, Missouri, when he was 28 years old. They have two children.

Bradly Len was born in Louisiana, Pike County, Missouri, on Thursday, August 29, 1974. He is the son of Leanard Niemeyer and Judy Twellman.

Children of Dawn Marie Deters and Bradly Len Niemeyer:

m   I. **Andrew Clemens Niemeyer** was born in Hannibal, Marion County, Missouri, on June 29, 2004.

f   II. **Lydia Catherine Niemeyer** was born at St. Lukes Hospital in Chesterfield, Saint Louis County Missouri, on September 29, 2008.

Family of David Deters and Amy Holtsman

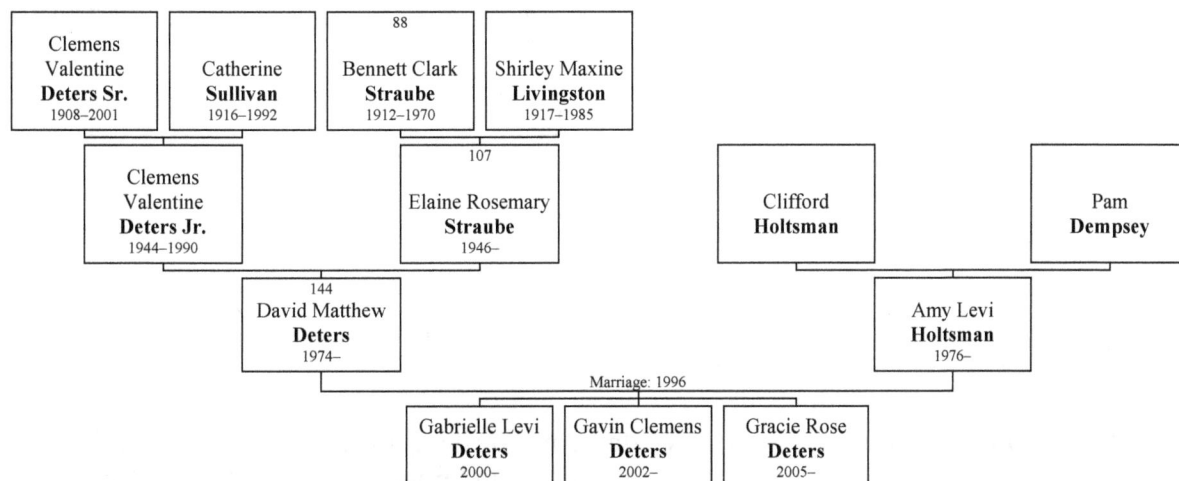

```
┌─────────────┐  ┌─────────────┐  ┌────88───────┐  ┌─────────────┐
│  Clemens    │  │             │  │             │  │Shirley Maxine│
│  Valentine  │  │  Catherine  │  │Bennett Clark│  │             │
│ Deters Sr.  │  │  Sullivan   │  │  Straube    │  │  Livingston │
│  1908–2001  │  │  1916–1992  │  │  1912–1970  │  │  1917–1985  │
└─────────────┘  └─────────────┘  └─────────────┘  └─────────────┘
      ┌────────────────┐        ┌────107────────┐
      │   Clemens      │        │               │     ┌──────────┐        ┌──────────┐
      │   Valentine    │        │Elaine Rosemary│     │ Clifford │        │   Pam    │
      │  Deters Jr.    │        │    Straube    │     │ Holtsman │        │ Dempsey  │
      │   1944–1990    │        │     1946–     │     └──────────┘        └──────────┘
      └────────────────┘        └───────────────┘
              ┌────144──────┐                              ┌──────────┐
              │David Matthew│                              │ Amy Levi │
              │   Deters    │                              │ Holtsman │
              │   1974–     │                              │  1976–   │
              └─────────────┘       Marriage: 1996         └──────────┘
        ┌──────────────┐  ┌──────────────┐  ┌──────────────┐
        │Gabrielle Levi│  │Gavin Clemens │  │  Gracie Rose │
        │   Deters     │  │   Deters     │  │    Deters    │
        │   2000–      │  │   2002–      │  │    2005–     │
        └──────────────┘  └──────────────┘  └──────────────┘
```

144. **David Matthew Deters** was born on Tuesday, August 13, 1974, in Hannibal, Marion County, Missouri. He is the son of Clemens Valentine Deters Jr. and Elaine Rosemary Straube (107).

At the age of 21, David Matthew married **Amy Levi Holtsman** on Saturday, July 13, 1996, in St. Clement, Pike County, Missouri, when she was 20 years old. They have three children.

Amy Levi was born on Thursday, May 13, 1976. She is the daughter of Clifford Holtsman and Pam Dempsey.

Children of David Matthew Deters and Amy Levi Holtsman:

f   I. **Gabrielle Levi Deters** was born at Barnes Jewish Hospital in Saint Peters, Saint Charles County, Missouri, on August 29, 2000.

m   II. **Gavin Clemens Deters** was born at Barnes Jewish Hospital in Saint Peters, Saint Charles County, Missouri, on January 21, 2002.

f   III. **Gracie Rose Deters** was born at Barnes Jewish Hospital in Saint Peters, Saint Charles County, Missouri, on February 03, 2005.

Family of Anthony Straube and Gloria Koehn

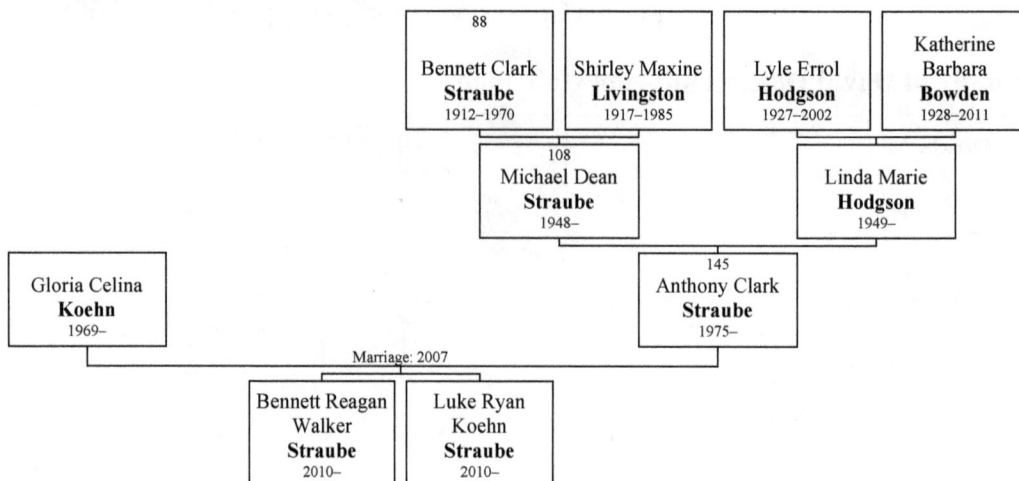

145. **Anthony Clark Straube** was born on Wednesday, April 02, 1975, in Mexico, Audrain County, Missouri. She is the daughter of Michael Dean Straube (108) and Linda Marie Hodgson. She is also known as **Andy**.

At the age of 32, Anthony Clark married **Gloria Celina Koehn** on Sunday, May 27, 2007, in Las Vegas, Clark County, Nevada, when he was 38 years old. They have two sons.

Gloria Celina was born in Key West, Monroe County, Florida, on Thursday, April 03, 1969.

Sons of Anthony Clark Straube and Gloria Celina Koehn:

    m   I. **Bennett Reagan Walker Straube** was born in Key West, Monroe County, Florida, on June 23, 2010.

    m   II. **Luke Ryan Koehn Straube** was born in Key West, Monroe County, Florida, on June 23, 2010.

Family of Jerrid Woodhurst and Stacy Weeks

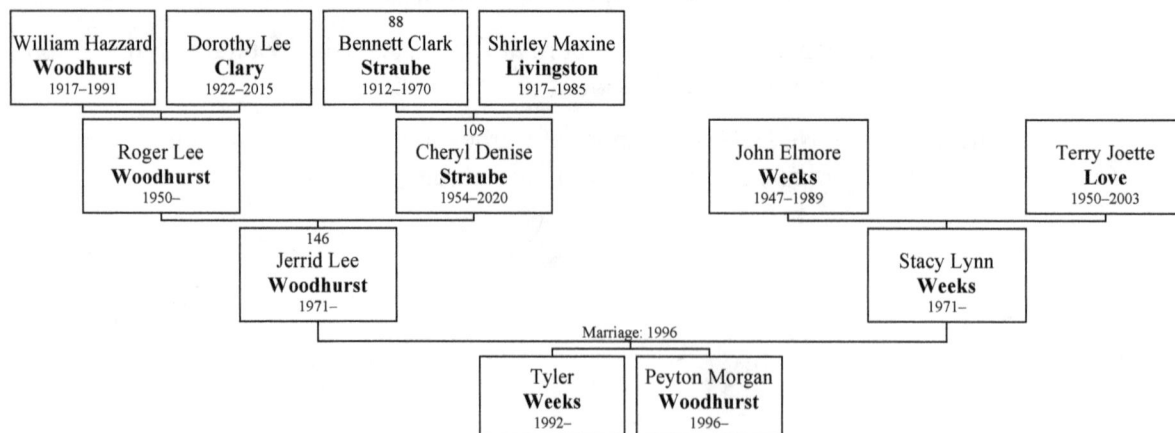

146. **Jerrid Lee Woodhurst** was born on Saturday, December 11, 1971, at St. Elizabeth Hospital in Hannibal, Marion County, Missouri. He is the son of Roger Lee Woodhurst and Cheryl Denise Straube (109).

At the age of 24, Jerrid Lee married **Stacy Lynn Weeks** on Saturday, June 22, 1996, when she was 24 years old. They have two sons.

Stacy Lynn was born in Louisiana, Pike County, Missouri, on Friday, November 19, 1971. She is the daughter of John Elmore Weeks and Terry Joette Love.

Sons of Jerrid Lee Woodhurst and Stacy Lynn Weeks:

m   I. **Tyler Weeks** was born on March 03, 1992.

m   II. **Peyton Morgan Woodhurst** was born in Lake St. Louis, Saint Charles County, Missouri, on October 29, 1996.

Family of Sherri Woodhurst and David Bruce

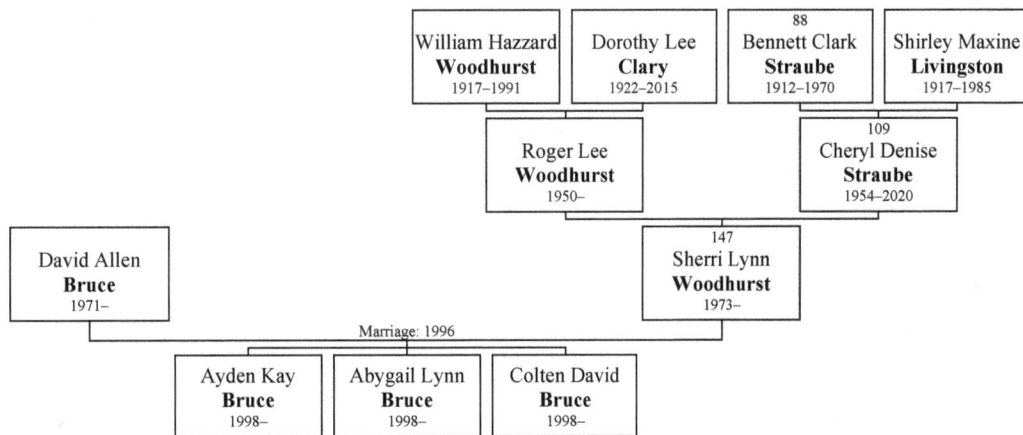

147.   **Sherri Lynn Woodhurst** was born on Friday, September 07, 1973, at St. Elizabeth Hospital in Hannibal, Marion County, Missouri. She is the daughter of Roger Lee Woodhurst and Cheryl Denise Straube (109).

At the age of 22, Sherri Lynn married **David Allen Bruce** on Saturday, January 06, 1996, in Perry, Ralls County, Missouri, when he was 24 years old. They have three children.

David Allen was born in Boonville, Cooper County, Missouri, on Monday, July 12, 1971.

Children of Sherri Lynn Woodhurst and David Allen Bruce:

f   I. **Ayden Kay Bruce** was born in Columbia, Boone County, Missouri, on November 05, 1998.

f   II. **Abygail Lynn Bruce** was born in Columbia, Boone County, Missouri, on November 05, 1998.

m   III. **Colten David Bruce** was born in Columbia, Boone County, Missouri, on November 05, 1998.

Family of Brandon Straube and Elizabeth Evans

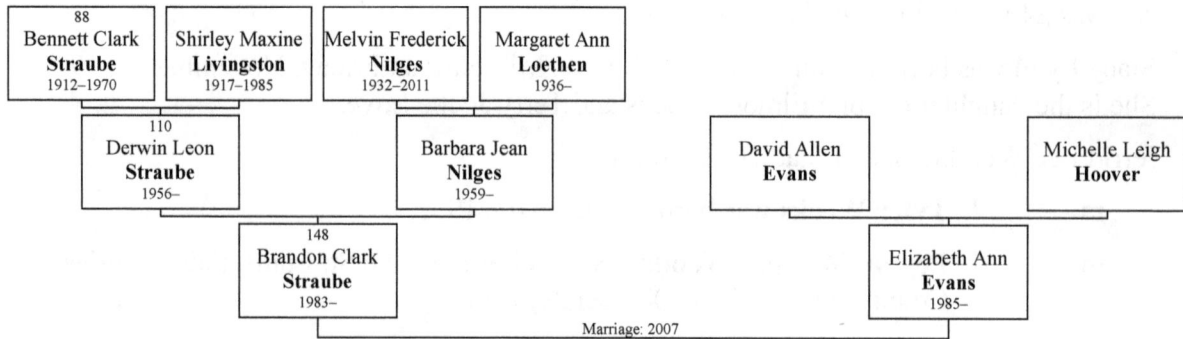

| 88 Bennett Clark **Straube** 1912–1970 | Shirley Maxine **Livingston** 1917–1985 | Melvin Frederick **Nilges** 1932–2011 | Margaret Ann **Loethen** 1936– | | | David Allen **Evans** | | Michelle Leigh **Hoover** |

110 Derwin Leon **Straube** 1956–   Barbara Jean **Nilges** 1959–

148 Brandon Clark **Straube** 1983–   Elizabeth Ann **Evans** 1985–

Marriage: 2007

148. **Brandon Clark Straube** was born on Sunday, October 16, 1983, in Hannibal, Marion County, Missouri. He is the son of Derwin Leon Straube (110) and Barbara Jean Nilges.

At the age of 23, Brandon Clark married **Elizabeth Ann Evans** on Saturday, October 06, 2007, in Vandalia, Audrain County, Missouri, when she was 22 years old. Elizabeth Ann was born in Mexico, Audrain County, Missouri, on Wednesday, April 24, 1985. She is the daughter of David Allen Evans and Michelle Leigh Hoover.

Samuel Hargadine

149. **Samuel Emmett Hargadine V** was born on Sunday, August 10, 1958, in Columbia, Boone County, Missouri. He is the son of Samuel Emmett Hargadine IV and Georganna Myers (111).

Samuel served in the U.S. Army from August 12, 1976 to August 12, 1979. Basic training was completed at Ft. Leonard Wood, Missouri. Military Police training was completed at Ft. McClellan, Alabama. Duty stations were in Amberg and Hanau, Germany. Honorably Discharged from Active and Reserve duty on June 15, 1982, at the rank of Specialist 4.

Samuel is an active Find a Grave Contributor #51090756

Marriages with Sheri Lynn Palmerton and Annette Sue Peddicord (Page 241) are known.

Family of Samuel Hargadine and Sheri Palmerton

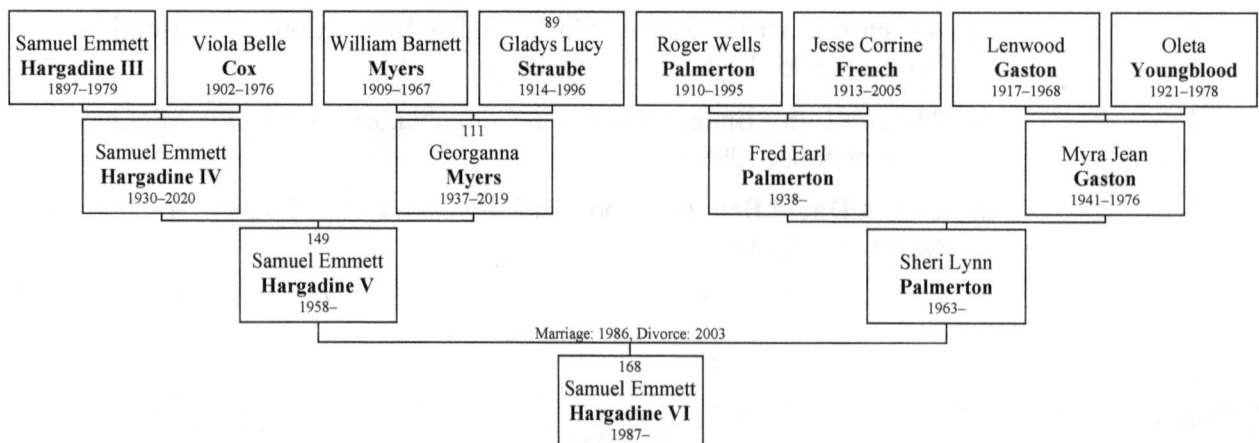

| Samuel Emmett **Hargadine III** 1897–1979 | Viola Belle **Cox** 1902–1976 | William Barnett **Myers** 1909–1967 | 89 Gladys Lucy **Straube** 1914–1996 | Roger Wells **Palmerton** 1910–1995 | Jesse Corrine **French** 1913–2005 | Lenwood **Gaston** 1917–1968 | Oleta **Youngblood** 1921–1978 |

Samuel Emmett **Hargadine IV** 1930–2020   111 Georganna **Myers** 1937–2019   Fred Earl **Palmerton** 1938–   Myra Jean **Gaston** 1941–1976

149 Samuel Emmett **Hargadine V** 1958–   Sheri Lynn **Palmerton** 1963–

Marriage: 1986, Divorce: 2003

168 Samuel Emmett **Hargadine VI** 1987–

Here are the details about **Samuel Emmett Hargadine V's** first marriage, with Sheri Lynn Palmerton. You can read more about Samuel Emmett on page 240.

At the age of 28, Samuel Emmett Hargadine V married **Sheri Lynn Palmerton** on Saturday, September 13, 1986, in Columbia, Boone County, Missouri, when she was 23 years old. They were divorced in Howard County, Missouri, on November 06, 2003. They have one son.

Sheri Lynn was born in St. Charles, St. Charles County, Missouri, on Wednesday, January 09, 1963. She is the daughter of Fred Earl Palmerton and Myra Jean Gaston.

Son of Samuel Emmett Hargadine V and Sheri Lynn Palmerton:

+ 168 m I. **Samuel Emmett Hargadine VI** was born in Columbia, Boone County, Missouri, on July 23, 1987. He is also known as **Sammy**.

Family of Samuel Hargadine and Annette Peddicord

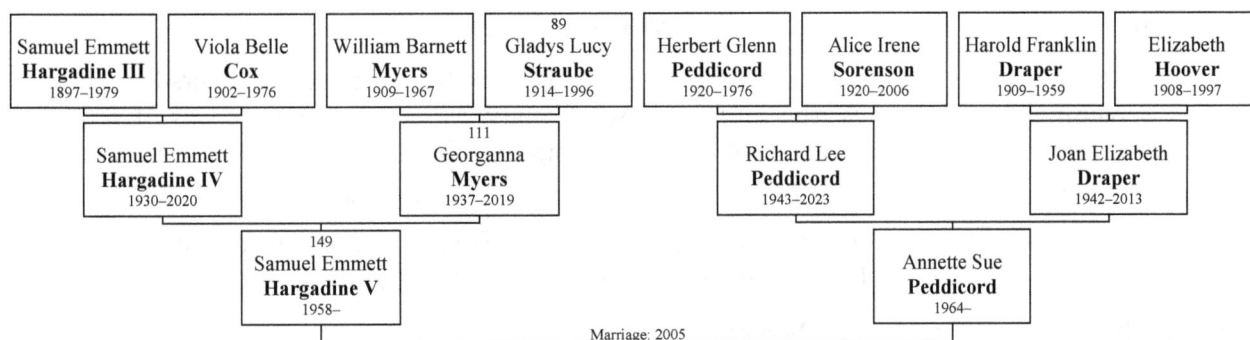

Here are the details about **Samuel Emmett Hargadine V's** second marriage, with Annette Sue Peddicord. You can read more about Samuel Emmett on page 240.

At the age of 47, Samuel Emmett Hargadine V married **Annette Sue Peddicord** on Friday, August 19, 2005, in Columbia, Boone County, Missouri, when she was 41 years old. Annette Sue was born in Belmond, Wright County, Iowa, on Friday, January 10, 1964.[77] She is the daughter of Richard Lee Peddicord and Joan Elizabeth Draper.

John Hargadine

150. **John Everett Hargadine** was born on Wednesday, March 21, 1962, at George Washington University Hospital in Washington D.C.. He is the son of Samuel Emmett Hargadine IV and Georganna Myers (111).

Named after John W. Willis and Everett James Straube and the subject of this book's dedication.

Marriages with Monelle Schriewer, Patricia A. Lehman (Page 242) and Mary Anne Elizabeth Niemeyer (Page 243) are known.

---

77 Ancestry.com, U.S., Index to Public Records, 1994-2019 (Lehi, UT, USA, Ancestry.com Operations, Inc., 2020), Ancestry.com.

Family of John Hargadine and Monelle Schriewer

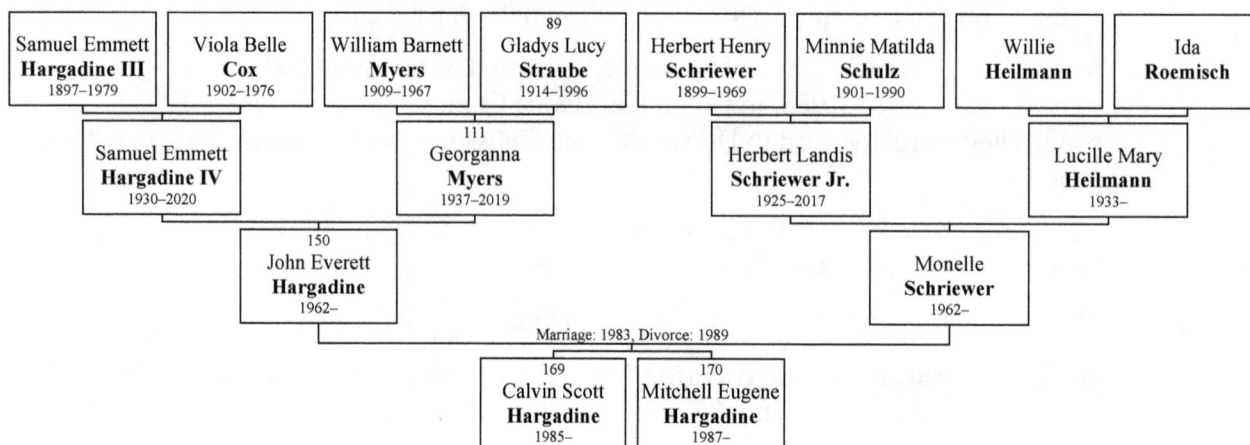

| Samuel Emmett **Hargadine III** 1897–1979 | Viola Belle **Cox** 1902–1976 | William Barnett **Myers** 1909–1967 | 89 Gladys Lucy **Straube** 1914–1996 | Herbert Henry **Schriewer** 1899–1969 | Minnie Matilda **Schulz** 1901–1990 | Willie **Heilmann** | Ida **Roemisch** |

| Samuel Emmett **Hargadine IV** 1930–2020 | 111 Georganna **Myers** 1937–2019 | Herbert Landis **Schriewer Jr.** 1925–2017 | Lucille Mary **Heilmann** 1933– |

150
John Everett
Hargadine
1962–

Monelle
Schriewer
1962–

Marriage: 1983, Divorce: 1989

| 169 Calvin Scott **Hargadine** 1985– | 170 Mitchell Eugene **Hargadine** 1987– |

Here are the details about **John Everett Hargadine's** first marriage, with Monelle Schriewer. You can read more about John Everett on page 241.

At the age of 21, John Everett Hargadine married **Monelle Schriewer** on Thursday, September 29, 1983, in Warrensburg, Johnson County, Missouri, when she was 21 years old. They were divorced in Columbia, Boone County, Missouri, in April 1989. They have two sons.

Monelle was born in New Braunfels, Comal County, Texas, on Tuesday, January 23, 1962. She is the daughter of Herbert Landis Schriewer Jr. and Lucille Mary Heilmann.

Sons of John Everett Hargadine and Monelle Schriewer:

+ 169 m I. **Calvin Scott Hargadine** was born in Sedalia, Pettis County, Missouri, on October 22, 1985.

+ 170 m II. **Mitchell Eugene Hargadine** was born in Columbia, Boone County, Missouri, on September 17, 1987.

Family of John Hargadine and Patricia Lehman

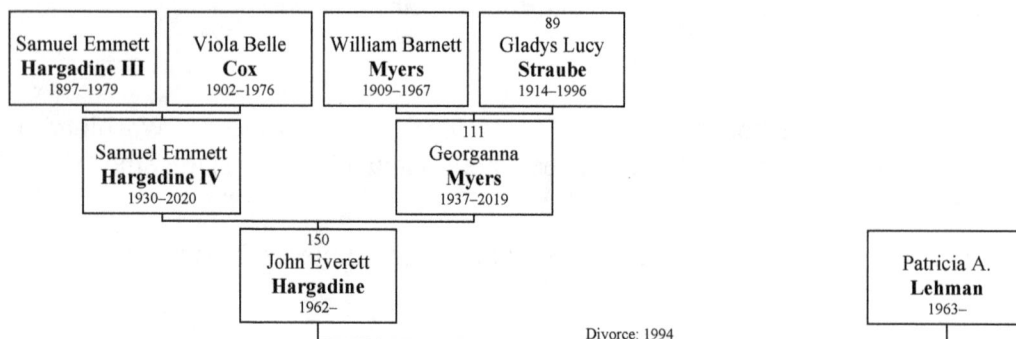

| Samuel Emmett **Hargadine III** 1897–1979 | Viola Belle **Cox** 1902–1976 | William Barnett **Myers** 1909–1967 | 89 Gladys Lucy **Straube** 1914–1996 |

| Samuel Emmett **Hargadine IV** 1930–2020 | 111 Georganna **Myers** 1937–2019 |

150
John Everett
Hargadine
1962–

Patricia A.
Lehman
1963–

Divorce: 1994

Here are the details about **John Everett Hargadine's** second marriage, with Patricia A. Lehman. You can read more about John Everett on page 241.

John Everett Hargadine married **Patricia A. Lehman**. They were divorced in Boone County, Missouri, on September 15, 1994.

Patricia A. was born in September 1963.

Family of John Hargadine and Mary Niemeyer

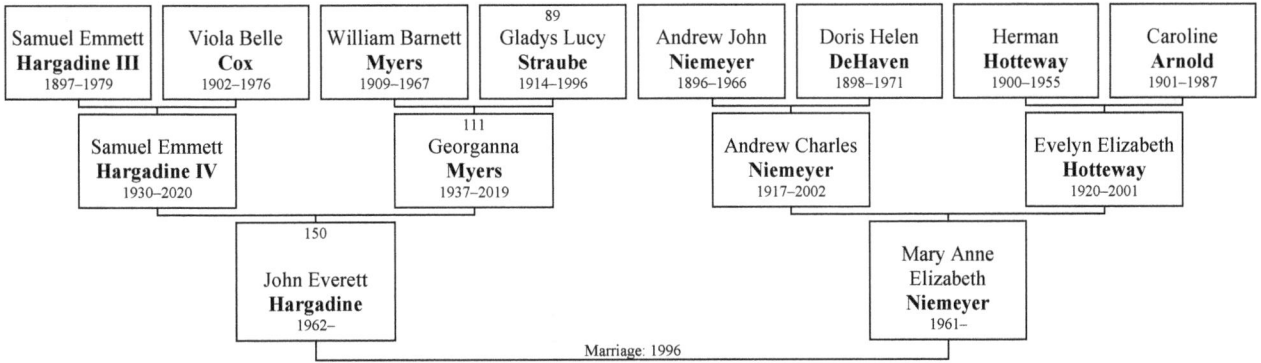

Samuel Emmett **Hargadine III** 1897–1979	Viola Belle **Cox** 1902–1976	William Barnett **Myers** 1909–1967	89 Gladys Lucy **Straube** 1914–1996	Andrew John **Niemeyer** 1896–1966	Doris Helen **DeHaven** 1898–1971	Herman **Hotteway** 1900–1955	Caroline **Arnold** 1901–1987

Samuel Emmett **Hargadine IV** 1930–2020

111 Georganna **Myers** 1937–2019

Andrew Charles **Niemeyer** 1917–2002

Evelyn Elizabeth **Hotteway** 1920–2001

150 John Everett **Hargadine** 1962–

Mary Anne Elizabeth **Niemeyer** 1961–

Marriage: 1996

Here are the details about **John Everett Hargadine's** third marriage, with Mary Anne Elizabeth Niemeyer. You can read more about John Everett on page 241.

At the age of 34, John Everett Hargadine married **Mary Anne Elizabeth Niemeyer** on Saturday, September 28, 1996, in Saint Louis, Saint Louis County, Missouri, when she was 34 years old. Mary Anne Elizabeth was born in Saint Louis, Saint Louis County, Missouri, on Monday, October 09, 1961. She is the daughter of Andrew Charles Niemeyer and Evelyn Elizabeth Hotteway.

Family of Laurie Straube and James Heckman

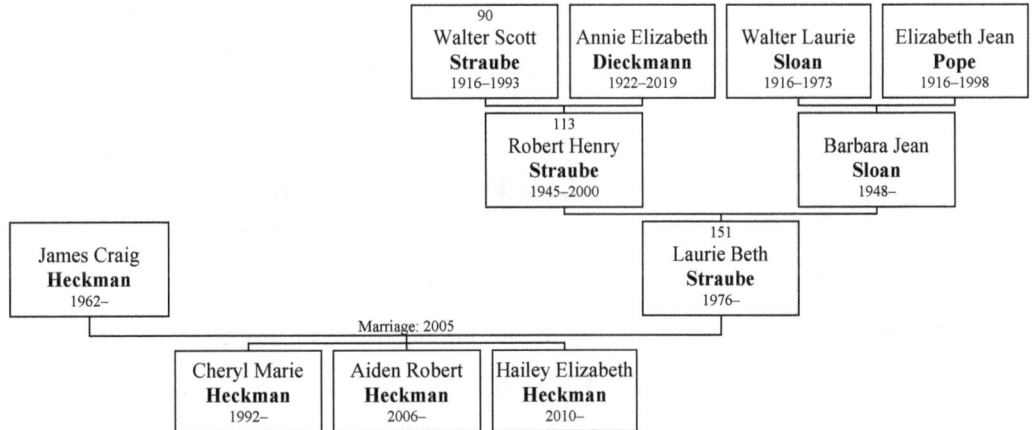

90 Walter Scott **Straube** 1916–1993	Annie Elizabeth **Dieckmann** 1922–2019	Walter Laurie **Sloan** 1916–1973	Elizabeth Jean **Pope** 1916–1998

113 Robert Henry **Straube** 1945–2000

Barbara Jean **Sloan** 1948–

James Craig **Heckman** 1962–

151 Laurie Beth **Straube** 1976–

Marriage: 2005

Cheryl Marie **Heckman** 1992–

Aiden Robert **Heckman** 2006–

Hailey Elizabeth **Heckman** 2010–

151.   **Laurie Beth Straube** was born on Monday, August 02, 1976, in Annandale, Fairfax County, Virginia. She is the daughter of Robert Henry Straube (113) and Barbara Jean Sloan.

At the age of 29, Laurie Beth married **James Craig Heckman** on Saturday, August 13, 2005, in Fayetteville, Cumberland County, North Carolina, when he was 42 years old. They have three children.

James Craig was born on Tuesday, November 27, 1962.

Children of Laurie Beth Straube and James Craig Heckman:

> f   I. **Cheryl Marie Heckman** was born in Fayetteville, Cumberland County, North Carolina, on November 30, 1992. Laurie Beth Straube is her stepmother.

> m   II. **Aiden Robert Heckman** was born in Fayetteville, Cumberland County, North Carolina, on August 22, 2006.

> f   III. **Hailey Elizabeth Heckman** was born on July 05, 2010.

Family of Nichole Pagnella and David Jensen

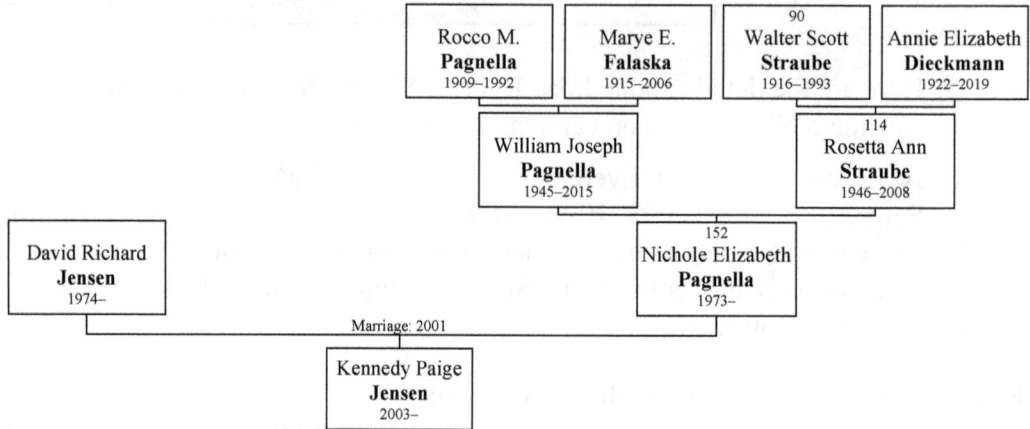

152.   **Nichole Elizabeth Pagnella** was born on Monday, February 19, 1973, in Alexandria, Virginia. She is the daughter of William Joseph Pagnella and Rosetta Ann Straube (114). She is also known as **Nicki**.

At the age of 28, Nichole Elizabeth married **David Richard Jensen** on Friday, July 06, 2001, when he was 27 years old. They have one daughter.

David Richard was born on Monday, May 06, 1974.

Daughter of Nichole Elizabeth Pagnella and David Richard Jensen:

> f   I. **Kennedy Paige Jensen** was born at St. John's Mercy Medical Center in City of Creve Coeur, Saint Louis County, Missouri, on November 15, 2003.

Family of Christiane Smith and John Hamai

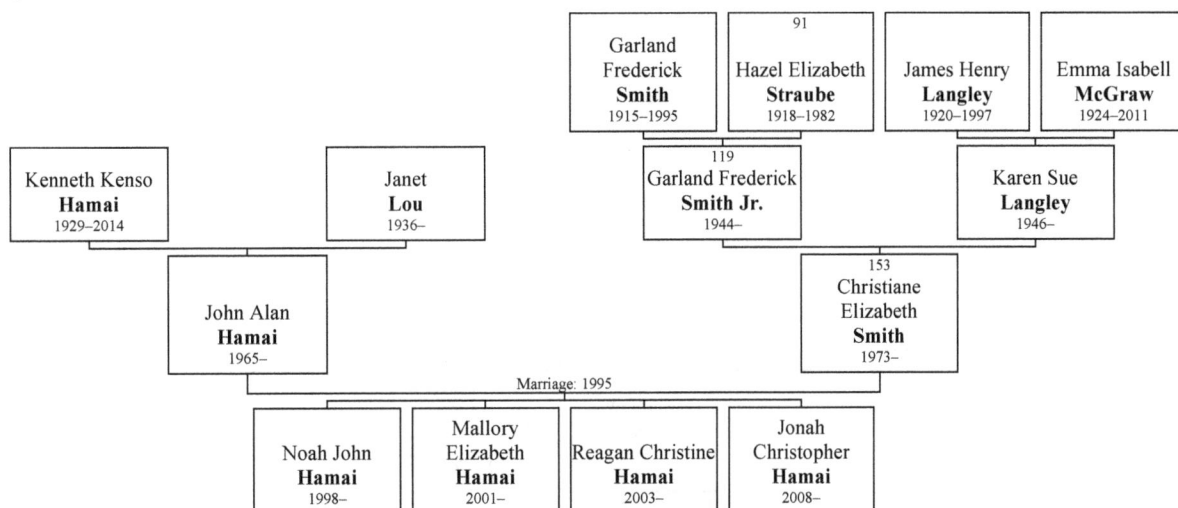

| | | 91 | | |
| Garland Frederick **Smith** 1915–1995 | Hazel Elizabeth **Straube** 1918–1982 | James Henry **Langley** 1920–1997 | Emma Isabell **McGraw** 1924–2011 |

| Kenneth Kenso **Hamai** 1929–2014 | Janet **Lou** 1936– | 119 Garland Frederick **Smith Jr.** 1944– | Karen Sue **Langley** 1946– |

| John Alan **Hamai** 1965– | 153 Christiane Elizabeth **Smith** 1973– |

Marriage: 1995

| Noah John **Hamai** 1998– | Mallory Elizabeth **Hamai** 2001– | Reagan Christine **Hamai** 2003– | Jonah Christopher **Hamai** 2008– |

153.   **Christiane Elizabeth Smith** was born on Friday, June 29, 1973, in City of Creve Coeur, Saint Louis County, Missouri. She is the daughter of Garland Frederick Smith Jr. (119) and Karen Sue Langley.

At the age of 21, Christiane Elizabeth married **John Alan Hamai** on Friday, May 26, 1995, at St. Angela Marici Catholic Church in Florissant, Saint Louis County, Missouri, when he was 30 years old. They have four children.

John Alan was born on Thursday, March 11, 1965. He is the son of Kenneth Kenso Hamai and Janet Lou.

Children of Christiane Elizabeth Smith and John Alan Hamai:

m   I.   **Noah John Hamai** was born at St. Johns Mercy Medical Center in City of Creve Coeur, Saint Louis County, Missouri, on May 20, 1998.

f   II.   **Mallory Elizabeth Hamai** was born at St. Johns Mercy Medical Center in City of Creve Coeur, Saint Louis County, Missouri, on January 30, 2001.

f   III.   **Reagan Christine Hamai** was born at St. Johns Mercy Medical Center in City of Creve Coeur, Saint Louis County, Missouri, on November 13, 2003.

m   IV.   **Jonah Christopher Hamai** was born at St. Johns Mercy Medical Center in City of Creve Coeur, Saint Louis County, Missouri, on October 31, 2008.

Family of Ian Smith and Lauren Buckingham

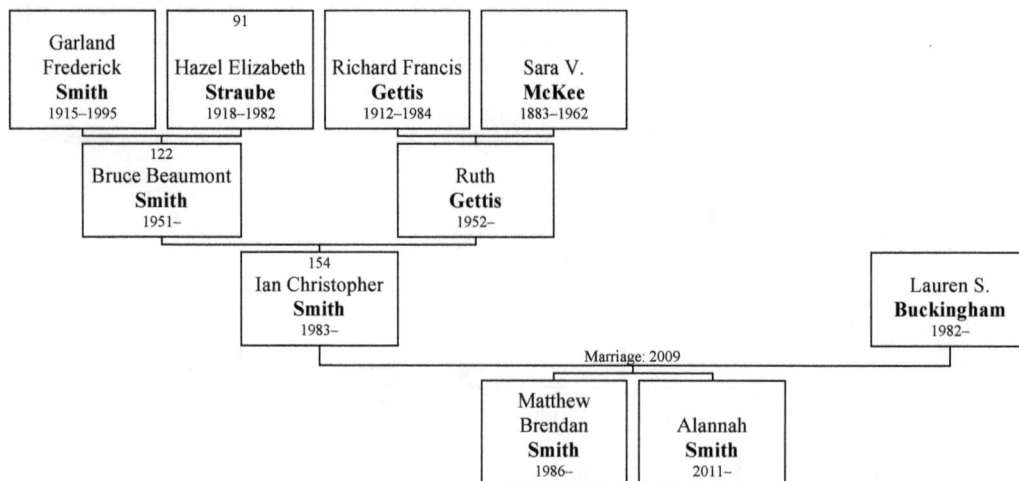

```
┌──────────────┐ ┌──────91──────┐ ┌──────────────┐ ┌──────────────┐
│   Garland    │ │    Hazel     │ │   Richard    │ │   Sara V.    │
│  Frederick   │ │  Elizabeth   │ │   Francis    │ │    McKee     │
│    Smith     │ │   Straube    │ │   Gettis     │ │  1883–1962   │
│  1915–1995   │ │  1918–1982   │ │  1912–1984   │ │              │
└──────────────┘ └──────────────┘ └──────────────┘ └──────────────┘
      ┌─────122─────┐              ┌──────────────┐
      │    Bruce    │              │    Ruth      │
      │  Beaumont   │              │   Gettis     │
      │    Smith    │              │   1952–      │
      │    1951–    │              │              │
      └─────────────┘              └──────────────┘
              ┌─────154─────┐                              ┌──────────────┐
              │    Ian      │                              │  Lauren S.   │
              │ Christopher │                              │ Buckingham   │
              │   Smith     │                              │   1982–      │
              │   1983–     │                              │              │
              └─────────────┘                              └──────────────┘
                          Marriage: 2009
              ┌──────────────┐ ┌──────────────┐
              │   Matthew    │ │   Alannah    │
              │   Brendan    │ │    Smith     │
              │    Smith     │ │    2011–     │
              │    1986–     │ │              │
              └──────────────┘ └──────────────┘
```

154. **Ian Christopher Smith** was born on Tuesday, August 09, 1983, in Annapolis, Anne Arundel County, Maryland. He is the son of Bruce Beaumont Smith (122) and Ruth Gettis.

At the age of 26, Ian Christopher married **Lauren S. Buckingham** on Saturday, October 10, 2009, in Elkton, Cecil County, Maryland, when she was 27 years old. They have two children.

Lauren S. was born in Monterey, Monterey County, California, on Saturday, September 11, 1982.

Children of Ian Christopher Smith and Lauren S. Buckingham:

    m   I. **Matthew Brendan Smith** was born in Annapolis, Anne Arundel County, Maryland, on May 13, 1986.

    f   II. **Alannah Smith** was born on January 30, 2011.

Family of Annice Allensworth and Randy Hays

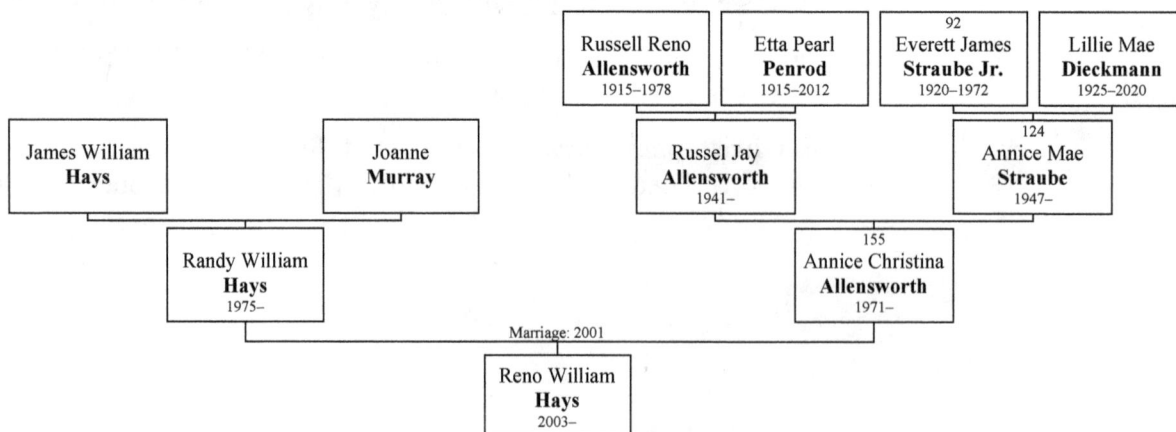

```
                          ┌──────────────┐ ┌──────────────┐ ┌──────92──────┐ ┌──────────────┐
                          │ Russell Reno │ │  Etta Pearl  │ │   Everett    │ │  Lillie Mae  │
                          │ Allensworth  │ │   Penrod     │ │    James     │ │  Dieckmann   │
                          │  1915–1978   │ │  1915–2012   │ │ Straube Jr.  │ │  1925–2020   │
                          │              │ │              │ │  1920–1972   │ │              │
                          └──────────────┘ └──────────────┘ └──────────────┘ └──────────────┘
┌──────────────┐ ┌──────────────┐       ┌──────────────┐       ┌─────124─────┐
│    James     │ │   Joanne     │       │  Russel Jay  │       │  Annice Mae  │
│  William     │ │   Murray     │       │ Allensworth  │       │   Straube    │
│    Hays      │ │              │       │   1941–      │       │   1947–      │
└──────────────┘ └──────────────┘       └──────────────┘       └──────────────┘
        ┌──────────────┐                        ┌─────155─────┐
        │    Randy     │                        │   Annice     │
        │   William    │                        │  Christina   │
        │    Hays      │                        │ Allensworth  │
        │   1975–      │                        │   1971–      │
        └──────────────┘                        └──────────────┘
                          Marriage: 2001
                  ┌──────────────┐
                  │    Reno      │
                  │   William    │
                  │    Hays      │
                  │   2003–      │
                  └──────────────┘
```

155. **Annice Christina Allensworth** was born on Monday, December 27, 1971, in Hannibal, Marion County, Missouri. She is the daughter of Russel Jay Allensworth and Annice Mae Straube (124). She is also known as **Tina**.

Annice Christina served in the U.S. Air Force.

At the age of 29, Annice Christina married **Randy William Hays** on Saturday, October 06, 2001, in Bowling Green, Pike County, Missouri, when he was 26 years old. They have one son.

Randy William was born in Hannibal, Marion County, Missouri, on Tuesday, August 05, 1975. He is the son of James William Hays and Joanne Murray.

Son of Annice Christina Allensworth and Randy William Hays:

> m   I. **Reno William Hays** was born at St. Joseph Hospital West in Lake St. Louis, Saint Charles County, Missouri, on August 26, 2003.

Family of Ricky Allensworth and Emilie Patton

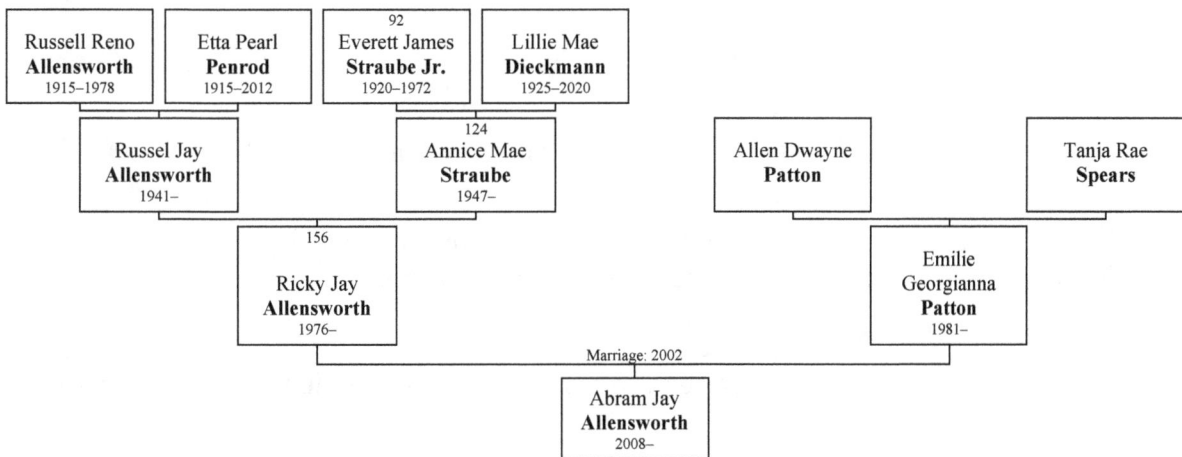

156.   **Ricky Jay Allensworth** was born on Wednesday, February 04, 1976, in Hannibal, Marion County, Missouri. He is the son of Russel Jay Allensworth and Annice Mae Straube (124).

At the age of 26, Ricky Jay married **Emilie Georgianna Patton** on Tuesday, June 18, 2002, when she was 21 years old. They have one son.

Emilie Georgianna was born in Louisiana, Pike County, Missouri, on Saturday, April 18, 1981. She is the daughter of Allen Dwayne Patton and Tanja Rae Spears.

Son of Ricky Jay Allensworth and Emilie Georgianna Patton:

> m   I. **Abram Jay Allensworth** was born in Lake St. Louis, Saint Charles County, Missouri, on January 27, 2008.

Family of Aaron Straube and Kelly Street

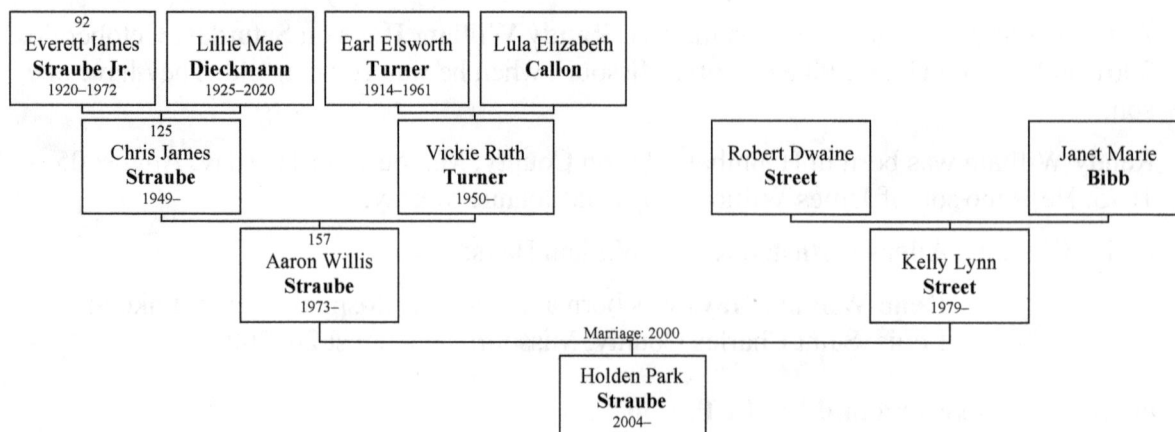

```
┌─────────────┐ ┌─────────────┐   ┌─────────────┐ ┌─────────────┐
│     92      │ │             │   │             │ │             │
│Everett James│ │ Lillie Mae  │   │Earl Elsworth│ │Lula Elizabeth│
│ Straube Jr. │ │ Dieckmann   │   │   Turner    │ │   Callon    │
│ 1920–1972   │ │ 1925–2020   │   │ 1914–1961   │ │             │
└─────────────┘ └─────────────┘   └─────────────┘ └─────────────┘
     ┌──────────────┐              ┌──────────────┐
     │     125      │              │              │
     │ Chris James  │              │ Vickie Ruth  │
     │   Straube    │              │    Turner    │
     │    1949–     │              │    1950–     │
     └──────────────┘              └──────────────┘
          ┌──────────────┐
          │     157      │
          │ Aaron Willis │
          │   Straube    │
          │    1973–     │
          └──────────────┘
```

```
┌─────────────┐                   ┌─────────────┐
│Robert Dwaine│                   │ Janet Marie │
│   Street    │                   │    Bibb     │
└─────────────┘                   └─────────────┘
          ┌──────────────┐
          │  Kelly Lynn  │
          │   Street     │
          │    1979–     │
          └──────────────┘
```

Marriage: 2000

```
          ┌──────────────┐
          │ Holden Park  │
          │   Straube    │
          │    2004–     │
          └──────────────┘
```

157. **Aaron Willis Straube** was born on Thursday, June 14, 1973, in Hannibal, Marion County, Missouri. He is the son of Chris James Straube (125) and Vickie Ruth Turner.

At the age of 26, Aaron Willis married **Kelly Lynn Street** on Saturday, May 20, 2000, in Bowling Green, Pike County, Missouri, when she was 21 years old. They have one son.

Kelly Lynn was born in Louisiana, Pike County, Missouri, on Thursday, May 10, 1979. She is the daughter of Robert Dwaine Street and Janet Marie Bibb.

Son of Aaron Willis Straube and Kelly Lynn Street:

    m   I. **Holden Park Straube** was born in Hannibal, Marion County, Missouri, on December 06, 2004.

Family of Sara Straube and Brian Anders

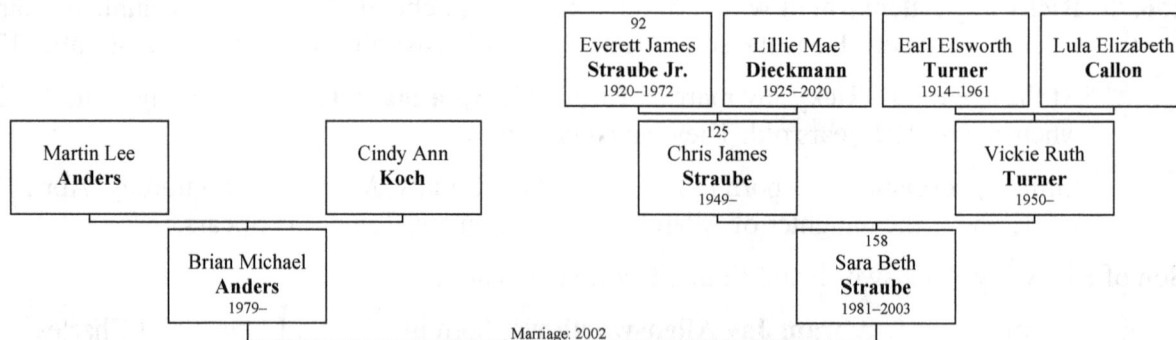

```
                        ┌─────────────┐ ┌─────────────┐   ┌─────────────┐ ┌─────────────┐
                        │     92      │ │             │   │             │ │             │
                        │Everett James│ │ Lillie Mae  │   │Earl Elsworth│ │Lula Elizabeth│
                        │ Straube Jr. │ │ Dieckmann   │   │   Turner    │ │   Callon    │
                        │ 1920–1972   │ │ 1925–2020   │   │ 1914–1961   │ │             │
                        └─────────────┘ └─────────────┘   └─────────────┘ └─────────────┘
┌─────────────┐ ┌─────────────┐              ┌──────────────┐              ┌──────────────┐
│ Martin Lee  │ │ Cindy Ann   │              │     125      │              │ Vickie Ruth  │
│   Anders    │ │    Koch     │              │ Chris James  │              │    Turner    │
│             │ │             │              │   Straube    │              │    1950–     │
└─────────────┘ └─────────────┘              │    1949–     │              └──────────────┘
     ┌──────────────┐                        └──────────────┘
     │Brian Michael │                             ┌──────────────┐
     │   Anders     │                             │     158      │
     │    1979–     │                             │  Sara Beth   │
     └──────────────┘                             │   Straube    │
                                                  │  1981–2003   │
                                                  └──────────────┘
                        Marriage: 2002
```

158. **Sara Beth Straube** was born on Tuesday, January 06, 1981, in Hannibal, Marion County, Missouri. She was the daughter of Chris James Straube (125) and Vickie Ruth Turner.

Sara Beth died at Barnes Hospital in Saint Louis, Saint Louis County, Missouri, on August 14, 2003, at the age of 22. Her cause of death was leukemia. Sara Beth was buried in Memorial Gardens Cemetery, Bowling Green, Pike County, Missouri, on August 17, 2003 (Find a Grave ID 68398672).

Born Sara Beth Straube on January 6, 1981. She is the daughter of Chris James Straube and Vickie Ruth Turner.

Sara got a degree in elementary education from Missouri Baptist. She married Brian Anders in 2002 and was just beginning her teaching career when diagnosed with acute leukemia. She passed away on August 14, 2003, at the age of 22 at the Siteman Cancer Center of Barnes-Jewish Hospital in St. Louis, Missouri. Services for Sara were conducted on August 17, 2003, at the Second Baptist Church, and burial was at Memorial Gardens in Bowling Green.

A fund to award an elementary teaching scholarship annually in Sara's memory was set up.

Sara is survived by her husband, Brian Anders; her parents, Chris and Vickie Straube; two brothers, Trent Straube of New York and Aaron Straube of Bowling Green;her sister-in-law, Kelly Straube; her grandmother, Mrs. E.J. (Lil) Straube, Jr. of Bowling Green and a host of relatives and friends.

At the age of 21, Sara Beth married **Brian Michael Anders** on Saturday, June 15, 2002, in Second Baptist Church, Bowling Green, Pike County, Missouri, when he was 23 years old. Brian Michael was born in Kirksville, Adair County, Missouri, on Saturday, May 05, 1979.

Anders-Straube

Mr. and Mrs. Chris Straube of Curryville announce the engagement and forthcoming marriage of their daughter, Sarah Beth Straube to Brian Michael Anders, son of Mr. and Mrs. Martin Anders of Bowling Green. Ms. Straube is a 1999 graduate of Bowling Green High School and is currently a senior at Missouri Baptist College and will graduate in December 2002 with a bachelor's degree in elementary education. She is currently employed by Perry State Bank. Mr. Anders is a 1997 graduate of Bowling Green High School and is a trooper with the Missouri State Highway Patrol and is assigned with the Marion and Ralls counties.

A 4 p.m., June 15 wedding is planned at the Second Baptist Church in Bowling Green. He is the son of Martin Lee Anders and Cindy Ann Koch.

Jason Straube

159.   **Jason Quinn Straube** was born on Saturday, February 23, 1974, in Hannibal, Marion County, Missouri. He is the son of Stanley Willis Straube (126) and Vicki Ann Burnett.

Marriages with Cynthia Ann Creech, Christi Lynn Gosnell (Page 250) and Wendy Marie Oberman (Page 251) are known.

Family of Jason Straube and Cynthia Creech

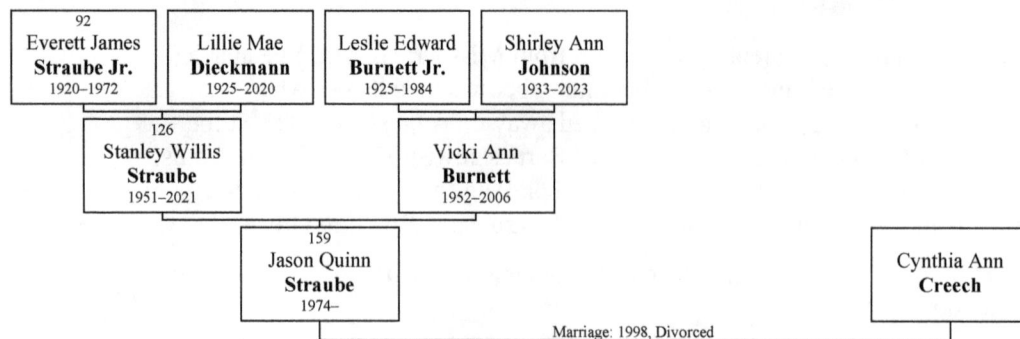

| 92 Everett James **Straube Jr.** 1920–1972 | Lillie Mae **Dieckmann** 1925–2020 | Leslie Edward **Burnett Jr.** 1925–1984 | Shirley Ann **Johnson** 1933–2023 |

126 Stanley Willis **Straube** 1951–2021

Vicki Ann **Burnett** 1952–2006

159 Jason Quinn **Straube** 1974–

Cynthia Ann **Creech**

Marriage: 1998, Divorced

Here are the details about **Jason Quinn Straube's** first marriage, with Cynthia Ann Creech. You can read more about Jason Quinn on page 249.

Jason Quinn Straube married **Cynthia Ann Creech** on Saturday, August 29, 1998, in Bowling Green, Pike County, Missouri. They are divorced.

Family of Jason Straube and Christi Gosnell

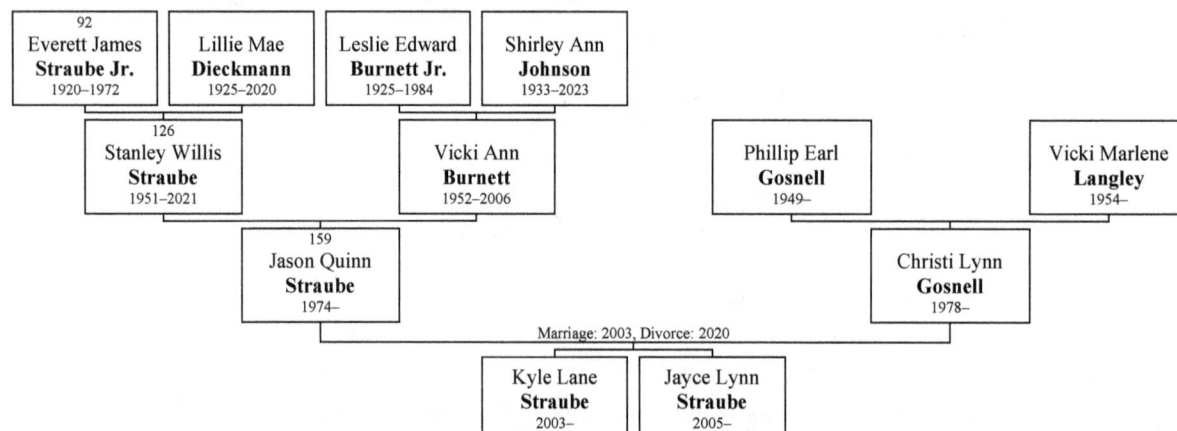

| 92 Everett James **Straube Jr.** 1920–1972 | Lillie Mae **Dieckmann** 1925–2020 | Leslie Edward **Burnett Jr.** 1925–1984 | Shirley Ann **Johnson** 1933–2023 |

126 Stanley Willis **Straube** 1951–2021

Vicki Ann **Burnett** 1952–2006

Phillip Earl **Gosnell** 1949–

Vicki Marlene **Langley** 1954–

159 Jason Quinn **Straube** 1974–

Christi Lynn **Gosnell** 1978–

Marriage: 2003, Divorce: 2020

Kyle Lane **Straube** 2003–

Jayce Lynn **Straube** 2005–

Here are the details about **Jason Quinn Straube's** second marriage, with Christi Lynn Gosnell. You can read more about Jason Quinn on page 249.

At the age of 29, Jason Quinn Straube married **Christi Lynn Gosnell** on Saturday, April 26, 2003, in Bowling Green, Pike County, Missouri, when she was 25 years old. They were divorced on October 05, 2020. They have two children.

Christi Lynn was born in Louisiana, Pike County, Missouri, on Friday, February 24, 1978. She is the daughter of Phillip Earl Gosnell and Vicki Marlene Langley.

Children of Jason Quinn Straube and Christi Lynn Gosnell:

m   I. **Kyle Lane Straube** was born on September 30, 2003.

f   II. **Jayce Lynn Straube** was born in Lake St. Louis, Saint Charles County, Missouri, on November 18, 2005.

Family of Jason Straube and Wendy Oberman

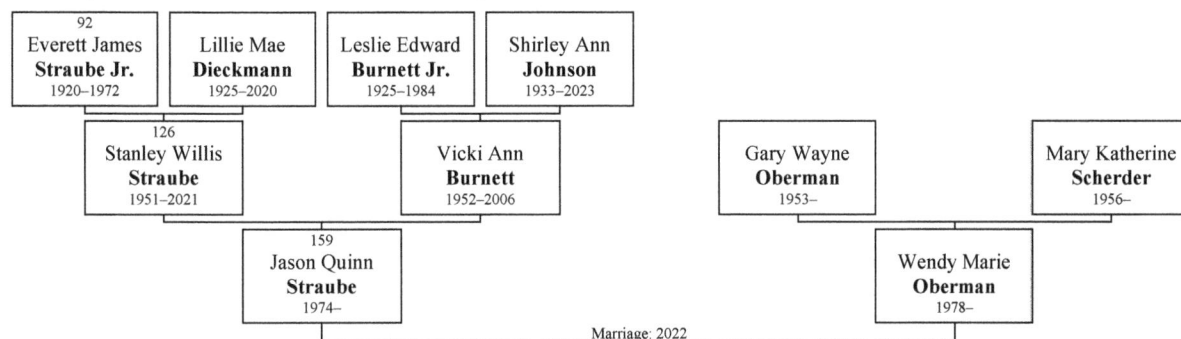

| 92
Everett James
Straube Jr.
1920–1972 | Lillie Mae
Dieckmann
1925–2020 | Leslie Edward
Burnett Jr.
1925–1984 | Shirley Ann
Johnson
1933–2023 |

| 126
Stanley Willis
Straube
1951–2021 | Vicki Ann
Burnett
1952–2006 |

Gary Wayne **Oberman** 1953–   Mary Katherine **Scherder** 1956–

159
Jason Quinn **Straube** 1974–

Wendy Marie **Oberman** 1978–

Marriage: 2022

Here are the details about **Jason Quinn Straube's** third marriage, with Wendy Marie Oberman. You can read more about Jason Quinn on page 249.

At the age of 48, Jason Quinn Straube married **Wendy Marie Oberman** on Monday, May 23, 2022, in Hermann, Gasconade County, Missouri, when she was 43 years old. Wendy Marie was born in Louisiana, Pike County, Missouri, on Thursday, September 28, 1978. She is the daughter of Gary Wayne Oberman and Mary Katherine Scherder.

Family of Carmen Straube and John Charlton

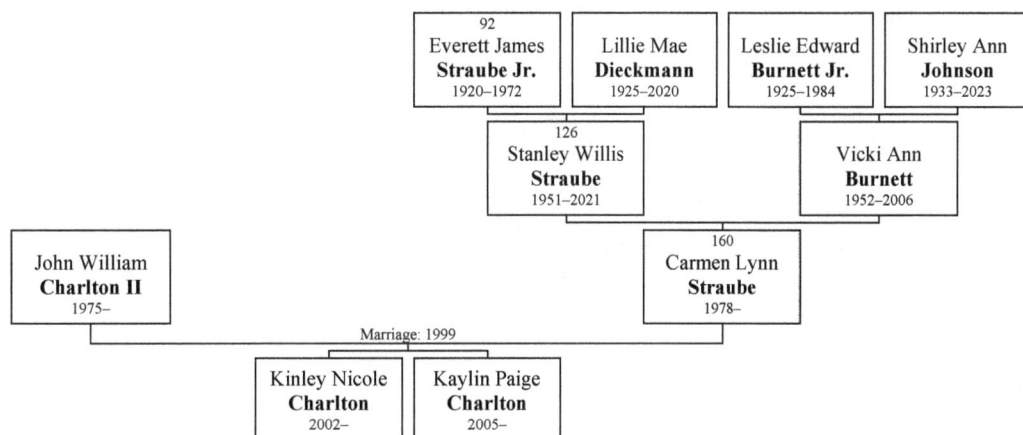

| 92
Everett James
Straube Jr.
1920–1972 | Lillie Mae
Dieckmann
1925–2020 | Leslie Edward
Burnett Jr.
1925–1984 | Shirley Ann
Johnson
1933–2023 |

| 126
Stanley Willis
Straube
1951–2021 | Vicki Ann
Burnett
1952–2006 |

John William **Charlton II** 1975–

160
Carmen Lynn **Straube** 1978–

Marriage: 1999

Kinley Nicole **Charlton** 2002–   Kaylin Paige **Charlton** 2005–

160.   **Carmen Lynn Straube** was born on Saturday, August 05, 1978, in Hannibal, Marion County, Missouri. She is the daughter of Stanley Willis Straube (126) and Vicki Ann Burnett.

At the age of 21, Carmen Lynn married **John William Charlton II** on Saturday, September 18, 1999, in Bowling Green, Pike County, Missouri, when he was 24 years old. They have two daughters.

John William was born on Thursday, June 12, 1975.

Daughters of Carmen Lynn Straube and John William Charlton II:

    f   I. **Kinley Nicole Charlton** was born in Mexico, Audrain County, Missouri, on June 26, 2002.

    f   II. **Kaylin Paige Charlton** was born on August 09, 2005.

Family of Seth Straube and Jeni Portwood

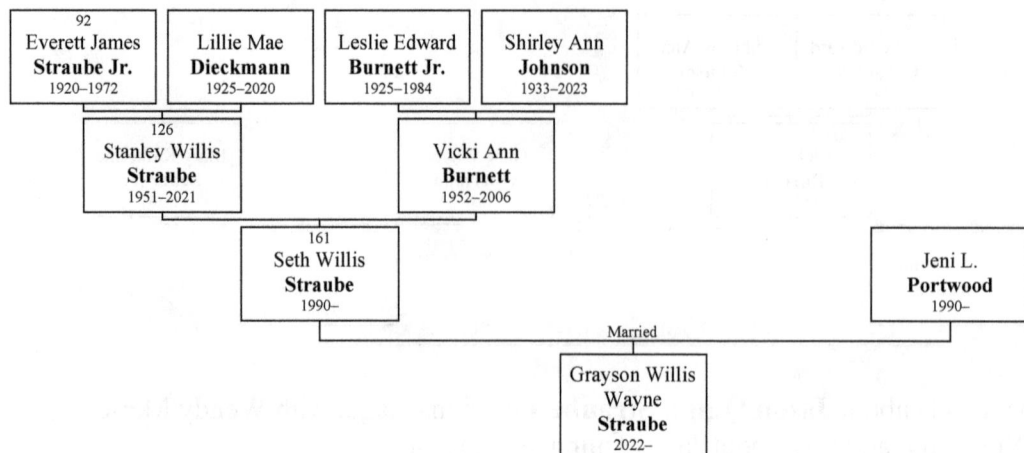

```
┌─────────────┐  ┌─────────────┐  ┌─────────────┐  ┌─────────────┐
│     92      │  │ Lillie Mae  │  │Leslie Edward│  │ Shirley Ann │
│Everett James│  │ Dieckmann   │  │ Burnett Jr. │  │  Johnson    │
│ Straube Jr. │  │ 1925–2020   │  │ 1925–1984   │  │ 1933–2023   │
│  1920–1972  │  │             │  │             │  │             │
└─────────────┘  └─────────────┘  └─────────────┘  └─────────────┘
      ┌──────────────────┐            ┌──────────────────┐
      │       126        │            │    Vicki Ann     │
      │ Stanley Willis   │            │    Burnett       │
      │    Straube       │            │    1952–2006     │
      │   1951–2021      │            │                  │
      └──────────────────┘            └──────────────────┘
              ┌──────────────────┐              ┌──────────────────┐
              │       161        │              │    Jeni L.       │
              │   Seth Willis    │              │   Portwood       │
              │    Straube       │              │    1990–         │
              │     1990–        │              │                  │
              └──────────────────┘              └──────────────────┘
                          Married
                   ┌──────────────────┐
                   │ Grayson Willis   │
                   │     Wayne        │
                   │   Straube        │
                   │    2022–         │
                   └──────────────────┘
```

161. **Seth Willis Straube** was born on Saturday, July 14, 1990, in Hannibal, Marion County, Missouri. He is the son of Stanley Willis Straube (126) and Vicki Ann Burnett.

He married **Jeni L. Portwood**. They have one son.

Jeni L. was born in July 1990.

Son of Seth Willis Straube and Jeni L. Portwood:

      m   I. **Grayson Willis Wayne Straube** was born on June 14, 2022.

Family of Eric Scherder and Kayla Bovard

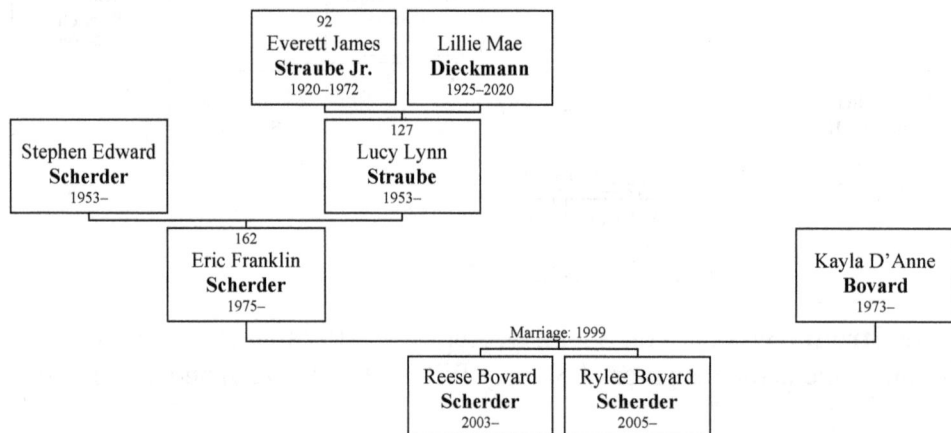

```
                 ┌─────────────┐  ┌─────────────┐
                 │     92      │  │ Lillie Mae  │
                 │Everett James│  │ Dieckmann   │
                 │ Straube Jr. │  │ 1925–2020   │
                 │  1920–1972  │  │             │
                 └─────────────┘  └─────────────┘
┌─────────────┐        ┌──────────────────┐
│Stephen Edward│       │       127        │
│  Scherder   │        │   Lucy Lynn      │
│   1953–     │        │    Straube       │
│             │        │     1953–        │
└─────────────┘        └──────────────────┘
        ┌──────────────────┐              ┌──────────────────┐
        │       162        │              │  Kayla D'Anne    │
        │  Eric Franklin   │              │    Bovard        │
        │    Scherder      │              │    1973–         │
        │     1975–        │              │                  │
        └──────────────────┘              └──────────────────┘
                     Marriage: 1999
          ┌──────────────┐  ┌──────────────┐
          │ Reese Bovard │  │ Rylee Bovard │
          │  Scherder    │  │  Scherder    │
          │   2003–      │  │   2005–      │
          └──────────────┘  └──────────────┘
```

162. **Eric Franklin Scherder** was born on Tuesday, December 30, 1975, in Hannibal, Marion County, Missouri. He is the son of Stephen Edward Scherder and Lucy Lynn Straube (127).

At the age of 23, Eric Franklin married **Kayla D'Anne Bovard** on Saturday, March 13, 1999, in Hopkins, Nodaway County, Missouri, when she was 25 years old. They have two sons.

Kayla D'Anne was born in Maryville, Nodaway County, Missouri, on Sunday, July 22, 1973.

Sons of Eric Franklin Scherder and Kayla D'Anne Bovard:

m   I. **Reese Bovard Scherder** was born in Fayetteville, Washington County, Arkansas, on April 11, 2003.

m   II. **Rylee Bovard Scherder** was born in Evansville, Vanderburgh County, Indiana, on October 21, 2005.

Family of Curtis Scherder and Christina Prunty

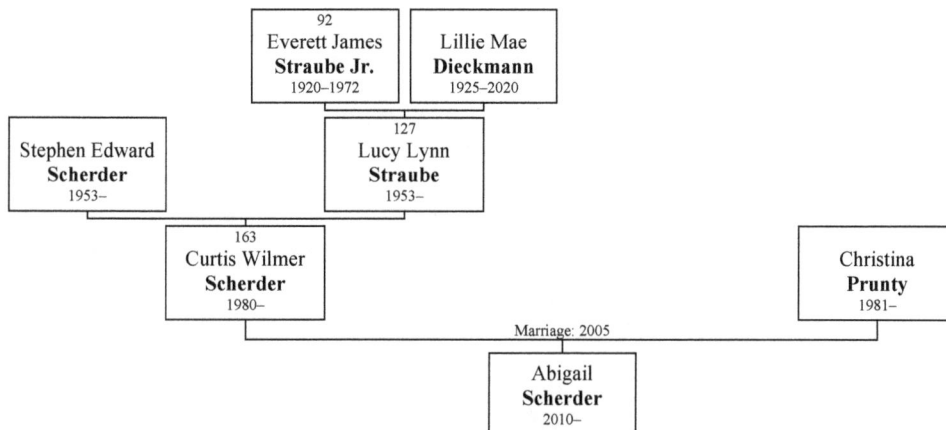

163.   **Curtis Wilmer Scherder** was born on Wednesday, February 20, 1980, in Mexico, Audrain County, Missouri. He is the son of Stephen Edward Scherder and Lucy Lynn Straube (127).

At the age of 25, Curtis Wilmer married **Christina Prunty** on Saturday, August 13, 2005, in Bowling Green, Pike County, Missouri, when she was 24 years old. They have one daughter.

Christina was born on Monday, February 16, 1981.

Daughter of Curtis Wilmer Scherder and Christina Prunty:

f   I. **Abigail Scherder** was born on December 08, 2010.

8th Generation

Family of John Doyle and Jamie Orel

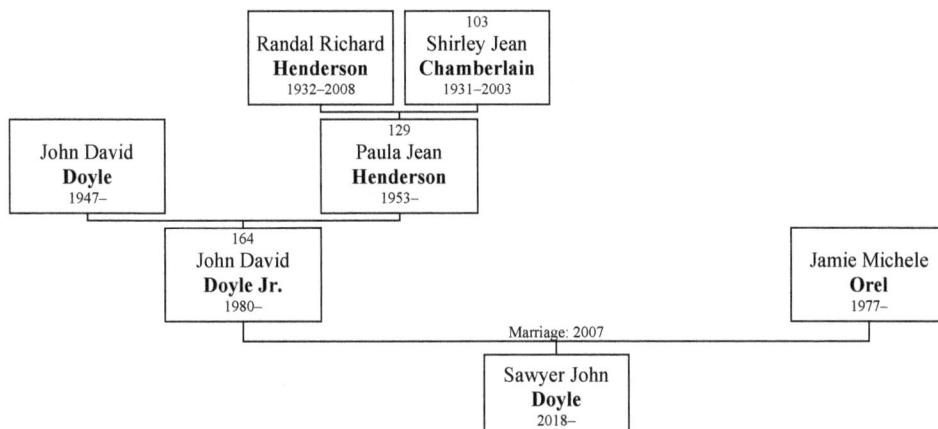

164. **John David Doyle Jr.** was born on Tuesday, August 12, 1980, in Dallas, Dallas County, Texas. He is the son of John David Doyle and Paula Jean Henderson (129).

John David married **Jamie Michele Orel** on Saturday, October 20, 2007. They have one son.

Jamie Michele was born in August 1977.

Son of John David Doyle Jr. and Jamie Michele Orel:

> m   I. **Sawyer John Doyle** was born on September 06, 2018.

Matthew McDill

165. **Matthew Wayne McDill** was born on Friday, September 21, 1984, in Plano, Collin County, Texas. He is the son of Jeffery Wayne McDill and Susan Luanne Henderson (131).

Relationships with Araceli Marie Galvan and Stacy Lopez (Page 256) are known.

Matthew McDill and Araceli Galvan

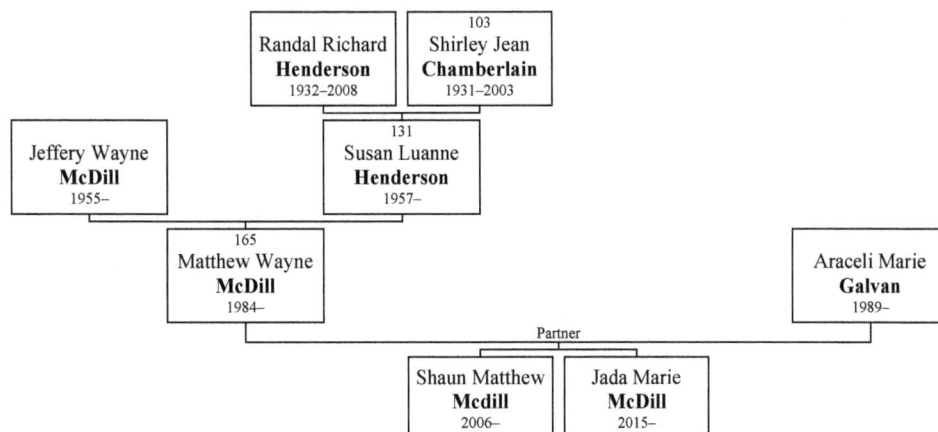

Here are the details about **Matthew Wayne McDill's** first relationship, with Araceli Marie Galvan. You can read more about Matthew Wayne on page 255.

Matthew Wayne McDill is partnered with **Araceli Marie Galvan**. They have two children.

Araceli Marie was born in Dallas, Dallas County, Texas, on Wednesday, January 18, 1989.[78]

Children of Matthew Wayne McDill and Araceli Marie Galvan:

m   I. **Shaun Matthew McDill** was born at Presbyterian Hospital in Plano, Collin County, Texas, on April 07, 2006.

f   II. **Jada Marie McDill** was born in Lewisville, Denton County, Texas, on May 19, 2015.

Family of Matthew McDill and Stacy Lopez

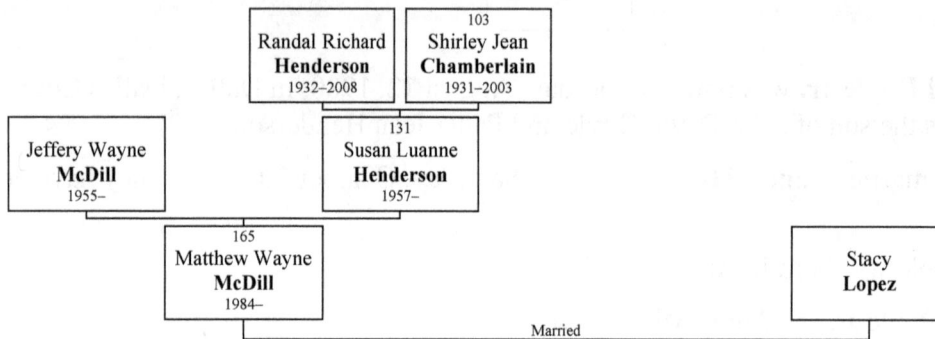

Here are the details about **Matthew Wayne McDill's** second relationship, with Stacy Lopez. You can read more about Matthew Wayne on page 255.

Matthew Wayne McDill married **Stacy Lopez**.

Family of Cody Mummert and Danielle Ashford

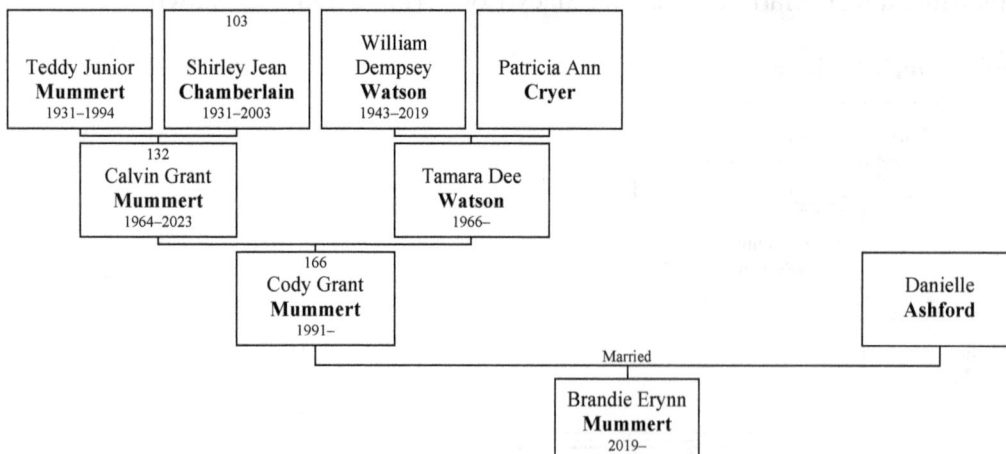

78   Ancestry.com, Texas, U.S., Birth Index, 1903-1997 (Lehi, UT, USA, Ancestry.com Operations Inc, 2005), Ancestry.com, Record for Araceli Marie Galvan. https://search.ancestry.co.uk/cgi-bin/sse.dll?db=8781&h=15622838&indiv=try.

166. **Cody Grant Mummert** was born on Monday, January 21, 1991, in Corsicana, Navarro County, Texas. He is the son of Calvin Grant Mummert (132) and Tamara Dee Watson.

He married **Danielle Ashford**. They have one daughter.

Daughter of Cody Grant Mummert and Danielle Ashford:

      f   I. **Brandie Erynn Mummert** was born in Arlington, Tarrant County, Texas, on February 12, 2019.

Family of Norman Manuere and Alina Halito

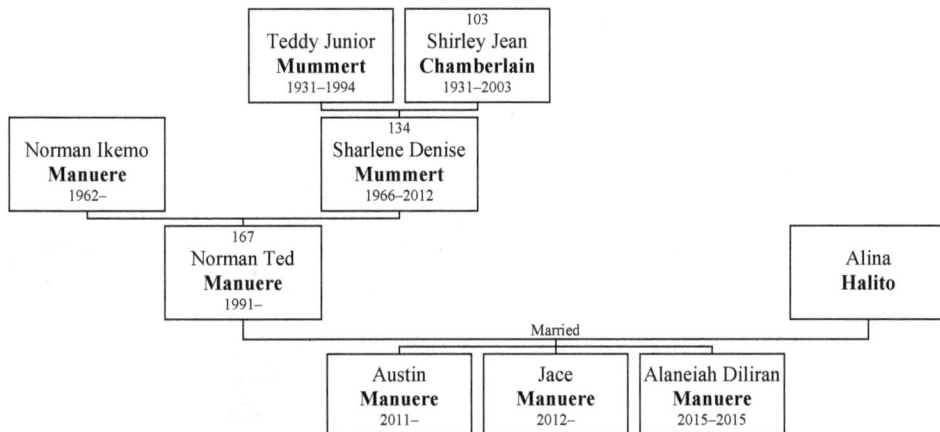

167. **Norman Ted Manuere** was born on Monday, November 18, 1991, in Fort Worth, Tarrant County, Texas. He is the son of Norman Ikemo Manuere and Sharlene Denise Mummert (134).

He married **Alina Halito**. They had three children.

Alina was born in Honolulu, Honolulu County, Hawaii.

Children of Norman Ted Manuere and Alina Halito:

      m   I. **Austin Manuere** was born in Corsicana, Navarro County, Texas, on March 27, 2011.

      m   II. **Jace Manuere** was born in Corsicana, Navarro County, Texas, on April 16, 2012.

      f   III. **Alaneiah Diliran Manuere** was born in Corsicana, Navarro County, Texas, on August 14, 2015. She died in Corsicana, Navarro County, Texas, on December 15, 2015. Alaneiah Diliran was buried in Hamilton Beeman Cemetery, Retreat, Navarro County, Texas, on December 20, 2015 (Find a Grave ID 156107498).

           Obituary for Alaneiah Diliran Manuere

              Alaneiah Dilran Manuere, four months of age, left this earth on Tuesday, December 15, 2015 at Navarro Regional Hospital in Corsicana. She was born on August 14, 2015 in Corsicana to Norman Jr. and Alina Manuere.

              She is survived by her parents, siblings Austin, and Jace Manuere; Aunts

Savannah Hernandes, Leila Manuere, Meroleen and Joncy Santos, Randa Mergen and Nekieisa Halito; Uncles Nathan, Caleb and Landon Manuere, Joyful, Jayson and Johnstone Santos, JFK and Douglas Halito. Grandparents Norman and Felisa Manuere, Sharlene Mummert, John and Ursula Santos, Christopher and Mary Halito.

Visitation will be 6-8 pm Friday, December 18, 2015 at Griffin-Roughton Funeral Home. Funeral service will be 3 pm Sunday, December 20, 2015 at Griffin-Roughton Funeral Home Chapel. Burial will follow at Hamilton-Beeman Cemetery.

Family of Samuel Hargadine and Hillery Wheeler

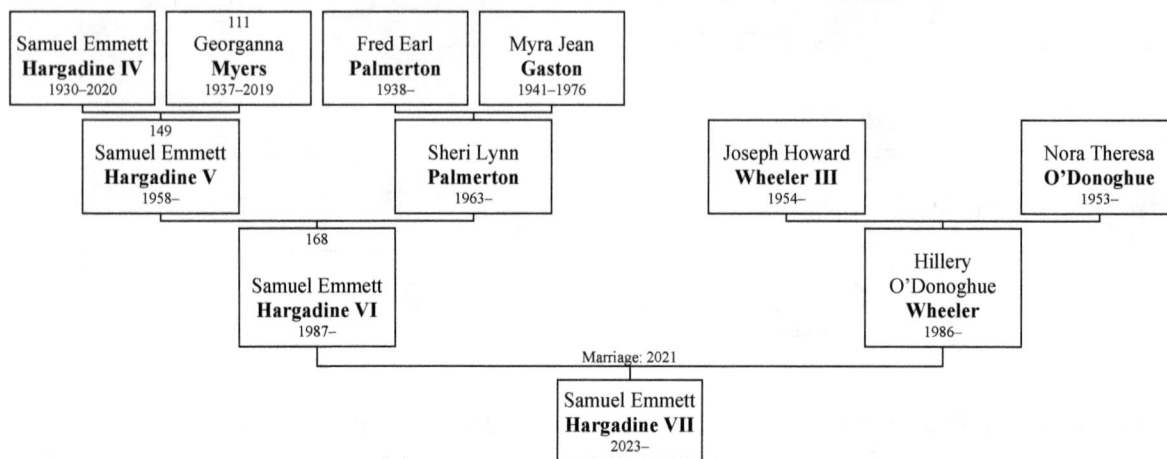

168. **Samuel Emmett Hargadine VI** was born on Thursday, July 23, 1987, at Boone Hospital Center in Columbia, Boone County, Missouri. He is the son of Samuel Emmett Hargadine V (149) and Sheri Lynn Palmerton. He is also known as **Sammy**.

At the age of 34, Samuel Emmett married **Hillery O'Donoghue Wheeler** on Saturday, July 31, 2021, at Civil Ceremony in Washington, District of Columbia, USA, when she was 35 years old. They have one son.

Hillery O'Donoghue was born in Hawaii, USA, on Saturday, June 28, 1986. She is the daughter of Joseph Howard Wheeler III and Nora Theresa O'Donoghue.

Son of Samuel Emmett Hargadine VI and Hillery O'Donoghue Wheeler:

m   I. **Samuel Emmett Hargadine VII** was born at George Washington University Hospital in Washington D.C. on December 16, 2023.

Family of Calvin Hargadine and Amber Beasley

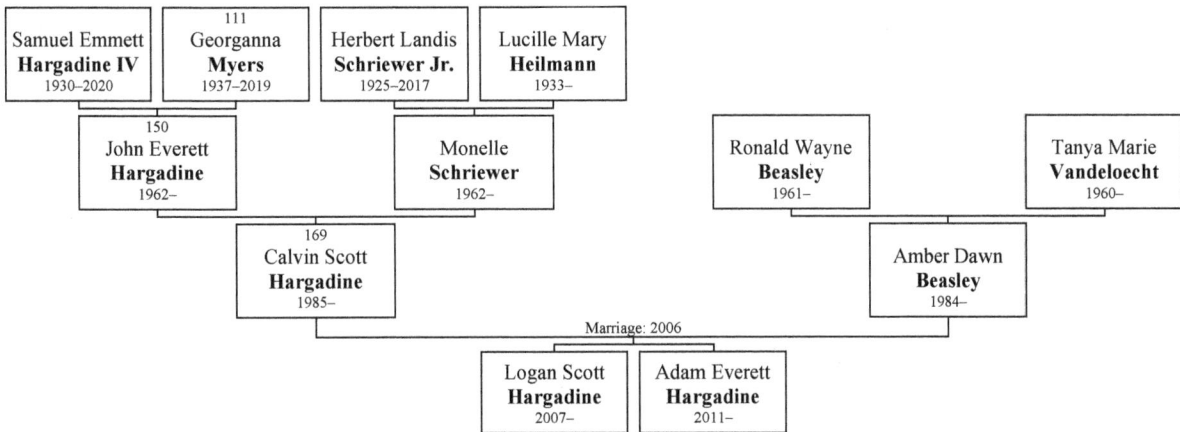

169. **Calvin Scott Hargadine** was born on Tuesday, October 22, 1985, in Sedalia, Pettis County, Missouri. He is the son of John Everett Hargadine (150) and Monelle Schriewer.

At the age of 20, Calvin Scott married **Amber Dawn Beasley** on Saturday, June 10, 2006, in Goose Creek, Berkeley County, South Carolina, when she was 21 years old. They have two sons.

Amber Dawn was born in Columbia, Boone County, Missouri, on Saturday, December 01, 1984.[79] She is the daughter of Ronald Wayne Beasley and Tanya Marie Vandeloecht.

Sons of Calvin Scott Hargadine and Amber Dawn Beasley:

m   I. **Logan Scott Hargadine** was born at Trident Hospital in North Charleston, Charleston County, South Carolina, on June 27, 2007.

m   II. **Adam Everett Hargadine** was born at Trident Hospital in North Charleston, Charleston County, South Carolina, on December 21, 2011.

Family of Mitchell Hargadine and Jenna McCracken

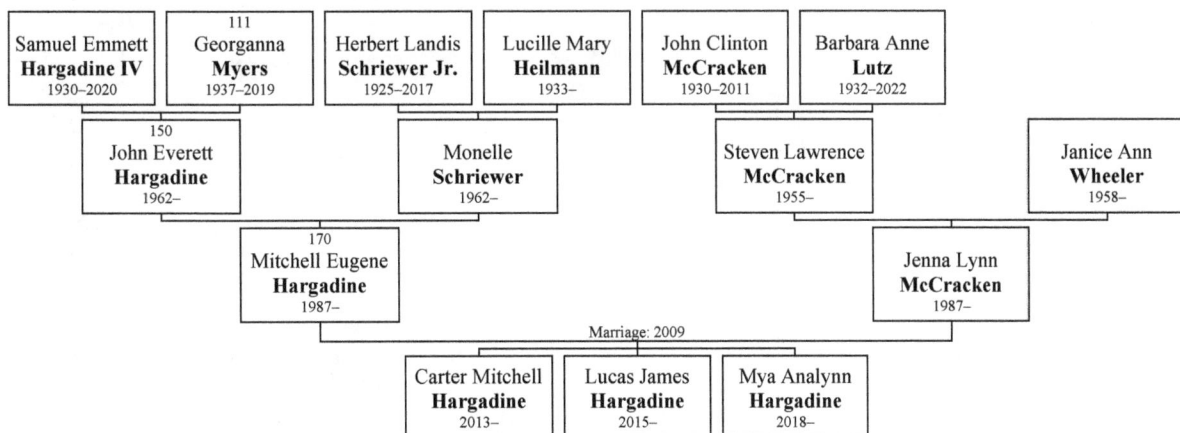

79   Interview with Amber Hargadine.

170. **Mitchell Eugene Hargadine** was born on Thursday, September 17, 1987, in Columbia, Boone County, Missouri. He is the son of John Everett Hargadine (150) and Monelle Schriewer.

At the age of 21, Mitchell Eugene married **Jenna Lynn McCracken** on Friday, May 22, 2009, in Saint Louis, Saint Louis County, Missouri, when she was 21 years old. They have three children.

Jenna Lynn was born in Fulton, Callaway County, Missouri, on Tuesday, September 01, 1987. She is the daughter of Steven Lawrence McCracken and Janice Ann Wheeler.

Children of Mitchell Eugene Hargadine and Jenna Lynn McCracken:

m   I. **Carter Mitchell Hargadine** was born in Concord, Cabarrus County, North Carolina, on April 24, 2013.

m   II. **Lucas James Hargadine** was born in Concord, Cabarrus County, North Carolina, on September 14, 2015.

f   III. **Mya Analynn Hargadine** was born in Concord, Cabarrus County, North Carolina, on September 12, 2018.

Index of Places

Bowling Green City Cemetery, Pike County, Missouri
(39.3473° N, 91.1945° W)

Bowling Green, Pike County, Missouri

Bracken County, Kentucky

Millwood, Lincoln County, Missouri

Missouri, USA
(38.2917° N, 91.6° W)

Moberly, Randolph County, Missouri

Monroe County, Missouri

Monterey, Monterey County, California

Montgomery City, Montgomery County, Missouri

Montgomery County, Missouri

Soldiers And Sailors Cemetery, Grand Island, Hall County, Nebraska
(40.9467° N, 98.3775° W)

South Bend, St. Joseph County, Indiana

Springfield Township, Franklin County, Indiana

Springfield, Franklin County, Indiana

St. Charles, St. Charles County, Missouri

St. Clair County, Illinois

St. Clement, Pike County, Missouri

Index of Individuals